Audio in the 21st Century

Scott Janus

INTEL
PRESS

621.3893
J268a

Copyright © 2004 Intel Corporation. All rights reserved.

ISBN 0-9717861-5-1

No part of this publication may be reproduced, stored in a retrieval system or transmitted in any form or by any means, electronic, mechanical, photocopying, recording, scanning or otherwise, except as permitted under Sections 107 or 108 of the 1976 United States Copyright Act, without either the prior written permission of the Publisher, or authorization through payment of the appropriate per-copy fee to the Copyright Clearance Center, 222 Rosewood Drive, Danvers, MA 01923, (978) 750-8400, fax (978) 750-4744. Requests to the Publisher for permission should be addressed to the Publisher, Intel Press, Intel Corporation, 2111 NE 25th Avenue, JF3-330, Hillsboro, OR 97124-5961. E-Mail: intelpress@intel.com.

This publication is designed to provide accurate and authoritative information in regard to the subject matter covered. It is sold with the understanding that the publisher is not engaged in professional services. If professional advice or other expert assistance is required, the services of a competent professional person should be sought.

Intel Corporation may have patents or pending patent applications, trademarks, copyrights, or other intellectual property rights that relate to the presented subject matter. The furnishing of documents and other materials and information does not provide any license, express or implied, by estoppel or otherwise, to any such patents, trademarks, copyrights, or other intellectual property rights.

Intel may make changes to specifications, product descriptions, and plans at any time, without notice.

Fictitious names of companies, products, people, characters, and/or data mentioned herein are not intended to represent any real individual, company, product, or event.

Intel products are not intended for use in medical, life-saving, life-sustaining, critical control or safety systems, or in nuclear facility applications.

Intel and the Intel logo are trademarks or registered trademark of Intel Corporation.

† Other names and brands may be claimed as the property of others.

This book is printed on acid-free paper. ♾

PACKARD LIBRARY

NOV 11 2005

THE COLUMBUS COLLEGE
OF ART AND DESIGN

Publisher: Richard Bowles
Editor: Lynn Putnam
Managing Editor: David B. Spencer
Content Manager: Stuart Goldstein
Text Design & Composition: Wasser Studios, Inc.
Graphic Art: Wasser Studios, Inc. (illustrations), Mandish Design (cover)

Library of Congress Cataloging in Publication Data:

Printed in the United States of America

10 9 8 7 6 5 4 3 2 1

First Printing, February 2004

Dedication

For Norm. As a grandfather, he taught me the virtues of common sense and told me stories about "tip and ring." He continues to be an inspiration to us all through his on-going efforts to learn about new technologies.

Contents

Preface

"Many suffer from the incurable disease of writing, and it becomes chronic in their sick minds."

— Juvenal

We live in exciting times! Today, we are at the point where you can buy a sound system that reproduces music more accurately than the human ear can discern. In other words, any differences between the original music and the reproduced music are so small as to be undetectable. Also readily available are portable players that allow you to store your entire music library in a device the size of a deck of cards. Sitting in front of a computer, we can listen to live music from the other side of the planet. Home theatres offer us surround-sound that immerses us into movies.

Today, mainstream audio technologies that simply did not exist even a few years ago provide us with innovative new products and usage models. However, these technologies have also brought with them unique challenges, such as how to protect high-value content from push-button piracy.

As a result of this explosion of audio topics, many engineers now find themselves building audio products. Sales and marketing personnel must position and pitch these products. Managers must oversee these projects. And consumers are trying to understand what all these new gizmos are and how they work.

Starting with basic concepts, this book introduces you to key audio technologies. I've designed this book to be read sequentially from cover to cover. Each chapter builds upon topics discussed in previous chapters. I have made an effort to present the content in an entertaining and easy-to-read manner. Many of the topics presented herein are difficult enough to understand without burdening you with the chore of reading dry prose.[1] You may, of course, also use this book as a random-access reference and just jump into topics of immediate interest as needed. I want this book to serve as a useful aid for all of those people who find themselves needing to know about audio technology.

It is important that this book is useful for you. To that end, if you find topics unclear, incomplete, or even completely missing, then please send me your questions and comments using the contact-the-author link at www.intel.com/intelpress/sum_audio.htm. I'll be posting errata, answers to readers' questions, and any new material for the book on that Web page.

Acknowledgements

For some authors, the process of writing is akin to a canoe gliding down a gentle mountain stream. Concepts are translated into actual words on the page with graceful ease. For other authors—such as those that write 1,000-page novels every year—writing is more like offshore powerboat racing. My metaphorical ship of writing, however, is more like an 18th century wooden sailing ship that is trapped in the ice at the 89th parallel. The masts have snapped off, the hull is being crushed, and food supplies are running low. At night, the ice weasels come.

For me, writing is difficult. Therefore, this book would not be in your hands today if it was not for the support and input that I received from numerous individuals. For starters, I must thank Brent Groves, Elizabeth Halt, and Mark Vaccaro for their detailed review of early drafts. Robin Basset, Phil King, and Scott McMillin provided useful validation of the penultimate draft. Lynn Putnam gave me very pertinent editorial feedback throughout the development of the book. David B. Spencer and Stuart Goldstein from the Intel Press deserve recognition for handling the logistics associated with actually getting the book published, leaving me free to focus on creating the contents.

Finally, thanks to my wife, Nikki Christison. She continued to provide me with valuable support even as she progressed through the later stages of her pregnancy. It's a boy!

---

[1] On the other hand, if you are a fan of dry prose, then please feel free to ignore the humorous asides sprinkled throughout this book.

Chapter 1

That Which Has Come Before

[I foresee] a marked deterioration in music and musical taste, an interruption in the musical development of the country, and a host of other injuries to music in its artistic manifestations, by virtue—or rather by vice—of the multiplication of the various music-reproducing machines.

—John Philip Sousa

Legend has it that in 590 BC, a messenger ran from the plains of Marathon to Athens to report the Athenian army's victory over Persian forces, as it was the fastest way to send a long distance communication. After delivering the message of victory, the messenger died from exhaustion after running some 25 miles.[1] Today, professional and amateur athletes run marathons for fun and profit. Race officials at the starting and finishing lines keep in touch with real-time voice communications via handheld radios. Runners can entertain themselves during the event by listening to their choice of pre-recorded music on lightweight players the size of a deck of cards.

The ability to record, play, and transmit sounds has progressed a great deal since ancient times. How did we get here from there?

---

1 Although it is doubtful the marathon origin legend is true, it is well documented that another professional courier by the name of Philippides ran from the plains of Marathon to Sparta, a distance of about 150 miles, in about two days. Luckily for today's athletes, the lesser distance of 26.2 miles is used for running marathons.

This book is not a history book, but it does start with a history chapter. This chapter provides a high-level overview of key events to help establish a context for current technologies that will be discussed in subsequent chapters. It is useful for us to know where we've been so we can make sure that where we're going is in the right direction! If you have no interest in the past, then you can safely skip this chapter.

Bear in mind that this brief synopsis of the history of audio technology only allows for the mentioning of key highlights. In fact, most technological innovations do not occur in a vacuum, but rely heavily on the ideas and efforts of inventor's contemporaries and predecessors. As Sir Isaac Newton said, "If I have seen further, it is by standing on the shoulders of giants."

Recorded Sound

In 1807, a man named Thomas Young created a device which recorded the vibrations of objects such as a tuning fork on a smoke-blackened cylinder. The cylinder was rotated as the fork vibrated, and a small stylus moved in response to the fork, removing soot from the cylinder. As a result, a crude depiction of the waveform of the sound made by the vibrating object was recorded.

Fifty years later in 1857, Édouard-Léon Scott de Martinville developed the phonautograph, the first general sound recording device. Whereas Young's device would only record the oscillations of a visibly vibrating object, Scott's phonautograph used a horn and a diaphragm to intensify and capture vibrations of the air itself. Sounds entering the horn would cause the diaphragm to move in sympathy; a hog whisker stylus attached to the diaphragm would remove soot from a smoke-blackened piece of paper wrapped around a cylinder, thereby tracing a waveform of the sound onto the paper. The device is shown in Figure 1.1.

The phonautograph was intended merely as a sound recording device; it had no playback capabilities. Scott theorized that famous people would have their voices recorded and the resulting piece of paper would be every bit as valuable as a traditional autograph.

Courtesy of the Courtesy of the National Museum of American History, Behring Center, Copyright © 2003 Smithsonian Institution

Figure 1.1 Scott's Phonautograph

Phonograph

In July of 1877, Thomas Edison was working on a device to record Morse code to paper disc. As a spin-off of such a device, he built a small toy which had a little cardboard figure of a man sawing wood. He hooked up the cardboard figure to a diaphragm through a series of pawls, pulleys, and cog wheels in such a way that if you spoke loudly into the diaphragm, the figure would move back and forth and appear to saw wood. Playing with the toy, it occurred to Edison that if he could record the movements of the diaphragm and later reproduce them, he would be able to reproduce sound.[2]

After much experimentation, he was able to build a device that recorded his voice and—for the first time in history—played back a discernable copy of the recording. Specifically, Edison recorded the nursery rhyme, "Mary Had a Little Lamb," which was the standard test phrase used in the Edison labs for sound equipment. The exact date of this momentous feat is a matter of some dispute. The official date is August 12, 1877. However, he did not file for the patent until December 24. Despite the ambiguity of the construction date, there is general consensus that Edison was the first person to design and construct a functional sound recording and playback device.

[2] This flash of inspiration is an excellent endorsement for people to continue playing with toys even after their childhood. I, for instance, have a preference for robots that transform into jet fighters.

Edison called his device the phonograph. Like Scott's phonautograph, it used a cylinder for recording, but in this case it was made of brass and wrapped in tinfoil. A stylus was placed against the tinfoil. The stylus was in turn connected to a diaphragm. Recording was accomplished by speaking into the diaphragm while rotating the brass cylinder. The stylus would create indentations in the foil that corresponded to the sound waveforms.

Playback was achieved using a different stylus and diaphragm. As the cylinder rotated, the stylus would move up and down following the recorded indentations. The playback diaphragm would move in sympathy, and cause the air to vibrate in such a way as to reproduce the original sounds.

At the time, Edison thought the phonograph would be nothing more than a novelty. By late 1878, he moved onto other projects, such as developing a viable electric light. The ability to record sound was revolutionary, but Edison's phonograph did not have an easy mechanism for creating copies of recordings. Also, the tinfoil recording would significantly degrade with each playback. Despite Edison's departure from the field, others were still hard at work trying to make better sound recording devices.

Graphophone

In 1881, Alexander Graham Bell, his cousin Chichester Bell, and Charles Tainter began experimenting with ways to improve upon Edison's phonograph. They called their improved version the graphophone. After much experimentation, they began using wax-covered paper tubes as the recording medium. Incidentally, the paper tubes developed for the graphophone have since been adapted for use in a myriad of applications, such as shipping tubes and paper towel spindles. An 1885 version of the graphophone is shown in Figure 1.2.

The inventors of the graphophone showed an advanced version of their device to Edison in 1887. They hoped to work together with him to further improve and commercialize the design. Edison rejected their proposal and instead set out to independently revisit and improve upon his original phonograph. The month-long project ended with a three-day marathon session, at the end of which Edison had an improved phonograph that used wax-covered cylinders as a recording media.

Courtesy of Dr. Steven Schoenherr

Figure 1.2 Graphophone 1885

As the 1880s closed, the battle between the Edison phonograph and the Bell-Tainter graphophone heated up. Each side had a patent that they felt gave them the right to produce their invention, and possibly the right to prevent the production of the competing product. A key point was that Edison's 1878 patent specified a process of "embossing or indenting," while Bell and Tainter's 1885 patent specified an "engraving technique," implying that material was actually being removed—as was the case when recording on wax.

The matter was resolved in 1888 when Jesse H. Lippencort became the sole licensee to sell both the phonograph and the graphophone. Edison and the American Graphophone Company retained manufacturing rights and responsibilities. Lippencort formed the North American Phonograph Company (NAPC) and positioned the two devices as office tools to augment or replace stenographers. Edison continued this marketing position when he got control of the company in 1890. He discouraged the use of record players for music and entertainment.

However, local subsidiaries of the NAPC began selling coin-operated players for public venues such as drug stores. These precursors to the jukebox proved to be immensely popular, and the record industry really began to take off.

The limited frequency range and short recording time of the wax media were not suited to many musical works. It was not feasible, for instance, to record orchestral pieces. However, brass instruments matched the frequency range of the cylinders well, so they comprised the majority of the first commercial records. Of particular popularity were recordings of the United States Marine Corps Band, as conducted by John Phillip Sousa.

At the time, there was no way to duplicate a cylinder. To make 100 copies of a song, they would place 10 recording devices in the same room as a brass band. An announcer would step very close to one of the recorders, start it recording, speak the name of the piece to be played, and then stop the recording. He would repeat this process with the other nine records. Then all 10 records would be started simultaneously and the band would play the selected piece—or at least the first two minutes of it. New wax cylinders would be inserted into the recorders and the whole process would be repeated nine more times. And thus would 100 copies of the recording be created.

Soloists had a harder time of it, as their quieter volume meant only three recorders at a time could be used. A soloist would thus need to play the same song over thirty times to create 100 copies.

Gramophone

At about the same time Edison, Bell, and Tainter were disputing each other's patents, yet another inventor—this one by the name of Emile Berliner—was revisiting Scott's phonautograph. Specifically, he explored photoengraving techniques as a method for adding playback capabilities. Wrapping and unwrapping the photoengravings from cylinders for duplication proved cumbersome, so Berliner began using a disc as his form factor.

Berliner's recording process entailed running a stylus over a soot-covered heavy glass disc. The disc rotated on a turntable, and clever gear work drove the stylus toward the center of the disc as it turned. Just like the phonautograph, the stylus would scrape away soot in a pattern matching the sound entering the recording diaphragm. After the recording was complete, Berliner would varnish the glass plate and then photoengrave the record in metal. By 1888 he had developed a film-covered zinc disc that used an acid bath to etch a durable groove in the record.

Berliner called his disc-based system the gramophone, a picture of which is shown in Figure 1.3.

Courtesy of Dr. Steven Schoenherr

Figure 1.3 Berliner's Gramophone

Berliner recognized the need to mass produce records, so he spent several years developing a process of making a negative mold of the master record and then stamping out an unlimited number of copies.

In 1895, the Berliner Gramophone Company began selling disc records and corresponding players. The seven-inch records were single-sided and provided about two minutes of playing time.

The Berliner discs went head to head against the already established cylinder industry. The discs had a big advantage in their ease of mass production. Whereas thousands of discs could be stamped from a master mold, it was just becoming possible to duplicate cylinders using a pantographic process that produced only 25 copies of a master cylinder.

The cylinder manufacturers naturally did not want to lose business to the upstart discs, so it is perhaps not surprising that a lengthy series of complex patent battles ensued. A 1900 American court decision resulted in the term gramophone being banned. Thus, record players would come to be known generically as phonographs to Americans, and gramophones to the rest of the world.

After many more court decisions, cross-patent licensing, and corporate reorganizations, several different companies in the U.S. and Europe had secured the rights to produce disc records and players in the early years of the 20th century.

The first decade of the 20th century saw a plethora of incompatible audio media. Discs and cylinders were quite incompatible with one another. Also, several different cylinder and disc rotation speeds were available, with rates up to 100 revolutions per minute (RPM).

Discs, especially the Berliner discs, eventually became the dominant medium. The rotation speed of discs was eventually standardized to 78.26 RPM. This rate of revolution is achieved using a motor running at 3600 RPM and a 46:1 reduction gear.

The discs came in different diameters. Seven-inch and 10-inch were the most common, although 8-inch and 12-inch sizes were also available. The large size of the groove on these 78s meant that even a 12-inch disc could only hold about four minutes of music. A recording of a symphony had to be stored across several discs. The resulting collection was bound together in a set of sleeves known as an album. Decades later, the term album would be used as a misnomer to describe a single long-playing record.

Electric Recording

As the 78s achieved dominance, an exciting new breakthrough was taking place. Prior to about 1915, all record players were acoustic; they relied on purely physical means to record and reproduce sounds. As such, the stylus had to be pressed very hard against the records, meaning the stylus needed to be replaced very frequently, and that only the loudest sounds could be recorded.

The limited sensitivity of acoustic systems posed harsh constraints on recording sessions. When recording symphonies, the traditional orchestra seating arrangement had to be discarded and the position of the instruments radically altered to meet the constraints of the recording device. It was not uncommon for musicians to be so tightly packed together that they would hit each other with their instruments during a performance. This crowding was further exacerbated by the need for individuals to run in front of the orchestra and lean very close to the recording horn during solos.

Experiments in using electric recording and playback for records began in the late 1910s, but it was not until 1925 that production systems become publicly available. With their introduction, it became possible to record orchestras in actual orchestra halls without any radical seating charts. Acoustic and electric records and players were completely interchangeable. For instance, electrically-recorded discs could be played on existing acoustic players. They sounded better than acoustically-recorded discs. The electrically-recorded discs would sound best, however, on electric players.

Beyond 78

One shortcoming of records was their brief playing time. In 1948, CBS introduced a new 33-1/3 RPM record format that addressed this limitation. The groove on these new records was known as a microgroove, because it was four times smaller than the one used on the 78. Rather than the natural shellac being used to manufacture contemporary 78s, these new records were made of polyvinylchloride (PVC). The microgroove and PVC construction meant that the sound quality of these long-playing (LP) records was better than the 78 and the 33-1/3 format from the previous decade. LPs could contain nearly 30 minutes of music per side. In fact, LPs as long as 45 minutes per side have been produced!

Also in 1948, RCA introduced a new 7-inch record format. Designed explicitly to replace the 78, these 45-RPM discs were also made of PVC and used a microgroove. They had a much large center hole than other records. These 45s were capable of playing 5.3 minutes of sound per side. As introduced, the two formats were not compatible with one another, and a Battle of the Speeds ensued.

Eventually, both the LP and 45s became widespread. The 1950s saw 45s become popular for recording singles and playing in jukeboxes. LPs were the format of choice for longer works such as symphonies and collections of popular songs. Record players were introduced that were able to play both 45 and LPs. The physical durability and quality of the new LP and 45 formats quickly rendered the 78 format obsolete.

Stereo and Quadraphonic Sound

For the first six decades of the record industry, the records only produced single-channel or monophonic sound. The single microphone and single speaker meant that to the two-eared human hearing system, the sound was always coming directly from the speaker. A monophonic recording of a symphony would provide no acoustical clues as to how the instruments were arranged on stage.

Two-channel or stereophonic sound used two microphones for recording and two speakers for playback. With stereo, a listener can identify sound as coming from the left speaker, the right speaker, or—and this is the real kicker—anywhere in between the two speakers. With a stereo recording of an orchestra, listeners could discern that the violins were on stage right and the violas were on stage left.[3]

In 1957, stereo records were introduced to the American mass market. The two signals needed to create stereo were stored on the two sides of the record groove. Credit for the development of this 45/45 system was given to Westrex, a Bell Laboratories subsidiary, but in fact the technique had been patented 26 years earlier by Alan Blumlein of Electro and Music Industries (EMI). Blumlein had previously experimented with using two styli to record two adjacent grooves on a single record, but his technique had the drawback of halving the recording time of the record.

Numerous competing four-channel or quadraphonic record systems were introduced in the 1970s. However, quadraphonic records never gained popularity, due in part to the lack of an industry standard. The different systems were all incompatible with one another. Even decades later, historical audiophile collectors have tracked down antique quad records and players only to find that the records are not compatible with their player.

Magnetic Recording

The phonograph and its cousins all stemmed from the concept of physically indenting a surface to store a signal corresponding to the sounds being recorded. In the 1890s, a completely different methodology for storing sound using magnetism was developed by Vlademar Poulsen. He was convinced that Bell's telephone would be much more useful in business settings if only there was some way of recording conversations. One day he accidentally discovered that he was able to draw patterns on the side of a tuning fork using a magnet. The patterns could be revealed by sprinkling iron filings onto the fork. From this incident, he decided it should be possible to record sound onto an iron media such as wire or tape.

By late 1898, he had created a practical demonstration of magnetic recording. He strung a wire across a room. He attached to the wire a recording device that consisted of a telephone transmitter, a battery, and an electromagnet. He would walk across the room pulling the recorder

[3] Assuming, of course, the listener knows the difference between the sound of a violin and a viola. I sure don't.

with him and saying "Yakob Yakob" into the transmitter. For playback, he would attach another device that consisted of a telephone receiver and an electromagnet. As the player was moved over the steel wire, the electromagnetic would react to the previously-recorded magnetic fields and generate electrical signals that would drive the telephone receiver to reproduce his speech.

The wire could be played back repeatedly without any significant degradation. Furthermore, it could be erased by running a permanent magnet along it, and then used to record new sounds all over again. These two capabilities were not to be found in phonograph technology.

Poulsen received a Danish patent for his work on December 1, 1898. He continued improving his invention, eventually coming to wrap the wire around a cylinder to create a magnetic recording device that looked similar to cylinder phonographs. He called the device a telegraphone. In 1900, Poulsen won the coveted Grand Prix at the World's Fair in Paris for the demonstration of the telegraphone. On November 13 of the same year, he was awarded a U.S. Patent for the device.

In the ensuing decades, magnetic recording technology improved. The media was changed from wire to steel tape, then to paper tape covered in magnetic film, and finally to plastic tape covered in magnetic film. Stereo was introduced on a wide scale in 1954.

These stereo tapes—and their monophonic predecessors—were only available in reel-to-reel format. The tape was originally wrapped on a supply reel. The end of the tape had to be manually threaded through the tape recorder and onto a take-up reel.

The 1960s saw the development of self-contained cartridges that required no external spools. The most popular of these was the 8-cartridge developed by Bill Lear, a man who also ran a little airplane company called Learjet. The 8-track tape contained four stereo tracks.

1963 saw Philips introduce the Compact Cassette tape format. The cassette was smaller than cartridges, and soon became the dominant consumer audio media format. It held that position until 1992, when the Compact Disc format began outselling it.

In 1987 Sony introduced a digital audiotape (DAT) format that provided sound quality equivalent to that of Compact Discs. DAT was never widely accepted by consumers, but found widespread use by professionals.

Magnetic recording has also found applications outside the field of audio; tapes have been developed for recording video, and discs for storing computer data.

Sound Transmission

Parallel with the development of sound recording and playback technologies, efforts were underway to transmit sound across large distances.

Telephone

The telegraph is a system that carried electric signals over wires. The electric signals were manually modulated by human operators, typically using Morse code. On the receiving end, another human operator would translate the dots and dashes of the transmitted code back into letters, numbers, and punctuation that could be read by laymen.

The first public demonstration of telegraphy was on January 6, 1838 when Alfred Vail sent the message, "A patient waiter is no loser," a distance of two miles. By the 1840s, long distance communication was publicly available via the telegraph. By 1861, transcontinental telegraph lines were in place across the United States.

In the 1870s, inventors were experimenting with ways to improve upon existing telegraphy. Many of them were trying to devise ways in which multiple transmissions could be concurrently sent over a single set of wires. One of these inventors was a man named Alexander Graham Bell.

In 1873, Bell used a set of electromagnets and tuning forks to transmit concurrent signals over a single wire pair. The following year it occurred to Bell that if he had a very large number of tuning forks, he would be able to transmit arbitrary sounds. Several years of experimentation followed, during which Bell was aided by his machinist Thomas A. Watson. On June 3, 1875, Watson built a machine, shown in Figure 1.4, designed by Bell via which they were definitely able to hear each other speaking even while on different floors of the same house. The transmitted sound, although recognizable as human speech, was not of sufficient quality for actual words to be discernable.

On March 10, 1876 they were testing a new version of the device when Bell said, "Mr. Watson, come here; I want you," and—for the first time—Watson was able to clearly discern the words. Variations on the quote are often attributed to Bell. The version here is the one written in Watson's original notebook.

Courtesy of Library of Congress, Prints and Photographs Division,
Detroit Publishing Company Collection

Figure 1.4 Model of Bell's 1875 Telephone

By the end of the year, Bell demonstrated that the telephone was capable of facilitating discernable vocal communications at a distance of a hundred miles over existing telegraph lines. He also held the first conference call, linking three receivers to a single transmitter. As such, Bell's telephone had many advantages over the existing telegraph.

As is often the case with disruptive technologies, litigation ensued among the inventors of the new device, other inventors who had been working on similar devices, and companies that owned a dominant stake in the current technologies that would be superseded by the new technologies. In the 11 years following Bell's invention, over 600 lawsuits would be filed against his patents.

In 1877, commercial telephone services began on a limited scale in the United States, even as litigation continued among the key players. By the following year, a workable manual exchange system was deployed that allowed calls to be arbitrarily routed between any two customers. The exchange system required a human operator to physically patch connections for every call.

In 1915, the first transcontinental telephone service was inaugurated by Bell in New York and Watson in San Francisco. They used replicas of their original telephones to repeat their first message: "Mr. Watson, come here; I want you." In 1926, the first commercial radio-based telephone service connected New York and London.

Today, of course, telephones are ubiquitous in most of the world. Although a 1911 book optimistically began, "Thirty-five short years, and presto! The newborn art of telephony is full-grown," there is evidence to suggest that telephony did not reach maturity in 1911, but has continued to develop. Cellular and satellite phones have made it affordable to communicate with very nearly anybody on the planet from nearly any location. Today's phones are growing beyond audio, and are now beginning to transmit video as well. But that is a story for another book.[4]

Radio

Radio is wireless broadcasting of an audio program to a large area over long distances. Radio got its start in 1864 when James Clerk Maxwell published a seminal paper "on the dynamical theory of the magnetic field." Starting with basic equations pertaining to electricity and magnetism, especially Faraday's work on induction, Maxwell mathematically arrived at the conclusion that energy could be transported through dielectric materials, such as air, organized as perpendicular waves of electricity and magnetism. Further, these waves were perpendicular to the energy's direction of travel, as shown in Figure 1.5. Maxwell also concluded that the waves moved at a finite speed, nominally the speed of light.

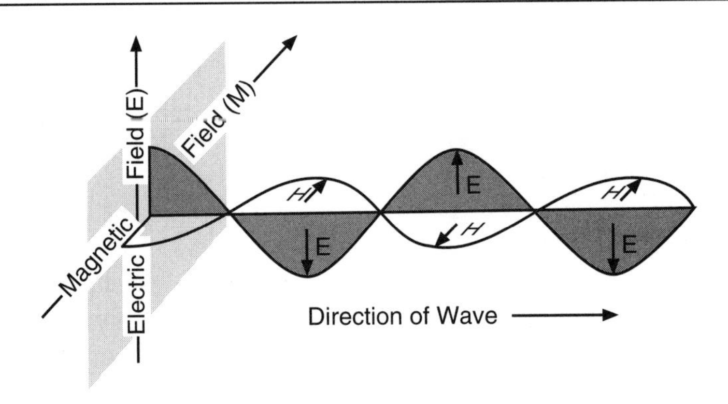

Figure 1.5 Maxwell's Electromagnetic Wave

[4] Such as *Video in the 21st Century* (Janus 2002).

At the time of publication, Maxwell's theories were very radical and were, therefore, rejected by the scientific community at large. The leading theory held that electricity and magnetism were separate forces, and that they were able to affect "action at a distance" instantaneously.

Maxwell did not devise any experiments to validate his mathematically-derived theories. It was not until 25 years later that Heinrich Hertz devised and conducted an elegant experiment that bolstered Maxwell's theories. After Hertz's experiment, other physicists were eager to replicate and expand his work. To this end, they needed devices that were capable of detecting electromagnetic (EM) waves.

One particularly sensitive EM detector called a coherer was developed by Oliver Lodge. In 1894, he demonstrated that the device could be used with a spark generator to transmit Morse code using Hertzian waves—as electromagnetic waves were known at the time. His demonstration sparked the interest of several inventors. Three of note were British naval officer Henry Jackson, the Russian Alexander Popov, and the Italian Guglielmo Marconi. All three of these men, and Lodge himself, experimented with methods for sending information using electromagnetic waves. All men were successful at demonstrating working wireless telegraphs within the next few years.

The most commercially successful of these inventors was Marconi. As the 19th century closed, he set up numerous demonstrations of his wireless devices. A key milestone in wireless telegraphy came on December 12, 1901 when Marconi reportedly received the first transatlantic wireless transmission. It was Morse code for the letter S repeated over and over again.

One of the early radio pioneers, American Reginald Fessenden, was very interested in the idea of wireless transmission of speech. He spent years developing new radio transmitters designed to carry speech. On Christmas Eve 1906, he made a famous broadcast that included a brief speech by himself, as well as Christmas music. The broadcast was heard by numerous radio operators on both military and civilian ships all over the Atlantic Ocean.

Radio really began to take off after World War I, when numerous amateur radio stations began transmitting with the cessation of the wartime broadcast ban. One of these stations was run by Frank Conrad. Normally, Conrad's broadcasts would consist of conversations about wireless equipment and technology. However, on October 17, 1919, Conrad instead broadcast music from a phonograph. He was subsequently flooded with requests for specific songs. He began bi-weekly music broadcasts. The programs mostly consisted of pre-recorded music, but occasionally included live broadcasts from his two young sons.

From these humble beginnings, radio broadcasting grew into a lucrative and pervasive industry. The first commercial station began broadcasting amplitude-modulated (AM) signals in 1921.

In 1939, American electrical engineer Edwin Armstrong experimented with a new radio technique. He was convinced that better sound quality was possible by modulating the frequency of the broadcast signal, rather than amplitude. His frequency modulation (FM) concept saw commercial deployment in 1941 in the United States. Twenty years later in 1961, FM broadcasting was extended to include stereo.

Today, radio remains ubiquitous. AM and FM stations broadcast music around the clock. New digital-based systems such as Digital Audio Broadcasting (DAB) are being deployed, and satellite-based services such as XM are also available.

It's a Journey, not a Destination

The past 125 years has seen the ability to record, play, and transmit sound move from fantasy to ubiquity. The progress we've made since those first crude experiments is remarkable. Edison's early wax cylinders were six inches across and could only store two minutes worth of low quality sound. Today, a 200-gigabyte hard drive of comparable size and weight can store over six *months* of high quality music. Sitting in a coffee shop in California, I can listen to a radio station in Europe over the Internet.

The following chapters of this book will explore today's dominant sound-related technologies. But remember that by no means has the field of audio reached its final instantiation. Industrious inventors are continually striving to improve upon the state of the art. Perhaps you, a reader of this book, will go on to be one of those who bring us cool audio technologies that no one else has even thought of yet!

Chapter 2

Sound

"Someone told me that each equation I included in the book would halve the sales."[1]

—Stephen Hawking, *A Brief History of Time*

If a tree falls in the forest, does it make a sound? Because it is a macroscopic event free of quantum mechanical effects, the answer is yes. But what precisely is sound?

A glib answer is that sound is what we hear. But then what is hearing? Hearing is the perception of sound. These circular definitions are a bit worrisome, but have no fear; we'll spend some time in this chapter and the next describing the physical characteristics of sound—acoustics—and how humans perceive that sound—psychoacoustics.

This chapter has a fair number of equations and graphs in it. These are intended to provide a comprehensive reference for audio engineers. If you are reading this book just to become familiar with different audio technologies, it may behoove you to skip to the summary at the end of the chapter. You should still be able to parse the remaining chapters without too much difficulty. However, I strongly encourage everyone to try to make it through this math chapter. Like the foundation of a house, a strong understanding of the fundamentals is required to support future concepts.

---

[1] If so, given a world population of 5 billion, the maximum number of equations you could put into a book and still have a least one reader would be $\log_2$(5 billion) or roughly 32 equations.

Intro to Sound

Sound is simply vibrations in matter. As such, sound requires a medium through which to propagate. By comparison, light requires no transport medium and can travel through vacuum. No matter what you may hear in most science fiction films, sound does not travel through a vacuum, no matter how big the explosion is.

Audible sounds are those vibrations that we humans can hear. Most of the sounds humans hear are transmitted through the air, although audible sounds can also be transmitted through liquid and solid matter. Airborne sound travels in the form of longitudinal waves.

Longitudinal Waves

Consider a long spring or Slinky† stretched out along a table. One end of the spring is fixed in place. The other end is attached to a crank-driven piston. If the crank is quickly turned, the piston compresses the coils of the spring nearest it. This region of compression propagates to the other end of the spring. As the crank continues to turn, the piston moves away from the spring, creating a region of decreased coil density in the coils nearest it. Again, this region of expansion or rarefaction propagates along the spring. This process is shown in Figure 2.1.

If we keep turning the crank, the piston continues oscillating, and in turn creates localized fluctuations in the coil density. These fluctuations are known as waves, and in this particular case are longitudinal waves because the waves oscillate in the same direction that they are traveling.

The Slinky example is very useful, as it is analogous to how sound behaves in air. Note that the slinky does not move. One end oscillates back and forth a short distance, but the spring as a whole does not make any forward progress.

Waves do move through the medium of the spring. These waves consist of alternating regions of compression and rarefaction. Compression refers to regions of higher density. Rarefaction refers to regions of lower density. Also note that there is an ambient coil density that the spring has before the piston begins moving.

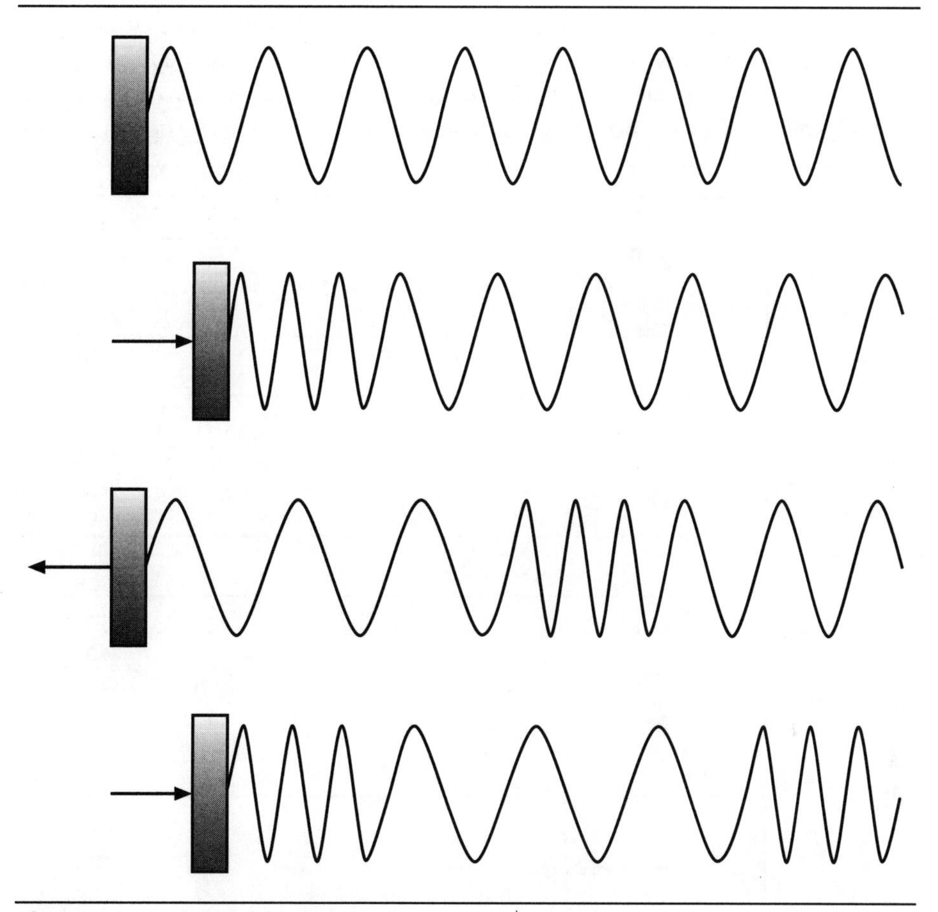

Figure 2.1 Longitudinal Waves in a Slinky†

In our thought experiment, the longitudinal waves are transmitted through the compressible medium of the spring. These are, technically, sound waves, although they are not audible to humans. The sounds we are most familiar with are those that move through air. These sounds consist of longitudinal waves passing through the media of air molecules.

Air has an ambient pressure. Sound waves are localized density fluctuations within this medium, as shown in Figure 2.2. Just as with our spring example, air molecules only oscillate when they are carrying sound; they do not move forward in the direction of the sound wave.

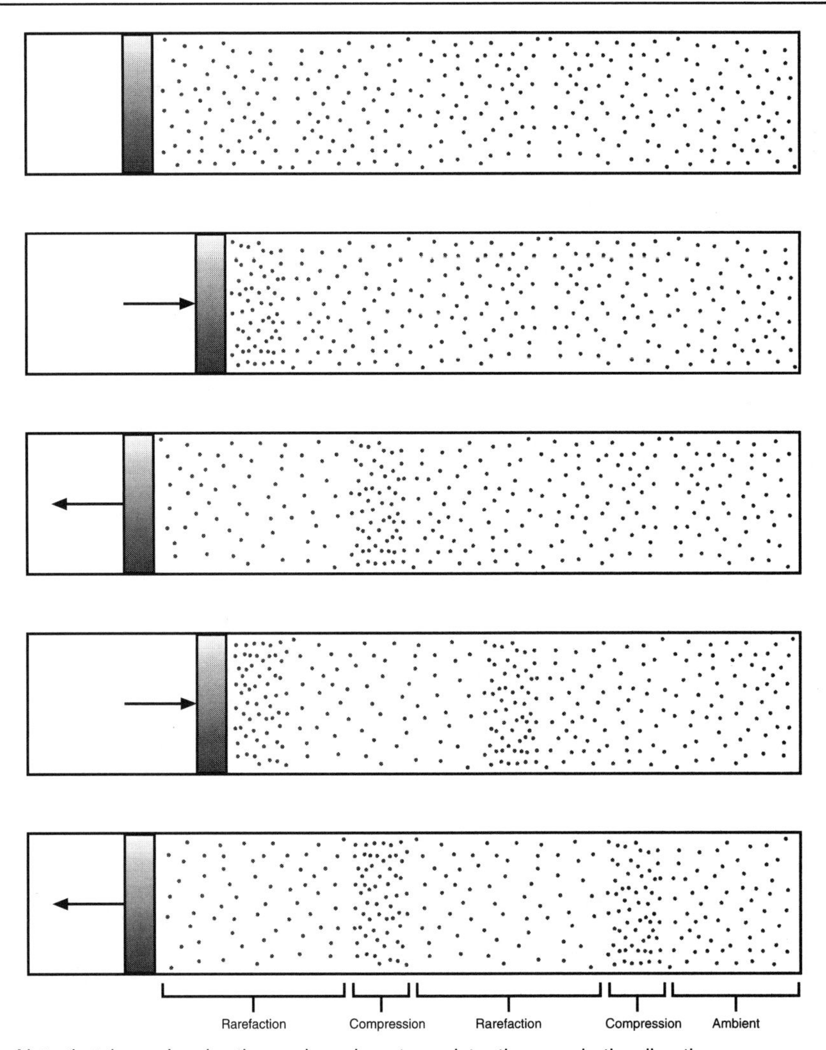

Figure 2.2 Air Molecules Carrying Sound Waves

Sound waves can travel through most types of matter. We are most familiar with sound moving through air, but it can move through other gases, as well as liquids and solids. In fact, the density of the universe was so great during its first 300,000 years that sound waves were able to ripple throughout it. The minute density fluctuations of these first sounds are thought to be responsible for the ultimate formation of galaxies and clusters. Alas, most sounds we hear today do not have the same import.

Waveforms

Now suppose we were to pick an arbitrary point in the pipe above and record the pressure over time. At first, we would just see the ambient atmospheric pressure. The pressure would then increase as the first compression region passed over the test point. Next, the pressure would decrease to below the ambient. If we were to plot our data, the result would look like Figure 2.3. Graphs such as this one in which we plot the pressure of a sound wave versus time are known as *waveforms*. We will be using them frequently as we discuss audio.

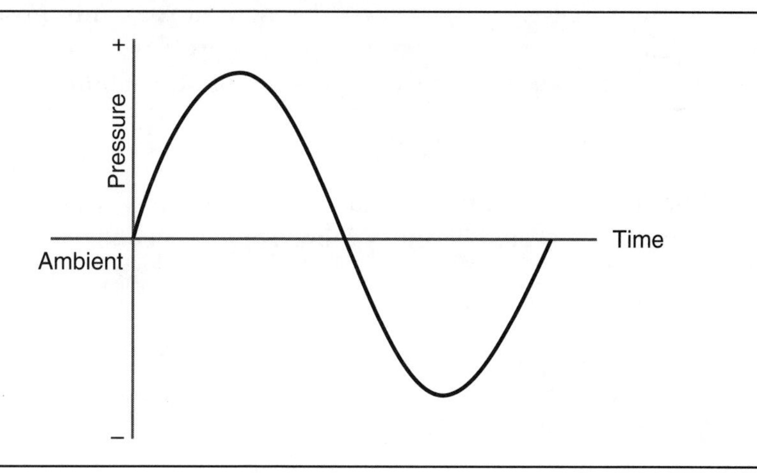

Figure 2.3 Waveform From the Pipe

Pure Tones

A simple type of sound is the pure tone. A pure tone is a sound with sinusoidal pressure fluctuations. In other words, the pressure waveform is a sine wave, as shown in Figure 2.4.

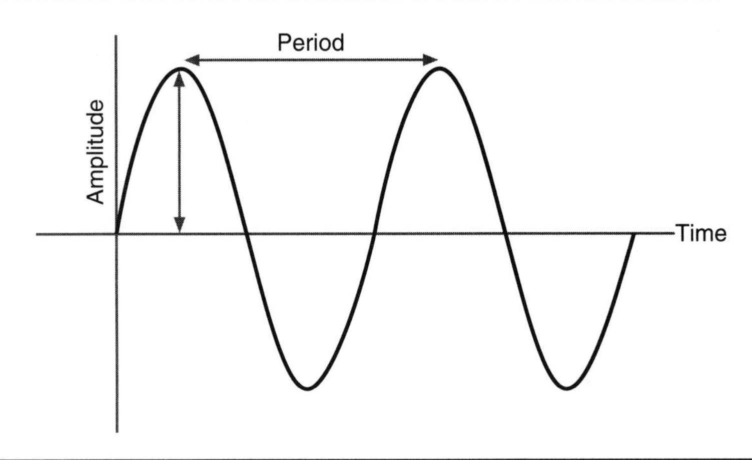

Figure 2.4 Pure Tone Waveform

The waveform of this pure tone has several characteristics of interest to us. The first is the magnitude. Zero amplitude in this case refers to the ambient pressure. Points of the sine wave with positive amplitude indicate increased pressure or compression. Points with negative amplitude indicate decreased pressure or rarefaction.

Period

The time required for a complete cycle is known as the ***period*** (T). The period is measured in units of time such as seconds.

Frequency

The ***frequency*** (f) is the rate at which the wave repeats. It can be derived from the period using Equation 2.1. Frequency is measured in units of per second, also known as ***hertz*** (Hz).

Equation 2.1 Frequency and Period

$$f=1/T$$

Example

Given a pure tone with a period of 1 ms, what is the frequency of the tone?

Solution

$f = 1/T$

$f = 1/(1\ ms)$

$f = 1/(0.001s)$

$f = 1000$ hertz

Phase

By definition a sine wave, and hence a pure tone, completes a cycle as its phase moves through a complete circle or 360 degrees. Figure 2.5 shows a sine wave moving through a complete cycle. It begins at a phase of 0 degree. The sine of 0 degree is 0, so the amplitude of the wave at that point is 0. The sine of 1 degree is ~0.017, so the wave begins moving upward. By 90 degrees the amplitude of the wave reaches a maximum of 1. It heads downward from there, crossing the zero-line again at a phase of 180 degree. It reaches the minimum value at 270 degrees. When the phase reaches 360 degrees we are back at zero amplitude and beginning a new cycle. A phase of 360 degrees is the same as a phase of 0 degree.

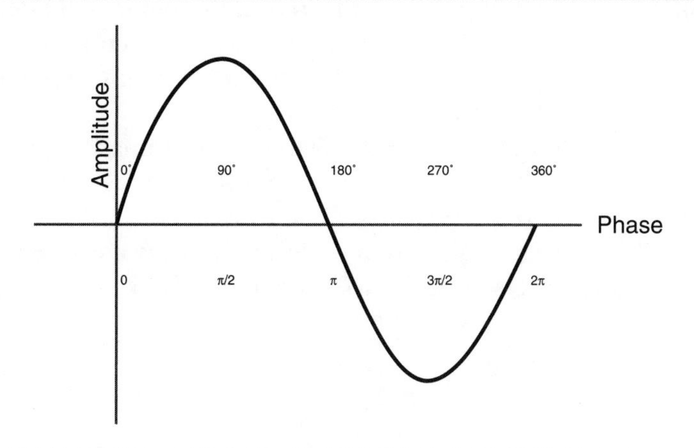

Figure 2.5 Phase

Phase is also measured in radians. Whereas 360 degrees are required to complete a full cycle, it takes 2π radians to complete a cycle. In other words, 2π radians = 360 degrees.

In addition to specifying a point within the cycle of a wave, phase can also be used to compare the alignment of two tones of the same frequency. For example, Figure 2.6 shows two waves of the same frequency that are offset by 90 degrees.

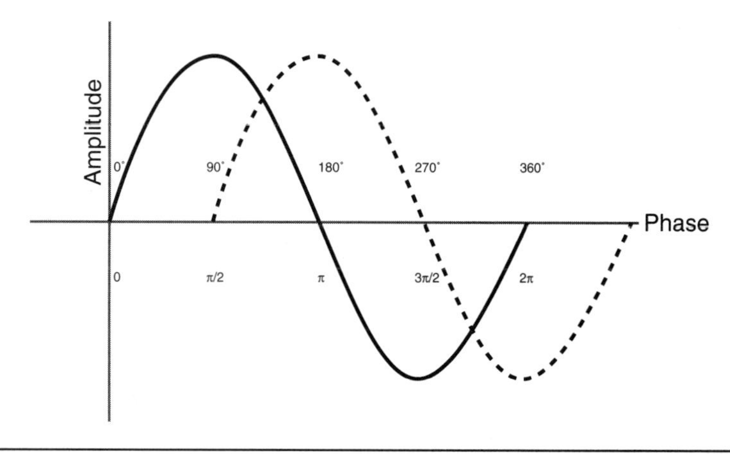

Figure 2.6 Phase Shift

This difference between two tones is known as a *phase offset* or *phase difference*. Phase offset is also loosely referred to as simply *phase*. Phase offsets are typically measured in the range −180 degrees to 180 degrees, rather than 0 degree to 360 degrees. When two waves have a non-zero phase offset, they are said to be *out of phase*. When two waves have zero phase offset, they are *in phase*.

When two waves are ±90 degrees out of phase, they are said to be in *phase quadrature*. When they are 180 degrees out of phase, the two waves are in *phase opposition*.

Phase plays an important role in sound wave interference and how humans localize sounds, as we will discuss later.

Example

Two pure tones with a frequency of 1,250 hertz are 45 degrees out of phase. What is their phase offset in units of time?

Solution

First, let's compute the period of the signals.

$f = 1/T$

$T = 1/f$

$T = 1/1250$ hertz

$T = .0008$ seconds $= 800$ microseconds (μs)

The two tones are 45 degrees out of phase. A complete cycle or period corresponds to 360 degrees. The phase offset is therefore $45/360 = 0.125$ of the total period. We can just multiply this fraction by the period to get the phase offset in units of time.

$t_{offset} = 800\ \mu s \times 0.125$

$t_{offset} = 100\ \mu s$

Propagation of Sound

We've examined some characteristics of sound from the vantage of a fixed point in space. Now we will consider how sound moves through space or propagates.

Diagramming Sound Movement

In diagramming how sound moves, we will be using two conventions: wave fronts and rays.

Wave Fronts

A convenient way to diagram the propagation of sound waves is by arbitrarily picking points of uniform density and plotting these wave fronts as lines. Plotting the wave fronts of our previous example would look like Figure 2.7.

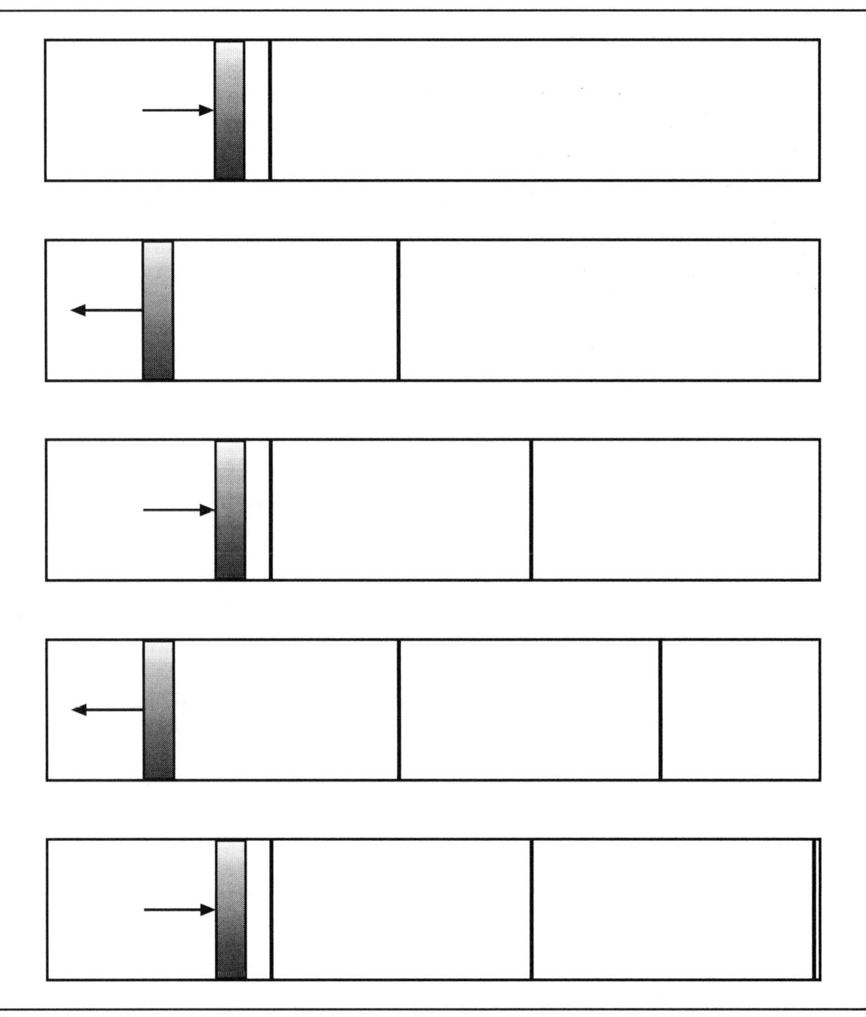

Figure 2.7 Planar Wave Fronts

The wave fronts in the preceding diagram are planar. Each successive wave front is parallel to one another.

Omnidirectional sounds are characterized by spherical wave fronts, as shown in Figure 2.8. For instance, the sound of a firework shell exploding in the air would create spherical wave fronts. The curvature of spherical wave fronts is very apparent close to the source of sound, but from very far away, the wave fronts would appear nearly planar in shape.

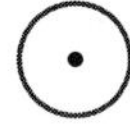
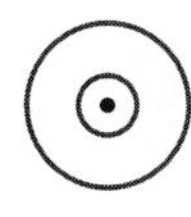
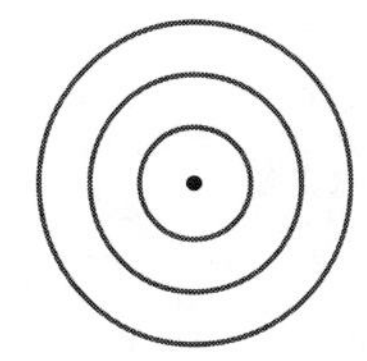

Figure 2.8 Spherical Wave Fronts

Wave fronts are a useful tool as we explore how sound moves through different types of environments.

Sound Rays

Although wave fronts are very useful for diagramming certain acoustic behavior, some concepts are more clearly illustrated using sound rays. These rays are arrows indicating the direction the sound is moving in. In the case of our pipe example, a sound ray would look like Figure 2.9.

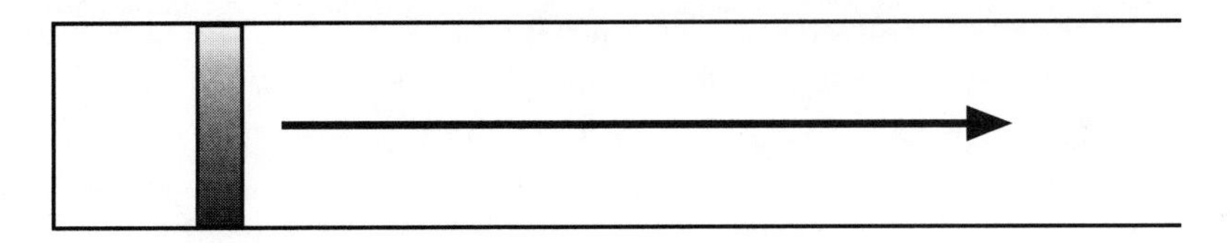

Figure 2.9 Sound Ray

Speed of Sound

So just how fast do sound waves move? The speed of sound varies depending on inertial properties such as density and the elasticity of the medium through which the waves are moving. As such, the speed at which sound moves through air depends upon the local atmospheric pressure, temperature, humidity, altitude, CO_2 concentration, and other related factors.

The speed of sound through air at standard temperature and pressure (STP), 20 degrees Celsius and 101.3 kilopascals, is 1,129 feet per second (344 meters per second). The speed of sound in some other materials is shown in Table 2.1.

Table 2.1 Speed of Sound in Various Materials

Material	c (ft/s)	c(m/s)
air (STP)	1,129	344
air (STP)	1,129	344
air (32°F, 0°C)	1,086	331
marble	12,500	3,810
cork	1,640	500
brick	11,975	3,650
water	4,911	1,497
seawater	5,023	1,531
paraffin	4,265	1,300
castor oil	4,845	1,477
oak	12,631	3,850

The speed of sound is designated with the letter *c*. The letter *c* is more commonly used to designate the speed of light. However, in this book *c* refers to the speed of sound unless otherwise noted.

The speed of sound is independent of the frequency or intensity of the sound. In general, all sounds move at the same speed within the same medium. For the sake of completeness, know that extremely loud sounds—sounds that will deafen a human—may have enough power to cause localized temperature fluctuations that may result in some frequencies moving at higher speeds than others.

Wavelength

Now that we know how fast sound is moving, let us consider how far apart the wave fronts are. The distance between adjacent wave fronts is known as the wavelength. The wavelength (λ) of a pure tone is inversely proportional to its frequency, as indicated by the relationship expressed in Equation 2.2.

Equation 2.2 Wavelength and Frequency

$$c = f \times \lambda$$

Note that wavelength of a sound at a given frequency also depends on the local speed of sound. The wavelength of a 1,000-hertz tone in air is different than the wavelength of a 1,000-hertz tone in sea water.

Example

Given a pure tone of 5,000 hertz in air at STP, what is the wavelength of the tone?

Solution

$c = f \times \lambda$

$\lambda = c/f$

$\lambda = (1125 \text{ feet/second}) / (5000 \text{ hertz})$

$\boldsymbol{\lambda = 0.225}$ **feet**

Reflection

Sound waves can reflect off objects. Waves hitting an acoustically reflective surface bounce off it in another direction. The direction of reflection is such that the angle at which it hits—the angle of incidence (θ_i)—equals the angle of reflection (θ_r), as demonstrated in Figure 2.10. The angles of incidence and reflection are measured with respect to the surface normal. The surface normal is a line perpendicular to the reflective surface.

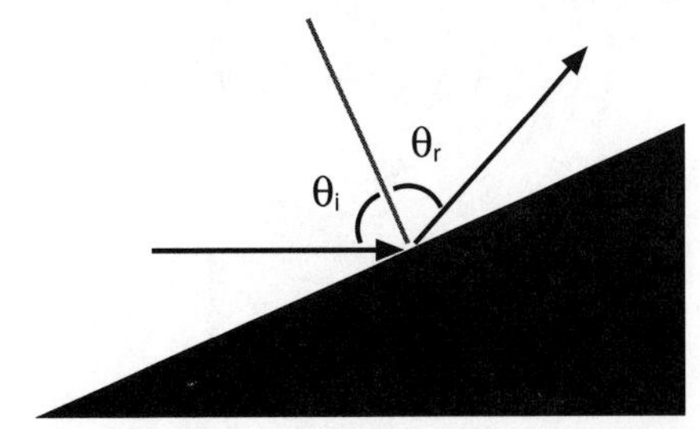

When sound hits a reflective surface, the angle of incidence equals the angle of reflection.

Figure 2.10 Reflected Sound Ray

We can draw diagrams of sound reflection using wave fronts, but they can be a bit more confusing to look at. Figure 2.11 is a diagram of reflecting parallel wave fronts.

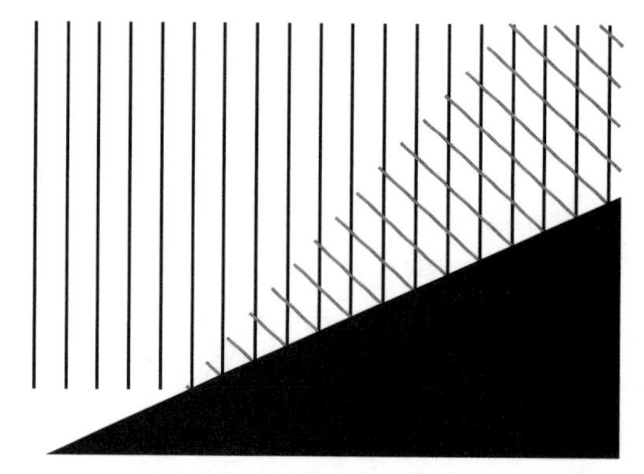

Black parallel waves come from the left and are reflected as gray parallel waves to the right.

Figure 2.11 Parallel Sound Waves Reflecting

Reflected spherical wave fronts create the auditory effect that they originate from a point source located behind the reflective surface, as shown in Figure 2.12.

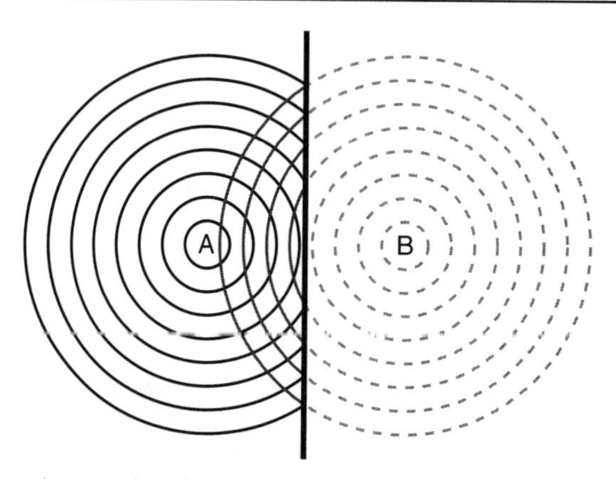

Sound source A generates the black spherical wave fronts. The dark gray reflected waves sound as if they are coming from a non-existent sound source located at point B, behind the reflective surface.

Figure 2.12 Reflected Spherical Wavefronts

We can focus sound by taking advantage of the way it reflects. A parabolic reflective surface redirects parallel rays of sound to a focal point, as shown in Figure 2.13. Because all the sound is being concentrated into a small region, the resulting pressure—and hence loudness—associated with the sound is greatly increased. This technique is used for amplifying distant sounds, as in the parabolic microphones used in recording on-field dialogue during football games.

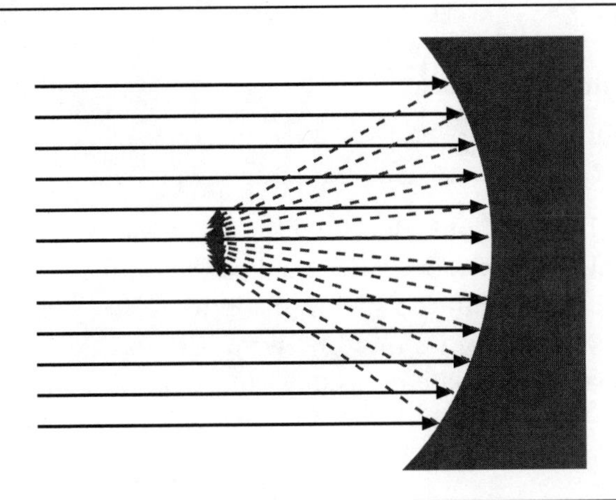

Figure 2.13 Focusing Sound

Refraction

Rather than reflecting off an object, some sound waves may refract through the object. Sound waves that are transmitted into the new media are bent, as shown in Figure 2.14.

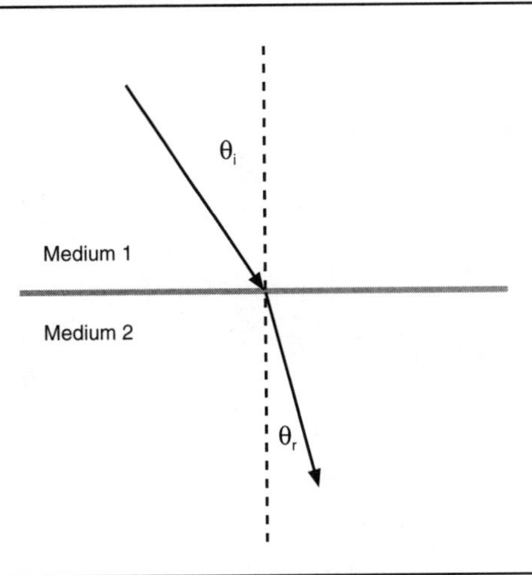

Figure 2.14 Refracted Sound Ray

In most cases, the angle of incidence does not equal the angle of transmission. The angle of transmission is dependent upon the angle of incidence and the speed of sound in the two materials. The relationship is quantified by Snell's Law, shown in Equation 2.3.

Equation 2.3 Snell's Law

$$\frac{\sin(\theta_i)}{\sin(\theta_r)} = \frac{c_i}{c_r}$$

Snell's Law holds that the ratio of the sine of the angle of incidence to the angle of transmission is equal to the ratio of the speed of sound in the original medium to the speed of sound in the refractive medium.

As sound hits the new medium, the frequency remains constant, but the wavelength changes, as diagrammed in Figure 2.15.

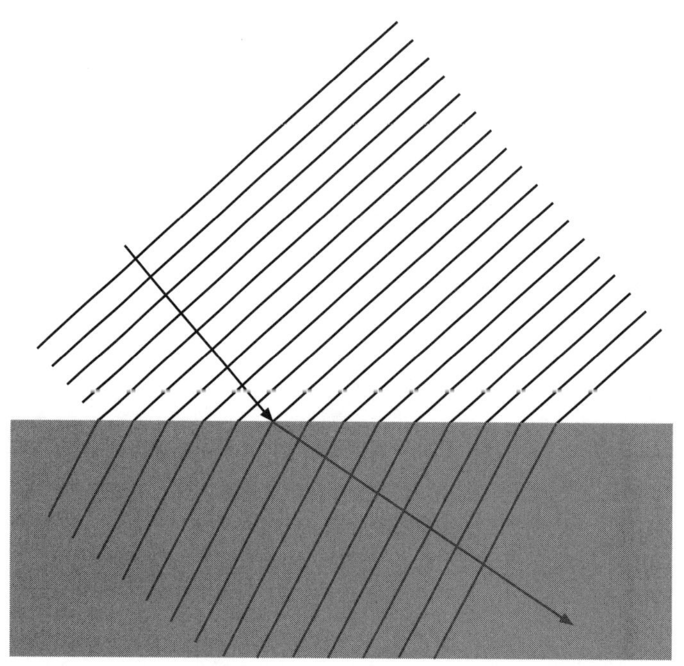

The wavelength of a sound increases as it refracts into a medium with a higher speed of sound.

Figure 2.15 Refracted Parallel Wavefronts

Example

A 100-hertz tone is traveling through air at STP in parallel wave fronts when it hits flat water at an angle of 10 degrees from vertical. What is the angle of transmission? What is the wavelength of the sound in the air? In the water?

Solution

Starting from Snell's Law, we know that:

$$\frac{\sin(\theta_1)}{\sin(\theta_2)} = \frac{c_1}{c_2}$$

$$\theta_2 = \sin^{-1}\left(\frac{c_2}{c_1}\sin(\theta_1)\right)$$

$$\theta_2 = \sin^{-1}\left(\frac{4921\text{ ft/s}}{1125\text{ ft/s}}\sin(10°)\right)$$

$$\theta_2 = \sin^{-1}(0.7596)$$

$$\boldsymbol{\theta_2 = 49.52°}$$

$\lambda_1 = c_1/f =$ (1125 ft/s) / (10 hertz) = **112.5 ft**

$\lambda_2 = c_2/f =$ (4921 ft/s) / (10 hertz) = **492.1 ft**

In addition to occurring across well-defined boundaries such as an air-water interface, refraction also occurs in regions with gradual velocity changes. For instance, in the evening, the air next to the earth is warm while the air higher up is cooler. Sound travels slower in the cooler air, causing sounds made near the ground to bend upwards. In such a situation, sound does not carry across the ground as far as it would in the daytime because it is being bent upwards. In the mornings, the reverse scenario can happen; cool air near the ground bends sound waves back towards the Earth. Spherical waves that would otherwise have traveled away from the ground are redirected downwards, causing sounds to be heard more clearly than they would have otherwise. These scenarios are diagrammed in Figure 2.16.

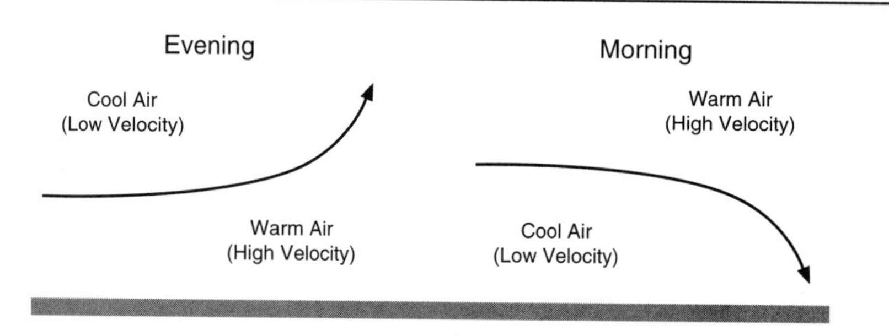

Figure 2.16 Sound Waves Bending in the Evening and Morning Air

Diffraction

In addition to reflection and refraction, energy carried as waves (including sound) also diffract. *Diffraction* is the tendency of waves to bend around obstructions in their path, as shown in Figure 2.17. As such, you can sometimes hear sounds even if there is an object between you and the source of the sound. The region behind the obstruction, which the sound waves do not reach, is the shadow zone.

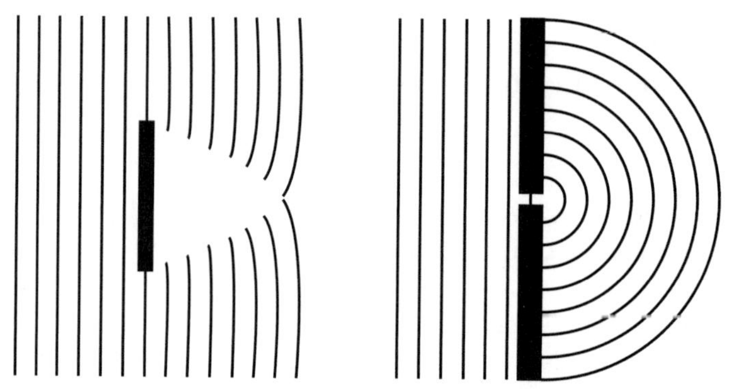

Sound waves diffract into the shadow zone of an obstruction (left). Sound waves also diffract spherically outward through a narrow opening (right).

Figure 2.17 Diffraction

The amount of diffraction depends upon the size of the obstruction and the wavelength of sound. If the wavelength is very large compared to the obstruction, then the diffraction is so great that there is almost no shadow zone at all. For instance, you can hear a tone with a 10-foot wavelength from behind a toothpick with no trouble at all.

Conversely, if the wavelength is small compared to the size of the obstruction, then there is a large region behind the obstruction that the sound waves cannot reach through diffraction.

As we will study in more detail in the following chapter, the diffraction of sound waves around the human head is one of the cues used for locating the position of sounds.

Interference

When sound waves occupy the same point in space, they interfere with one another. The resultant intensity of coincident waves is simply the sum of the intensities of the individual waves, a principle known as superposition.

If two identical waves interfere with each other, the resulting wave has the same frequency as the original waves, but is twice as intense, as shown in Figure 2.18. Such a combination is known as constructive interference.

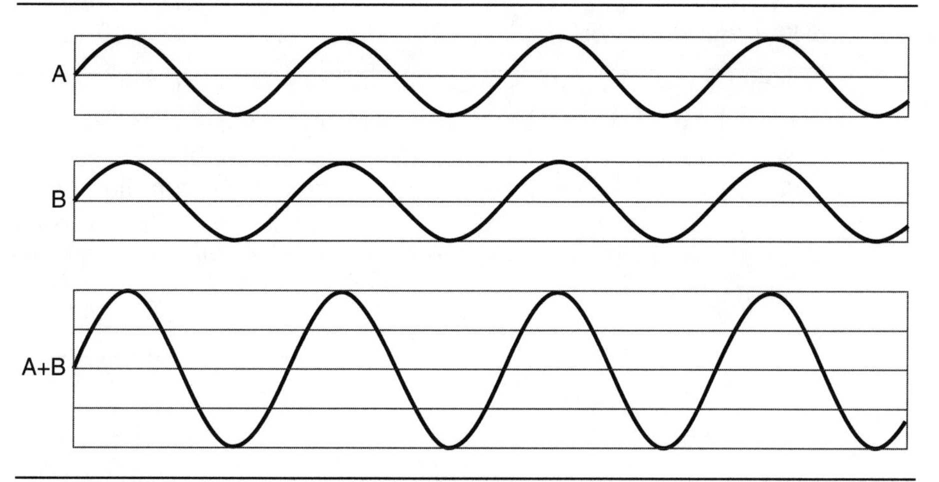

Figure 2.18 Constructive Interference

Now suppose one of the waves is in phase opposition to the other. When these two waves are added together, they cancel each other out, resulting in no waves, as seen in Figure 2.19. This nullification is known as destructive interference. It may seem odd that playing two sounds of equal intensity results in a net silence, but it is a very real phenomenon.

In fact, it is used by pilots, and now consumers, in noise-canceling headphones that cancel out ambient sounds.[2]

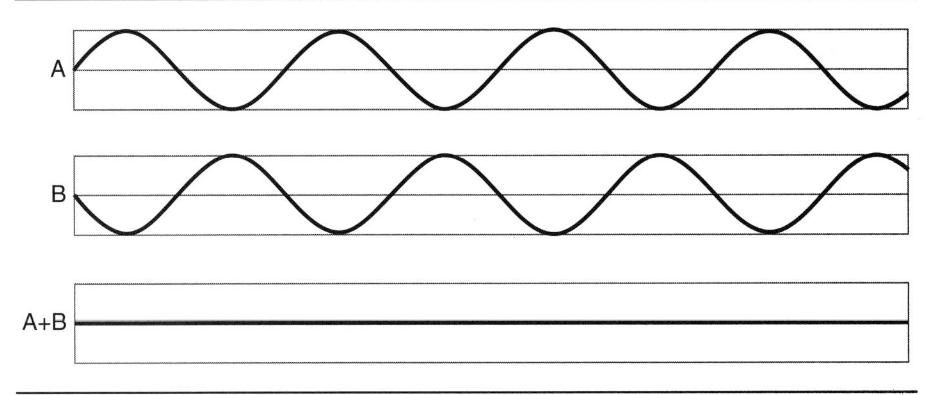

Figure 2.19 Destructive Interference

Beat Frequency

When two waves with similar frequencies interfere with one another, they exhibit what is known as a beat frequency. Even though the two original signals have a constant intensity, the combined signal's intensity sinusoidally varies between zero intensity and the combined intensity of the original two signals. The rate of this intensity oscillation is known as the *beat frequency*. The beat frequency for two signals is determined by Equation 2.4.

Equation 2.4 Beat Frequency

$$f_{beat} = f_{high} - f_{low}$$

[2] In a 1954 short story, Arthur C. Clarke posited a noise-cancellation device called the Fenton Silencer. Alas, the device ultimately exploded due to a design flaw brought about by the inventor's poor understanding of sound and energy. The reader is thus encouraged to read this chapter very carefully!

A diagram of beat frequencies is shown in Figure 2.20.

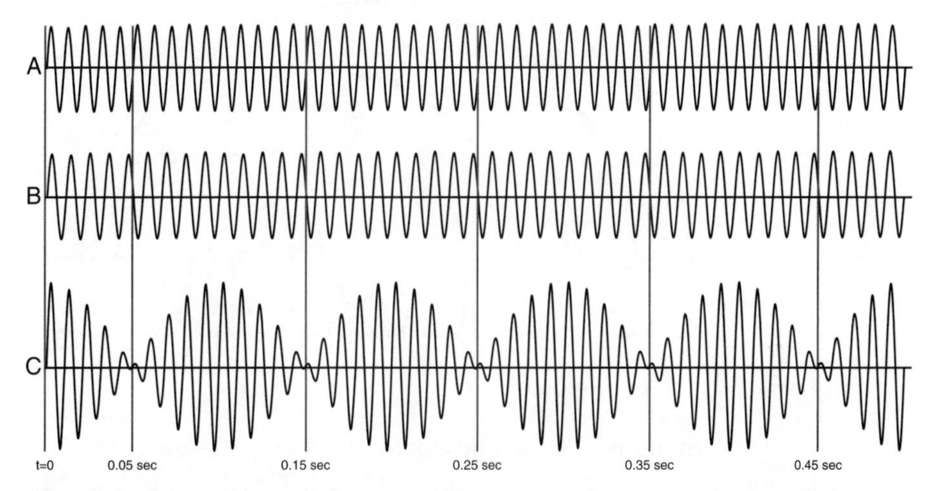

When combined, a 100-hertz tone (top) and a 90-hertz tone (middle) combine to produce a signal (bottom) with a beat frequency of 100 - 90 = 10 hertz. The 10-hertz beat frequency means that the sound has zero intensity every 0.01 seconds, as evidenced on the diagram at time 0.05 s, 0.15 s, 0.25 s ...

Figure 2.20 Beat Frequency

The beat frequencies are used by musicians to tune their stringed instruments. If they play a reference tone from a tuning fork or electronic tuner, and then pluck the string being tuned, an out-of-tune string has a beat frequency. The higher the beat frequency, the more out of tune the string is. By adjusting the tension on the string until the beat frequency becomes zero and disappears, they can bring the string into tune.

Doppler Effect

When a fire engine races past us, the frequency of its siren seems to change. Obviously, the frequency produced by the siren remains constant. Firemen riding in the truck hear the same constant frequency. However, to stationary observers, the frequency is higher as the truck approaches and is lower when the truck recedes.

What is happening is that the truck's motion is compressing the wave fronts in front of the vehicle and spreading them out behind, as shown in Figure 2.21. Because frequency is inversely proportional to the wavelength, the siren's frequency is higher to stationary observers in front of the moving truck, and lower to stationary observers behind the truck.

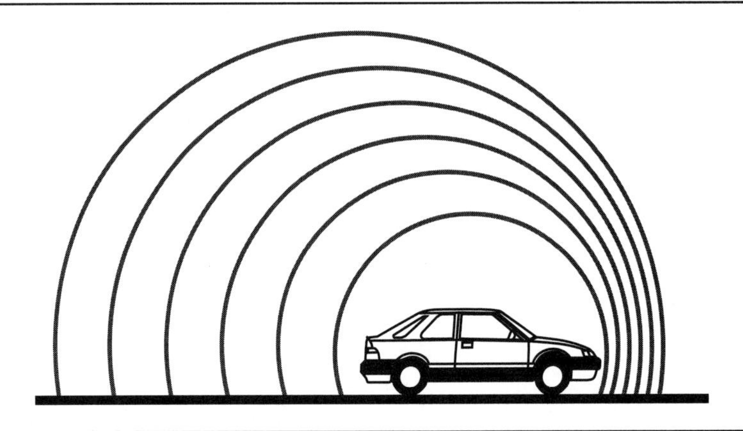

Figure 2.21 The Doppler Effect

This phenomenon is known as the Doppler Effect, after Christian Doppler, who conceived the idea in 1842. The Doppler Effect holds true for other waves, such as light. Indeed, one of the biggest breakthroughs in astronomy came in 1929 when Edwin Hubble examined the Doppler shift of the light being produced by nearby galaxies and found that almost all of them are moving away from us at very high speed.[3] The Doppler Effect for a stationary observer is quantified in Equation 2.5.

Equation 2.5 Doppler Effect for Stationary Observer and Moving Sound Source

$$f' = \left(\frac{1}{1 \pm \frac{v}{c}} \right) f$$

where f is the frequency of the sound source

v is the velocity of the sound source with respect to the observer

c is the speed of sound

f' is the frequency heard by the station observer.

With regards to the ± term: + is used if the source is moving away from the observer; - is used if the source is moving towards the observer.

[3] This datum raises the perplexing question of what these other galaxies know that we don't.

The Doppler Effect also applies to moving observers and stationary sound sources. However, the amount of frequency shift for an observer moving past a stationary source at a given speed is different than the frequency shift of a sound moving at that same speed past a stationary observer. In other words, the siren sounds different if the truck is moving towards you at 50 miles per hour (MPH), than if you were moving towards it at 50 MPH. The precise relationship is given in Equation 2.6.

Equation 2.6 Doppler Effect for Moving Observer and Stationary Sound Source

$$f' = \left(1 \pm \frac{v}{c}\right) f$$

With regards to the ± term: + is used if the observer is moving toward the source; - is used if the observer is moving away from the source.

Example

A sound generator is producing a 1,000-hertz tone. What frequency does a stationary observer hear when the generator moves towards him at 100 feet per second? What frequency does the observer hear when he moves toward the stationary generator at the same speed?

Solution

For the first case,

$$f' = \left(\frac{1}{1 - \frac{v}{c}}\right) f = \left(\frac{1}{1 - \frac{100\,ft/s}{1125\,ft/s}}\right) 1000Hz = 1098Hz$$

In the second case,

$$f' = \left(1 + \frac{v}{c}\right) f = \left(1 + \frac{100\,ft/s}{1125\,ft/s}\right) 1000Hz = 1089Hz$$

Sound Intensity and Power

We've discussed how sound moves through a medium, and we've also discussed some characteristics of sound such as frequency, wavelength, and speed. We will now explore another characteristic of sound: intensity.

As we will soon learn in this chapter, humans can hear sound with a wide range of intensities. The range is so vast that it is often unwieldy to deal with the intensity values if they are all arranged evenly. Furthermore—as we will discuss in great detail in the next chapter—human perception of sound is non-linear. A small change in intensity of a low intensity sound is much more noticeable than the same amount of change in a high intensity sound. For these reasons, we often apply logarithms to acoustic measurements. Logarithms have the advantage of compressing higher numbers close together.

Logarithms

It used to be that the only way to figure out a logarithm was by buying an expensive reference book and looking up the answer in a table. The advent of the slide rule meant that with just a little training, anyone could readily compute a logarithm by sliding bits of wood and plastic from side to side with great precision. The tricky bit was keeping track of the power of ten. Was the answer 0.0125 or was it 0.00125? Today, of course, to compute the logarithm of a number, you just type in the number into a scientific calculator and press the log button.

A logarithm or log is defined to be $\log_b(x) = y$, such that $b^y = x$. For instance, $\log_{10}100 = 2$, because $10^2 = 100$.

Unless explicitly stated otherwise, the base of a logarithm is assumed to be 10, because that's how many fingers we have. As such, rather than writing $\log_{10}(x)$, we often just write $\log(x)$.

You may sometimes see $\log_e(x)$ (where e is ~2.7182818). This logarithm is known as a natural log, and is typically abbreviated $\ln(x)$. Also, logarithms with a base of 2 are common, and $\log_2(x)$ is often abbreviated as $\lg(x)$.

Decibels

There are many examples in the field of sound where we take the logarithm of a ratio of values. Being a ratio, the number is unit-less. However, to provide a descriptor of what the number is, the term Bel is used. The Bel is named after Alexander Graham Bell.

For example, if we wanted to compare a 100-watt (W) power source to a 20-watt power source, we would say the logarithm power ratio is log(100W/20W) = log (5) = 0.699 Bels.

For common sound measurements, the Bel is too large a unit, so we instead use a tenth of a Bel, also known as a deciBel (dB). The capital B is often omitted when writing out the term, giving us decibel. However, the abbreviation properly maintains the capital B (dB).

We will explore the concept of decibels in greater detail after we first introduce the types of measurements that use decibels.

Sound Power

When something makes a noise, it is using energy to create oscillations in the air. Because energy is conserved, what is really happening is that energy of one form is being converted into another form. For instance, a loudspeaker converts electrical energy into the kinetic energy of a vibrating diaphragm. The rate at which energy is converted over an interval of time is known as power. When the energy in question is being used to create sounds, the power is known as acoustic power or sound power.

In the field of acoustics, power is most often measured in units of the watt (W). Many of us are familiar with watts as a measurement of the power consumption of light bulbs. The acoustic power examples are shown Table 2.2.

Table 2.2 Acoustic Power of Some Common Objects

Item	Max Acoustic Power (Watts)
Boeing 777 at full throttle	8,000
75-piece orchestra	75
250 watt cinema loudspeaker	7.0

Many sound devices, such as speakers and amplifiers, are often described with a wattage value, as in 30-watt speakers. Almost invariably, the wattage listed is referring to the electrical power the device can handle. The acoustic power the device can produce is always much less than the electrical power.

The sound power of a device is sometimes measured against a reference sound power of 10^{-12} W. The logarithm of this ratio is taken to give the Sound Power Level, which has the somewhat counterintuitive acronym of PWL. The PWL is defined in Equation 2.7.

Equation 2.7 Sound Power Level

$$\text{PWL (dB)} = 10 \log (W/W_0), \text{ where } W_0 = 10^{-12} \text{ watts}$$

The 10 in Equation 2.7 is there to convert from Bels to decibels. As we will soon see, PWL is not the only measurement to use decibels. As such, to clarify that a particular decibel measurement is of the Sound Power Level, the number is often annotated as dB-PWL.

Example

What is the sound power level of a 100W loudspeaker that is producing 3.0W of acoustic energy?

Solution

$\text{PWL} = 10 \log(W/W_0)$

$\text{PWL} = (3 \text{ watts}/10^{-12} \text{ watts})$

$\text{PWL} = 10 \log (3\times10^{12})$

PWL = 125 dB-PWL

Sound Intensity

A measurement of sound power level does not vary with distance from the sound source. By analogy, a 75-watt light bulb always has a power level of 75 watts. It does, however, appear brighter when you are one foot away from it compared to when you are five light years away from it. Similarly, sound intensity is a measurement which is very much dependent on distance from a sound source. The closer you are to a sound power source, the higher the sound intensity is.

Sound intensity is formally defined as the acoustic power applied over an area, as shown in Equation 2.8. Humans can hear sound intensities ranging from roughly 10^{-12} W/m^2 to 1 W/m^2.

Equation 2.8 Sound Intensity

sound intensity = acoustic power / area

For a simple case, imagine an omnidirectional sound generator located in a free space where we don't need to worry about reflections. At a distance r from the source, the power would be applied over the surface area of a sphere of diameter r. Given that the surface area of a sphere $4\pi r^2$, the intensity of this sound would be given by Equation 2.9.

Equation 2.9 Sound Intensity of an Omnidirectional Transmitter in a Free Field

sound intensity = acoustic power / $(4\pi r^2)$

We see from Equation 2.9 that intensity is inversely proportional to the square of the distance from the source. If we double our distance from the sound source, the intensity of the sound is quartered. This relationship is also known as the inverse squares law. It holds with our everyday experience of sounds: the further away we are from a sound generator, the less its intensity is.

In the real world, not all sounds are omnidirectional. A loudspeaker, for instance, directs most of its power toward the front and very little to the rear. Furthermore, most sounds do not occur in a free field, but reflect off the ground, trees, walls, ceilings, or other obstructions. These same objects can cause the sound waves to refract and diffract, further altering the distribution of acoustic power. It is subsequently very difficult to accurately measure sound intensity in the real world. It is, however, relatively easy to measure sound pressure.

Pressure

As we've discussed earlier, sound consists of localized fluctuations in the ambient pressure.

Pressure is a force acting over an area. A common pressure measurement we use in everyday life is measuring the pressure of the tires on our car or bicycles. Most automobile tires are inflated to a pressure on the order of 30 pounds per square inch (psi). Every square inch inside the tire feels as much pressure against it as would be exerted by the gravitational force of a 30 pound weight.

Of course, most of the world is still using the metric system. The metric unit of force is the Newton. Pressure is thus measured in units of Newtons per square meter (N/m^2). The Pascal (Pa) is a unit of pressure defined to be 1 N/m^2.

The pressure change required for a sound to be audible to humans is quite small. In fact, humans can hear sound pressure differences as small as 20 microPascals (µPa). By comparison, atmospheric pressure is 101.3 kiloPascals (kPa). That means we can hear variations in pressure that are five billionths smaller than the ambient air pressure. If we had the same accuracy in visually detecting changes in distance as we do detecting changes in ambient pressure, we would be able to discern variations in the moon's distance from the Earth on the order of three inches!

Although it is much easier to measure sound pressure than sound intensity, intensity is a more useful measurement. It turns out that sound intensity is proportional to the square of pressure. If we wanted to get a measurement of intensity, we could derive it from the pressure by applying a little math:

$10 \log(\text{Intensity}_1/\text{Intensity}_0) =$

$10 \log ((\text{Pressure}_1/ \text{Pressure}_0)^2) =$

$20 \log (\text{Pressure}_1/ \text{Pressure}_0)$

This last step comes courtesy of the equality $\log(x^y)= y \log x$. From this exercise, we have derived a useful acoustical measurement known as the Sound Pressure Level (SPL). The SPL provides sound intensity by comparing the measured pressure against a reference pressure associated with the quietest sound a human can hear (known as the threshold of hearing), as shown in Equation 2.10.

Equation 2.10 Sound Pressure Level

$$SPL = 20 \log (P_1/P_0), \text{ where } P_0 = 20\ \mu Pa$$

To clarify that a particular decibel measurement is of the sound pressure level, the number is often annotated as dB-SPL.

Example

A handheld sound level meter indicates that a nearby jackhammer has a sound pressure level of 85 dB-SPL. What is the sound pressure of the jackhammer?

Solution

$SPL = 20 \log (P_1/P_0)$
$(SPL/20) = \log (P_1/P_0)$
$10(SPL/20) = P_1/P_0$
$P_1 = P_0 \times 10^{(SPL/20)}$
$P_1 = 20\ \mu Pa \times 10^{(85/20)}$
$P_1 = 20\ \mu Pa \times 10^{(85/20)}$
$P_1 = 347$ *milliPascals*

Remember that the SPL is dependent on distance from the sound source, as well as the geometry and location of reflective and refractive objects in the environment. Keeping that in mind, Table 2.3 provides a list of the SPL of some common sounds in typical situations. Note that prolonged exposure to sounds above 100 dB result in permanent hearing loss.

Table 2.3 SPL of Some Common Objects

Sound	SPL (dB)
Whispering	10-20
Quiet Library	30
Ordinary conversation (at 1.5 feet)	65
Vacuum cleaner	75
Heavy traffic	85
Siren (at 100 feet)	100
Rock Concert	120
Threshold of Pain	120
Jet engines (at 100 feet)	140

Decibels Revisited

Now that we've introduced Sound Power Level (PWL) and Sound Pressure Level (SPL), let's spend some more time getting familiar with measuring them in decibels.

Remember that decibels are logarithmic ratios. As such, you cannot simply add them. For example, a 15 dB-PWL sound source combined with another 15 dB PWL sound source does not result in a PWL of 30 dB. Instead, the combined PWL is 18dB, as we shall see in the following example.

Example

Suppose you have two sound sources which each have a PWL of 15dB. What is the combined PWL of the two sources?

Solution

For starters, let's compute the PWL of the first speaker.

$$PWL = 10 \log (W_1/W_0)$$
$$(PWL/10) = \log (W_1/W_0)$$
$$10^{(PWL/10)} = W_1/W_0$$
$$W_1 = W_0 \times 10^{(PWL/10)}$$
$$W_1 = W_0 \times 10^{(15/10)}$$
$$W_1 = 31.6 \times 10^{-12} \text{ W}$$

We know that the two sound sources have the same PWL, so $W_2 = W_1$. The total power is just the sum of the two individual power sources.

$$W_{TOTAL} = W_1 + W_2.$$
$$W_{TOTAL} = 63.2 \times 10^{-12} \text{ W}$$

Right, so now let's compute the PWL of the two sound sources.

$$PWL_{TOTAL} = 10 \log (W_{TOTAL}/W_0)$$
$$PWL_{TOTAL} = 10 \log (63.2 \times 10^{-12} \text{ W} / 10^{-12} \text{ W})$$
$$\mathbf{PWL_{TOTAL} = 18.0 \text{ dB}}$$

Note that doubling the power resulted in a PWL increase of 3dB (from 15.0 dB-PWL to 18.0 dB-PWL). In fact, doubling any power level results in a 3 dB increase in PWL. Conversely, halving a power level results in a 3 dB decrease in PWL.

The same doubling-3dB relationship holds true for SPL as well, with some caveats. When we are dealing with random noise, the relationship holds. However, we have already discussed that sound waves interfere with one another. If you added two coherent sine waves with 15 dB-SPL together, and they were exactly out of phase, they would cancel each other out. The resultant pressure from the two sounds would be zero, resulting in an SPL of $-\infty$ dB. Such scenarios are not common in most real world situations.

Example

Two sound sources have a combined SPL of 50 dB. Turning off the first sound source reduces the SPL to 45 dB. What would be the SPL if just the first sound source was turned on?

Solution

First, let's figure out the total pressure.

$$P_{TOTAL} = P_0 \times 10^{(SPL/20)}$$
$$P_{TOTAL} = 20\ \mu Pa \times 10^{(50/20)}$$
$$P_{TOTAL} = 6324\ \mu Pa$$

Now let's figure out the pressure from the second sound source.

$$P_2 = P_0 \times 10^{(SPL/20)}$$
$$P_2 = 20\ \mu Pa \times 10^{(45/20)}$$
$$P_2 = 3557\ \mu Pa$$

Next we can determine the pressure from the first sound source.

$$P_1 = P_{TOTAL} - P_2$$
$$P_1 = 6324\ \mu Pa - 3557\ \mu Pa$$
$$P_1 = 2767\ \mu Pa$$

Finally, we can compute the SPL in dB above the reference.

$$SPL_1 = 20 \log (P_1/P_0)$$
$$SPL_1 = 20 \log (2767\ \mu Pa / 20\ \mu Pa)$$
$$\mathbf{SPL_1 = 42.8\ dB}$$

The Frequency Domain

When studying the propagation of sound earlier in this chapter, we plotted sound pressure over distance. This can be considered the spatial domain. We also plotted sound intensity over time as waveforms. Such graphs occupy the temporal domain. It is also very useful to plot sound intensity versus frequency. Such diagrams are of the frequency domain.

Let us consider some simple examples. Figure 2.22 shows some simple waveforms in the temporal domain and the corresponding plot of the sounds in the frequency domain. Such a graph of intensity versus frequency is known as a *spectrum*.

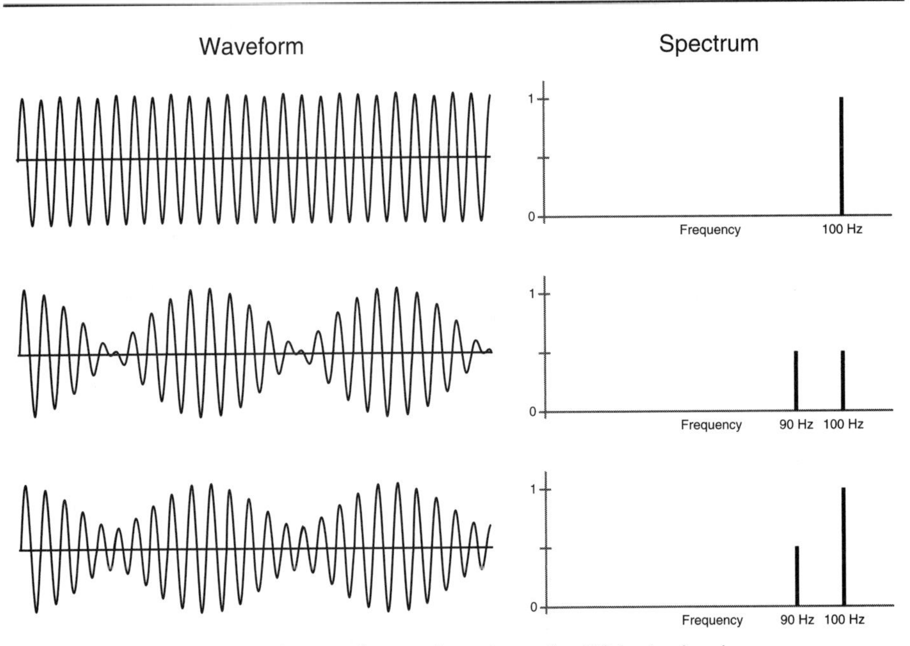

The top diagrams show the waveform and spectrum of a 100-hertz signal. The middle diagrams show a sound consisting of a 90-hertz and 100-hertz tone at the same intensity. The bottommost diagrams show a sound again made by combining a 90-hertz and 100-hertz tone, but in this case the 100-hertz tone is twice as intense as the 90-hertz tone.

Figure 2.22 Sample Spectra

Spectra are useful because they provide information about a sound that is not immediately obvious from visual inspection of a complex waveform. Specifically, a spectrum shows the frequencies a sound contains.

It is difficult to directly measure sound spectra. Spectra are usually created by recording the sound's waveform (intensity vs. time) and then mathematically deriving the frequency intensities using techniques such as Fourier transforms.

We have spent much of this chapter focusing on pure tones. These period signals do not change over time. A 60-hertz pure tone at time index zero is still a 60-hertz pure tone at time index infinity. As such, the spectrum of a pure tone does not change, and remains constant across all time. Real world signals, however, often vary a great deal over time. For instance, consider the sound depicted in Figure 2.23. The waveform tells us that the sound is varying in intensity in a complex fashion with no discernable pattern.

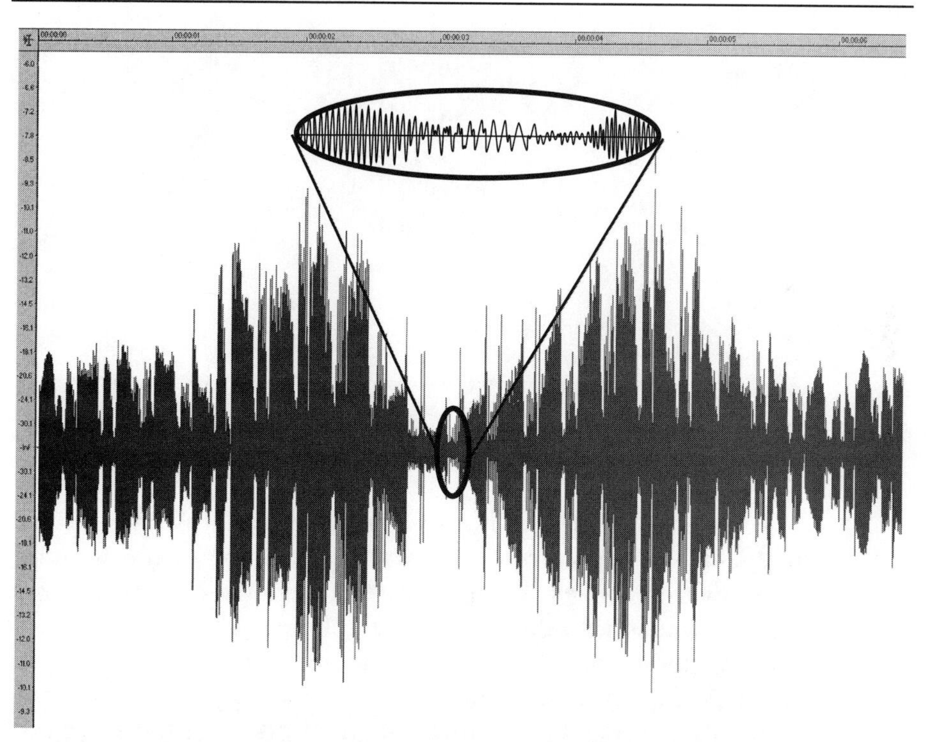

Note that this waveform is a line graph, not a filled graph. The lines are so close together they appear as filled space. The callout in the center of the graph zooms in on the graph to reveal that this is indeed just a single-lined waveform.

Figure 2.23 Waveform of a Complex Sound

A frequency analysis of the sound gives us the spectrum shown in Figure 2.24. This spectrum applies to the entire music sample, roughly seven seconds long. The spectrum shows a lot of activity ranging from 150 to 2,500 hertz. There is no significant contribution to the spectrum above 6,000 hertz.

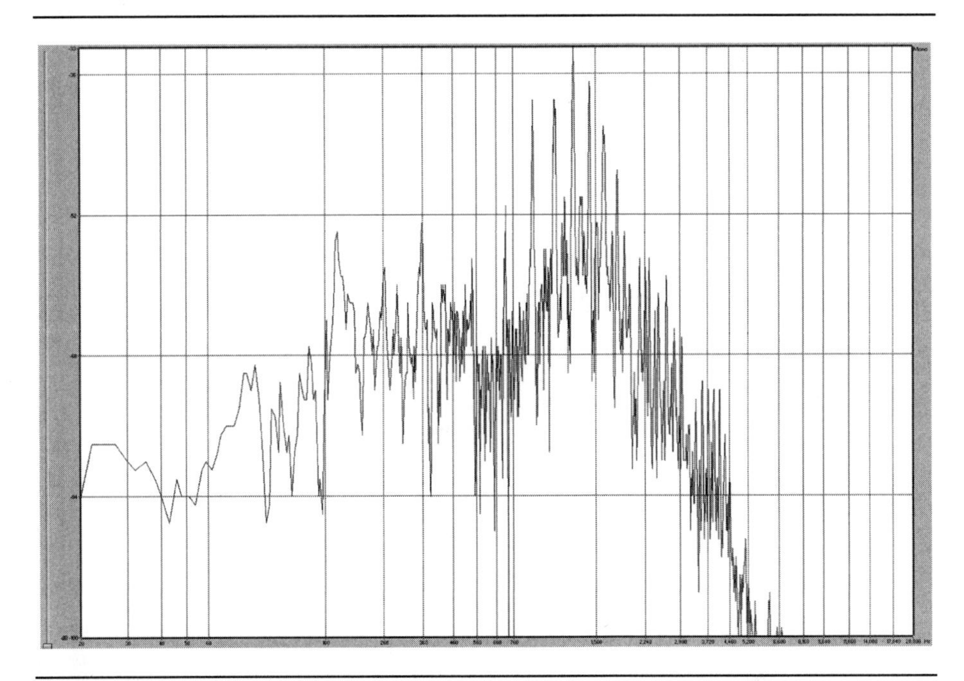

Figure 2.24 Spectrum of a Complex Sound

Focusing on different portions of the waveform reveals much different spectra. The spectrum of the very beginning of the sound reveals a lot of low frequencies. A snippet from the middle of the song reveals very little low frequency information, but a lot of high frequency information, as shown in Figure 2.25. This technique of calculating the spectrum for only a portion of a waveform is known as applying a window to the sound. The analogy here is that only the portion of the waveform that is inside the window can be seen.

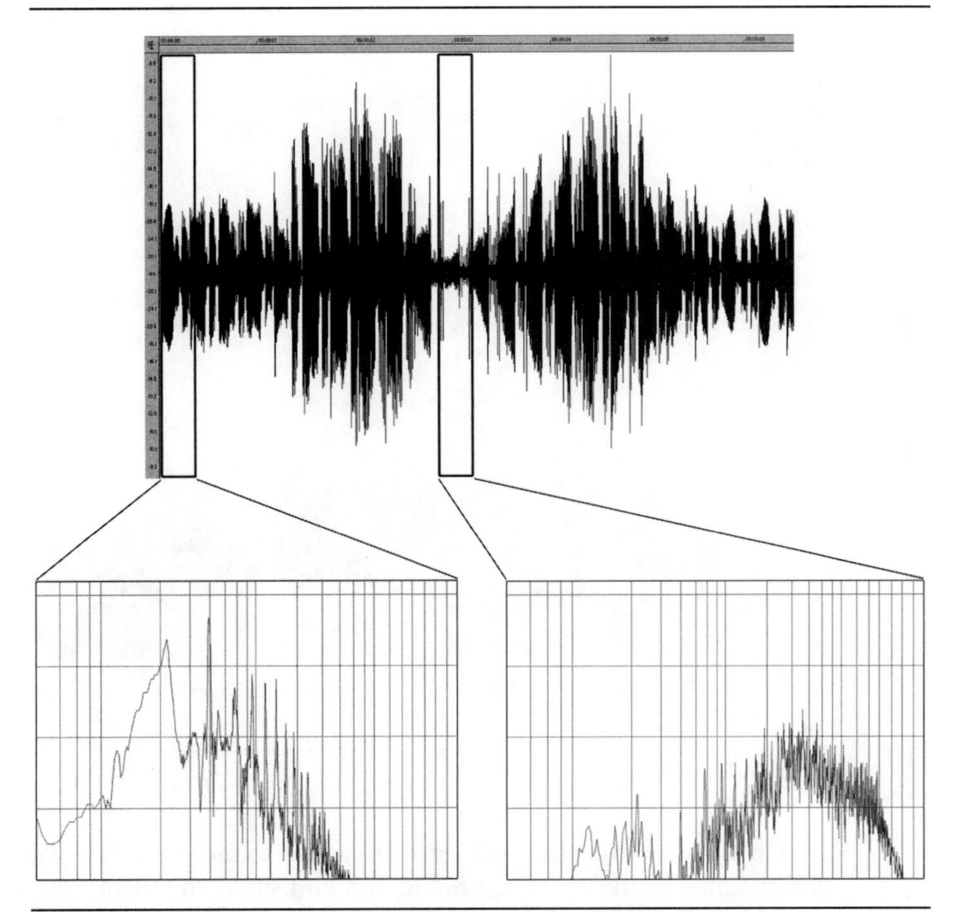

Figure 2.25 Spectra of Different Windows of a Complex Sound

If we wanted to see how the spectrum changes through time, we can slice up the sound into small intervals and place the spectra for each of these slices side by side. Such a graph is known as a *sonogram*. A sonogram for our waveform from Figure 2.23 is shown in Figure 2.26.

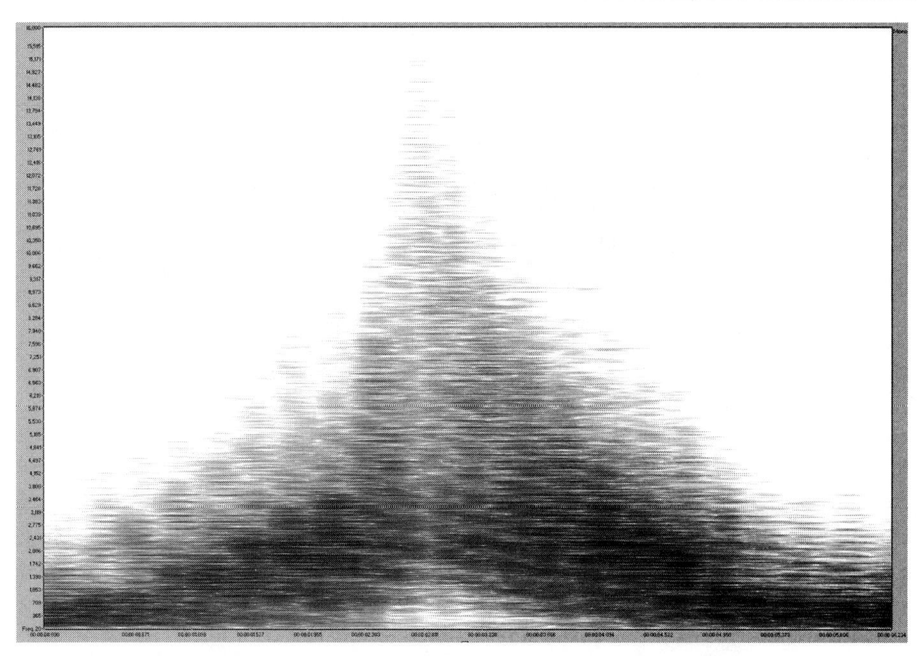

The darker the region, the greater the intensity of the corresponding frequency at that time

Figure 2.26 Sonogram

We can see from this sonogram that the sound has a lot of low frequency information at its beginning and end. By comparison, the middle time portion of the sound is composed of higher frequencies.

Although spectra—and sonograms—describe the frequencies that constitute a sound, they do not provide any information about the phase of those frequencies. Therefore, different waveforms can have the same spectrum. The spectrum of a 1,000-hertz pure tone consists of a spike at 1,000 hertz, regardless of the phase of that tone. A more complex example is shown in Figure 2.27.

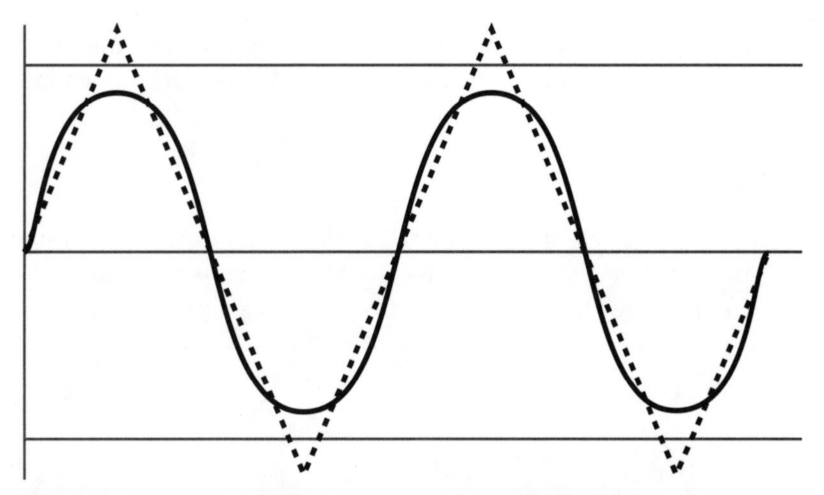

These two waveforms have the same spectra—that of a triangular wave, as shown in Figure 2.22. The waveform depicted here with a dotted line here is indeed a triangular wave. It is created by combining together an infinite number of sine waves in the manner of

$$\sin(x)-\frac{1}{3^2}\sin(3x)+\frac{1}{5^2}\sin(5x)-\frac{1}{9^2}\sin(9x)+\ldots$$

The alternating polarity of the sine waves correspond to phase shifts of 180 degrees. The curved line in the diagram may look like a sine wave, but in fact it is composed by again combining an infinite number of sine waves:

$$\sin(x)+\frac{1}{3^2}\sin(3x)+\frac{1}{5^2}\sin(5x)+\frac{1}{9^2}\sin(9x)+\ldots$$

Figure 2.27 Many-to-one Mapping of Waveforms to Spectra

Sounds of Interest

Certain sounds make recurring appearances in the field of acoustics. We have already discussed sine waves, a.k.a. pure tones, in some detail.

Nineteenth century French mathematician Jean-Baptiste Fourier proved that any "reasonably behaved" periodic signal could be represented by summing together a series of sine waves. Such a series is known today as a Fourier series. Fourier series often contain an infinite number of elements. Most of the elements in a Fourier series are multiples of a base frequency known as a *fundamental*.

Frequencies that are multiples of the fundamental are known as *harmonics*. A frequency twice as large as the fundamental is known as the second harmonic. The third harmonic is three times larger than the fundamental. And so on.

Sine Waves

It's pretty easy to put together a series of sine waves to form a sine wave! You just need the sine wave itself. A sine waveform and spectrum is shown in Figure 2.28.

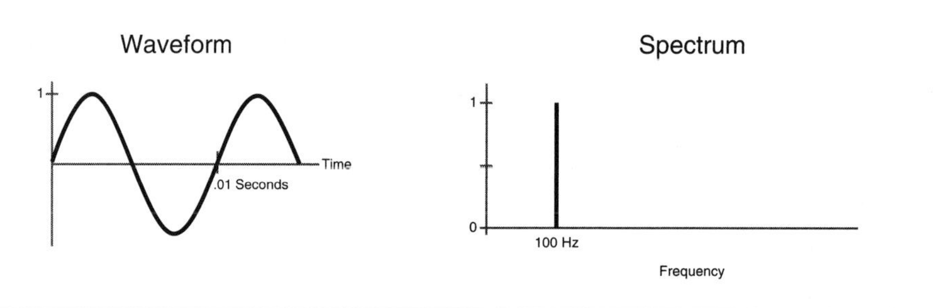

Figure 2.28 Yet Another Sine Wave

Square Waves

Looking at Figure 2.29, it's easy to see how a square wave gets its name. It's surprising to learn that this sound—which has a waveform consisting of perpendicular lines—can be created by adding together curvy sine waves. Mind you, it does take an infinite number of them! A square wave can be composed by adding together odd harmonics (h = 1, 3, 5, ...). Each odd harmonic h that is added needs a magnitude of $1/h$.

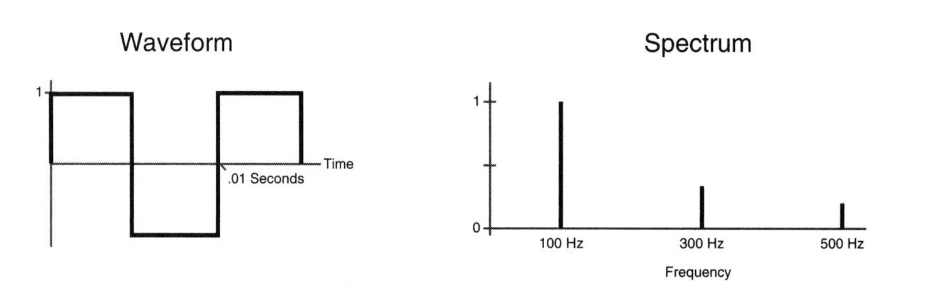

Figure 2.29 Square Wave

Triangular Waves

Triangular waves are periodic signals that can be decomposed into odd harmonics, with each odd harmonic h having a magnitude of 1/h2, as shown in Figure 2.30.

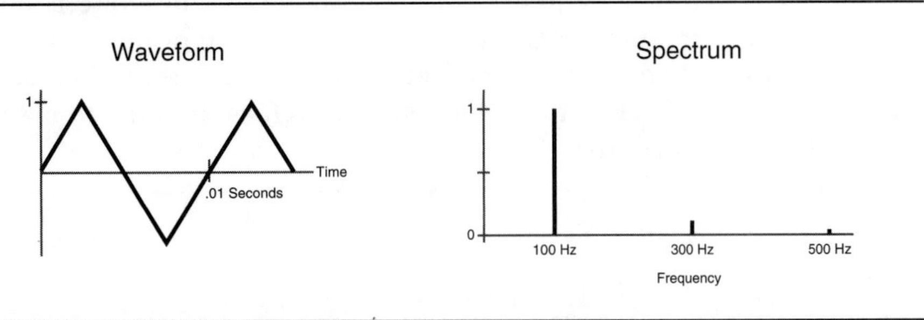

Figure 2.30 Triangular Wave

Saw-tooth Waves

Another common periodic wave is the saw-tooth, shown in Figure 2.31. Saw-toothed patterns are composed of odd and even harmonics, with the *h*th harmonic scaled by $1/h$.

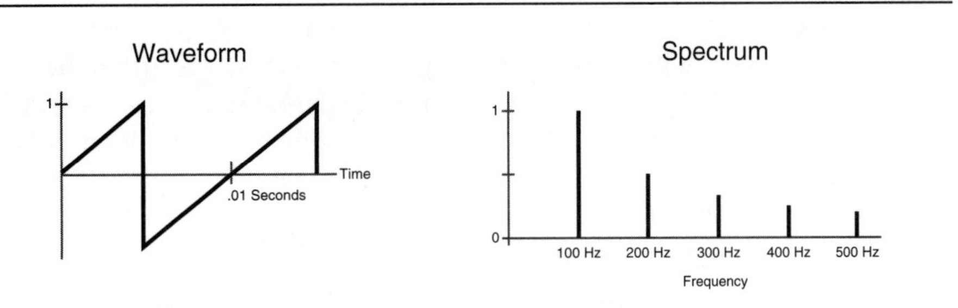

Figure 2.31 Saw-tooth Wave

White Noise

White noise has equal energy at all frequencies. In this sense, it is analogous to white light, which consists of all frequencies of visible light. An example of white noise is shown in Figure 2.32. White noise is a class of sound that is not a periodic signal. Because white noise is not periodic, Fourier's theorem does not apply, and we cannot derive a series of sine waves that create an exact match for the waveform. We can, however, get arbitrarily close to a white noise waveform in order to mathematically derive the spectrum shown.

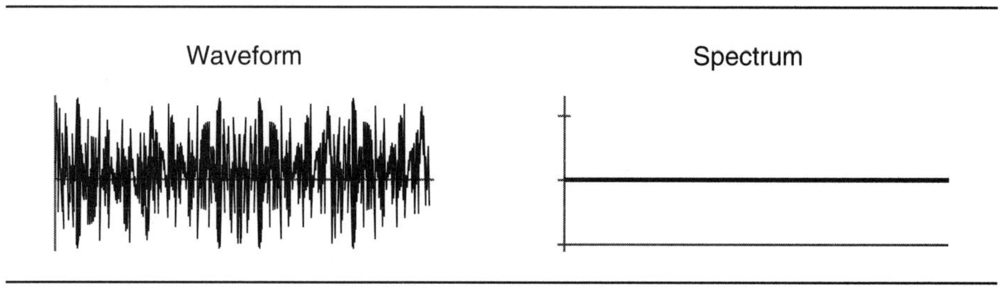

Figure 2.32 White Noise

Pink Noise

Whereas white noise has equal energy at all frequencies, the energy of pink noise decreases inversely proportional to the frequency, as shown in Figure 2.33. For this reason, it is also known as 1/f noise. Pink noise is interesting because the amount of energy per octave is constant (whereas with white noise the amount of energy per octave is twice the energy in the preceding octave).

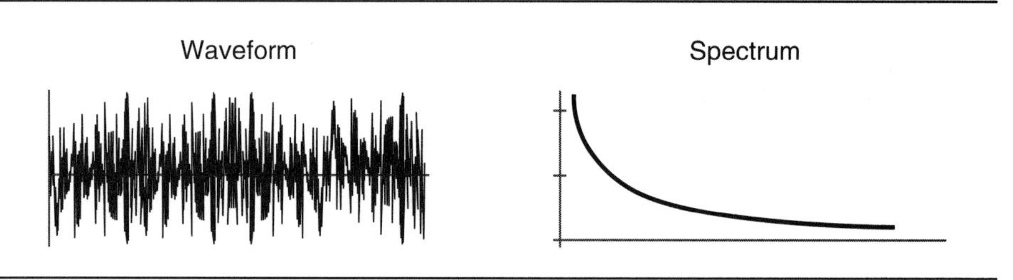

Figure 2.33 Pink Noise

Measuring Sound Quality

Audio is the technology of producing sounds. These sounds are often reproductions of real-world sounds. For instance, we may record an orchestra playing and play it back later. Given the chaotic and noisy universe in which we live, the reproduction always contains some errors. It is not an exact replica of the original sound.

Most audio solutions strive for high quality, although some may need to sacrifice quality to meet other project constraints such as time and money. Even though audio reproduction can never be completely perfect, we may be able to achieve sufficient quality that the errors are undetectable to the human hearing system.

It is therefore useful to have some tools for measuring just how accurate our reproduction is. This section will describe a few such metrics.

Harmonic Distortion

When presented with a signal, most real world audio systems introduce harmonics of the original frequencies. This corruption is known as harmonic distortion. Harmonic distortion is typically not desired behavior, but a side effect of being constrained to using a finite number of imperfect components.

Third Harmonic Distortion

In the context of audio, even-numbered harmonics (2nd, 4th, etc.) are not usually easily detectable to the human ear. Odd-numbered harmonics are more noticeable and somewhat less pleasant to hear. The first odd harmonic is the third harmonic, which usually has the highest amplitude of all the odd harmonics in the context of harmonic distortion. Hence, third harmonic distortion (TDH) is sometimes used as a measurement of sound quality.

TDH is also of interest because when solid-state circuitry is driven with too high a signal, it introduces odd harmonic distortions. Conversely, when vacuum tubes overload, they introduce even harmonic distortions.

TDH can be measured by sending a pure tone into the system being tested and measuring the amplitude of the third harmonic that comes out. The value is typically reported as a percentage of the fundamental.

For instance, if a system is fed a 1,000-hertz tone at 1 volt and the output has a 3,000-hertz signal with a magnitude of 0.05 volts, the system has a third harmonic distortion of 5%. The value is most accurately reported by referencing the test conditions. To wit: 5% TDH (1,000 hertz, 1 volt).

Total Harmonic Distortion

Another common measurement distortion is total harmonic distortion (THD). As implied by its name, THD measures the impact of all the unwanted harmonics. It is calculated using Equation 2.11.

Equation 2.11 THD

$$\mathrm{THD} = \frac{\sqrt{V_2^2 + V_3^2 + V_4^2 + \cdots}}{\sqrt{V_1^2 + V_2^2 + V_3^2 + V_4^2 + \cdots}}$$

Where V_1 is the amplitude of the fundamental, V_2 is the amplitude of the second harmonic, V_3 is the amplitude of the third harmonic, and so on.

THD is practically measured by taking the distorted output signal and removing the fundamental input signal from it. The resulting signal can be analyzed to derive the THD. This technique also measures the noise generated by the signal passing through the system. Such a measurement is more accurately referred to as a total harmonic distortion and noise (THD + N).

Signal to Noise Ratio

The signal to noise ratio (SNR) is, quite simply, the ratio of the desired signals strength to the strength of any unwanted noise. If, for instance, the signal and noise are both measured as voltages, the SNR in decibels can be calculated by Equation 2.12.

Equation 2.12 SNR

$$\mathrm{SNR\ (dB)} = 20 \log (V_{signal} / V_{noise})$$

In most cases, it is desirable to have the highest SNR possible. In the case of an audio system, you would ideally want to have a SNR that was as good as that afforded by the human hearing system. The signal to noise ratio of some common audio systems is shown in Table 2.4.

Table 2.4 SNR Values

System	SNR (dB)
Compact disc player	100
Human ear (in quiet room)	90
Record player	70-80
Tape player	65-70
FM radio	60
AM radio	50

Dynamic Range

The dynamic range is a measure of the largest signal a system can handle compared to the smallest signal it can handle. It is often reported in decibels, as can be calculated from Equation 2.13. In some cases, the smallest signal an audio system can generate is below the noise floor, in which case the dynamic range is the ratio of the loudest signal to the noise floor.

Equation 2.13 Dynamic Range

$$\text{Dynamic Range (dB)} = 20 \log (V_{high} / V_{low})$$

The dynamic range of some common audio systems is shown in Table 2.5.

Table 2.5 Dynamic Range Values

System	Dynamic Range (dB)
Compact disc player	96
Human ear	120
Symphony orchestra	100
Record player	50
Tape player	60
FM radio	50
AM radio	30

Summary

Sound is caused by the vibration of objects within a medium. We typically are concerned with sound in air, where the vibrations cause alternating regions of compression and rarefaction. These pressure changes are very small compared to the ambient air pressure.

When sound waves hit an object, they are reflected and/or refracted. Sound waves may curve around some obstructions; this property is known as diffraction.

The amount of energy an object is using to make sounds is known as *acoustic energy*. Acoustic energy is measured in watts or as a Sound Power Level (PWL) that indicates the dB above a reference power level of 10^{-12}W.

Sound intensity is the acoustic power applied over an area. It is dependent on distance from the sound source. For an omnidirectional sound source, sound intensity is inversely proportional to the square of the distance from the sound source.

It is difficult to directly measure sound intensity; but relatively easy to measure sound pressure. Sound intensity is measured in terms of pressure as Sound Pressure Level (SPL), which indicates the number of dB above a reference pressure of 20 μPa.

A plot of the intensity of a sound over time is known as a waveform. A plot of the intensity of a sound's frequency components is known as a spectrum. A plot of a how a sound's spectra changes over time is known as a sonogram.

Chapter 3

Hearing

ARTHUR: It looks like the sea front at South End.

FORD: Hell, I'm relieved to hear you say that.

ARTHUR: Why?

FORD: I thought I must be going mad.

ARTHUR: Perhaps you are. Perhaps you only thought I said it.

FORD: Well, did you say it or didn't you?

ARTHUR: I think so.

FORD: Well, perhaps we're both going mad.

—Douglas Adams, *Hitchhiker's Guide to the Galaxy*

The human auditory system is a fascinatingly complex collection of components that enables us to hear a wide range of sound frequencies and intensities. Our hearing is the result of literally hundreds of millions of years of evolution, dating all the way back to when the first vertebrates crawled out of the sea to take a stab at living on land.[1] Although fish have long had the ability to hear sounds underwater, such sense mechanisms did not work well in the air. A bone which was originally used to support gills eventually evolved to become first a jawbone and then an ear bone which we still carry with us today in our middle ears.

[1] Then, as now, oceanfront property was prime real estate.

Sound waves are well-understood physical phenomena with properties that we can unequivocally measure and behavior that we can reliably predict. Human perception of those waves is a different matter. Although the gross characteristics of human hearing are well understood, many subtleties remain uninvestigated. Perception of sound varies based on a wide number of environmental factors, and, furthermore, varies from one person to another.

Why do we care about perception? One reason is that it helps us as engineers to build efficient sound systems. If we know humans can only hear frequencies in the range 20 to 20,000 hertz, then we know we don't need to spend time and effort making sure our system is capable of producing 100,000-hertz sounds. Similarly, if we know that sounds in excess of 200 dB-SPL liquefy a person's internal organs, we may want to put safety mechanisms in place to prevent anyone from turning their CD player up to that level. We will also see how some quirks of the human auditory perception system allow us to discard pieces of a sound with no change in perceptual quality.

Useful Concepts

Before we begin our exploration of the physical structure and perceptual characteristics of the human hearing system, we will first have a brief overview of two topics: non-linearity and filters. These topics are relevant because the human hearing system has a nonlinear response to stimuli and is sometimes modeled as a set of overlapping auditory filters.

Nonlinearity

In a linear system, a fixed change in the input always has the same amount of effect on the output. In a nonlinear system, a fixed change to the input has a different effect on the output, depending on where the change is made. This abstract definition may not be immediately edifying, but fear not: I have a practical example.

Consider a large box of negligible weight and a large number of identical five-pound bricks. If I increase the number of bricks in the box from one to two, the overall weight of the box and its contents increases by five pounds. If I have 999 bricks in the box and add one more, the overall weight still increases by five pounds. Regardless of how many bricks are in the box, each time I add a brick to the box, the weight increases by five pounds. As such, the relationship between the number of bricks in the box and the overall weight are linear.

This thought experiment may seem simplistic and a matter of common sense, but in fact most human senses are not linear. For instance, even if the box were closed, it would be very easy for you to distinguish the heaviness of a one-brick box compared to a two-brick box. However, it would be virtually impossible for you to distinguish the difference in heaviness between a 999-brick box and a 1,000-brick box. In both scenarios, there is a five-pound difference between the two boxes. However, the human sense of heaviness is much more sensitive to changes in objects of low weight compared to extremely high weight. The relationship between the number of bricks and perceptual heaviness is thus nonlinear.

A good rule of thumb for determining whether a relationship is linear or nonlinear is to graph it. If the resulting graph is straight, the relationship is linear. If it's curved, it's nonlinear. If, for instance, we were to graph the weight of our box of bricks versus the number of bricks, we would get the graph shown in Figure 3.1.

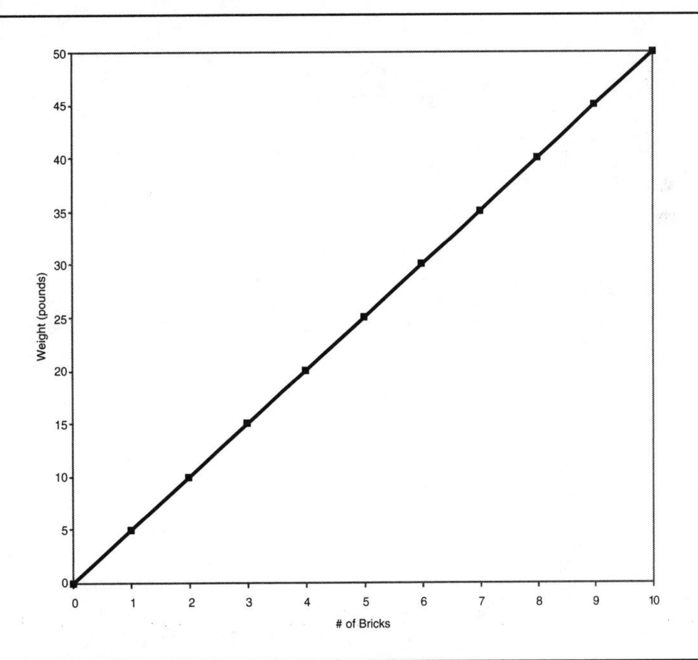

Figure 3.1 Plot of Number of Bricks vs. Weight of Box

More formally, a system defined by $f(x)$ is linear if and only if $f(a) + f(b) = f(a+b)$. Thus, $f(x) = 5x$ would be linear, because: $5a + 5b = 5(a+b)$. On the other hand, $f(x) = x^2$ would not be linear, because $a^2+b^2 \neq (a+b)^2$

for all values of a and b. For instance, for a = 1 and b = 0.5, $a^2+b^2 = 1.25$, but $(a+b)^2 = 2.25$. The fact that the plot of $f(x) = x^2$ in Figure 3.2 exhibits a definite curve is further evidence that the function is indeed nonlinear.

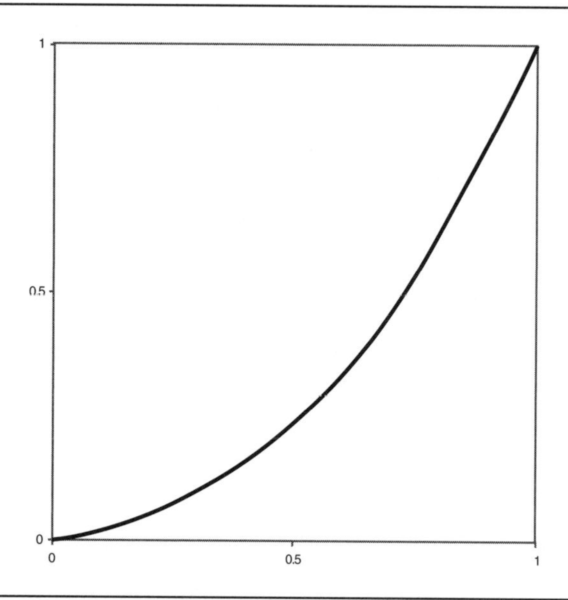

Figure 3.2 Plot of $f(x) = x^2$

Example

Given a 1-watt omnidirectional sound source in a free field, by how much does the sound intensity change between 1 foot and 2 feet away? What's the difference from 999 feet to 1,000 feet? Is the relationship between sound intensity and distance linear or nonlinear?

Solution

Assuming that our sound source has constant power, we can derive from Equation 2.9 that:

$\Delta_{intensity}(r_1,r_2) = (1 \text{ watt}/4\pi)/ (r_2^2-r_1^2)$

$\Delta_{intensity}(1,2) = (1 \text{ watt}/4\pi)/(2^2-1^2)= 26.5 \text{ mW}$

$\Delta_{intensity}(999,1000) = (1 \text{ W}/4\pi)/(1000^2-999^2) = .0398 \text{ mW}$

In both cases, the distance change is one foot. However, the change in intensity is much larger from 1 foot to 2 feet than it is from 999 feet to 1,000 feet. This relationship is therefore non-linear.

Filters

A filter is a system that takes a signal as input and reduces the intensity of certain frequency ranges of that signal. One type of filter only permits low frequencies to pass through it. All frequencies above a fixed frequency—known as the *cutoff frequency*—are stopped by the filter. Frequencies below the cutoff frequency are passed through the filter unaltered. This type of filter is known as a low-pass filter. As with all filters, it is graphically represented by a diagram of its responsiveness to a white noise signal, as shown in Figure 3.3.

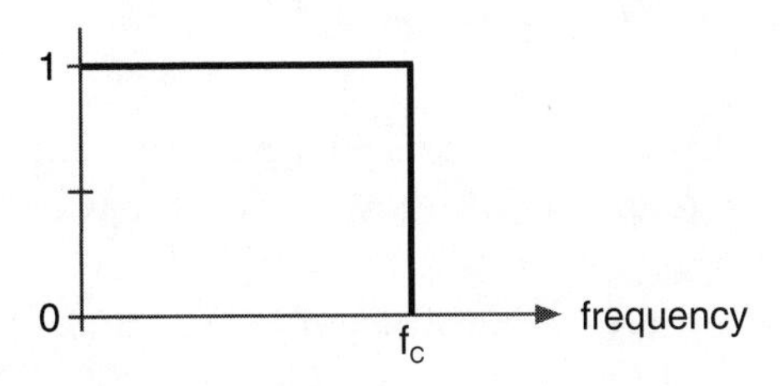

Figure 3.3 Rectangular Low-Pass Filter

The effects of a low-pass filter on a sample signal are shown in Figure 3.4. The low frequencies are passed through, while the higher frequencies are completely blocked.

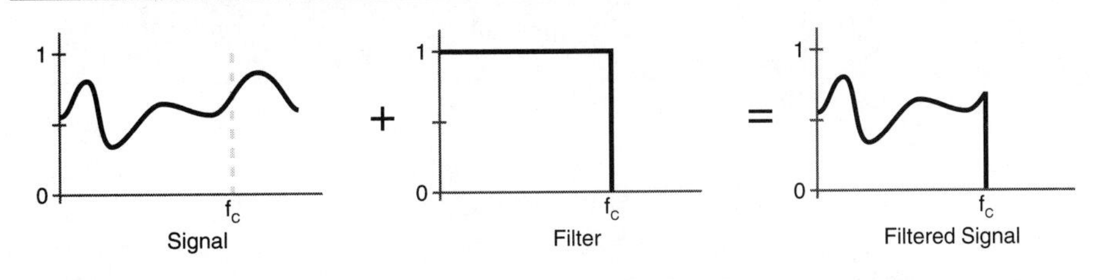

Figure 3.4 Effects of Low-Pass Filter on a Signal

Another type of filter is the high-pass filter. As its name implies, all frequencies below the cutoff frequency are blocked, as shown in Figure 3.5.

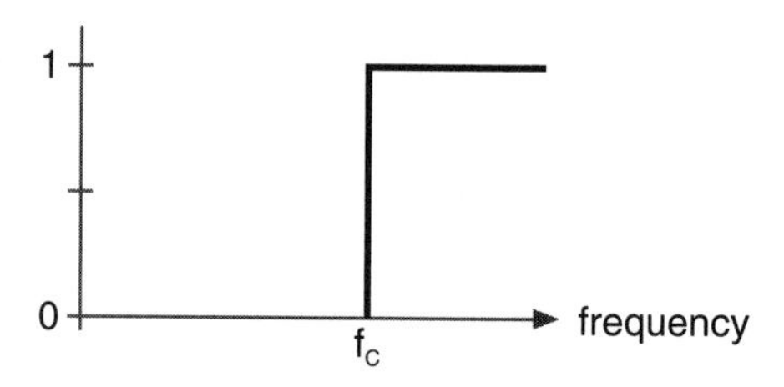

Figure 3.5 Rectangular High-Pass Filter

If you were to combine a low-pass filter and a high-pass filter where the cutoff frequency of the low-pass filter was lower than the cutoff frequency of the high-pass filter, you would get a band stop filter. Frequencies between the two cutoff frequencies (f_L and f_H) would be completely stopped by the filter, as shown in Figure 3.6.

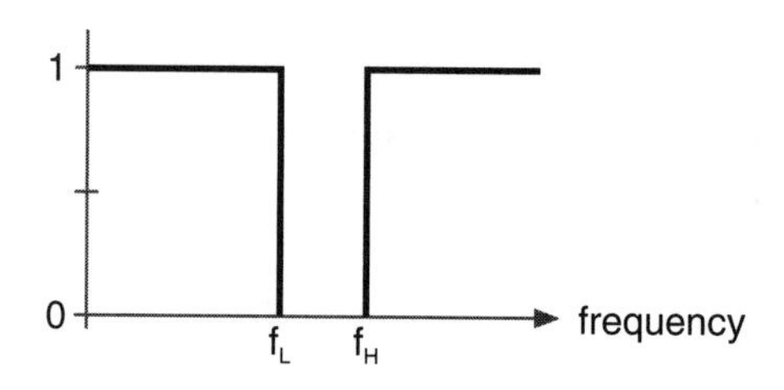

Figure 3.6 Rectangular Band Stop Filter

In the other case of combining a low- and high-pass filter, the cutoff frequency of the low-pass filter is greater than the cutoff frequency of the high-pass filter. In this case, the resulting filter is a band-pass filter. It only allows frequencies between f_L and f_H to pass. All others are stopped, as shown in Figure 3.7.

The midpoint between f_L and f_H is known as the center frequency (f_C). The distance between f_L and f_H is called the bandwidth of the filter.

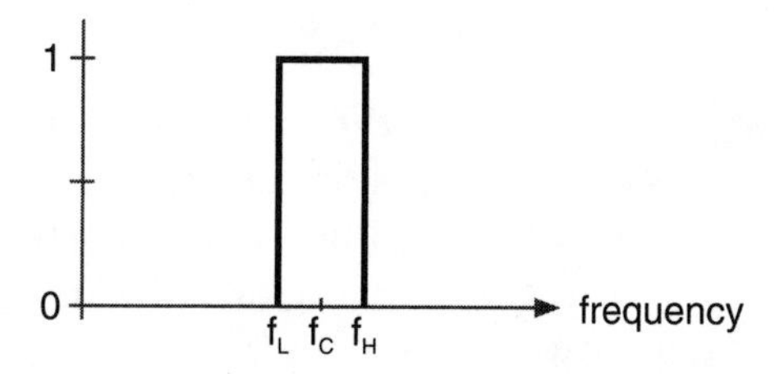

Figure 3.7 Rectangular Band-Pass Filter

Although rectangular filters can be very useful, it turns out that it very difficult to build a perfectly rectangular filter in the real world. It is more practical to build filters with sloped edges, such as the trapezoidal band-pass filter shown in Figure 3.8.

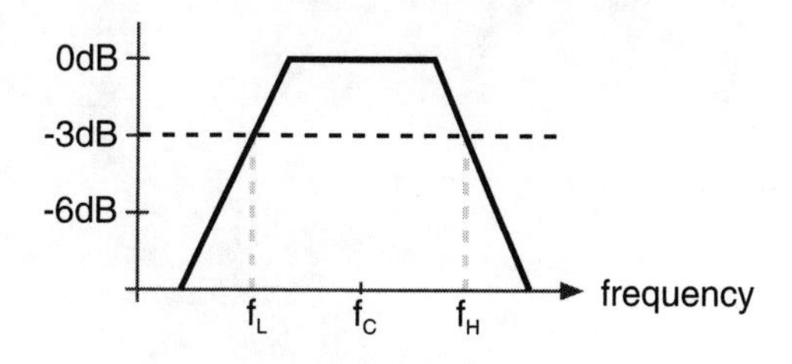

Figure 3.8 Trapezoidal Band-Pass Filter

As soon as the edge of a filter is sloped, it does not make sense to measure the cutoff frequency at the point where the attenuation begins. Frequencies around this point undergo very little reduction. Instead, the cutoff frequency is typically measured at the point where the filter has attenuated the signal by 3 dB.

The rate at which these filters attenuate frequencies is known as the slope. The slope is typically measured in the number of decibels of attenuation that occurs when the frequency increases by a factor of 10, also called a decade. For example, if a filter has a 3-dB reduction at 1,000 hertz and a 10-dB reduction at 10,000 hertz, the slope of the filter is 10 - 3 = 7 dB/decade. Simple trapezoidal filters have slopes on the order of 20 dB/decade; more sophisticated—read expensive—filters can have much steeper slopes.

Trapezoidal filters are still approximations of the behavior of real world filters. They are much more accurate models than rectangular filters, but do not take into account all the little ripples and curves that are characteristic of real world filters.

Physiology

Now that we have reviewed the concepts of non-linearity and filters, we will begin examining how the human hearing system works, starting with physical structures. Hearing is accomplished by sense organs known as ears. The ear has three main regions: the outer ear, the middle ear, and the inner ear, as shown in Figure 3.9.

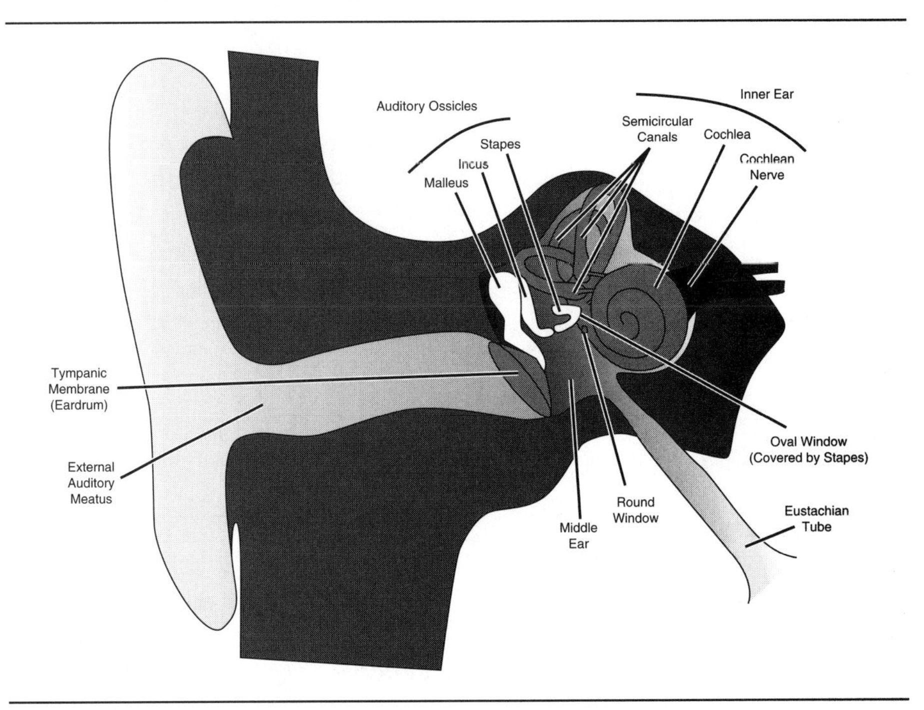

Figure 3.9 Human Ear

Outer Ear

Most people are familiar with the outer ear, as it is easily visible. The purpose of the outer ear is to focus pressure waves using folds collectively known as the pinna. As we will discuss in more detail later, the pinna also encodes information about the direction of sound sources.

Sounds collected by the pinna are focused down a tube-like structure known as the external auditory canal, also known as the external meatus.

Middle Ear

The external auditory canal ends with the eardrum, also called the tympanic membrane. The eardrum marks the start of the middle ear. The eardrum is a taut membrane that vibrates in sympathy with the sounds directed down the canal.

Attached to the eardrum is a series of three bones known collectively as the ossicles. These three bones are the hammer, anvil, and stirrup, also known by their Latin equivalents: malleus, incus and stapes. The eardrum is connected to the hammer bone. The hammer bone is connected to the anvil bone. The anvil bone is connected to the stirrup bone. The stirrup bone is connected to the oval window, a membrane covering the entrance to the inner ear.

The main purpose of the middle ear is to transport airborne sounds from the outer ear to the fluid-filled inner ear. If the airborne sounds were to pass directly to the oval window, most of the acoustical energy would reflect and not be transferred to the inner ear. You may have taken advantage of this phenomenon as a child by diving under water when your parents were yelling that it was time to leave the pool. Your parent's airborne voices would have mostly been reflected off the water's surface, due to the impedance mismatch between the two media.

The middle ear acts as an impedance matching device, converting the airborne pressure waves for efficient transport through the larger resistance of the inner ear's fluid. This impedance matching is done in part through the lever action of the ossicles and by the fact that the oval window is smaller than the eardrum.

The ossicles have tiny muscles attached to them that contract when the ear is exposed to very loud sounds. This middle-ear reflex is too slow to provide protection against impulsive sounds such as gunshots, but it does activate right before we begin talking. If it were not for this reflex, the direct conduction of our voices to our middle ears would tend to drown out any external sounds.

The middle ear is sealed at one end with the eardrum and at the other with the oval window. Differences in the ambient pressure of the middle ear and the outside world can be painful and even damaging. Luckily, pressure equalization of the middle ear can be accomplished via the Eustachian tube, which connects to the back of the throat. When you rapidly change altitude and your ears pop, that pop is from the middle ear equalization through the Eustachian tubes.

Inner Ear

Whereas the primary function of the outer and middle ears is to efficiently transport acoustic energy from the outside world, the inner ear is where the acoustic energy stimulates nerves which result in the sensation of hearing. The inner ear also provides the sensations of linear and angular acceleration. A diagram of the inner ear is shown in Figure 3.10.

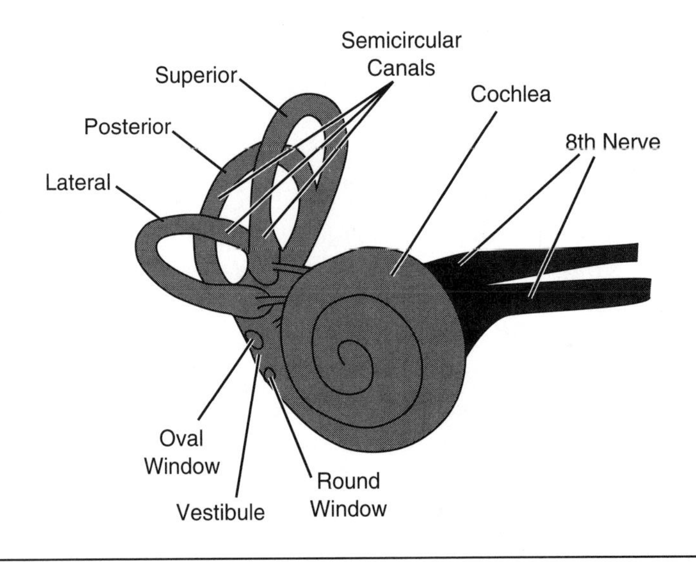

Figure 3.10 Inner Ear

The main hearing structure of the inner ear is the cochlea. The cochlea is a rigid tube coiled into a spiral, much like a snail's shell. Indeed, cochlea is Latin for snail shell. The cochlea itself is filled with a nearly incompressible liquid that transmits pressure waves from the middle ear.

The beginning of the cochlea is known as the base. The end is known as the apex. The base of the apex contains the oval window, a membrane that attaches to the middle ear's stirrup. Right below the oval window is a smaller membrane known as the round window. The round window acts as a sort of pressure valve for the cochlea. When the oval window is pushed inward by the stirrup, the round window bulges outward.

Suspended inside the cochlear fluid is the basilar membrane. When pressure waves travel down the cochlear fluid, they push against the basilar membrane. The deformation of the basilar membrane stimulates its hair cells, triggering electrical impulses that are sent to the brain—and interpreted as sound!

The basilar membrane, therefore, is where the rubber hits the road. An interesting feature of the membrane is that each region only responds to certain frequencies. The membrane near the base only reacts to high frequency sounds, whereas the membrane near the apex only reacts to low frequency sounds.

Brain

The brain has the responsibility of converting the raw electrical impulses generated by deformations of the basilar membrane into coherent sounds. A great deal of research has been conducted to determine precisely how the brain does this conversion, but many of the details remain unknown. But even without a complete understanding of how the brain processes the electrical stimuli, we do have a good understanding of the end result.

There are only certain sounds we can hear, and which ones we can hear depend on a wide number of factors. The capabilities and limitations of human hearing have been determined primarily through practical experimentation: exposing people to a wide variety of sounds under different conditions and asking them what they heard.

Intensity and Loudness

As has been discussed in the previous chapter, intensity is a quantifiable characteristic of sound. By comparison, a sound's perceived intensity as registered by the human hearing system is very subjective. This perceptual value is known as *loudness*.

Intensity

In an otherwise silent environment, humans can hear sounds as faint as 0 dB-SPL. This *threshold of hearing* varies from person to person, and is also frequency dependent. It should be noted that such perfectly quiet environments are very hard to find in the real world. As a result, background noise is usually the limiting factor in preventing us from hearing faint sounds, rather than our absolute sensitivity.

The most intense sounds humans can hear are on the order of 120 to 130 dB-SPL. Sounds with intensities above this level cause feelings such as prickling and pain. As such, this level is also known as the *threshold of feeling*. Intensities of 160 dB-SPL are powerful enough to perforate the eardrum!

Intensity Discrimination

When studying the human perception, it is common to measure the smallest consistently perceivable change for a given stimulus. This value is known as the *just noticeable difference* (JND). For broadband noises, the JND between two sound intensities is about 1 dB.

Loudness

If you were to double the intensity of a noise, it would not necessarily sound twice as loud. *Loudness* is the subjective equivalent of intensity. As such, it varies from person to person and it is not directly measurable. It also turns out that loudness is frequency dependent. The American National Standards Institute (ANSI) has defined it thus: "Loudness is defined as the attribute of auditory sensation in terms of which sounds can be ordered on a scale extended from quiet to loud."

Sones

To determine the qualities of loudness, human test subjects are asked to compare or adjust tones to meet certain criteria. One such test presents subjects with a tone, and then has them adjust the intensity of a second tone at the same frequency until it is twice as loud.

To measure the results, a unit called the sone was created. A sone is defined to be the loudness of a 1,000-hertz tone at 40 dB-SPL. A sound with a loudness of two sones would be twice as loud. Experimental results suggest that a 2-sone 1,000-hertz tone has to have an intensity of 50 dB-SPL. In other words, increasing the intensity by a factor of ten results in only a doubling of its loudness!

Phons

Another useful loudness metric was developed by Fletcher and Munson in their seminal 1933 paper "Loudness, its definition, measurement, and calculation." The phon, as it is called, is again anchored to a 1,000-hertz reference tone. Any noise that sounds as loud as a 1,000-hertz 40-dB-SPL tone has a loudness of 40 phons. Similarly, 50 phons is the loudness of a 1,000-hertz 50-dB-SPL tone. There is a one-to-one mapping between phons and dB-SPL at 1,000 hertz, so you may at first wonder why we would bother defining a new unit. The answer becomes apparent as you measure the loudness of different frequency tones, which is precisely what Fletcher and Munson did.

The resulting graph of their data, shown in Figure 3.11, dramatically reveals how well humans hear different sound frequencies.

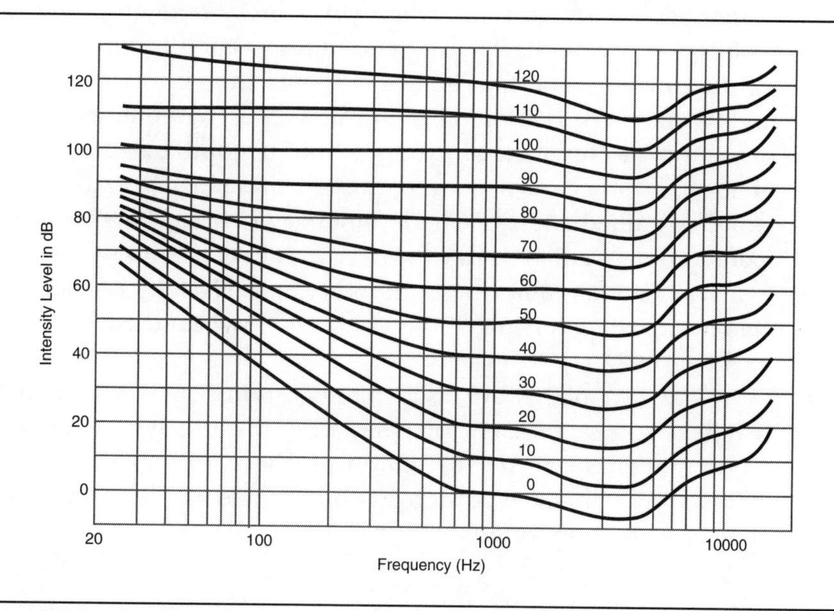

Figure 3.11 Fletcher-Munson Equal Loudness Contours

Each of the lines on the graph is known as an equal loudness contour. All sound intensities that lie along a contour have the same loudness. Looking at the 40-phon contour, we see that a 1,000-hertz tone at 40-dB-SPL has the same loudness as a 100-hertz tone at 60 dB-SPL and a 3,000-hertz tone at 37 dB-SPL.

In short, the graph reveals that we are most sensitive to frequencies in the range of 700 to 4,000 hertz. We are less sensitive to low frequencies and high frequencies outside this range. Generally, the farther away a tone is from the 3,000-hertz sweet spot, the less sensitive we are to it. To make a low and high frequency noises sound as loud as mid-range frequencies, their intensities must be increased.

This effect is not as pronounced for high-intensity sounds. A look at the 90-phon contour reveals it to be fairly flat for low frequencies, indicating that low frequencies in the 90-dB-SPL range sound just about as loud as 90-dB-SPL tones in the mid-range. In contrast, humans are much less sensitive to low frequency sounds at low intensities. A look at the 10-phon contour shows that a 30-hertz tone would need an intensity of nearly 70 dB-SPL to match the loudness of a 3,000-hertz tone at 2 dB-SPL.

This intensity-dependent sensitivity to low frequency sounds is in fact the motivation behind the loudness switches on many older sound systems. The theory was that when you were listening to your radio at low volume, you would activate the loudness switch to increase the intensity of the low frequencies. The music would then hopefully sound the same at low intensity as it did at high intensities. Without compensation, low frequency noises such as drums would become inaudible when the volume was turned down, even though mid-range sounds like a singer's voice remained audible. The loudness switch has been re-titled on many contemporary audio devices with names like bass boost.

The Fletcher-Munson graph has been revised by further experiments, and an updated version of the curves is now standardized in ISO Recommendation 226.

Note that phons are used for measuring sounds of equal loudness, whereas sones are used for comparing the relative loudness of sounds. There is nothing in the definition of phons that relates the loudness of two different phon levels; a 40-phon sound is not necessarily twice as loud as a 20-phon sound.

Weighting Curves

If I told you that there was a tone playing at 50 dB-SPL in room, would you mind having to work in that room for eight hours a day? Your answer would probably depend on the frequency of the tone. If it was a 20-hertz tone, it would be imperceptible to you. But if it was a 2,000-hertz tone, it would be clearly audible and likely to be quite annoying.

Providing only a sound's intensity level is not enough information to determine how loud it is going to sound to the average person. We also need to know the frequency information. But because most real-world noises are more complex than a pure tone, we would need to provide a full spectrum of the noise. By correlating the intensities of the different frequencies with the sensitivity of human sensitivity to those frequencies, we could then get a good feel for the loudness of the environment.

It would be very useful if we could encapsulate all this information into a single number.[2] In fact, that is precisely what sound meters do. They sample a wide range of frequencies and then weight the intensities to match our sensitivity to the different ranges. The decibel value provides a

[2] Much like a student's four years of accomplishments at high school can be boiled down to a single number determined by a standardized multiple-choice test.

reasonable estimate of the loudness of broadband sounds. Three different weighting curves are commonly used, as shown in Figure 3.12.

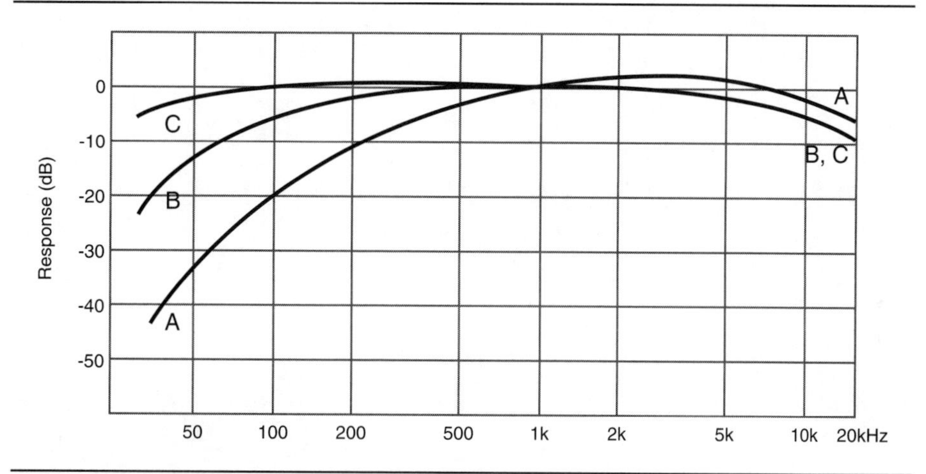

Figure 3.12 Sound Meter Weight Curves

The A-curve is designed to be used for low intensity sounds, the B-curve for middle intensity sounds, and the C-curve for high intensity sounds. The different shape of the curves reflects our intensity-dependent sensitivity to low frequencies. In fact, the A-curve is roughly the inverse of the 40-phon equal loudness contour. Similarly, the B-curve and the C-curve are inverses of the 70-phon and 100-phon contours, respectively. Such weighted intensities are designated as dB-A, dB-B, and dB-C to indicate which weight curve was used to make the measurement.

Effects of Duration

The loudness of a sound also depends on the duration of that sound. Consider a sound of fixed intensity. If the sound lasts two seconds, it sounds just as loud if it had lasted only one second. However, as the duration of the sound falls below 200 milliseconds, its loudness decreases, even though its intensity remains fixed! A 10-millisecond sound may sound half as loud as a 200 millisecond sound of the same intensity. A graph of this effect is shown in Figure 3.13.

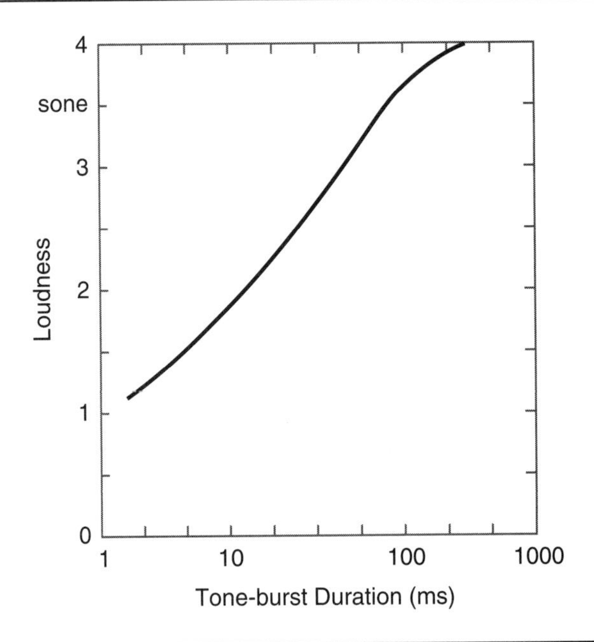

Figure 3.13 Loudness vs. Duration

Steady sounds lasting tens of seconds also decrease in loudness. This characteristic of hearing is known as *loudness adaptation*. Constant intensity sounds may decrease in loudness by as much as 25 percent over the course of several minutes.

Frequency and Pitch

In the previous chapter we discussed the characteristic of sound known as frequency. In this section, we will examine the frequencies we can hear as well as our subjective interpretation of those frequencies.

Frequency

Humans can hear frequencies in the nominal range of 20 to 20,000 hertz. The exact frequency range varies from person to person. Furthermore, for any given person, the range of frequencies they can hear decreases over time. In particular, people lose the ability to hear higher frequencies as they age.

Frequency Selectivity

Our perception of different sound frequencies is markedly different than our perception of different light frequencies. When our eyes are simultaneously presented with two frequencies of light, we see only a single color. For instance, if we see a light containing red and blue frequencies, we see the color purple. By contrast, when our ears are presented with two markedly different audio frequencies, such as a 1,000-hertz and a 10,000-hertz tone, we hear two distinct tones.

Only when two audio frequencies are very close together are they merged into a single perceptible sound. The ability to differentiate two pure tones is known as *frequency selectivity* or *frequency resolution*. Frequency resolution varies based on the frequencies involved, as well as the intensity of the sounds. For tones around 200 hertz, we can discriminate between two frequencies as close together as 1 hertz. In other words, we are able to distinguish between a 200-hertz and a 201-hertz tone. For higher frequencies, our frequency selectivity degrades. For a 10,000-hertz tone, typical frequency selectivity is on the order of 200 hertz.

Pitch

The frequency components of a sound are objective. Two devices measuring a pure tone always agree on its frequency. However, two humans hearing a pure tone unaided may disagree on the frequency of that same pure tone. Furthermore, a person hearing a 1,000-hertz tone followed by a 2,000-hertz tone may not think that the second tone sounds exactly twice as high as the previous.

The subjective equivalent of frequency is *pitch*. Pitch has been defined by ANSI as "that attribute of auditory sensation in terms of which sounds may be ordered on a scale extended from high to low." Pitch is measured using a unit known as a *mel*. The value of 1,000 mels has been arbitrarily defined to be the pitch of a 1,000-mel tone. A 2,000-mel tone is one that sounds to a listener twice as high as a 1000-hertz tone. A 500-mel tone is one that sounds twice as low as a 1,000-mel tone.

The correlation between an average person's measurement of pitch versus frequency is shown in Figure 3.14. The graph reveals a distinctly nonlinear relationship between pitch and frequency. This simplified diagram notwithstanding, the relationship between pitch and frequency varies based on the intensity and duration of the sounds.

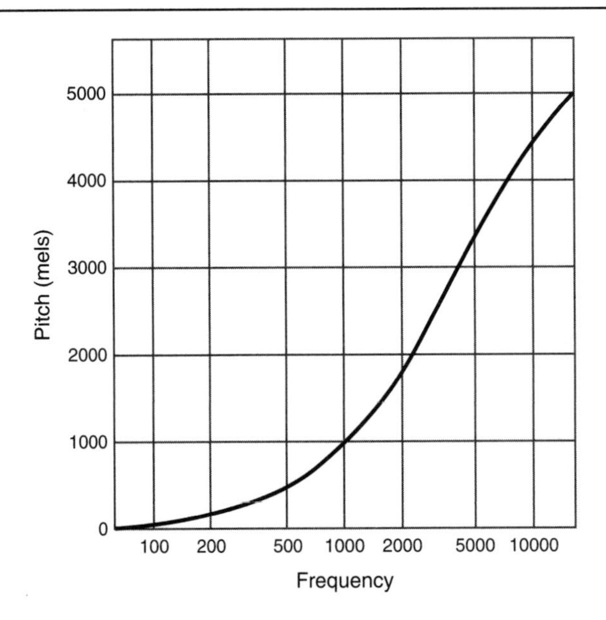

Figure 3.14 Frequency vs. Pitch

For complex sounds such as those produced by musical instruments, people tend to key off the fundamental frequency. Regardless of the distribution and intensity of the harmonics, pitch is determined by the fundamental.

When presented with an arbitrary tone, most people cannot determine the pitch of a tone. Most of us cannot, for example, identify a tone as being 2,000 mels without first being presented with a 1,000-mel tone for comparison. A small percentage of the population, however, can indeed identify pitch fairly accurately without a reference. This capability is known as *perfect pitch*. Those with perfect pitch typically identify tones as musical notes, such as middle C, rather than using mels.

Timbre

Timbre is defined by ANSI as "that attribute of auditory sensation that allows us to judge two sounds similarly presented with same loudness and pitch as being different." This definition is akin to saying that summer is that season which is not winter, fall, or spring. Timbre is that quality that allows us to distinguish between a piano playing a note and a violin playing that same note. Although the two sounds have the same fundamental pitch, their spectra are quite distinguishable.

Whereas sounds can be ordered from high to low with regard to pitch and loudness, timbre has no concept of ordering. You cannot say that one sound has more or less timbre than another.

Masking

Masking is the effect of one sound being obscured by another. For instance, a loud engine can mask the sound of a quiet car radio. There are many different forms of masking that occur in the context of the human hearing system.

Masking is an important phenomenon for us to understand. Because masked sounds are undetectable, there is no reason for us to reproduce those sounds in any audio system we might be designing. A clear understanding of masking can help us design an audio compression algorithm that is perceptually lossless.

When masking occurs, there are two sounds involved: the signal, or probe, and the masker. The signal is the sound that the subject is trying to hear. The masker is the interfering sound that is making the signal harder or impossible to detect. Both the signal and the masker can be any type of sound: pure tones, narrowband noise, wideband noise, or other complex sounds. The masking effects vary depending on the types of noise involved.

Simultaneous Masking

Simultaneous masking is the effect of one sound obscuring another concurrent sound. For instance, one study showed the threshold of hearing for a 5,000-hertz pure tone to be about 10 dB-SPL. When 38-dB-SPL white noise was introduced as a masker, the pure tone was no longer audible. Indeed, the intensity of the pure tone had to be increased to 25 dB-SPL before it could be detected. Simultaneous masking is used by a type of hearing aid known as a tinnitus masker. The device produces low intensity noise to mask the patient's tinnitus, a persistent ringing in the ears.

We have already mentioned a similar phenomenon earlier in this chapter. When two tones are below the frequency selectivity threshold, we can only hear a single sound. Precisely speaking, this effect is not masking, but instead a different effect known as *fusion*.

Binaural Masking

The concept of simultaneous masking is easy to grasp, as we have everyday experiences demonstrating it, such as not being able to hear the phone when the vacuum cleaner is turned on. However, some counterintuitive simultaneous masking can occur when different sounds are presented to each ear. Indeed, the masking threshold of a signal can be lower when listening with both ears than with just one. This phenomenon is known as binaural masking level difference (BMLD).

Consider a pure tone that is combined with masking noise so that the tone is just below the threshold. When the identical combined sound is presented to both ears, the pure tone cannot be heard. It is masked. However, if the pure tone presented to one ear is given a 180-degree offset, then the pure tone can be heard! See Figure 3.15.

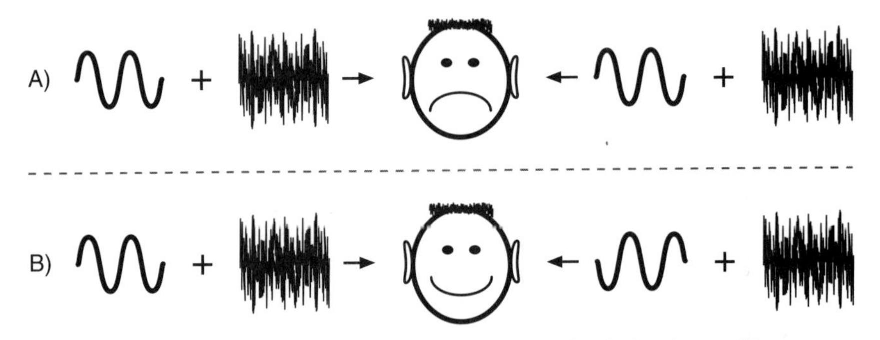

When both ears are presented with an identical pure tone just below the masking threshold of the white noise (A), the tone cannot be heard. However, if the tone presented to one of the ears is offset by 180 degrees (B), then the tone can be heard.

Figure 3.15 Binaural Masking Level Difference with Phase Offset

Perhaps even more counter-intuitively, a masked tone presented to one ear can be unmasked by applying just noise to the other ear, as shown in Figure 3.16.

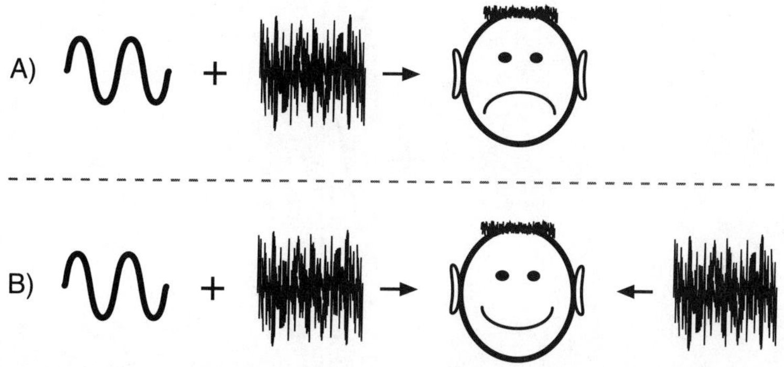

When one ear is presented with a pure tone just below the masking threshold of the white noise (A), the tone cannot be heard. However, if the masking noise alone is subsequently presented to the other ear (B), the tone can be heard.

Figure 3.16 Binaural Masking Level Difference with Asymmetric Masking

Non-simultaneous Masking

When two sounds are presented one after the other with a very small interval between them, one of the sounds may be masked by the other. Such masking is known as non-simultaneous or temporal masking.

When the masker comes before the signal, it is known as *forward masking*. When the signal comes before the masker, it is known as *backward masking*.

Non-simultaneous masking can be quite pronounced and can result in raising the threshold of sounds by over 30 dB, as can be seen in Figure 3.17.

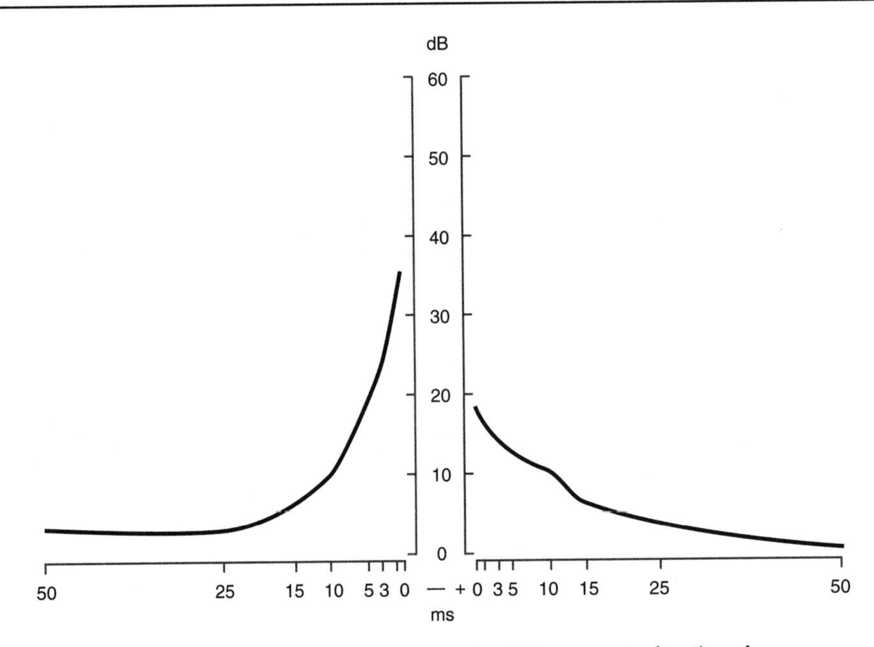

The graphs demonstrate how the masking threshold changes as a function of the time interval between masker and signal. The graph on the left shows backward masking. The graph on the right shows forward masking.

Figure 3.17 Non-simultaneous Masking

Critical Bands

Early investigation into simultaneous masking led Fletcher to hypothesize that a portion of the human hearing system behaves as if it is a set of continuously overlapping bandpass filters. Each of these filters is thought to correspond to a physical location on the basilar membrane. Specifically, each filter maps to a section of the basilar membrane roughly 0.9-mm long. The range of filters that stimulate the same portion of the basilar membrane is known as a *critical band*. The width of a critical band is known as the *critical bandwidth*.

Although some papers describe an explicit number, such as 24, of critical bands with well-defined limits, further studies have suggested that the auditory system truly has a set of continuous filters, and that it is appropriate to place a critical band around any arbitrary audible frequency.

Simultaneous masking only occurs for sounds within a critical band. For instance, if a 1,000-hertz tone is being played and a narrowband noise is being simultaneously presented in the range of 4,000 to 5,000 hertz, no masking of the tone occurs. However, if the noise is changed to be in the range of 500 to 1,500 hertz, then masking does occur.

Loudness is also linked to the critical bands. For instance, narrowband noise at constant intensity has a constant loudness as long as the bandwidth of the noise remains within a critical band. If the bandwidth of the noise spans critical bands, then loudness increases, as shown in Figure 3.18.

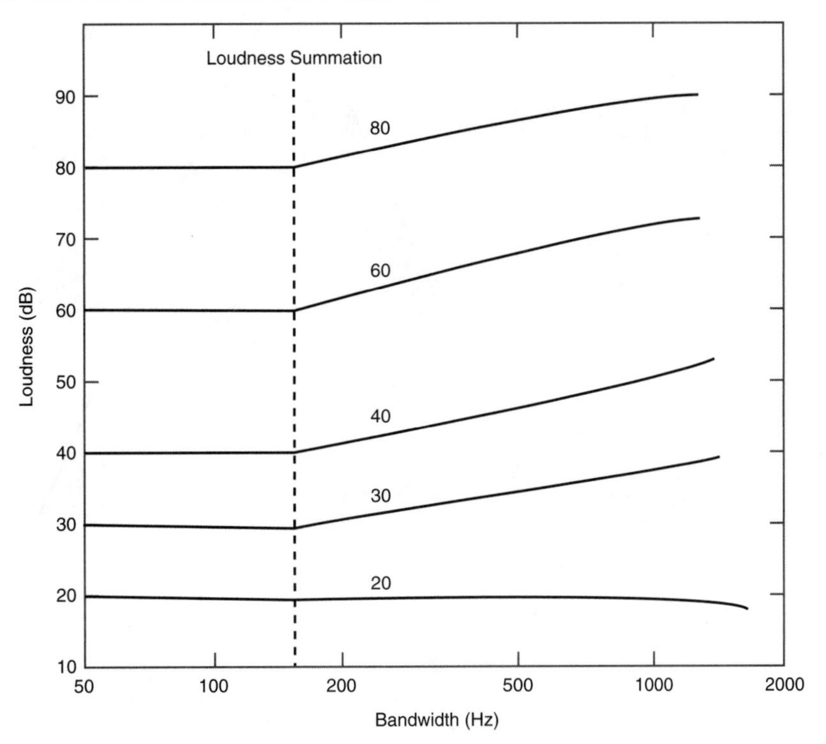

This graph shows to results of a 1956 study. Subjects were presented with noises at fixed intensities—20, 30, 40, 60, and 80 dB-SPL. The noise was centered at 1,000 hertz. As the bandwidth of the noise was increased, the intensity in phons remained constant, until the bandwidth reached 160 hertz. At this point, the intensity began to increase as the bandwidth increased. In other words, the fixed-intensity noise seemed louder when it began to span multiple critical bands.

Figure 3.18 Loudness as a Function of Bandwidth

In the mid 1970s, R.D. Patterson ran a series of experiments in which he had listeners try to detect a test tone with varying types of masking noise. The noise had a spectral hole around the frequency of the test tone. By varying the width of the hole, he was able to determine the responsiveness of the basilar membrane within a critical band. In other words, he was able to determine the shape of the auditory filters. The auditory filters are not rectangular, but rather have rounded tops and sloped edges, as shown in Figure 3.19. The critical bandwidth is a measure of the effective bandwidth of the auditory filters.

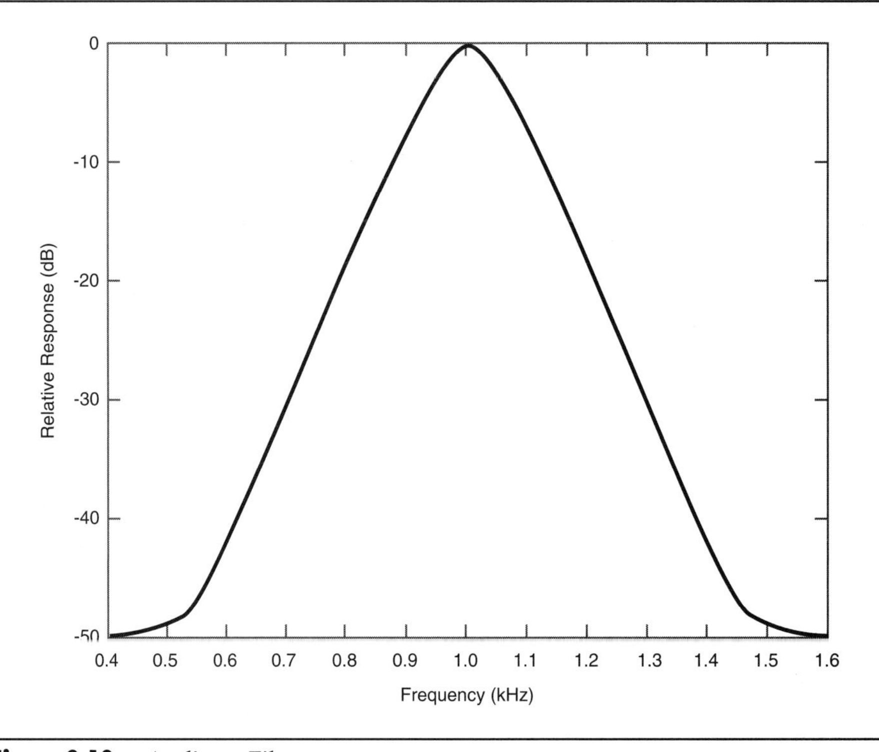

Figure 3.19 Auditory Filter

Temporal Resolution

When presented with very short sounds, or clicks, we can perceive them as distinct sounds as long as they are separated in time by a few milliseconds. If the gap between the clicks is shorter than a few milliseconds, we can no longer hear the individual clicks. Instead, they seem to be a continuous sound. On a related note, when presented with a continuous sound, we cannot hear any gaps in that sound unless they are longer than 2 to 3 milliseconds. In other words, if you insert very short amounts of silence into a sound, the silences are undetectable.

Sound Localization

A very useful thing to do with sound is to locate where it is coming from. If your mate was calling you, you would want to know where she was so you could go to her. If a saber-toothed tiger was growling nearby, you would want to know where it is so you could run away from it.[3] By studying the characteristics of localization, we can design surround sound systems that effectively reproduce spatial cues, and thus allow us to hear sound effects like bullets flying past us in the comfort of our own home.

In general it is difficult to locate very short sounds. Longer sounds are easier to pinpoint.

The spatial perception of sounds is accomplished by two types of cues: monaural and binaural. Monaural cues require the use of a single ear, whereas binaural cues require both ears.

Monaural Cues

The primary monaural localization cue is the loudness of the sound. In short, the louder the sound is, the closer it is to you. This cue works most effectively for sounds with which we are familiar. For instance, if we hear people talking nearby, we have a good idea of how far away they are. Conversely, if we hear an artificially generated 1,000-hertz pure tone, it is very difficult to determine how far away it is, because we have no idea of the intensity of the signal. It might be a 120-dB-SPL source located far away, or a 10-dB-SPL source located within arm's reach.

The accuracy of localization under these conditions can be improved by slight head movements. By comparing the loudness of the sound at slightly different positions, we instinctively use the inverse square law to estimate the distance of the sound. If the loudness of the sound changes dramatically during subtle head movements, the inverse square law implies that the sound is nearby. If there are no discernable changes in loudness, the sound is probably far away.

---

[3] Or vice versa, depending on the state of your marital bliss.

The louder a sound is, the closer it is perceived to be, but that does not necessarily mean that the loudest sound is the closest one. For instance, a butterfly fluttering a foot away is going to be quieter than an F5 tornado 100 feet away.

Binaural Cues

Binaural localization is our ability to determine the position of a sound using sound cues presented to both ears. Our brains compare differences in the sound that reach each of the ears and process the information to localize the sound.

Binaural localization is one of the few capabilities of the human hearing system that require use of both ears. We are able to detect pitch, loudness, and timbre using only one ear.

Time Differences

One binaural cue is the arrival time of a new sound. If a sound originates directly in front of a person, then the sound waves reach each ear at the same time. However, if the sound is slightly to the right, the sound waves reach the right ear slightly before the left ear, as shown in Figure 3.20. Humans can perceive interaural time differences as small as 10 microseconds.

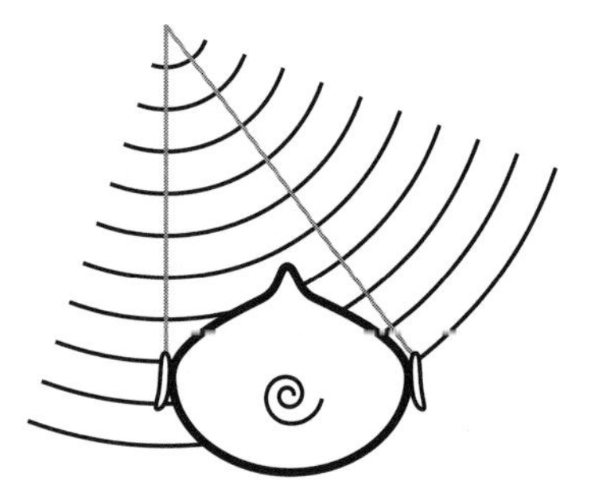

Figure 3.20 Time Differences

Note that time difference cues have a positional ambiguity of 180 degrees. Sounds reaching the ears simultaneously may be directly in front of the listener, but they may just as well be originating directly behind the listener. Similarly, a sound originating 10 degrees to the right of forward has the same time differences as a sound origination 10 degrees to the left of backward.

Intensity Differences

We are thick-headed. Sufficiently so that our heads are acoustically opaque; sounds can generally not propagate through them. Sound originating to one side of the head is able to reach the ear on that side unobstructed. However, the head is in the way of the sound reaching the ear on the other side of the head. While low frequency sounds may be able to diffract, or bend, around the head, the high frequency sounds are blocked by the head, as shown in Figure 3.21.

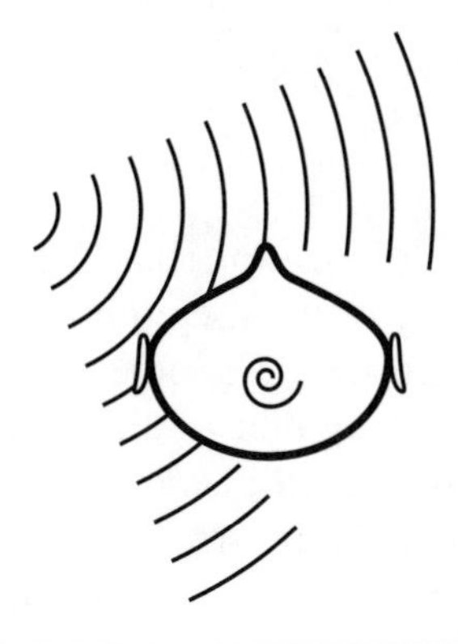

Figure 3.21 Intensity Differences

The resulting interaural intensity differences provide additional cues that aid us in localizing sounds. The physics of waves means that the shadowing effect only occurs for frequencies with a wavelength longer than the obstruction; in this case, the head. Experimentation suggests that interaural intensity differences are only useful for frequencies above 1,500 hertz. The wavelength of a 1,500-hertz tone is about nine inches, which is indeed about the size of an average head.

Phase Differences

For frequencies below 1,500 hertz, the longer wavelengths mean that the sound diffracts around the head and is able to reach both ears. For these lower frequencies, the difference in phase is a useful localization cue, as shown in Figure 3.22.

For frequencies above 1,500 hertz, the phase difference cues become ambiguous. For instance, the phase difference between the ears might be 180 degrees, but it would not be clear if the signal reaching one ear was half a phase ahead or half a phase behind the other.

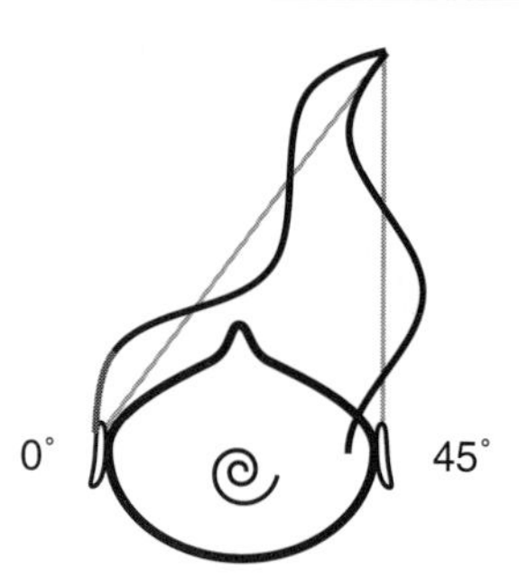

Figure 3.22 Phase Differences

Pinna Effects

The pinna plays an important role in localization. The many folds of the pinna reflect sound toward the auditory canal. The clever bit is that each fold acts as a filter, reflecting some frequency ranges more strongly than others. The practical upshot of this characteristic is that a sound has a slightly different spectrum reflecting off the pinna depending on its direction. Furthermore, faint intra-pinna echoes are also directed down the auditory canal. These echoes are also directionally dependent. As such, the pinna effectively stamps a unique signature onto a sound that the brain can decode to determine the location of the sound.

Researchers have filled test subject's pinna with clay and observed a corresponding decrease in localization precision. Although you may not care to stuff your ears with clay, you can observe the pinna effects by moving them about with your fingers. Pulling the pinna out and forward emphasizes the lower frequencies and makes the sound louder. Holding the pinna flat against your head makes sounds quieter and tinnier.

Another interesting experiment was done by placing small microphones in the auditory canals of people and feeding the recorded sound directly into other people's auditory canals with headphones. What the study found is that people were able to learn how to localize the sounds, even though the pinna-generated effects came from somebody else's pinna!

Precedence Effect

Although you may not realize it, we live in a world filled with echoes. Consider, for example, the scenario depicted in Figure 3.23. Apart from the direct path from the sound source to an ear, there are also numerous indirect paths where the sound first bounces off one or more walls.

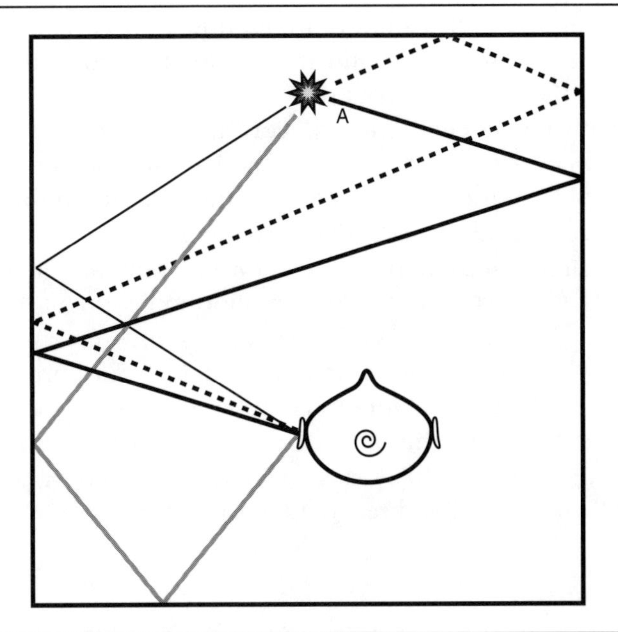

Figure 3.23 Echo Paths

The reason that we are often oblivious to this prevalence of echoes is that our auditory system is very effective at filtering out echoes. If two transient sounds reach a listener's ears in a short time interval, they are fused together by the auditory system and heard as a single sound. The time span between the two sounds can be as large as about 40 milliseconds for complex sounds, but only about 5 milliseconds for a single click.

When the two sounds are fused together in this fashion, the localization of the sound is determined primarily by the first sound that reaches the ear. This localization behavior is known variously as the *precedence effect*, the *Haas effect*, and the *law of the first wave front*.

The arrival time of the second sound does have an effect on localization. As the gap between the first and second sound increases, the closer the overall sound seems to be coming from the second source location.

The precedence effect is most likely to occur for cases in which the two sounds are similar. For instance, if the two sounds are an identical whistle, then the precedence effect merges the echo into a single perceived sound. However, if one sound is a whistle and the other is a door slamming shut, the two sounds are perceived as two independent noises, each with a unique location.

Even if the two sounds are identical, the precedence effect does not occur if the second sound is substantially more intense, perhaps 10 to 15 dB, above the first sound.

The precedence effect is very useful in that it allows us to localize sounds even in an acoustically active environment. This ability is very handy in situations such as when you wake up in the middle of the night and hear a saber-toothed tiger prowling about in your cave.

You may have gotten a taste for just how full of echoes the world is if you have ever listened to a monophonic home video taken inside a crowded restaurant. While actually in the restaurant yourself, we can usually hear everyone clearly at our table, but during playback of the recording, all of the echoes become very obvious and make it much harder to hear anything. The precedence effect does not operate while we're listening to the tape playback, because the sound reaching our left ear is identical to the sound reaching our right ear.

Summary

The human auditory system provides us with a subjective experience of sound waves. Although the capabilities of hearing vary from person to person, the average young adult can discern frequencies in the range from 20 to 20,000 hertz, ranging in intensity from zero to 120 dB-SPL.

We are most sensitive to mid-range frequencies. As sounds get further away from 3,000 hertz, either higher or lower, they become increasingly more difficult to hear.

Pitch is the subjective analog of frequency. Pitch is measured in mels.

Loudness is the subjective analog of intensity. Loudness is measured in sones and phons. As a rule of thumb, a 10-dB increase in intensity results in the loudness of the sound doubling.

One sound may mask another sound. Masking can occur if the masker and signal are simultaneous, but also if one precedes the other.

In terms of frequency selectivity, the human hearing system behaves as if it is a series of overlapping auditory filters. Although the auditory filters have rounded tops with sloping edges, they may be approximated by rectangular passband filters. The width of these hypothetical filters corresponds to the critical bandwidth.

Sound localization is accomplished by using time and intensity differences between the two ears, as well as spectral effects caused by the pinna and head shadowing.

Chapter 4

Speakers

"Yes, Archchancellor." Ponder cleared his throat. "Sound, you see, comes in waves—"

He stopped. Wizardly premonitions rose in his mind. He just knew that Ridcully was going to assume he was talking about the sea. There was going to be one of those huge bottomless misunderstandings that always occurred whenever anyone tried to explain anything to the Archchancellor. Words like "surf," and probably "ice cream" and "sand" were just...

"It's all done by magic, Archchancellor," he said, giving up.

"Ah. Right," said Ridcully. He sounded a little disappointed. "None of that complicated business with springs and cogwheels and tubes and stuff, then."

"That's right, sir," said Ponder. "Just magic. Sufficiently advanced magic."

—Terry Pratchett, *Hogfather*

One of the most critical elements in any sound system is the speaker. Regardless of how a sound signal is created, stored, and transmitted, it eventually needs to be converted into audible pressure waves. This conversion is handled by a device known as a speaker. In this chapter, we will examine the different types of speakers and the components needed to construct them.

Speakers are devices that convert electrical signals into sound pressure waves. Sending an appropriate signal to a speaker creates sounds that are a very good approximation of the original source.

A speaker typically consists of three elements: *drivers*, a *crossover*, and an *enclosure*. We will examine these components in more detail below and explore different configurations of these components.

Drivers

Drivers are the speaker components that actually convert electrical signals into sound pressure waves. Sometimes drivers are also referred to as speakers. This book consistently uses the term *driver* to refer to the actual component that converts electrical signals into sound waves. The term *speaker* is used in reference to a collection of one or more drivers assembled within an enclosure.

Drivers are also referred to as *transducers*, because they convert energy from one medium—electric—to another—air.

Driver Types

There are many different driver types. A few of the more common ones are discussed here.

Dynamic Drivers

The most common driver design in the world today is known as a dynamic moving-coil driver, shown in Figure 4.1. Such transducers are often referred to simply as dynamic drivers, even though there are types of dynamic drivers that do not use a moving coil.

Dynamic drivers move air through the action of an electromagnetic linear motor. The two components of this motor are a toroidal permanent magnet and a cylindrical electromagnet, located inside the hole of the permanent magnet. When power is applied to the electromagnet, it generates a magnetic field. This field interacts with the field of the permanent magnet and repels the electromagnet away from the permanent magnet.

The electromagnet is known as the *voice coil*: coil, because it is built by wrapping a tightly coiled wire around a former; voice, because the varying electrical signals applied to the coil provide the initial physical impetus that creates sounds. The voice coil and permanent magnet do not actually touch, but are separated by a small space known as the *field gap*.

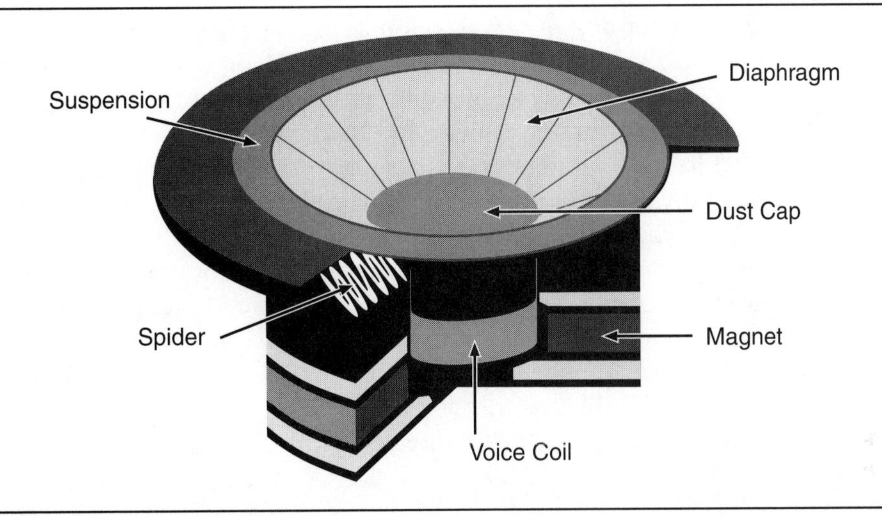

Figure 4.1 Driver Design

The piece of the driver which actually creates airborne pressure waves is the *diaphragm*. It may be made of materials as mundane as paper or as exotic as polyethylene naphthalate. Most diaphragms are shaped like a flat cone with the tip removed, although some small diaphragms are hemispherical. The inside edge of the truncated cone is attached to the voice coil. This attachment point—as well as the field coil itself—is shielded from the outside environment by a *dust cap*.

The outer rim of the diaphragm is attached to the frame of the driver by the *suspension*. The suspension determines the maximum range of motion of the diaphragm. This displacement distance is known as the *excursion*. Most diaphragms have an excursion on the order of a few millimeters, but specialized sub-woofers may have excursions in excess of two inches!

When a diaphragm is driven by very intense signals outside the maximum excursion, damage to the diaphragm and or suspension can occur. This condition is known as overshoot when the diaphragm is pushed too far outward and as undershoot when it is pulled too far inward.

The voice coil is attached to the frame by a flexible construct known as the *spider*. The spider keeps the voice coil centered within the permanent magnet. The spider also acts in opposition to the linear push of the activated coil, constantly pulling the coil back toward its starting position inside the permanent magnet. Today's spiders are typically corrugated sheets, but the original ones were discrete elastic bands which superficially resembled the legs of a spider.

This driver design was developed in a 1925 paper by Chester W. Rice and Edward W. Kellog working at General Electric. At the time, available permanent magnets were not powerful enough. Instead, they used a stationary electromagnet called the field coil. This static electromagnet needed its own power supply, so early drivers had four connectors: two to carry the audio signal to the voice coil, and another two carrying a DC voltage to energize the field coil.

World War II saw the development of more powerful permanent magnets. Eventually all post-war drivers replaced the field coil with these magnets. Apart from this one change, the majority of today's drivers still adhere to that fundamental 1926 design. The materials used to construct the component have improved dramatically in the intervening decades, providing ever-increasing fidelity.

Horns

A variation of the dynamic driver is the horn, shown in Figure 4.2. A horn is simply a dynamic driver with a waveguide attached over the diaphragm. The cross-section of the waveguide is about the size of the diaphragm at the attachment point, but then flares out much wider. The design of the waveguide is such that sound waves are focused in a tighter pattern than they would be otherwise. Sound within this field is more intense than it would be without the waveguide.

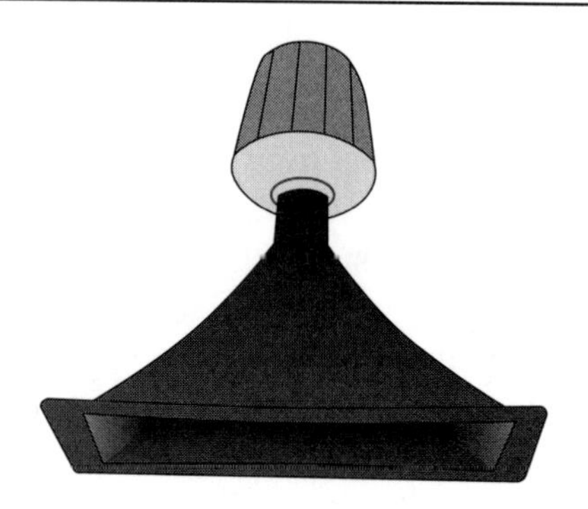

Figure 4.2 Horn Driver

As an analogy, consider a simple flashlight. The light bulb corresponds to the driver and the parabolic reflector to the waveguide. The flashlight produces an intense and highly directional beam. If we remove the parabolic reflector, the resulting light beam is spread across a much wider area, but the intensity at a point directly in front of the flashlight is much less than it was with the reflector intact. In both cases, the power of the light bulb itself remains constant.

So, a horn allows the overall sensitivity of a dynamic driver to be increased, but at the expense of having a smaller sound field. Indeed, the sensitivity of a horn may be over 6 dB higher than the sensitivity of the same dynamic driver without the waveguide. As such, a less powerful amplifier can be used to create the same sound intensity.

Horns are primarily used in public address (PA) systems or other situations where a large volume of space needs to be filled with sound. For large scale multi-driver speaker systems, as you might find at an amplified music concert, horns are often used for drivers that reproduce high and medium frequency sounds. Low frequency drivers, however, rarely sport waveguides, sine low frequency sounds readily diffract.

Electrostatic

Another type of transducer is the electrostatic driver. The electrostatic driver is constructed of two parallel metal plates separated by a spacer. These rigid plates, a.k.a. stators, are filled with small holes to allow air to pass. In between the stators is a thin, electrically conductive membrane, shown in Figure 4.3.

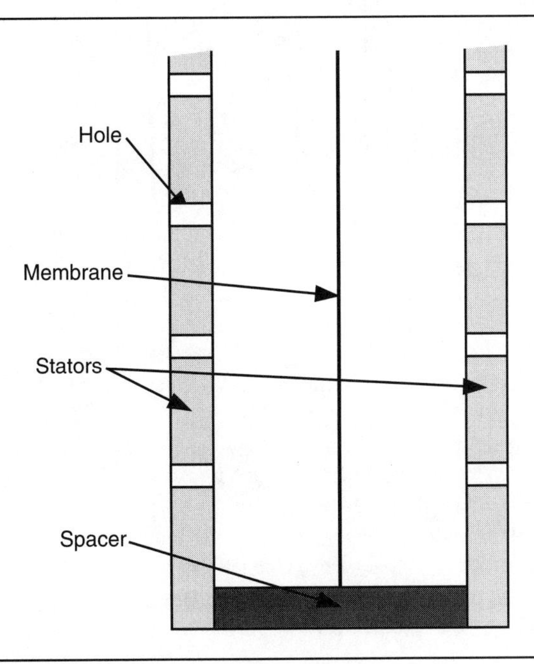

Figure 4.3 Electrostatic Driver Components

Electrostatic drivers produce sounds by moving the membrane. The membrane movement is accomplished by first applying a charge of thousands of volts to the stators and applying an opposite charge to the membrane. Recall that opposite charges attract. Because the two stators are equally charged, the membrane is equally attracted to each of them, and hence remains stationary in the middle.

To generate sound, the polarity of the stators is changed one at a time with a magnitude proportional to the input sound signal. The membrane is electrostatically attracted to one stator and repelled by the other, as shown in Figure 4.4. The subsequent movement of the membrane creates sound waves.

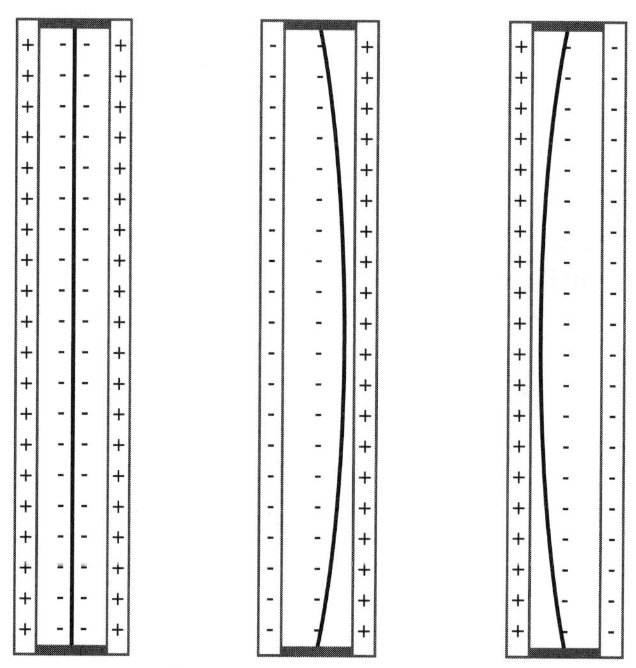

Left: In the neutral state, both stators have a positive charge. The membrane has a negative charge.

Center: To move the membrane to the right, a negative charge is applied to the left stator. The negatively-charged membrane is repelled by the left stator and attracted to the right stator.

Right: Restoring the positive charge to left stator and applying a negative charge to the right stator moves the diaphragm to the left.

Figure 4.4 Electrostatic Drivers in Action

The uniform movement of the membrane allows for very crisp reproduction of sounds. Indeed, the first time I heard electrostatic speakers, it sounded as if the singer was actually standing in the room with me, rather than simply having her voice reproduced on speakers. The low mass of the membrane means that electrostatic drivers have very good transient response. Electrostatic speakers are also very flat, and can be built to take up very little floor space. Some are even designed to be wall-mounted.

They are not, however, without their drawbacks. The high voltages mean that dust is actively drawn to them. Also, the speakers must prevent excessive excursions of the membrane; if the membrane moves so far as to touch the stators, it creates a short circuit.

Because the membrane has a small range of motion, it is difficult for the driver to create intense low frequency sounds. One way to increase the low frequency response is to increase the area of the membrane. A more common solution is to couple the electrostatic speaker with a cone woofer.

Planar Magnetic

Planar magnetic drivers are very similar to electrostatic speakers. Indeed, assembled planar magnetic speakers look just like electrostatic speakers.

Like electrostatic speakers, planar magnetic speakers also consist of two rigid, perforated metal plates separated by a spacer. Attached to the plates are permanent magnets. There is a thin membrane between the two plates. The membrane is not in and of itself conductive, but it does hold a wire coil. The electrical audio signal is run through this wire, generating electromagnetic fields that are attracted and repelled to the static magnetic field of the permanent magnets. The membrane moves as a result of the electromagnetic interactions, thus producing sound waves, as shown in Figure 4.5.

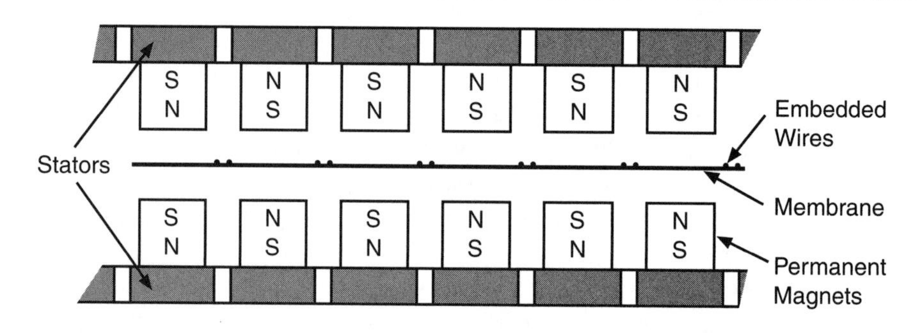

Figure 4.5 Planar Magnetic Driver Components

The performance and capabilities of planar magnetic speakers is very similar to electrostatic speakers. The planar magnetic speakers have the added advantage of not attracting dust, because they do not generate large potentials.

Driver Characteristics

Regardless of the type, drivers have some common characteristics that describe the details of how they reproduce sound. In this section we will examine some of the more common driver properties.

Frequency Response

One of the characteristics of a driver is the range of frequencies it can accurately reproduce. Typically, there is not a well-defined point in the spectrum where a driver suddenly stops reproducing frequencies. Instead, there is a gradual roll off at the upper and lower frequencies. Reference to the frequency range of a driver must therefore include an indicator of how much the sound intensity varies over that range.

Consider the frequency response graph shown in Figure 4.6. We see that compared to a measured reference level at 1,000 hertz, the response of the drivers at 30 hertz is 3 dB below that reference. Similarly, the response is 3 dB down at 10,000 hertz. Between these two frequencies, the response of the driver dips up and down, but it is always within 3 dB of the reference level. We can therefore say that the frequency response of this driver is 30 to 10,000 hertz ±3 dB.

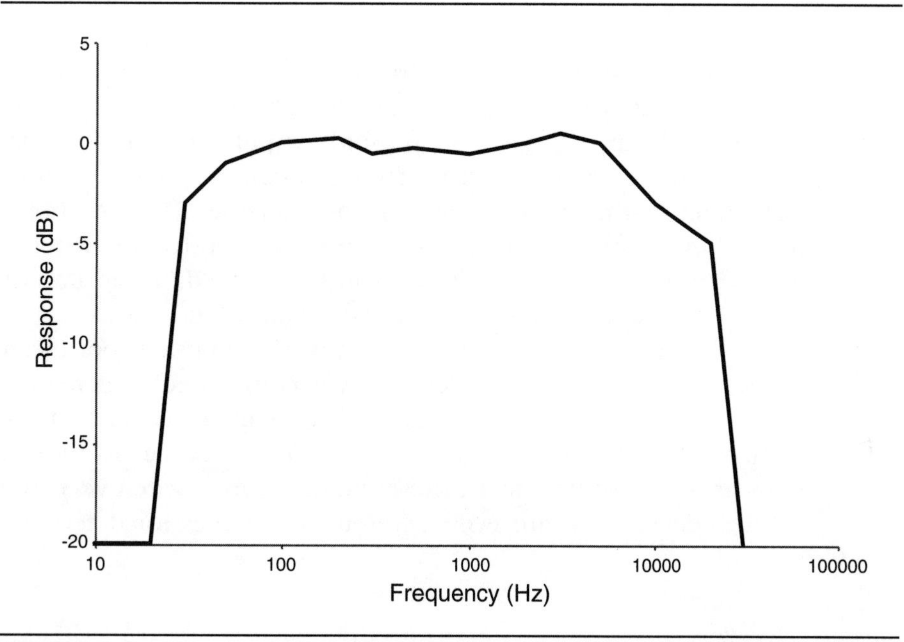

Figure 4.6 Frequency Response Graph

Merely specifying a frequency range without specifying the variation in the response is meaningless. We could arbitrarily say that the frequency range of the above driver is 20 to 30,000 hertz. And, indeed it is, if you allow a ±20 dB variation in the response. But remember from our study of psychoacoustics that a 20-dB decrease in intensity corresponds to a 75 percent reduction in loudness. Most listeners would not find it acceptable for these supposedly supported frequencies to be played at one-fourth of the loudness of the rest of the spectrum.

Another interesting question is how was the data for the above graph generated? One method is to place a microphone a fixed distance in front of a driver and adjust the amplitude of a 1,000-hertz test signal until it measures 100 dB-SPL. That is your reference level. By measuring the resulting microphone levels from input signals of the same magnitude but different frequencies, you can derive a frequency response graph. But such a graph only measures the response of signals in the range of 100 dB-SPL. The frequency response of the driver at 50 dB-SPL might be substantially different.

Power Handling

The power handling of a driver refers to the maximum electrical power that can be dissipated by the driver without it failing. Failure is usually in the form of clipping: given a sinusoidal input signal, the driver instead creates a square wave. Extreme failure conditions include tearing of the diaphragm or thermal damage from overheating. As a side note, one of the selling points of very high-powered automotive sub-woofers is the ease with which new diaphragms can be installed; it's an important feature for consumers looking to create extremely loud noises

Power handling is usually listed in watts as both a root mean square (RMS) value and as a peak. RMS power is intended to convey the constant power levels the drivers can handle, while peak is meant to convey the fact that the driver can handle higher powered signals for short durations of time. Just how short these durations are is often very vaguely defined. Indeed, there are even different techniques for determining RMS values.

Impedance

You may already know that electrical ***resistance*** is the opposition of an object to the flow of current. Specifically, resistance is the opposition to the flow of direct current. ***Impedance*** is opposition to the flow of alternating current. Like resistance, impedance is measured in ohms. Impedance is one of the common measurements made of a driver, with most drivers having an impedance on the order of 8 ohms.

Sensitivity

A driver's sensitivity refers to how effectively it can transform electrical power into sound. Sensitivity is usually measured by driving a driver with a 1-watt signal and measuring the intensity at a distance one meter from the driver. Average drivers have a sensitivity of around 90 dB-SPL

The fact that sensitivity is reported in units of dB-SPL has apparently led to the fairly widespread and erroneous use of the term SPL as a synonym for sensitivity.

Ideally the sensitivity of a driver should be measured in an anechoic chamber. Because the walls of the specialized room absorb all sound, the sensitivity measurement is not tainted by any echoes. However, sometimes driver sensitivity is done ***in room***, meaning the measurement was done in a typical room in which echoes are indeed present. The echoes contribute to the overall level being measured at the point one meter in front of the driver, resulting in a higher sensitivity. The actual increase of in-room sensitivity over anechoic sensitivity of course varies based on the characteristics of a room. As a rule of thumb, however, in-room sensitivity is typically 3 dB higher than the anechoic.

A driver's sensitivity can have a substantial impact on the design of an audio system. Consider that a driver with 90 dB-SPL sensitivity is able to generate *twice* the intensity of a driver with an 87 dB-SPL sensitivity, given the same power input. Remember that a difference of 3 dB corresponds to a 2× change in intensity. As such, you may be able to get the same performance with a 50-watt amplifier attached to the more sensitive drivers as you would with a 100-watt amplifier attached to the less sensitive drivers.

Sensitivity in and of itself is not an indicator of the overall quality of the driver. While it is true that inexpensive drivers tend to be less sensitive than more expensive ones, some performance drivers that are *very* expensive have a low sensitivity; they require a lot of power to deliver the fidelity that they do.

Woofers and Tweeters

Drivers that are capable of producing frequencies across the entire domain of human hearing are known as *full range* drivers. It is very difficult and expensive to make a single driver that is truly capable of reproducing the full range of frequencies. Materials and topologies that can efficiently generate 20,000-hertz tones tend to be less adept at producing 20-hertz tones. One way to overcome this difficulty is by using multiple drivers to produce sounds. A different driver is used for different frequency ranges.

This concept of using multiple drivers was commercialized in 1931 when such speakers were first deployed in cinemas. The field of cinematic sound was growing rapidly in the wake of the 1927 talkie *The Jazz Singer*. The poor frequency response of existing single-driver speakers made for the rapid transition to sound systems using frequency-specific drivers. Such systems remain the standard in cinemas and are often found in the home as well.

Drivers designed to create high frequency sounds are known as *tweeters*. Drivers designed to produce low frequency sound are called *woofers*. Tweeters are named in reference to the high-pitched sounds made by birds. Woofers are named after the low-pitched barks of dogs.

No standard frequency range is defined for either tweeters or woofers. However, a woofer and tweeter paired together into a two-driver speaker need to have compatible ranges. You would not, for instance, want to have a 30- to 2,000-hertz (+/- 3dB) woofer and a 5,000 to 20,000-hertz (+/- 3 dB) tweeter make up your speaker, as the frequency range of 2,000 to 5,000 hertz would have poor fidelity.

Some speakers use three drivers to create sounds. The driver used to generate the range of frequencies between the woofer and the tweeter is known as the *mid-range*. Mid-range drivers were originally known as squawkers. Although this term meshes nicely with woofers and tweeters, it has not persisted as a commonly used audio term.[1]

A single speaker may contain multiple mid-ranges. Each may have responsibility for reproducing a unique frequency range, or multiple mid-range drivers could both be used to reproduce the same middle range.

Drivers capable of producing very high frequency sounds are sometimes given the label of super tweeters. Drivers capable of producing very low frequencies are known as subwoofers. Again, there are no standard definitions for the frequency range needed to qualify as super tweeter or a subwoofer. Subwoofers can produce frequencies so low that you don't so much hear them, as feel them. Some super tweeters are capable of producing frequencies in excess of 40,000 hertz, well above the range of human hearing. Such super tweeters exist because some audiophiles feel that reproduction of ultrasonic frequencies is important. Even though we cannot hear the ultrasonics themselves, they maintain that we can hear the interactions they have with audible frequencies.

In general, tweeters are smaller than mid-ranges, and mid-ranges are smaller than woofers. This relationship of sizes derives from the fact that to create sounds of the same intensity, you have to move more air around for lower frequencies than for higher frequencies. The volume of air a driver can displace is a function of the excursion and area of the diaphragm. Design constraints mean that the increased volume needed for lower frequencies is achieved primarily by increasing the diameter of the diaphragm.

Beaming

Another reason for using multi-driver speakers is to help alleviate a phenomenon known as *beaming*. When using a single driver, sound becomes increasingly directional as the frequency of the sound increases.

---

[1] Perhaps because marketing folks felt it gave a bad impression!

Specifically, when the wavelength is about the same as the diameter of the driver, the sound is radiated in a very narrow beam. Such high directivity is usually not desirable because it means that there is only a very small area where a listener is able to hear the full range of frequencies, even though they can hear lower frequencies in a much larger area.

One way to reduce the beaming effect is to use a smaller diameter driver. However, small drivers are not very good at generating the large displacement volumes needed for low frequencies. Building a speaker with a tweeter and a woofer reduces the beaming effect of higher frequencies while still allowing for a good low-frequency response.

Another way to decrease beaming is to use a hemispherical diaphragm instead of a conical one. Dome drivers, as they are called, are used nearly exclusively in tweeters, because they handle the high frequencies that have the most beaming.

Crossovers

In a multi-driver speaker, each driver is specifically designed to reproduce a certain range of frequencies. As such, you only want to send signals to the drivers that are in its range of reproducibility. The device responsible for partitioning a full-range signal into driver-specific ranges is known as a *crossover*. A crossover is a series of two or more filters.

A crossover that splits a full-range signal into two ranges—one for the tweeter and one for the woofer—is known as a two-way crossover. It consists of a low-pass filter and a high-pass filter, as shown in Figure 4.7. The output of the low-pass filter is sent to the woofer; the output of the high-pass filter is sent to the tweeter. Because it is impractical to build filters with perpendicular slopes, there is a frequency range in which a portion of the original signal is sent to both the tweeter and the woofer. In other words, if you were to play a pure tone and increase its frequency, there would be a gradual crossfade between the sound being played on the woofer and the tweeter. The mid-point of this transition is known as the crossover frequency.

Crossovers must be designed to match the frequency response range of the drivers. For instance, if you had a woofer that was able to produce frequencies of 40 to 5,000 hertz ± 3 dB and a tweeter that was able to produce frequencies of 5,000 to 20,000 hertz ± 3 dB, you would want your crossover to have a crossover frequency of 5,000 hertz.

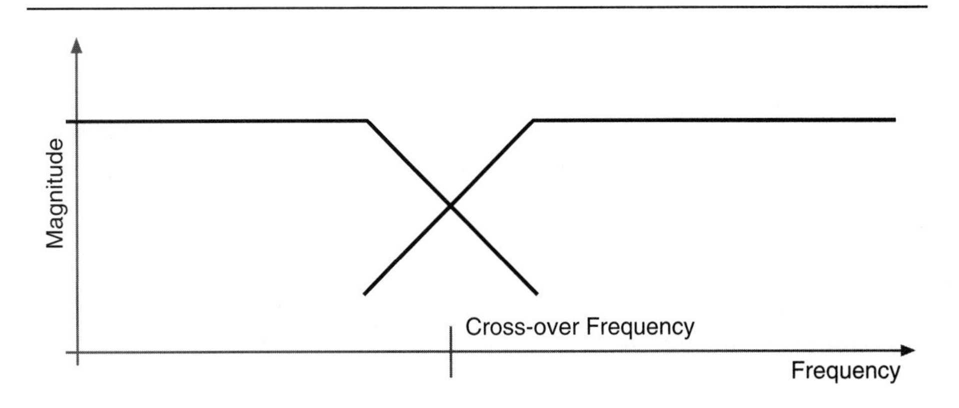

Figure 4.7 Crossover Frequency Response

Speakers using three drivers—woofer, mid-range, and tweeter—use a three-way crossover. Three-way crossovers use three filters to partition the original signal: a low-pass, a band-pass, and a high-pass, as shown in Figure 4.8.

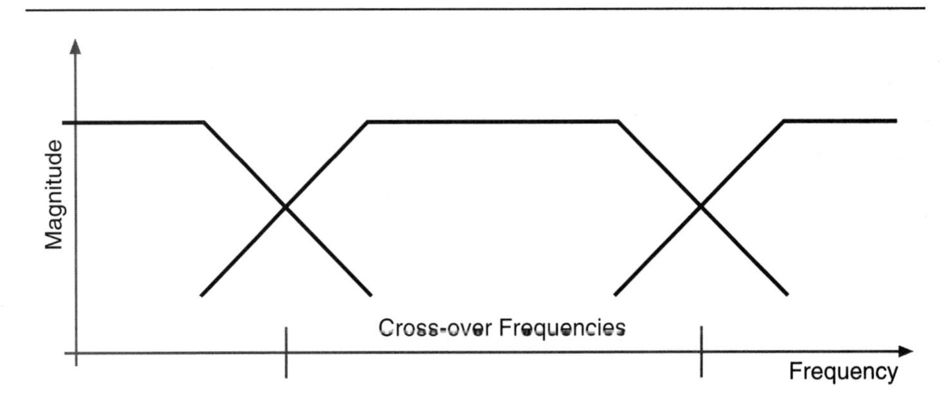

Figure 4.8 Three-way Crossover

The steeper the slope of the filters, the less overlap there is between drivers. In other words, the steeper the slope, the faster the transition occurs between woofer and tweeter as the frequency increases.

Crossover slopes are a multiple of 6 dB per octave. A crossover with a 6-dB per octave slope is known as a first order crossover. A crossover with a 12-dB per octave slope is known as a second order crossover. And so forth. Most speakers today use first through fourth order crossovers.

Although higher order crossovers have steeper slopes and are more expensive, there is not necessarily a correlation between crossover order and speaker performance. Care must be taken to use drivers that are compatible with one another and the crossover, but a high performance speaker can be built with any order.

Enclosures

The enclosure is the super structure of the speaker, as shown in Figure 4.9. The drivers and crossovers are attached to the enclosure. Although some speaker enclosures may look like a simple box, a lot of engineering effort goes into the design of enclosures. The exact shape of the box and the composition of its walls dramatically affect the sounds produced by the drivers.

Figure 4.9 Speaker Enclosure

Materials

The ideal speaker enclosure would be infinitely inert. Regardless of the intensity of the pressure waves generated by the drivers, it would remain motionless. Such immobility is desirable because any distortion of the enclosure's shape during playback distorts the sound. Alas, such a material is purely hypothetical, but reasonable real-world compromises have been found.

In particular, medium density fiberboard (MDF) is a popular enclosure material. Much like Pringles† are constructed from potato fragments, MDF consists of wood chips packed densely together and joined with glue. While it can be tooled much like raw wood, it is denser than most woods, and substantially cheaper than wood of corresponding density. It is also more uniform than raw wood, being free of knots and grains.

High density plastic is also used for enclosures, especially in speakers designed for outdoor use.

The enclosure exteriors are typically given an aesthetic treatment. It may be as simple as paint on a plastic enclosure. Most MDF enclosures destined for home use are covered in a thin plastic or vinyl coating, often designed to look like real wood.[2] Some very high-end speakers may be covered in thin strips of actual wood.

Topology

The majority of enclosures are shaped externally like rectangular parallelepipeds. Or as most people would say, like a box. The side of the box to which the drivers are mounted is known as the baffle. It is important for movement of the baffle to be minimized, so many enclosures brace the baffle with internal walls and struts. Some enclosures are filled with damping materials that muffle sound waves inside the enclosure.

There are many enclosures that deviate wildly from the box structure. Some outdoor enclosures are shaped like rocks. One imaginative sub-woofer uses an enclosure shaped just like a nitrous oxide tank.

In addition to the external shape of the enclosure, the internal placement of the drivers and the baffle also has a great impact on the overall characteristics of the speaker. The reason the interior topology is so important is that the driver diaphragm not only affects the air in front of it, but the air behind it as well. The sound wave created by the front of the driver is known as the *front wave*, and the wave created by the back of the diaphragm is known as the *rear wave*, as shown in Figure 4.10.

[2] But more often looking like a thin sheet of plastic.

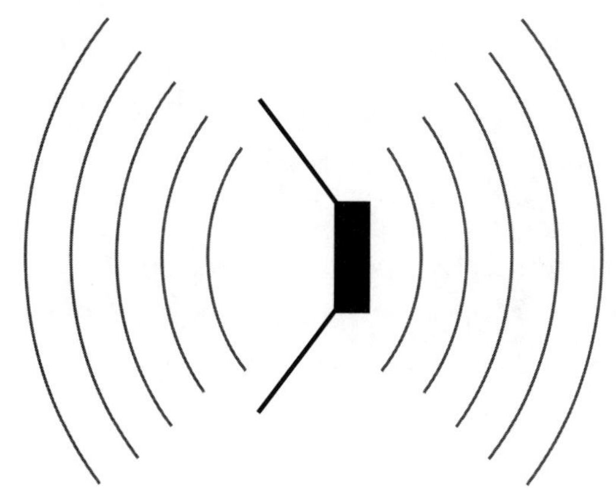

As a diaphragm moves, it creates a front wave, shown on the left, and, simultaneously, a rear wave.

Figure 4.10 Front and Rear Waves

The rear wave is identical to the front wave, but shifted 180 degrees in phase. The rear wave has just as much power as the front wave, so its effects can have a profound impact on speaker performance. Indeed, the waves can cancel each other out. The interference is most pronounced at lower frequencies, because they have the most refraction, as shown in Figure 4.11.

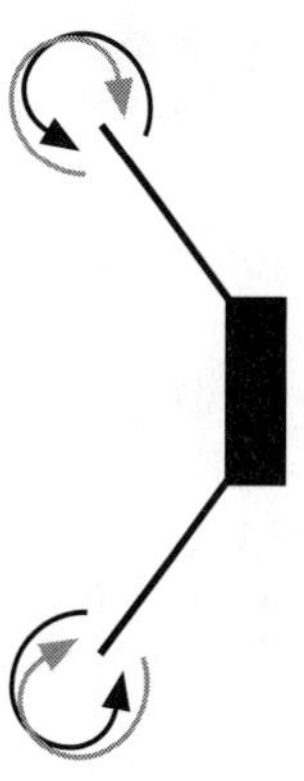

Low frequency sound waves from the front and rear waves can diffract around a speaker in free air and interfere with one another.

Figure 4.11 Interference

Because the interface between the front and rear waves is minimal at higher frequencies, most enclosure designs focus on the behavior of low frequencies.

Sealed Box

One of the most common enclosure designs is the sealed box. It is also referred to as a sealed acoustic suspension or air suspension. As shown in Figure 4.12, the space behind the baffle is enclosed. Air therein cannot escape.

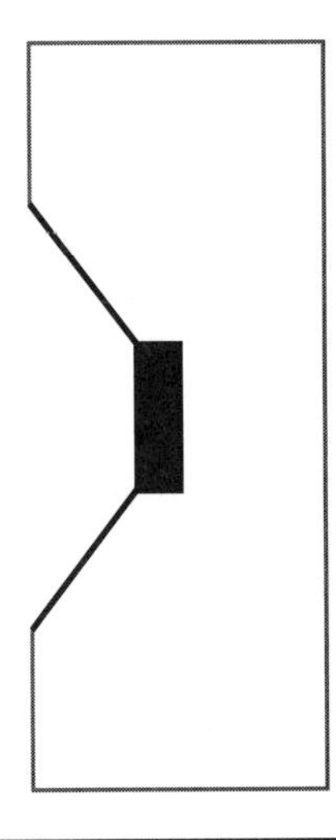

Figure 4.12 Sealed Acoustic Suspension Design

When the diaphragm moves forward, it creates a region of compression in front of the diaphragm. At the same time, the movement creates a region of rarefaction behind the diaphragm, as shown in Figure 4.13.

Because the box is sealed, the air pressure inside the box is less than the atmospheric pressure outside the box. The decreased internal pressure is due to the fact that number of air molecules inside the box has remained constant, but the volume of the box has increased slightly due to the outward displacement of the speaker.

Because the external air pressure is higher than the internal, the external air pushes on the diaphragm, trying to achieve pressure equilibrium.

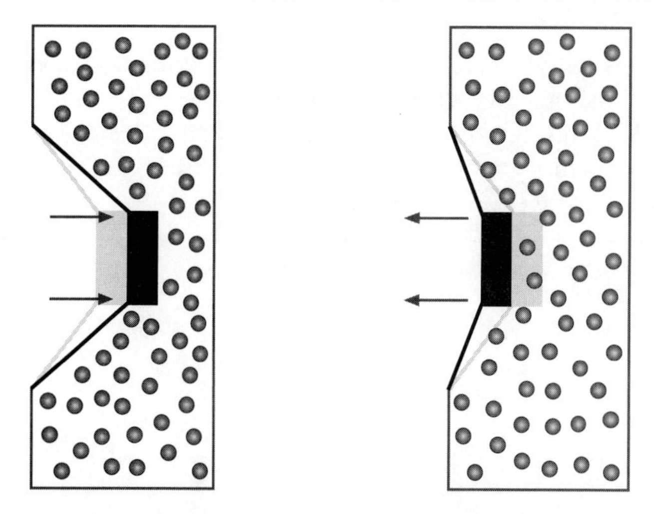

Figure 4.13 Compression and Rarefaction in Sealed Enclosure

Conversely, when the diaphragm moves into the enclosure, it raises the pressure inside the box higher than the ambient pressure. In this scenario, the internal air pushes the diaphragm outward, again trying to achieve equilibrium.

As such, the pressure differential is always trying to push the diaphragm back to the neutral position. This behavior is the same as that of the driver's suspension, which is why this enclosure design is known as an acoustic or air suspension.

The additional restorative force offered by the sealed enclosure makes this design one of the most accurate. It produces very tight, or well-defined, bass. Acoustic suspensions are also very easy to make; small errors in construction do not adversely affect the overall performance. The design is very good at handling large amounts of power. The air spring offered by the sealed enclosure helps protect the diaphragm from undershoot and overshoot.

This same air spring, however, means that the design is not very efficient. Compared to an open system, additional energy must be applied to the driver to overcome the restorative force of the acoustic suspension.

Infinite Baffle

One way to ensure that the rear wave does not interfere with the front wave is to completely isolate the two. Such isolation can be accomplished through the use of an infinite baffle design, shown in Figure 4.14. As implied by its name, a very large baffle is used to separate the front and rear waves.

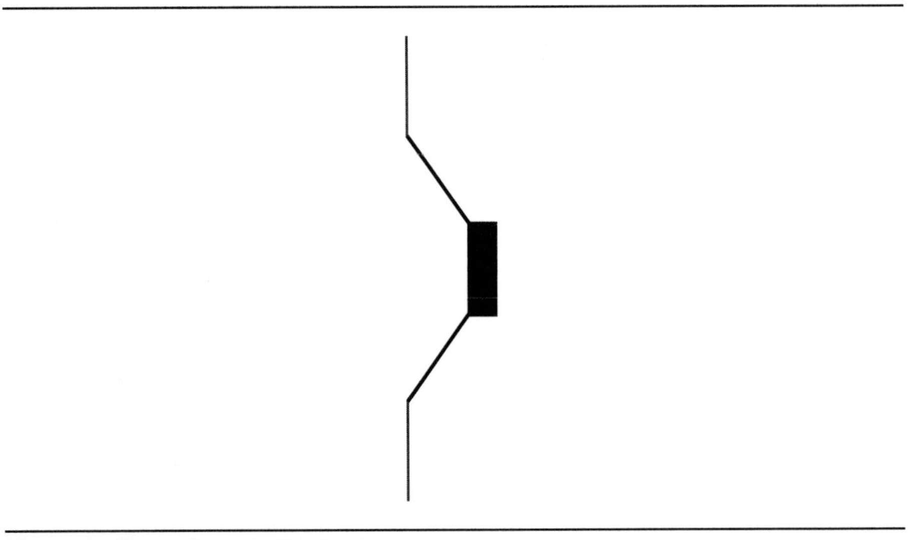

Figure 4.14 Infinite Baffle Design

Now, it is not always practical to build an enclosure that is actually infinite in size. Luckily, the behavior of an infinite baffle can be approximated using finitely sized enclosures. For instance, a driver mounted on the rear deck of a sedan can be an infinite baffle design. The front wave radiates into the car's interior, while the rear wave radiates into the car's trunk. The two waves do not interact.

At first glance, such a configuration might seem to be a sealed acoustic suspension. However, because the compliance, or springiness, of the air inside the trunk is much less than the compliance of the driver's suspension, no substantial pressure differentials are created between the front and back of the speaker. The air inside the trunk does not have a restorative effect on the diaphragm.

As a rule of thumb, for an enclosure to be an effective sealed acoustic suspension, the enclosure needs to be small enough so that the compliance of the air inside is greater than the compliance of the driver's physical suspension. If the air spring's compliance is several times weaker than the driver's suspension, then the design is effectively an infinite baffle.

With no air spring, the infinite baffle has greater efficiency than a sealed box. For the same reason, infinite baffle designs have less protection against undershoot and overshoot.

Reflex

Another common speaker design is the reflex enclosure, shown in Figure 4.15. The ported design is also known as bass reflex, vented, or ported.

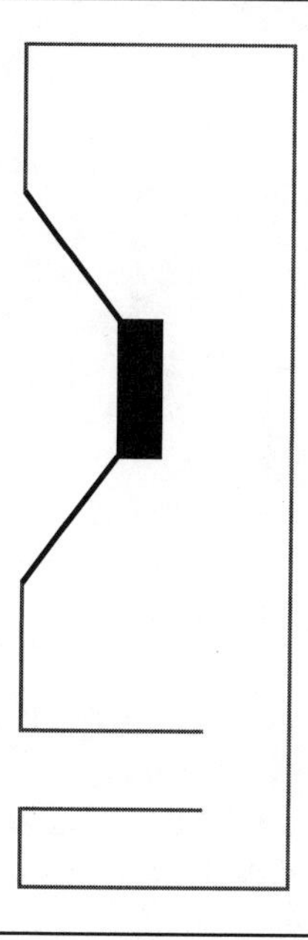

Figure 4.15 Reflex Design

Unlike the other designs we've considered so far, the reflex configuration allows the rear wave to directly interact with the front wave via a hole in the baffle. The hole can simply be cut out of the baffle, in which case it is known as a vent. More commonly, a tube is coupled with the hole to create a port.

The air inside the port acts as a membrane. The back wave radiating inside the enclosure strikes the air inside the port, causing a phase-inverted copy of the wave to be radiated out the front of the port. This wave reinforces the front waves, as shown in Figure 4.16. This augmentation extends the low frequency response of the speaker.

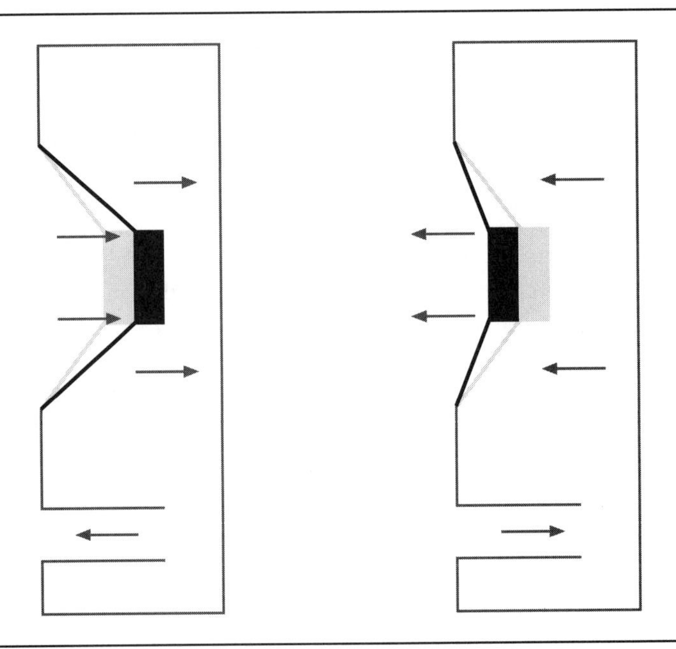

Figure 4.16 Reflex Action

The port, like all the other physical parameters of the enclosure, must be carefully designed. Because only certain frequencies can pass through the port, it is said to be tuned.

Ported designs are more difficult to construct than sealed enclosures; minor errors in the physical parameters can have a substantial impact on the overall performance of the speaker.

Compared to a sealed box, a ported design with the same driver is more efficient. The ported design does not have to fight against the air spring, and the energy of the back wave is used to reinforce the front wave. Again, the lack of an air spring means the driver is not protected from excessive excursions.

A variation of the ported design is the passive radiator. Here, the port is replaced by a driver with no voice coil, as shown in Figure 4.17.

The rear wave strikes the passive radiator, causing it to move and generate its own front wave that reinforces the primary front wave being generated by the powered diaphragm, the active radiator. The passive radiator design is a compromise between a sealed and ported design, and its performance characteristics lay between them. It is less efficient than a ported design and less accurate than a sealed design.

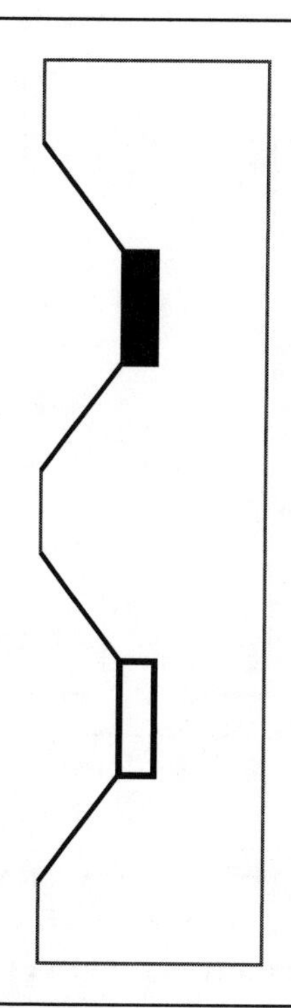

Figure 4.17 Passive Radiator Design

Compound

Sealed and ported designs can be combined to create compound designs. These designs are also known as bandpass designs. Whereas the previously-discussed enclosures behave as high-pass filters, with output that declines rapidly below the cutoff frequency, compound designs behave as bandpass filters. They also have a relatively low upper frequency limit above which the output rapidly declines.

Given the fact that they only respond well to low frequencies, compound designs are most commonly used as subwoofer enclosures.

One type of compound enclosure is the single-vented band-pass design shown in Figure 4.18. It essentially consists of a sealed box coupled with a ported enclosure. It is also known as a fourth order design, because both the low-pass and high-pass fall-off slopes are second order (12 dB per octave). This design is complex, but has excellent power handling in a small box. It is not quite as efficient as a reflex.

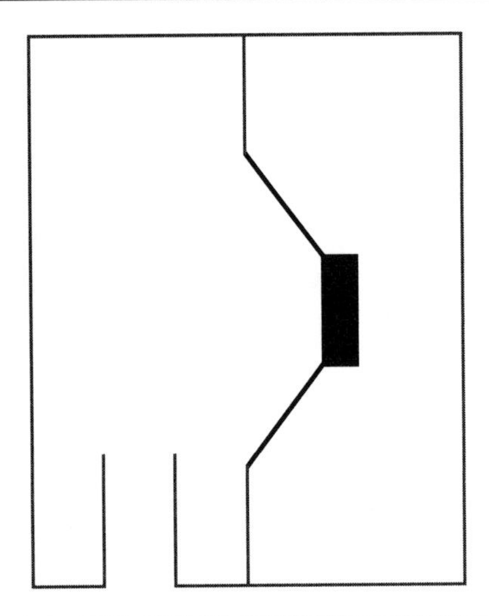

Figure 4.18 Single-Vented Bandpass

Even more complex is the dual-vented band-pass design, shown in Figure 4.19, also known as a sixth order band-pass design. Dual-vented boxes can be extremely small, yet are capable of handling massive amounts of power to produce incredibly loud sound. These designs tend to be one-note wonders, useful for making large booming sounds but not much else.

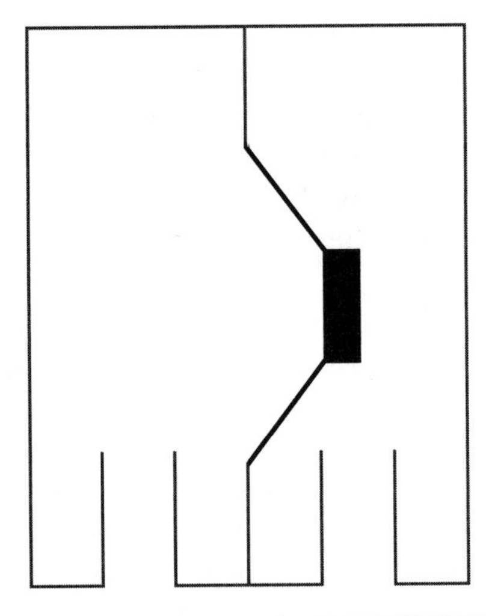

Figure 4.19 Double-Vented Bandpass

Transmission Line

Another design is the transmission line (TL) , shown in Figure 4.20. It uses a long guide path known as, yes, a transmission line. The transmission line can be folded; in such a configuration, it is also known as a labyrinth.

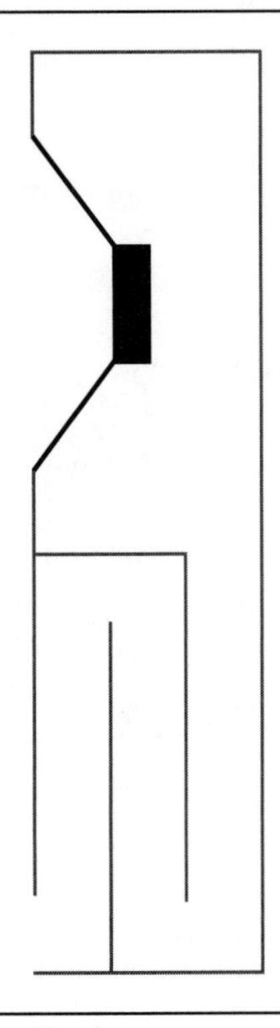

Figure 4.20 Transmission Line Design

Superficially, the TL may resemble a port. Ports, however, are relatively short and hold a membrane of air that is excited by the rear wave to reinforce the front wave. The purpose of the much longer TL is to actually neutralize the rear wave. Ideally, the TL would be infinitely long, so as to completely dissipate the energy of the rear wave.

Real-world designs have TLs of finite length. For higher frequencies, the rear wave is completely absorbed by the TL, and the enclosure effectively acts like an infinite baffle. However, for lower frequencies with wavelengths on par with the length of the TL, the back wave emerging from the end of the TL reinforces the front wave.

TLs are commonly designed to have a length one quarter of the wavelength of the fundamental resonance of the driver. As such, the reinforcement effect occurs at the point where the native output of the driver is falling off. In other words, the effective cutoff frequency of the TL speaker is lower than the native driver.

Practical Application

The enclosure topologies described above are simple to diagram, but building real-world speaker enclosures is substantially more complex. If the volume of an enclosure was too large, a sealed enclosure could easily behave as an infinite baffle. Making the port hole too small on a reflex design could result in a horrible bass response. A mistake in the length of a transmission line could result in the back waves canceling out the low frequency front waves.

Although the basic enclosure topologies were developed in the 1930s, speaker design was still very much a matter of trial and error for several decades. The different parameters such as suspension compliance, port diameter, port length, and enclosure volume all had to be carefully orchestrated to produce a good speaker. Much of the guesswork has been removed from basic speaker design thanks to work done in the 1960s and early 1970s by Neville Thiele and Richard Small. They defined a framework of interrelated parameters that approximate how speakers behave. These Thiele-Small parameters are still used today. And, indeed, numerous shareware programs that allow hobbyists to design their own speakers using these variables are available on the Internet.

Polarity

Speaker enclosures for cone drivers are examples of direct radiating systems. The drivers are all arranged on the front of the enclosure, as shown in Figure 4.21. This speaker configuration is also referred to as a monopole.

Because all of their energy is directed forward, direct radiating speakers are very good at focusing sounds at a specific region. They provide very good imaging. Conversely, there is a relatively small area where a listener has the optimum listening experience.

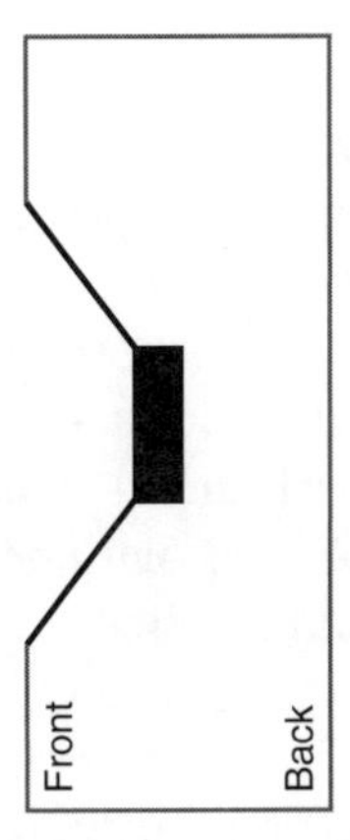

Only a single driver is shown in this diagram, but a direct radiating speaker could in fact contain multiple drivers, such as a tweeter, mid-range, and woofer, all arranged on the front of the speaker.

Figure 4.21 Direct Radiating Speaker

Another speaker configuration places an active driver on both the front and the rear of the enclosure, as shown in Figure 4.22. If the drivers are wired in phase with one another, it is known as a bipolar speaker. Because the drivers are in phase, whenever the front driver moves outward, the rear driver also moves outward. When the front driver moves inward, the rear driver also moves inward.

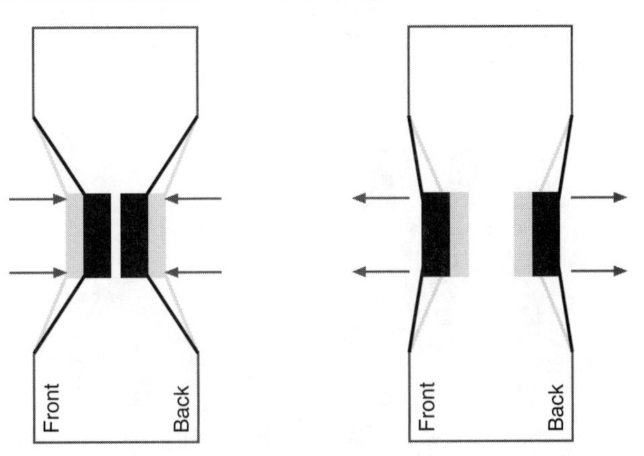

When the front driver moves inward, the rear driver also moves inward (left).
When the front driver moves outward, the rear driver also moves outward (right).

Figure 4.22 Bipolar Speaker

Compared to direct radiating speakers, bipolar speakers have a much more diffuse sound. Although the bipolar speakers have a forward driver that acts like a direct radiator, the rear driver also generates sound waves that reflect off environmental objects such as wells before reaching the listener. The resulting sound field has a much larger sweet spot or zone in which listeners receive an optimal sound experience. This diffuse field makes the sound more difficult to localize, and, as such, the imaging is not as precise as it is with direct radiating speakers.

These qualities make bipolar speakers well suited for use as surround channels in home theatres. Bipolars are also sometimes used as primary or front speakers. However, direct radiators are the most common form of speakers. One factor is price: bipolar speakers are more expensive than their direct radiator equivalents because they have twice as many drivers.

Dipolar speakers are very similar to bipolar speakers. Indeed, there are speakers available that can be converted from dipole to bipole by the flip of a switch. Again, dipolar speakers have drivers on both the front and back of the enclosure. However, the front and back drivers are wired out of phase. That is, when the front driver moves outward, the rear driver moves inward, and vice versa, as can be seen in Figure 4.23. Planar speakers also behave as dipoles.

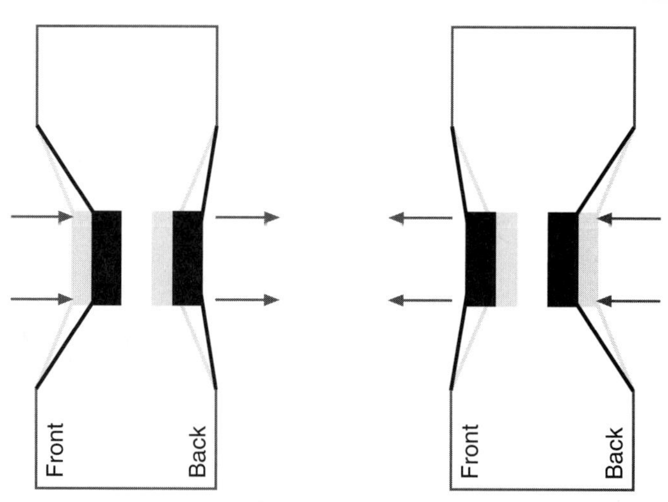

When the front driver moves inward, the rear driver moves outward (left).
When the front driver moves outward, the rear driver moves inward (right).

Figure 4.23 Dipolar Speaker

Dipole speakers create an even more diffuse sound field than bipole speakers, making them very well suited for reproducing surround channels.

The broad sound generated by dipole comes at the cost of poor imaging. As such, dipoles are very poorly suited for serving as main speakers.

Speaker Types

Speakers come in a wide variety of shapes and are used for a wide variety of applications. They may be as simple as a tiny piezoelectric used to make your computer go beep when you turn it on, or they could be as complex as a stadium array designed to clearly carry a singer's high note to 10,000 fans, even as their chest cavities are shaken by the amplified bass line.

In this section, we will briefly discuss a few of the more common form factors.

Passive vs. Active

Speakers may be either passive or active.

The electrical audio signals sent to passive speakers are passed down to the speaker's drivers with no further amplification. As such, passive speakers must be driven by a dedicated amplifier to create adequate electrical power to drive the passive speakers at a usable volume. Directly attaching passive speakers to the low-level line-out electrical signals generated by non-amplified audio equipment, such as a CD player, only generates very low-volume sounds.

Active, or powered, speakers contain a built-in amplifier. As such, they can receive low-intensity electrical signals and internally amplify them to sufficient power levels to drive the speaker's drivers at usable volume levels.

Both passive and active speakers need connectors to receive the audio signals, typically handled by two wires. Because active speakers create amplified signals and are bound by the first law of thermodynamics, they need a power source. This power can be handled by batteries mounted inside the speaker or—as is more typically the case—by an external AC power source which gets converted to DC either inside or outside of the speaker.

When using active speakers, it is important not to mix the sound inputs with the power inputs, otherwise you get a very loud and very brief 60-hertz tone right before your drivers tear themselves to pieces. Luckily, the connectors for sound signals and power supplies are usually shaped quite differently!

Applications

Speakers come in a wide variety of shapes and sizes. Their morphology is often unique to the intended use of speaker. A few of the more common speaker applications are discussed here.

Bookshelf Speakers

Bookshelf speakers are typically box-shaped enclosures which are small enough to be placed on a bookshelf, as shown in Figure 4.24. These speakers are usually designed to be used for reproducing stereo sound and for casual listening. They are meant to be full-range speakers, and therefore commonly include a tweeter and woofer. Their relatively small size and the fact that they are usually passive means they cannot create loud intensities; however, they are quite adequate for the average listener.

Figure 4.24 Bookshelf Speakers

Bookshelf speakers are meant to be elevated. For ideal performance, they should be placed above the ground at about the same height as the listener's ears.

Floor-Standing Speakers

Floor-standing speakers are larger in size but similar in shape to bookshelf speakers. Their larger size generally makes them more expensive but also allows them to generate louder sounds, especially the lower frequencies. Floor-standing speakers as often as not include one or more mid-range drivers in addition to a tweeter and woofer.

These speakers are usually designed specifically to sit on the floor; their enclosures are created to take into account the audio reflections of the nearby floor.

Floor-standing speakers often produce higher quality sound than bookshelf speakers. They are targeted at people who want more precise and/or louder sound reproduction. Floor-standing speakers are typically deployed in pairs to reproduce stereophonic sound. They may also serve as the front speakers in a surround sound system.

Sub-woofers

Sub-woofers, shown in Figure 4.25, are designed to reproduce only low frequencies. They typically contain a single driver. They can be used to augment full range speakers, where they produce very low frequencies at high volume. They are commonly used in surround sound systems where they reproduce the low frequency effects (LFE) common in many of today's movies. Subwoofers are available in both passive and active varieties.[3]

Figure 4.25 Subwoofer

[3] Perhaps one of the most interesting subwoofer instantiations is that of the BMW Z4 roadster, which includes a tuned tube that carries low frequency engine noise into the driving compartment so you can hear it go VROOM VROOM.

Satellite Speakers

Satellite speakers, shown in Figure 4.26, are small passive speakers designed to reproduce the surround channels in surround sound systems. Because surround channels are often used to create ambient sounds rather than primary sounds, satellite systems may not need to create sounds as loud or clear as the primary speakers.

Figure 4.26 Satellite Speaker

Satellite speakers may be full-range, but some satellite systems use very small speakers the size of coffee mugs to reproduce the upper frequencies and rely on a subwoofer to reproduce the lower frequencies.

Center Channel Speakers

Some surround sound systems make use of a front center channel. This channel actually reproduces the majority of the sound in the system, and so it needs to be reproduced by a powerful full-range speaker. Center channel speakers are often magnetically shielded so they can be placed on top of television sets without distorting the picture.

Computer Speakers

The increasing ubiquity of computers has brought with it a relatively new breed of speakers designed specifically for use with personal computers (PCs). Designed to sit on either side of a computer monitor, these active speakers ideally include shielding to prevent magnetic and electric interference with the PC components.

Recent years have seen a great deal of innovation in computer speakers. Although sophisticated two-way speakers have been available for quite some time, recent instantiations include novel configurations such as arrays of tiny drivers and powered subwoofers.

Headphones

The above-mentioned speaker types allow for multiple listeners. Headphones, on the other hand, provide a unique single-person listening experience. Headphones consist of a two drivers, each of which is mounted near an ear.

Because headphones are designed to be worn on the head, the drivers are necessarily small. Headphones are full-range speakers, even though their drivers may be smaller than the tweeter on a floor-standing speaker. Headphones are able to generate a full-range of audio sounds because they only need to create very low intensities due to their close proximity to the human ear.

There are a wide variety of headphones available. The largest ones, as shown in Figure 4.27, include large padded cups that completely enclose the pinnae. Such headphones filter out ambient sounds and focus the full power of the drivers into the ears. They are known as studio, closed cup, and circumaural headphones. Although these headphones produce very pure sound, they tend to be heavier than other styles. Also, the tight seal around the ear can become uncomfortable during long sessions.

Figure 4.27 Studio Headphones

Medium-sized headphones have foam pads that rest against the pinnae. The majority of the sound energy is still focused on the listener's ears, but an appreciable fraction of the sound energy escapes outward. As such, other people are able to hear some of the sound. Also, a person wearing these headphones can still hear external noises. Headphones of this type are light and comfortable to wear for extended periods of time.

The smallest type of headphones are earbuds. These are very tiny drivers that fit directly onto the opening of the ear canal. The diminutive speakers make it very difficult to reproduce a full range of sound. However, earbuds are well-suited to a physically active listener as they tend to stay in place regardless of your body's orientation or movement. They are also extremely compact.

Summary

Speakers convert electrical energy into sound waves. They typically have three main components: the driver, a crossover, and an enclosure.

The driver is the element that actually converts the electrical signal into pressure waves. The most common driver, the cone driver, uses an electromagnetically-driven diaphragm to generate the pressure waves.

A crossover splits the input signal into different frequency ranges, so that each range can be driven by a driver suited to that range. Speakers which contain a single driver have no crossover.

The enclosure holds the other elements of the speaker together. Its shape can have a tremendous impact on the overall intensity and frequency response of the drivers.

Chapter 5

Microphones

"You can't make up anything anymore. The world itself is a satire. All you're doing is recording it."

—Art Buchwald

Microphones are transducers that convert air pressure waves into electrical signals. As such, they are the opposite of speakers. In fact, most speakers can be used as crude microphones, and vice versa. Microphones are also known as mikes or mics.

Transducer Types

The crucial element of the microphone which performs the actual transduction of sounds into electrical signals is known aptly enough as the transducer. It is also referred to as a *capsule*. There are several different capsule types; most of them are very similar to the types of speaker drivers.

Capsules typically contain a diaphragm that gathers sound waves. The movement of the diaphragm is converted into electrical signals that are dependent upon the capsule type.

Note that microphone diaphragms are usually much smaller than speaker diaphragms. Microphone diaphragms are quite often less than an inch across, whereas most speakers are several inches across. The smaller mike diaphragm gives a better frequency response, because external sounds have less mass to excite to generate a signal. Also, keeping the diaphragm size small with respect to the sound wavelengths being captured limits the distortion caused by diaphragm resonance.

Dynamic

One of the most common capsule types is the dynamic moving-coil, as shown in Figure 5.1. It is very similar to a dynamic driver. A coil of wire is attached to the diaphragm. As the diaphragm moves back and forth in response to sound waves, the coil is also moved back and forth. Because the coil is suspended within a magnetic field generated by a permanent magnet, an electrical signal is inducted.

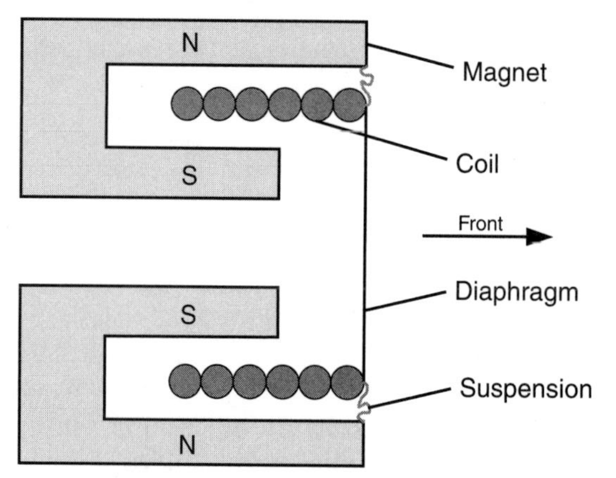

Figure 5.1 Moving-coil Schematic

Moving-coil mikes are sturdy, inexpensive, and good for capturing high intensity sounds. However, due to the relatively large mass of the coil assembly, they are not as good at capturing high frequencies as other capsule styles are.

Ribbon

Ribbon capsules, shown in Figure 5.2, are similar to moving-coil dynamic capsules. The diaphragm in this case is a thin metal sheet that vibrates in response to sound waves within a permanent magnetic field. An electrical signal is thus generated by induction. Because ribbon mikes use electromagnetic induction, they are also technically dynamic mikes. However, colloquial usage of the term dynamic mike refers to the moving-coil variety.

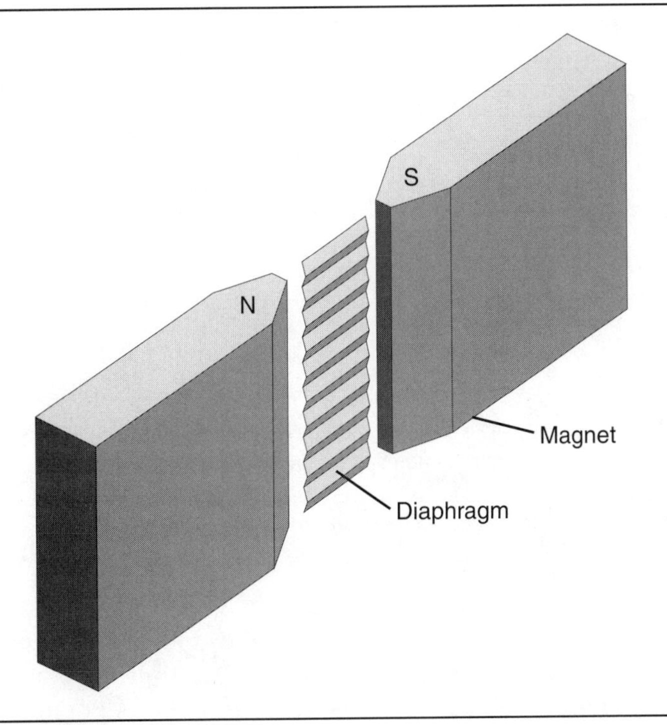

Figure 5.2 Ribbon Schematic

The mass of the ribbon is low compared to that of a moving-coil assembly, so ribbon capsules are better at recording high frequency sounds. However, they are much more fragile. Early ribbon mikes could be permanently damaged by high intensity sounds such as those produced by drums at a close range. Today's ribbon mikes are much more robust and not nearly as susceptible to damage from loud noises.

Condenser

Another common capsule type is the condenser. It is also known a capacitor capsule, for the simple reason that it is effectively a capacitor. A capacitor consists of two parallel conductive plates separated by either a small air gap or insulating material. The ability of the capacitor to store a charge—its capacitance—is a function of the width of this gap.

In a condenser capsule, the diaphragm is used as one of the two plates. The other plate is fixed in place, as shown in Figure 5.3. As sound waves impinge upon the diaphragm, the distance between the two plates varies, and, as such, the capacitance of the plates changes. The capsule uses an external power source to convert the varying capacitance into a voltage-varying electrical signal representing the original sound.

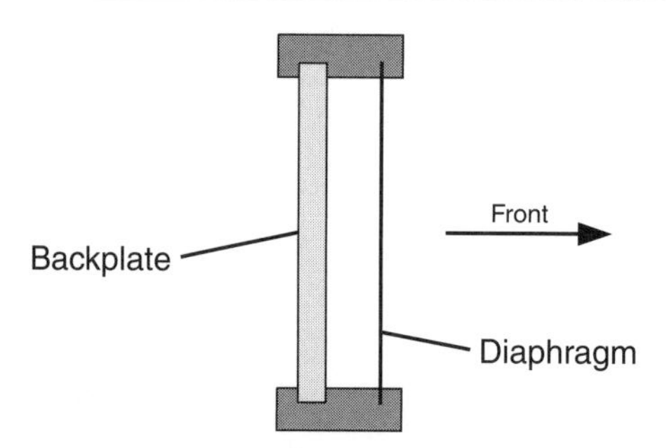

A condenser mike can be designed so that rearward sounds strike the back of the diaphragm by perforating the backplate.

Figure 5.3 Condenser Schematic

Condenser microphones generally give a very natural and clear response. They are especially good at picking up transient sounds.

However, condenser microphones require a power source to function. First, a voltage difference needs to be generated between the diaphragm and the backplate. Second, because the impedance of the condenser capsule is so high, a dedicated head amplifier must be used to create a signal with impedance suitable for transmission across external microphone cables.

In the early days of microphones, the circuits were constructed using vacuum tubes, which meant that condenser mikes used large, heavy, external AC-driven power sources. The introduction of the transistor meant that the bias voltage and the internal amplifier could both be powered by a smaller DC power source.

Today, the DC power is supplied by either an internal battery or by a very elegant technique known as *phantom power*. Phantom power supplies power to the microphone over the very same lines the mike uses to transmit the sound signals. The phantom power system does not disrupt the audio signals in any way, and furthermore, is designed in such a way that it does not affect the operation of microphones that do not require external power—for example, dynamic mikes. As such, the power is there when it is needed, but effectively disappears when it is not: hence the term phantom.

The charge that condenser mikes maintain means that they tend to accumulate dust and other foreign matter over time. Also, in a moist environment, condensation can actually short out the microphone. Despite these limitations, condenser mikes are very popular and provide the best recording quality for many situations.

Electret

The electret condenser is a specialized type of condenser microphone. Rather than charging one of the capacitance plates from a separate power source, it is instead given a permanent electrical charge. Such a plate is known as an *electret*. It is the electrical equivalent of a permanent magnet.

Because the electret implicitly carries a charge, it does not need to draw on a power supply to create a bias voltage. However, an electret microphone still needs a power source to drive the head amp.

Electret capsules are less susceptible to arcing and can achieve better signal-to-noise ratios than standard condensers.

Over time, the electret charge slowly degrades, and eventually the microphone will no longer function. Contemporary electret microphones can last over a decade before losing their charge.

Piezoelectric

Certain crystals physically change shape when electricity is applied to them. Conversely, changing a crystal's shape causes it to generate electricity. Such crystals are said to be *piezoelectric*. Attaching piezoelectric material to a diaphragm results in a piezoelectric transducer. The vibrations of the diaphragm compress and expand the crystal, causing it to generate an electric signal representing the original sound. Microphones based on this type of capsule are known as piezoelectric, crystal,[1] or quartz mikes.

Such mikes are inexpensive, but they do not have very good fidelity.

Carbon

The first telephones used carbon transducers for microphones. A diaphragm was attached to a thin packet of carbon. As the carbon was compressed and expanded by diaphragm movement, the resistance of the

[1] The first microphone along these lines used Rochelle salt, or potassium sodium tartrate. You can grow your own Rochelle salt crystals using only baking soda and cream of tarter. Mmm...science is tasty!

dust changed. A voltage-varying signal was generated by running current through the variable resistance dust.

Such microphones require a separate power source and do not have a very good response. As such, they are rarely found today, although some telephones still use them.

Laser

Laser microphones are unique in that they do not have an inherent diaphragm.[2] Instead, a laser is focused on an external object such as a window. As that object vibrates in response to local sound waves, the physical displacement of the object is measured using the laser. Internal circuitry processes the measurement data to produce a voltage-varying electrical signal representing the original sound.

Because the window can be several hundred yards away from the laser mike, the device allows you to hear what is happening inside a distant room. At the same distance, a more traditional microphone would not be able to resolve those same sounds, because the pressure waves from the window at such a distance would be negligible. With this capability, the laser mike is used almost exclusively for surveillance by police and military forces.

Characteristics

The behavior of a microphone varies based on the transducer type, the materials used to construct it, the physical arrangement of the elements, and any electric support circuitry. Several different characteristics are used to describe how a particular mike performs.

Impedance

Microphones are available with widely varying impedances. The different values have different tradeoffs.

The very low impedance mikes (50 ohm) have good resistance to electrostatic interference. They are, however, susceptible to electromagnetic interference. In particular, they pick up a 60-hertz hum from AC power lines. Fifty-ohm mikes are effective for cable lengths up to 100 feet, beyond which point the signal to noise ratio degrades.

---

[2] They're also a bit unique in that they use a laser!

Low impedance mikes (150 to 250 ohm) are less susceptible to electromagnetic interference but more sensitive to electrostatic interference than very low impedance mikes. The electrostatic interference can be lessened by using balanced audio signals, a concept we will discuss in more detail in Chapter 7. Low impedance mikes can be used with cables that are hundreds of feet long.

High impedance mikes (20 to 50 kilohm) are the most sensitive to electrostatic interference, but are the most immune to electromagnetic interference. High impedance mikes must use cables that are shielded against electrostatic interference. These cables can only be on the order of 25 feet long. Beyond that point, higher frequencies are rapidly attenuated by the cable impedance.

Most contemporary microphones are low impedance, as they allow for long cable lengths and can be reasonably protected against electrostatic and electromagnetic interference. High impedance mikes were more common in the era of vacuum tubes.

Sensitivity

A microphone's sensitivity is usually reported as the RMS voltage it generates in response to a given sound intensity. Somewhat confusingly, there are several different ways of actually documenting sensitivity.

One common reference sound level is a 1,000-hertz pure tone at 74 dB-SPL, which is equivalent to a pressure of 1 microbar (μB).

So a sensitivity measurement may look like: 1 mV / μB. In other words, in response to a sound pressure of one microbar, the microphone generates a voltage signal with an RMS intensity of 1 millivolt (mV). The same sensitivity may alternatively be reported as 1 mV μB^{-1} or 1 mV (74 dB-SPL).

Instead of reporting a direct voltage, sensitivity is sometimes reported as the number of decibels below 1 volt. So, the 1 mV / μB sensitivity may alternatively be written as -60 dBV / μB because it is 60 decibels below 1 volt.

The other commonly used reference level is 94 dB-SPL, a level equivalent to 10 μB and also 1 Pascal. As such, you may also see sensitivities reported as 5 mV/ Pa, 5 mV (94 dB-SPL), or -46 dBV Pa^{-1}. All three of these measurements indicate the same amount of intensity.

Suppose you want to compare the sensitivity of one microphone measured using a 74 dB-SPL reference and another with a 94 dB-SPL reference. Because 94 dB-SPL has 10 times the pressure as 74 dB-SPL (10 μB compared to 1 μB), microphones with a perfectly linear response would generate a voltage signal 10 times greater. Real world microphones typically do not have a perfectly linear response, but the 10× multiplier does serve as a reasonable approximation for converting sensitivities. Thus, a 1 mV (74 dB-SPL) sensitivity is roughly the same as a 10 mV (94 dB-SPL) sensitivity.

Frequency Response

The spectrum of sound that a mike is capable of recording is known as its *frequency response*. It can be specified as a range of frequencies with a variation in sensitivity, such as 20 to 20,000 hertz ± 3 dB.

Alternatively, the frequency response may be described graphically, as shown in Figure 5.4.

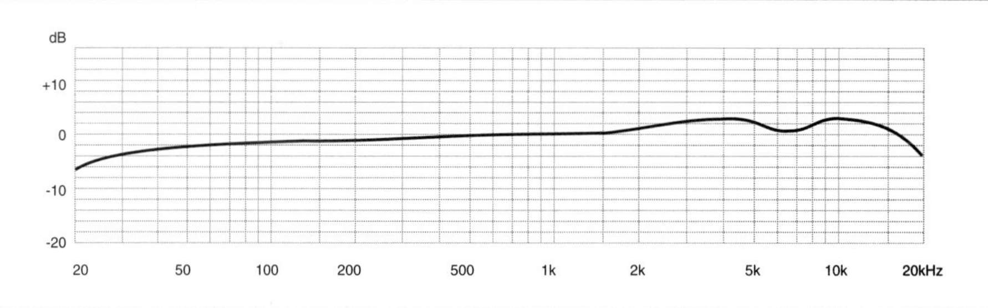

Figure 5.4 Microphone Frequency Response Curve

The graphical approach is particularly apt given that some microphones use a rising response. These mikes are more sensitive to high frequencies than they are to lower ones. Such a response results in bright, clear sound and is good for recording loud drums and guitars.

Other microphones strive for a flat response, which gives a natural tone quality in most situations.

Polar Patterns

In addition to being frequency dependent, the sensitivity of a microphone often varies depending on the direction from which the sounds originate. Sounds that originate directly in front of the microphone are said to be *on-axis*. Sounds from other directions are considered *off-axis*. Some microphones are equally sensitive to both on-axis and off-axis sounds, while other microphones are distinctly more sensitive to on-axis sounds.

Graphs of the direction-dependent sensitivity are known as *polar patterns* , pickup patterns, or polar diagrams. A blank polar graph is shown in Figure 5.5. Zero degrees on the graph corresponds to directly in front of the microphone; 180 degrees is directly behind. The sensitivity of the microphone is plotted as a function of distance from the center of the graph. The on-axis sensitivity is always assumed to be the maximum value, and serves as a reference for all other directions. The graphs are typically measured in decibels, so the outside of the graph is marked at 0 dB. Any points along this circle mean the microphone is just as sensitive in the corresponding direction as it is in the 0 degrees direction.

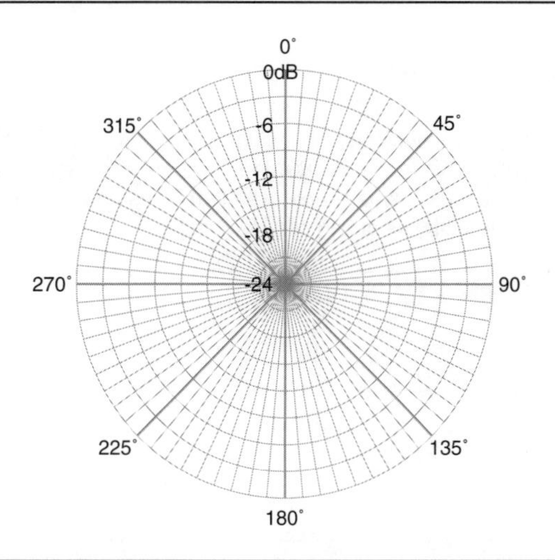

Figure 5.5 Polar Graph

Five polar patterns are common: omnidirectional, bidirectional, cardioid, supercardioid, and hypercardioid.

Omnidirectional

Consider the microphone topology shown in Figure 5.6. The diaphragm is backed by a sealed enclosure, much like sealed acoustic suspension speaker design. Sounds impinging from the front of the mike directly strike the diaphragm. Sounds coming from behind the microphone bend around the enclosure and also strike the diaphragm. This design is therefore receptive to sounds from all angles.

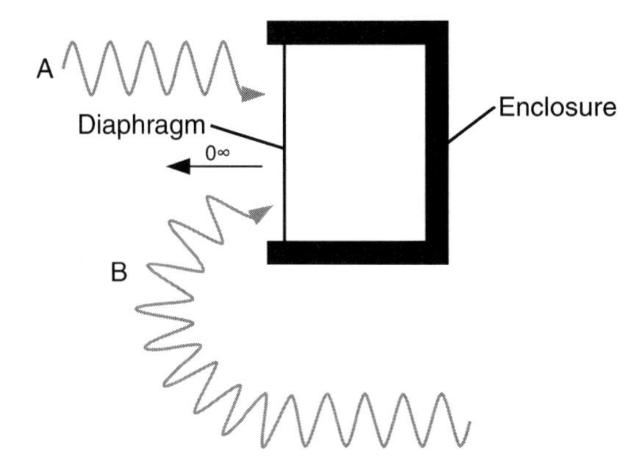

Sound from the front (A) and from the back (B) are able to reach the diaphragm.

Note that practical designs also include a very small vent used to gradually equalize the air inside the cavity due to gradual changes in the ambient pressure. The vent is small enough so that it has no effect on the pressure waves generated by incoming sounds.

Figure 5.6 Pressure Operation

Mikes using this design are known as pressure operation microphones. Because this design is equally sensitive in every direction, it has an omnidirectional polar pattern, as shown in Figure 5.7. The omnidirectional response is simply a circle when plotted on a polar graph.

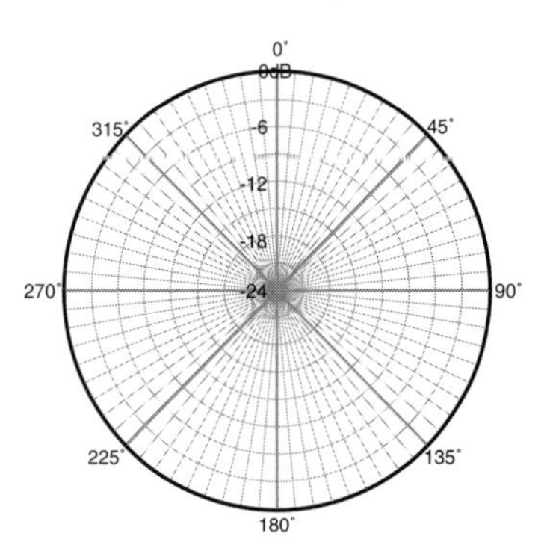

Figure 5.7 Omnidirectional Pattern

It is worth remembering that diffraction decreases as frequency increases. As such, high frequency sounds with wavelengths on par with the enclosure size do not bend and hit the microphone. Thus, the frequency response of an omnidirectional microphone is not truly equal in all directions for higher frequencies.

Bidirectional

Now consider a microphone design, like the one shown in Figure 5.8, in which both sides of the diaphragm are open to the air, as is the case with a ribbon microphone.

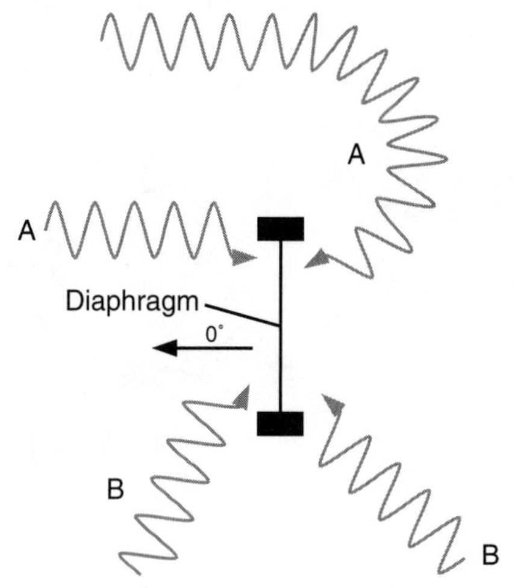

Sounds from the front (A) and from the back (B) are able to reach the diaphragm.

Figure 5.8 Pressure Gradient Operation

Sounds from the front strike the front of the diaphragm as well as bending around and hitting the rear. Sounds from the rear strike the rear of the diaphragm and bend to hit the front. In both cases, the diffracting sound waves have to travel a longer distance than the direct sound waves. This additional distance results in a phase shift in the diffracting wave such that it and the direct wave have an additive effect for most frequencies. When the direct wave is creating a region of compression adjacent to the diaphragm, the diffracting wave is creating a region of rarefaction. For these sounds, a pressure gradient is created. And, indeed, microphones using this type of assembly are sometimes known as pressure gradient microphones.

To put it simply, the diaphragm moves a lot when the sound is coming from straight ahead or straight behind the mike.

Conversely, if the sounds are coming from the side, waves strike the front and back of the diaphragm in phase because both waves travel the same distance. Because both waves have the same phase, they create the same pressure on both sides of the diaphragm. The diaphragm therefore does not move. In other words, sounds coming from the sides do not elicit a response.

This type of sensitivity is known as a bi-directional polar pattern, as shown in Figure 5.9. Mikes with this sensitivity pattern readily pick up sounds directly in front and directly behind, but reject sounds from the sides. This pattern is also known as a figure-eight.

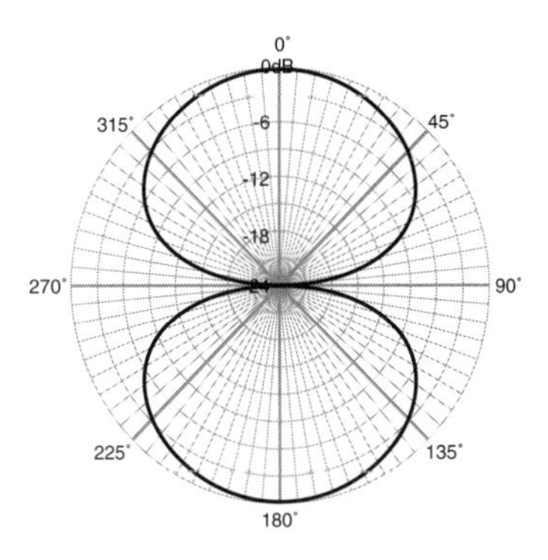

Figure 5.9 Bi-directional Pattern

Cardioid

Omnidirectional and bidirectional mikes can be very useful, but there are times when you want to be able to record only the sounds that are coming from the front of the mike. For instance, you may be recording a singer during a live concert and want to capture her voice but not the sounds of the audience.

If you were to take an omnidirectional response and combine it with a bidirectional response, the resulting overall response is a cardioid, shown in Figure 5.10. Looking at the omnidirectional pattern and the bidirectional pattern, it may not be immediately obvious how one ends up with the cardioid shape. The tricky bit is that, on a bidirectional mike, the signals generated by rearward sounds have the opposite polarity of signals generated by forward sounds. The polarity of the signals for rearward sounds on a bidirectional mike is also the opposite of all signals generated by an omnidirectional mike. These opposing polarities mean that the rearward sensitivities of the two patterns cancel each other out.

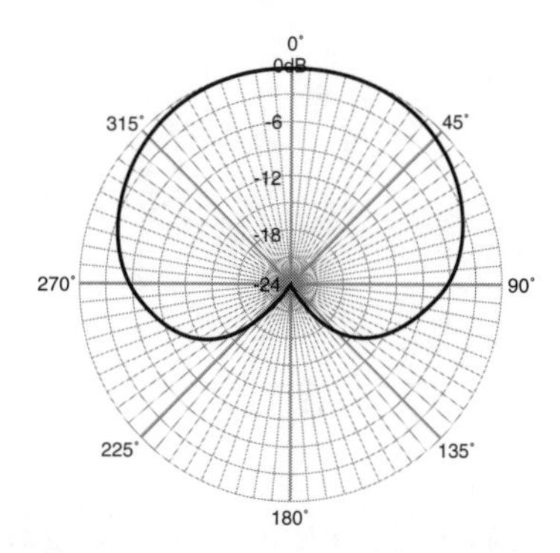

Figure 5.10 Cardioid Pattern

The cardioid is very receptive to sounds from in front of the mike, but increasingly less receptive to sounds as they move toward the back of the mike. Indeed, directly behind the mike there is a lobe where the microphone cannot sense sounds at all.

A microphone with a cardioid response is known as a unidirectional microphone. There are, in fact, several different types of cardioid responses. The one we have just discussed can be obtained by combining an omnidirectional and bidirectional response in equal portions. It is accurately, but rarely, known as a pure cardioid to clearly differentiate it from the other types of cardioid patterns we are about to discuss.

Supercardioid

Combining an omnidirectional and bidirectional response in a ratio of $1{:}\sqrt{3}$ creates a pattern known as a supercardioid, shown in Figure 5.11. Again, this response is a unidirectional pattern in that it is very receptive to forward-originating sounds but is much less so to sounds from the rear.

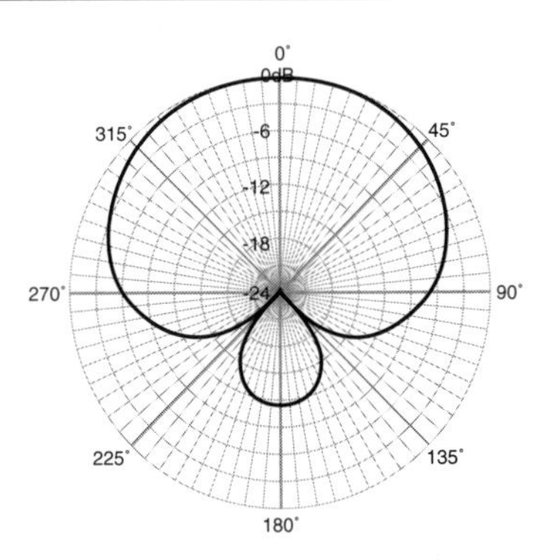

Figure 5.11 Supercardioid Pattern

So why a ratio of 1:√3? It may not be immediately obvious from visual inspection of the polar pattern, but if you do the math,[3] you'll find that of all the cardioids, the supercardioid pattern has the highest unidirectional index. The unidirectional index is a measure of directivity we will discuss in more detail shortly.

Unlike a pure cardioid, the supercardioid *can* detect sounds that originate directly behind it, at 180 degrees. It does have its own blind spots or null points, specifically at approximately 125 degrees and 235 degrees, also written as ±125 degrees.

Hypercardioid

Another common polar pattern is the hypercardioid, shown in Figure 5.12, which can be formed by combining an omnidirectional and bidirectional response in a ratio of 1:3.

You may be thinking that the 1:3 ratio was not arbitrarily chosen. If so, you are correct![4] It turns out that of all the cardioid patterns, the hypercardioid has the highest distance factor. Distance factor is, again, a measure of directivity that we will discuss in more detail shortly.

[3] And indeed *you* will need to do the math. I'm not putting it in here. But rest assured that lots of numbers and squiggly little lines are involved.

[4] If not, well, don't worry. As George Bernard Shaw said, "A life spent making mistakes is not only more honorable, but more useful than a life spent doing nothing."

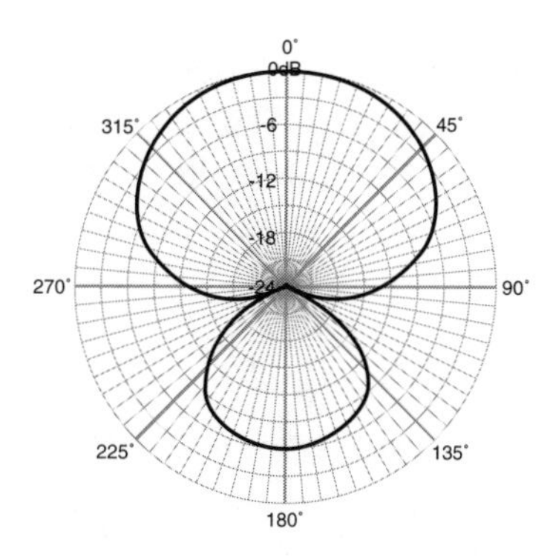

Figure 5.12 Hypercardioid Pattern

Single Element Cardioid Designs

As noted previously, microphones originally created cardioid responses by electrically combining the signal of two capsules: one with an omnidirectional and one with a bidirectional response. This practice continues today, and some microphones continue to use multiple capsules that can be altered by the flip of a switch or the twist of dial to give a wide range of responses.

However, many of today's cardioid microphones achieve their response using only a single element, thanks to the 1937 efforts of Ben Bauer of Shure. He devised a design he called unidirectional/phase shift or uniphase, shown in Figure 5.13.

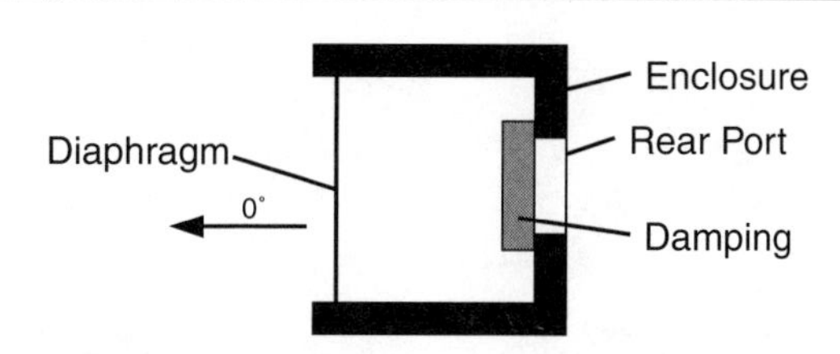

Figure 5.13 Uniphase Design

We have seen that if waves hit only the front of the diaphragm, we get an omnidirectional response. If all the waves are allowed to hit the front and back of the diaphragm, we get a bidirectional response. The uniphase design achieves a cardioid response by adding a delay to the waves that enter from the rear. The delay is achieved by adding a damping material that has a slower speed of sound than air or by using a labyrinth. Multiple rear port pathways may be created to get the desired response over a large frequency domain.

Cardioid mikes built using a single capsule in this fashion can be made smaller than microphones that use multiple capsules.

Polar Patterns in the Real World

All of the polar patterns we have shown so far are mathematically generated ideal responses. Actual microphones have pickup patterns that vary from the ideal. This variation comes from the fact that the microphone has a nonzero size, and thus gets it its own way when receiving sound waves from certain directions. Also, sound waves diffract differently depending on their wavelength. The higher the frequency, the less the wave bends.

An example of an actual omnidirectional microphone's frequency-dependent polar pattern is shown in Figure 5.14.

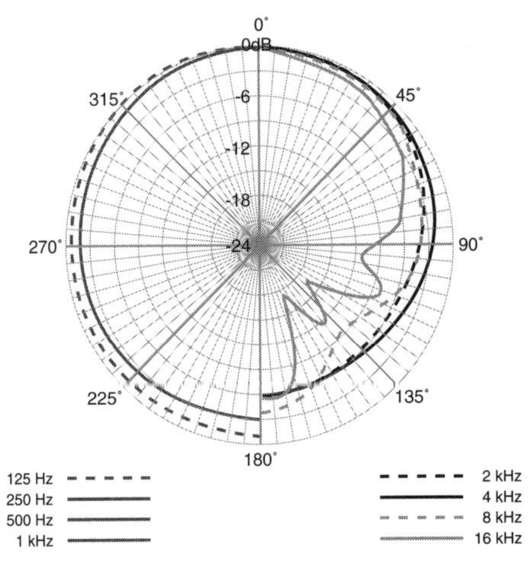

Note that this diagram takes advantage of the symmetry of the polar diagrams by placing half a plot on each side of the diagram, to more clearly show more frequency lines.

Figure 5.14 Frequency Dependency of Pickup Pattern

The ideal polar plots are still very useful tools, despite their deviation from reality. Knowing that—for instance—a mike has a cardioid response instead of an omnidirectional response, we know that it rejects a lot of sounds from the rear, especially those from directly behind the microphone.

Knowledge of the frequency-specific practical plots also aids us in our usage of microphones. For instance, if we are using an omnidirectional microphone with the response depicted above, we know that it is insensitive to higher frequency off-axis sounds. Thus, if we were recording a sound that came across as too trebly, we could turn the mike to color the response.

Off-axis Colorization

Off-axis colorization is the term used to describe the tendency of microphones to have an increasingly distorted frequency response as sounds originate further away from on-axis. When filtered by the off-axis response, sounds are said to be colored. In other words, they have a non-uniform frequency response. Most off-axis colorization is characterized by an uneven attenuation of the higher frequencies.

Proximity Effect

The frequency response of pressure gradient microphones is further affected by a phenomenon known as the *proximity effect*. Pressure gradient mikes become increasingly sensitive to low frequencies as the sound source nears the diaphragm.

For distant sounds, the diaphragm only experiences the phase difference between the sound striking the front and the sound striking the rear of the diaphragm. Sounds traveling the two paths have the same intensity.

However, for closer sounds there is a notable pressure difference between the front and rear sound paths. At higher frequencies, the pressure difference does not greatly affect the microphone's response, because there is still a substantial phase difference between the two sound paths. But for lower frequencies the phase difference between the two paths is much less; hence, the pressure difference has a large impact.

The proximity effect means that sound originating close to the microphone have more bass than they do in real life. Some microphones include additional electric or acoustic filters to counteract the bass response. These filters are often switchable: you would want the filters active if the mike was being used by a singer or orator, but would want the filters off if the mike was being used to capture more distant sounds.

Omnidirectional mikes—which use pressure operation—are immune to the proximity effect.

Three Dimensional Plots

All of the polar patterns we have shown so far have been two-dimensional. Of course, we live in a world of three dimensions.[5] To truly diagram the response of a microphone, we would need to plot it in three dimensions, such as the plot of a supercardioid response shown in Figure 5.15.

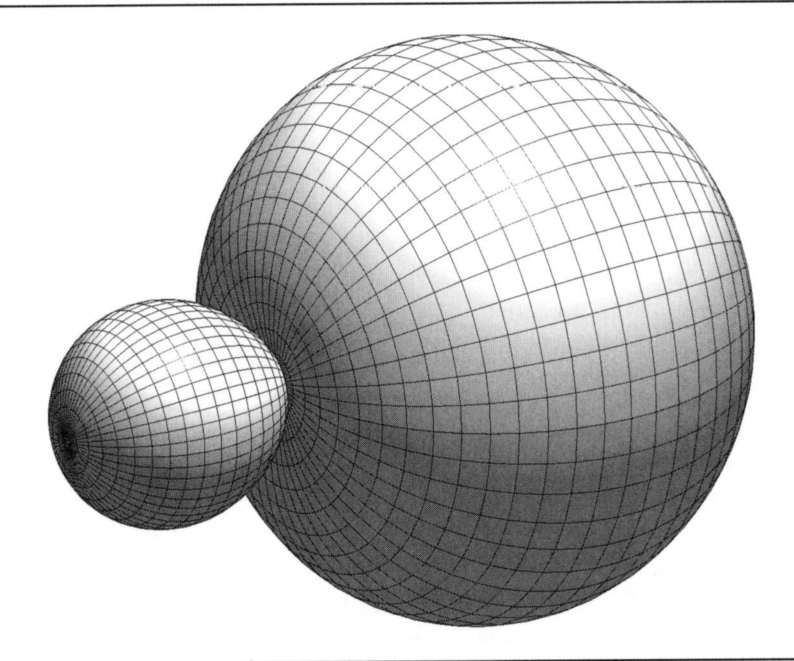

Figure 5.15 Hypercardioid in 3D

Three-dimensional graphs are much harder to draw and interpret. Luckily, the ideal microphone response is symmetric. The two dimensional polar plots we have been examining apply for any plane. They are accurate for the horizontal plane, the vertical plane, and any plane in between. With this understanding, the two-dimensional polar patterns accurately convey the response in three-dimensional space.

[5] Well, three immediately obvious spatial dimensions. There's also a temporal dimension, plus some theories suggest there may be half a dozen more spatial dimensions so tiny that we just don't notice them.

For actual microphones that do not have a symmetric response, the three-dimensional response can be roughly described by using a polar pattern for the horizontal plane and a different polar pattern for the vertical plane.

Measuring Directivity

Polar patterns are but one way to convey the directional sensitivity of a microphone. There are several other interrelated measurements of directivity. All of the measurements we are about to discuss are conveyed by a single unitless number, as compared to polar patterns, which are an involved graphical representation of directivity. All of the following measurements are ratios to the omnidirectional response, which has a value of 1.0 for all of these metrics. Values for the common polar patterns are summarized at the end of the chapter.

Random Energy Efficiency

Random energy efficiency (REE) is the measurement of a mike's ability to pick up sounds from the front direction while rejecting ambient noises. An omnidirectional mike has an REE of 1.0. More directional mikes have a lower REE. The lower the number, the more directional it is. The hypercardioid pattern has the lowest random energy efficiency (0.25).

REE can be calculated for ideal patterns through the use of some simple calculus. It can be practically calculated by placing a test microphone in a diffuse sound field and measuring its voltage output. This test value is divided by the voltage level of a reference omnidirectional microphone in that same sound field.

The REE really is a measure of how efficient a microphone is at capturing diffuse sounds. The omnidirectional mike has the highest REE because it is most efficient at capturing diffuse sounds. Other patterns are less efficient. If you consider that they all have null points, it is sensible that their REE is less—there are some regions of the diffuse field that they cannot even detect.

A low REE is not necessarily a bad thing. We often do not want to capture ambient sounds, but instead to just capture sounds directly in front of a microphone. That, indeed, is the whole point of having unidirectional mikes!

Diffuse sound fields for measurements such as REE are created in a *hard room*. A hard room is a specially designed room with acoustically reflective walls. Regardless of where a sound is generated in the room, its intensity is generally the same throughout the room due to all the reflections. Diffuse sound fields for measurements such as REE are created in a *hard room*. A hard room is a specially designed room with acoustically reflective walls. Regardless of where a sound is generated in the room, its intensity is generally the same throughout the room due to all the reflections.

Directivity Factor

The *directivity factor* (DRF) of a microphone is the ratio of its response to a diffuse sound field versus an on-axis sound. The DRF can be directly measured by placing a microphone in a diffuse sound field and measuring its voltage output, and then dividing that value by the voltage output of the microphone in the presence of an on-axis sound of the same intensity.

Another, perhaps easier way to calculate the directivity factor is to just take the reciprocal of the REE. At the risk of yet again halving the book's readership, Equation 5.1 provides the equation form:

Equation 5.1 Directivity Factor

$$DRF = 1 / REE$$

Because the directivity factor is the inverse of the REE, directional mikes have a higher directivity factor than an omnidirectional mike. The pattern with the highest directivity factor is the hypercardioid mike (4.0).

Measurements requiring purely on-axis sounds are carried out in an *anechoic* chamber. Such a chamber is the opposite of the hard room, in that all its walls absorb sound. There are no reflections, and, hence, no diffuse sounds.

Distance Factor

The *distance factor* (Q or sometimes DSF) is yet another measure of a microphone's directivity. The distance factor is a measurement of a microphone's *reach*: the point at which the pickup of direct sounds and ambient sounds is equal.

Thought of another way, the distance factor indicates how much further away from a direct sound source you can place a directional microphone compared to an omnidirectional microphone, yet still get the same voltage output. For instance, a cardioid mike has a distance factor of 1.73. This means it can record a person speaking 1.73 feet away just as well as an omnidirectional mike can from a distance of 1 foot away.

The distance factor can be measured by placing the test microphone and a reference omni-directional microphone in a reverberant chamber. A test sound is generated, and the test microphone is moved away from the sound source until the output level of the two mikes is equal. The distance factor is calculated by dividing the distance from the test mike to the sound source by the distance from the reference mike to the sound source.

The distance factor can be calculated by simply taking the square root of the directivity factor, as shown in Equation 5.2.

Equation 5.2 Distance Factor

$$Q = \sqrt{DRF}$$

The use of a square root makes sense, if you consider the fact that sound intensity is regulated by the inverse square law.

Unidirectional Index

Okay, here's one more directivity measurement that is related to the REE. The unidirectional index is a measurement of a mike's ability to accept sounds from the forward direction while rejecting sounds from the backward direction. It is calculated by determining the random energy efficiency for the hemisphere in front of the microphone and dividing that value by the REE for the hemisphere behind the microphone, as shown by Equation 5.3.

Equation 5.3 Unidirectional Index

$$UDI = REE(front)/REE(back)$$

Because omnidirectional mikes are equally adept at hearing sounds in the two hemispheres, it is not surprising that they have a unidirectional index of 1. The supercardioid pattern has the highest unidirectional index (13.8).

Angle of Acceptance

The *angle of acceptance* is the angle within which the microphone picks up sounds within a specified sensitivity. Sounds originating from outside the angle of acceptance are detected much less readily by the microphone.

Because the roll-off in sensitivity outside the angle of acceptance is gradual, it is necessary to specify how much of a drop in sensitivity occurs at the point where the angle is measured.

The angles of acceptance with a 3 dB drop from center for various patterns are shown in Figure 5.16.

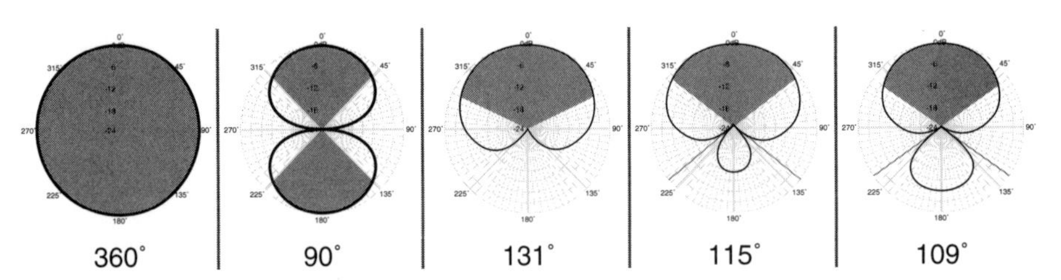

The ideal angles of acceptance for some classic microphone pickup patterns.
The angle is defined at a 3dB drop below the on-axis response.

Figure 5.16 Angles of Acceptance

Self Noise

All microphones have a certain amount of noise inherent in the signals they generate. This *self noise* is the amount of sound a microphone generates when it is placed in an absolutely quiet environment. In moving-coil and ribbon microphones, most of the noise originates from electrons moving within the coil and ribbon themselves. For condenser microphones, most of the noise comes from the head amplifier.

The self-noise is usually reported as an *equivalent noise level*, which is also known as *equivalent noise rating*. The equivalent noise level is the intensity an external sound source would need to have to generate a voltage level in the mike equal to the voltage the mike generates as self noise.

The equivalent noise level is typically measured in dB-SPL. It is commonly A-weighted—weighted with respect to the A-curve we discussed in Chapter 3.

Maximum Input Level

Microphones have a maximum sound level they can record without distortion. As sound intensity rises above this maximum input level, distortion continues to increase. Because the distortion increases gradually, it is proper to specify the max level along with the distortion at that point.

For instance, a mike might have a maximum input level of 110 dB-SPL with 1 percent THD.

This practice is very similar to the need for specifying the variation in intensity when indicating a frequency range.

Microphone Types

Microphones come in a variety of form factors. Each one has different strengths and weaknesses.

Standard

The most common microphone form factor is the standard hand-held microphone, such as the one shown in Figure 5.17. Mikes such as these are designed to be either held in the hand or mounted on a stand. They are general purpose microphones, used by singers and orators.

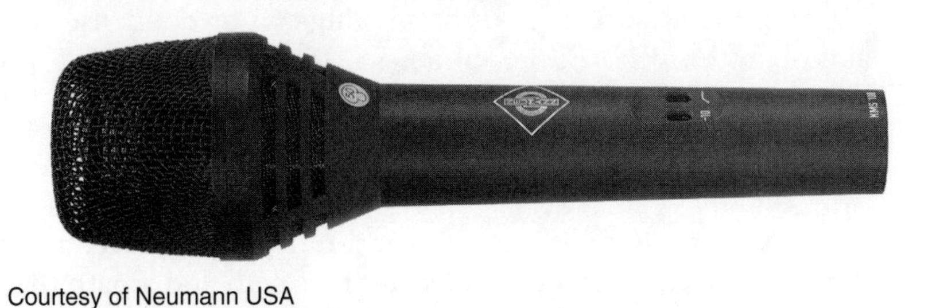

Courtesy of Neumann USA

Figure 5.17 Handheld Microphone

These microphones typically contain dynamic or condenser capsules. All the popular polar patterns are supported by these mikes. Sometimes a single mike supports multiple polar patterns that can be selected by a switch or dial.

Lapel

Lapel microphones are so small that you can wear them on, yes, your lapel. They are also known as lavaliere mikes, as they can alternately be worn on a loop around the neck like a lavaliere. Figure 5.18 shows a typical mike and clip.

Figure 5.18 Lapel Microphone

Lavalieres are often used in situations where you need some freedom of movement or the microphone needs to be indiscrete. While small, they do have the disadvantage of picking up the sound of body and clothing movement, because they are typically worn close to the body. They are often used in video productions and television shows.

These mikes are built using moving-coil or condenser capsule. They almost exclusively feature either an omnidirectional or a pure cardioid response.

Boundary

When a microphone is placed near a reflecting surface, a sound reaches the mike via two different paths: a direct path and a path that reflects off the surface, as shown in Figure 5.19.

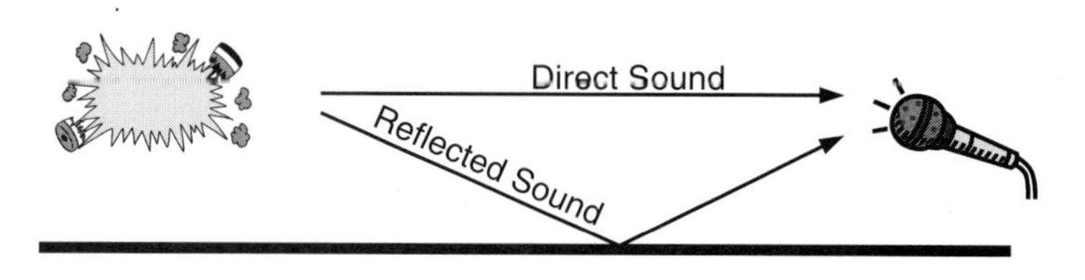

Figure 5.19 Multiple Sound Paths

After traveling the two paths, the sounds interfere with one another. At some frequencies, the interference is constructive, and the combined sound has twice the pressure (+ 6 dB intensity) as the direct sound. For other frequencies the two sounds destructively interfere, and the combined sound has no intensity. The resulting frequency response looks like Figure 5.20.

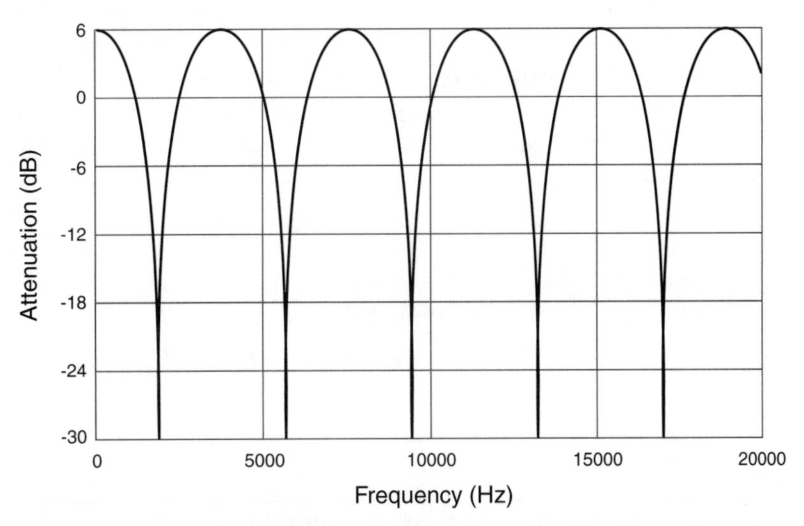

The comb filter gets its name from the fact that it looks—vaguely—like a comb, but only if you plot the frequencies on a linear scale.

Figure 5.20 Comb Filter Response

As such, sound recorded near a reflective surface does not have a uniform response. Depending on how close the microphone is to the reflector, the fidelity can be downright terrible. However, a carefully designed microphone is able to reap the 6-dB intensity gain for distant sounds.

A type of microphone known as a *boundary microphone*, shown in Figure 5.21, actually takes advantage of this effect to create a uniform frequency response. These mikes are also known as *boundary layer microphones* or *pressure zone microphones* (PZM).

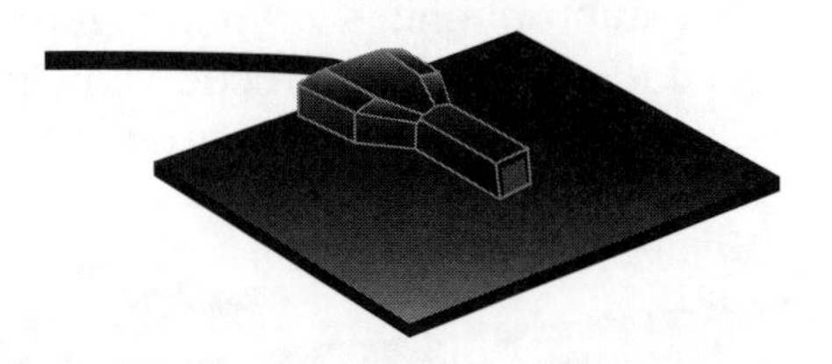

Figure 5.21 Boundary Microphone

Boundary mikes work by placing a capsule very close to a reflective plate, as shown in Figure 5.22. The plate is fixed in place and is an integral part of the microphone. The capsule diaphragm is close enough to the plate so that direct sounds and reflected sounds reach it nearly simultaneously. Because the distance of the two paths is virtually identical, the sound waves constructively interfere. In other words, the boundary microphone receives twice the pressure as other types of microphones, making it 6 dB more sensitive than the same capsule without the housing.

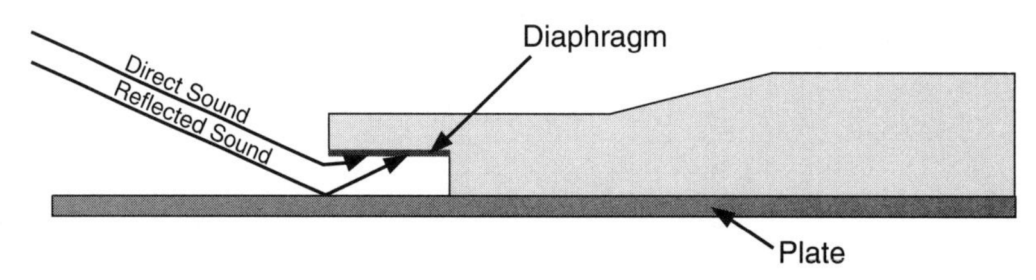

Direct and reflected sound waves reach diaphragm at same time, doubling the pressure on the diaphragm.

Figure 5.22 Boundary Microphone Design

Cancellations between the two wave paths occur for sufficiently high frequencies. The trick is to make sure those frequencies are high enough so as not to negatively affect the microphone's response. To have a response at 20 kilohertz that is only 3 dB down, the diaphragm would need to be mounted 0.085 inches above the plate.

Boundary mikes typically use an omnidirectional condenser capsule. They have less off-axis coloration than other omnidirectional microphones and are well suited to applications where the microphone must be positioned near a reflective surface.

Shotgun

A shotgun or line microphone, shown in Figure 5.23, is a specialized type of mike designed to have a very directional response. They are very good at picking up sounds on-axes and rejecting off-axis noises.

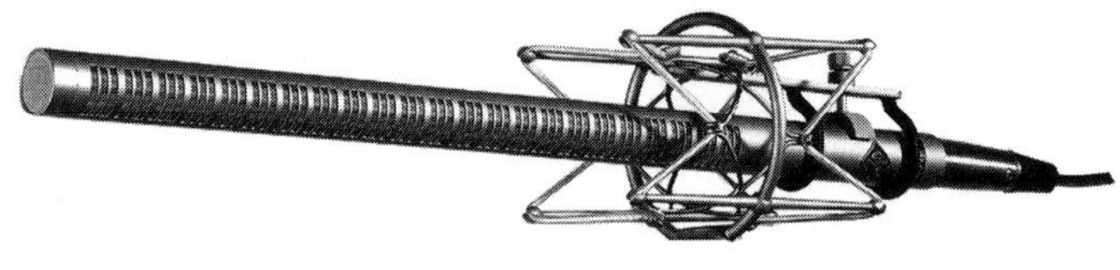

Courtesy of Neumann USA

Figure 5.23 Shotgun Microphone

Shotgun mikes are created by placing a long interference tube in front of a typical omnidirectional capsule, as shown in Figure 5.24. The interference tube contains many openings along its length. Sounds arriving on-axis have a direct path to the capsule. However, sounds arriving off-axis follow many different paths through the interference slits before reaching the capsule. The barrel is carefully designed so that for most frequencies the off-axis sounds cancel each other out.

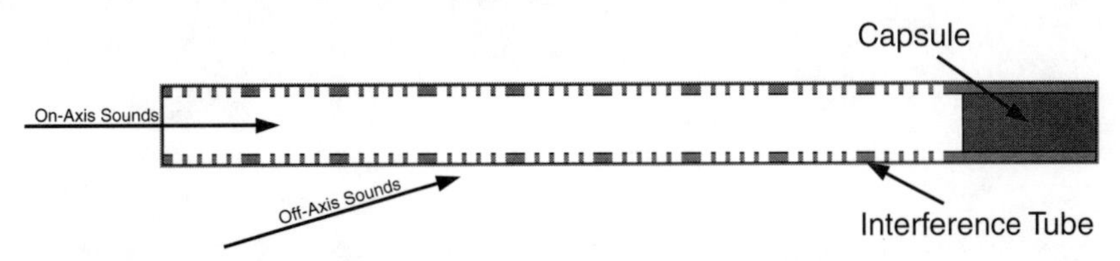

On-axis sounds have a direct path to the capsule. Off-axis sounds have multiple paths through the interference tube that tend to cancel out such sounds.

Figure 5.24 Shotgun Microphone Design

Their directivity is a function of the length of the long interference tube that gives them their name. Shotgun mikes are thus divided into two categories: short barrel and long barrel, although there is no hard and fast rule for the cross-over point between a short and long barrel. A short barrel may have two to three times the reach of normal cardioid microphone, whereas a long barrel may have over ten times the reach of a normal cardioid. Short barrel microphones are often mounted on booms and used to record sound for film or video production. Long barrel microphones are usually reserved for special situations where a distant sound needs to be captured.

As you might expect, different frequencies behave differently as they pass through the interference tube. The effectiveness of the tube at rejecting off-axis sounds is indeed frequency dependent, as can be seen in Figure 5.25.

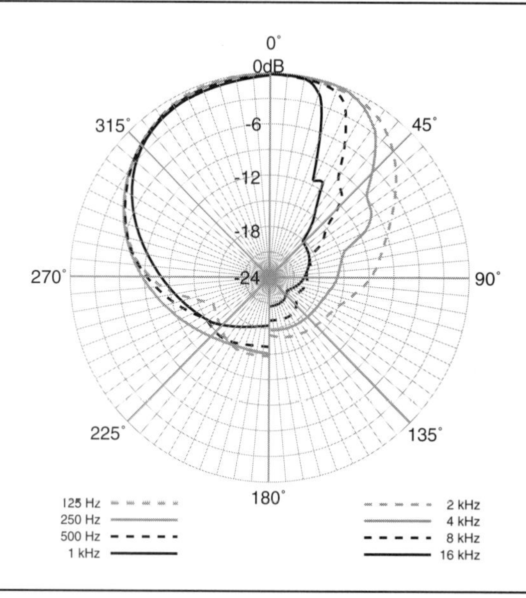

Figure 5.25 Shotgun Microphone Polar Pattern

Shotgun microphones are sometimes erroneously referred to as rifle microphones. Rifle microphones are actually a distinct design. They achieve a high order of directionality through the use of several tubular waveguides of differing lengths, as shown in Figure 5.26. Rifle microphones are rarely used today, having been superseded by shotgun mikes.

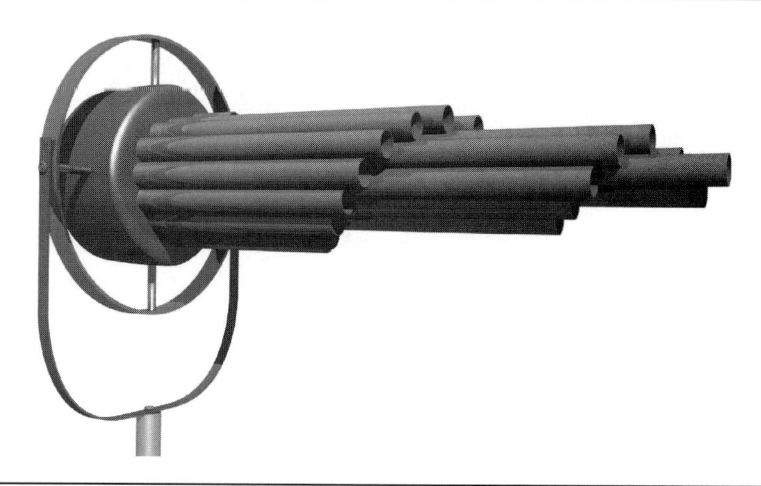

Figure 5.26 Rifle Microphone

Parabolic

The parabolic microphone depicted in Figure 5.27 is another mike design intended to capture distant sounds. Its most notable component is a large parabolic dish, typically in the range of 1.5 to 3 feet across. Such mikes can often be seen on the sidelines of large field sporting events such as football or soccer. They are also used to record the sounds of wildlife that you either can't get close to, such as birds, or that you do not want to get close to, such as lions.

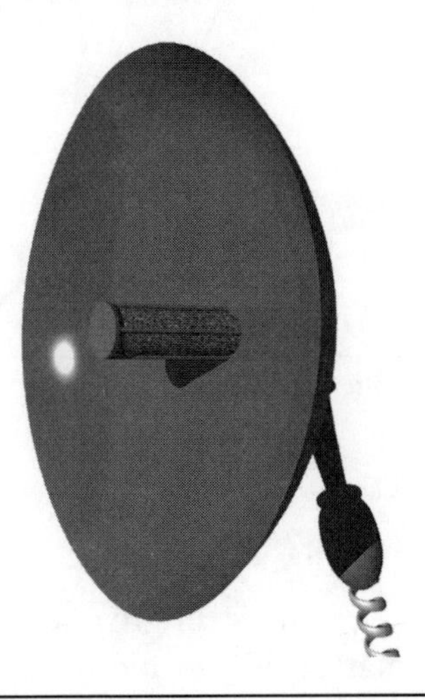

Figure 5.27 Parabolic Microphone

Parabolic mikes work by placing a capsule at the focal point of a parabolic dish, as shown in Figure 5.28. Sounds hitting the dish are reflected to the focal point. Waves that would normally encompass a wide area, the diameter of the dish, are all focused onto the diaphragm. Whereas other designs merely reject off-axis sounds, the parabolic design actually amplifies on-axis sounds. It is quite feasible for practical designs to achieve a 15-dB gain of on-axis sounds.

Not surprisingly, the polar response of parabolic mikes is also frequency dependent. For lower frequencies, the sensitivity decreases as the wavelength becomes comparable to the diameter of the dish.

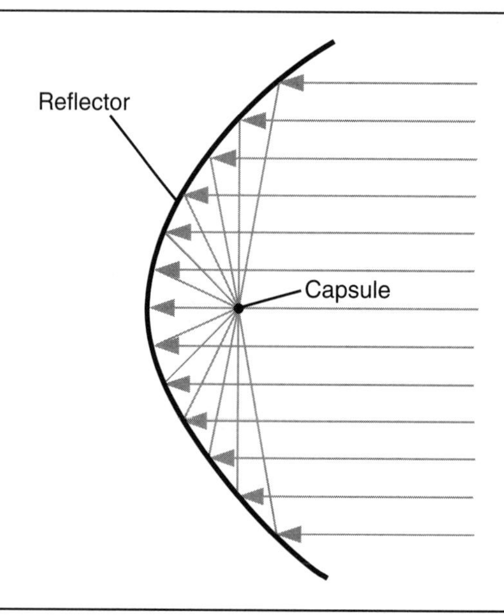

Figure 5.28 Parabolic Microphone Design

Which Microphone is Best?

Every microphone has its strengths and weakness. Choosing the proper microphone is a matter of considering all the different aspects of the recording environment and comparing the desired results with the capabilities of the different microphone types. However, there is rarely a microphone that is unequivocally the best one for the job. When it comes to choosing between a condenser and a moving-coil capsule, a cardioid and supercardioid response, or transistors and vacuum tubes, the answer often hinges just as heavily on the person's experience and personal preferences as it does the technical details of the mike itself.[6]

[6] Similar to how for some people the best vehicle for picking up groceries is a fuel-efficient compact car, but for others it is a gas-guzzling sport utility vehicle. Mine has four-wheel drive and snow tires!

Summary

Microphones are transducers that convert sound pressure waves into a voltage-varying electrical signal. In this chapter we examined the different types of capsules that form the heart of every microphone. These capsules included the dynamic moving-coil and the condenser.

We also examined different microphone characteristics such as directivity. A summary of these different directivity values for common polar patterns is shown in Table 5.1.

Table 5.1 Polar Pattern Summary

Name	Omni-directional	Bi-directional	Cardioid	Super-cardioid	Hyper-cardioid
Polar Pattern	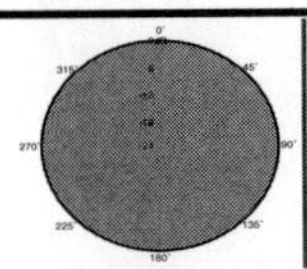	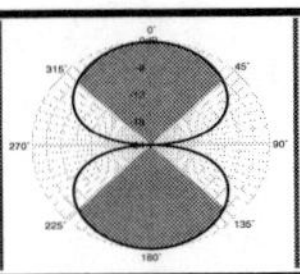	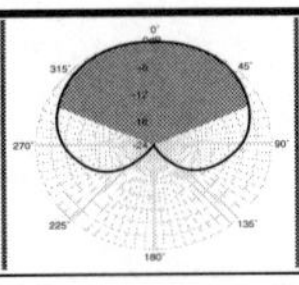	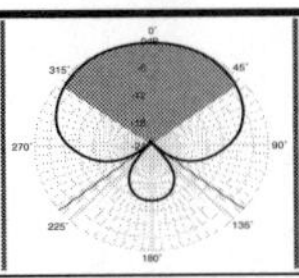	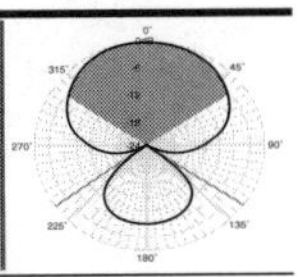
Distance Multiplier	1.0	1.7	1.7	1.9	2.0
Angle of Acceptance (-3 dB)	360°	90°	131°	115°	105°
Null Points	n/a	± 90°	±180°	±125°	± 109°
REE	1.00	0.33	0.33	0.27	0.25
DRF	1.00	3.00	3.00	3.73	4.00
DSF	1.00	1.73	1.73	1.93	2.00
UDI	1.00	1.00	6.99	13.83	6.96

In the next chapter, we will discuss the details of how microphones are used to record different types of sound such as stereo.

Chapter 6

Multichannel Sound

"If you don't make it, can I have your stereo?"

—Jack O'Neill, Stargate SG-1

In the beginning, all audio systems consisted of a single sound signal. The monophonic sound these systems generated was incapable of reproducing spatial auditory cues. For instance, you could not tell whether the original sound had been to the left or the right of the microphone. To overcome this limitation, most of today's sound systems use two or more channels, thus creating a more immersive listening experience.

Monophonic Sound

Sound represented as a single channel is known as *monophonic*—literally: one sound—or *mono* for short. Mono sound is captured by a single microphone and can be reproduced by a single speaker. Monophonic sound reproduction can accurately convey the loudness, pitch, and timbre of the original source.

What mono cannot do is reproduce spatial cues that allow the sound to be localized. Instead, all the sounds seem to come from the speaker. In a monophonic reproduction of a symphony, the cellos, the flutes, the cannons, and even in the guy in the audience yelling, "Tchaikovsky rocks!" all seem to originate at the same point in space. However, the original sounds were obviously located at different places.

The localization limitations of mono sound were recognized early on, and much experimentation was done in the beginning of the 20th century to produce two-channel, or stereo, sound systems.

For a variety of reasons, however, monophonic systems persisted for decades. First off, they were a huge improvement over the previous audio reproduction technology, which was none at all. Mono was also a good solution for reproducing single source sounds, like an orator or a soloist. Stereo systems were also more expensive, because they required twice as many speakers as a mono system. You also had the matter of compatibility. Most consumers with a collection of monophonic records would be unwilling to buy a new sound stereo system that did not play their existing library.

It was not until the 1957 introduction of stereo records that monophonic sound began to be phased out of consumer space. These new stereo records elegantly solved the compatibility issue by using a groove technique that allowed mono and stereo records to be interchanged.

Stereophonic Sound

Stereophonic (or stereo) sound uses two sound channels (left and right). These two channels may contain sounds that differ in amplitude, phase, and time. All three of these cues are used by the human hearing system for sound localization. As such, a stereophonic recording can fool us into hearing spatially diverse sounds that are reminiscent of the sound's original environment.

Playback

Stereo playback is accomplished by two speakers, one for each channel. One speaker is called the left and the other is called the right. The labeling is done from the vantage point of the listener, as shown in Figure 6.1. As a historical note, early experiments into spatial sound used many speakers arranged in a line. The number was eventually dropped to two to balance the tradeoff between cost and spatial image accuracy.

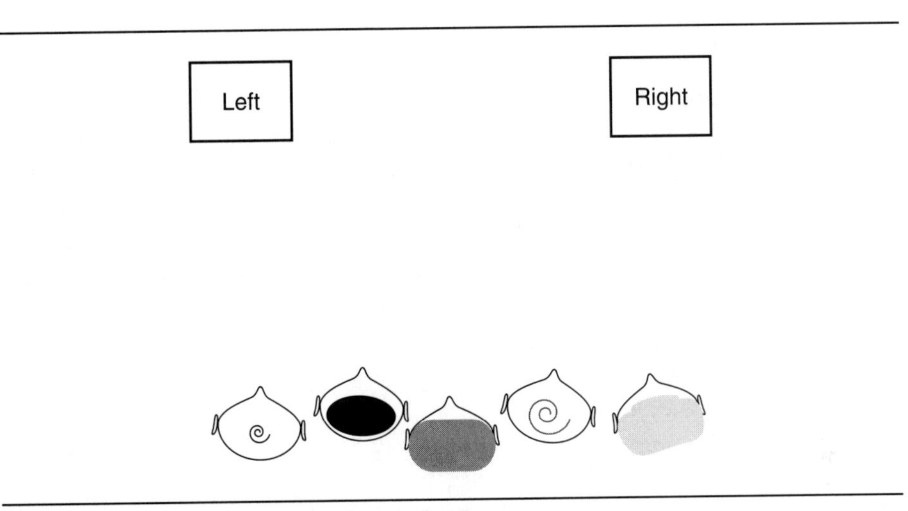

Figure 6.1 Speaker Configuration for Stereo

As was the case with mono, a sound originating solely from the left speaker is localized by a listener as coming from the left speaker. Similarly, a sound originating solely from the right speaker is localized as coming from the right speaker. So far, it's all very obvious. But here's where it gets interesting: a sound coming from both speakers at the same time with equal intensity seems to come from the point midway between the speakers, even though there is not actually a speaker there! In fact, a sound can be positioned anywhere on the line between the two speakers by changing the intensity of the sound's components on the left and right speakers.

The stereo effect can also be created by delaying the sound on one of the channels. Playing the identical sound on both channels at the same intensity, but playing one of them a fraction of a second later than the other, results in the human perception that the sound originated off to the side, rather than the mid-point.

Another way to create the stereo effect is by altering the phase of the sounds. Indeed, altering the phase of sounds can create the impression that they are coming to the left of the right speaker, and to the right of the left speaker, an effect not possible by simply altering the left vs. right intensity. This phase alternation technique is the method by which some stereo playback equipment provides the capability of stereo expansion, which alters the phase of the recorded sound to create a stereo image that appears to be larger than the two speakers.

Headphones

Although headphones consist of two speakers, they cannot, strictly speaking, reproduce a stereophonic sound system. You can certainly listen to a stereo recording on headphones,[1] but it does not accurately reproduce the stereo image. Rather than seeming to come from a point in front of you, sounds are instead lateralized: they seem to come from inside your head along a line between your ears. Very few real world sounds come from this location. Indeed, if you are listening to a symphony on headphones, it seems unlikely that the entire orchestra would fit inside your head.

To create a properly formed spatial sound image using headphones, a different sound technique known as ***binaural*** needs to be used. We will discuss it in greater detail shortly.

Now, all that having been said, the majority of the world's sound recordings are done in stereo, and people routinely listen to them using headphones.

Recording

Recording stereo sound is tricky business. It requires the use of multiple capsules. These multiple capsules may be located within a single microphone or may be contained in multiple microphones. Because these capsules exist in different spatial locations, there is a risk that certain sound waves cancel each other out if their signals are combined.

Keeping this complexity in mind, we will briefly cover some of the more common stereophonic recording techniques.

A-B Pair

The A-B pair technique uses two widely separated identical microphones to capture stereo sound. This method is also known as the *spaced pair* technique. The microphones are usually omnidirectional, but directional mikes can be used as well.

Because the mikes are located at substantially different locations, they capture amplitude and time-based localization cues. For example, sounds originating closer to the left mike have a higher intensity on the left channel than on the right channel. These sounds appear on the left channel before they do on the right channel.

---

[1] Indeed, that's what I'm doing as I write these words. Specifically, *Halo Soundtrack*, track 16: Rock Anthem for Saving the World.

A drawback of the A-B technique is that if the microphones are placed too far apart from one another, there is an audio hole when they are played back on speakers. This hole can be filled through the use of a third microphone placed between the A-B pair.

A good rule of thumb for A-B placement is the three to one rule: the mikes should be placed at least three times as far apart from each other as they are to the sound source. The three to one rule helps minimize phase cancellations between the two channels.

X-Y Pair

The X-Y pair technique refers to the class of methods wherein two microphones are placed close together and each microphone captures a single stereo channel. There are many different subcategories of X-Y pair recording; they vary based on the directionality and position of the microphones used.

Coincident pair techniques refer to situations in which two microphone capsules are located at the same point in space. In other words, they are coincident. Of course, microphones have non-zero size, and thus two of them are never truly coincident, but the thought here is to get them as close together as possible.

Because the two mikes occupy nearly the same point in space, sounds reach them at the same time. There are no phase differences in the two channels of captured sound, so there are few problems with cancellation. When using directional microphones, the only major difference between the sound captured for left and right channels is their amplitude.

The coincident pair technique is useful for recording a small sound source such as a soloist or small group, but may not capture a good stereo image of a larger sound source such as an orchestra.

One particular instantiation of the coincident pair is the Blumlein pair, named after Alan Dower Blumlein, who was a pioneer in the field of stereo recording. In a Blumlein pair, two bidirectional microphones are used with a separation of 90 degrees. The Blumlein pair captures very natural sound, but it is just as sensitive to sounds from the rear as it is to sounds to the front.

Another category of the X-Y pair is the near-coincident pair technique. Near-coincident refers to situations where the microphones are placed several inches apart, nominally equivalent to the distance between a person's ears. One particular instantiation of the near-coincident technique is the ORTF method, named after the French Radio Television Organization. The ORTF technique uses two cardioid mikes arranged at a

110-degree angle separated by 17 centimeters. This configuration yields a good stereo image. In addition to the intensity differences, the separation of the mikes also captures time-based localization cues.

M-S Pair

The M-S, or middle-side, technique also uses coincident microphones, but it is very distinct from the X-Y technique. In X-Y, each microphone captures a single channel. In the M-S technique, each microphone captures elements of both stereo channels.

The M component is captured using a directional capsule, such as a cardioid. The S component is typically captured using a bidirectional capsule. However, this capsule is rotated 90 degrees from the directional capsule. These M and S signals are obviously two channels, but they do not correspond to left and right stereo channels. If the M and S signals are added together, however, a left channel signal is created, as shown in Figure 6.2. If S is subtracted from M, a right channel signal is created.

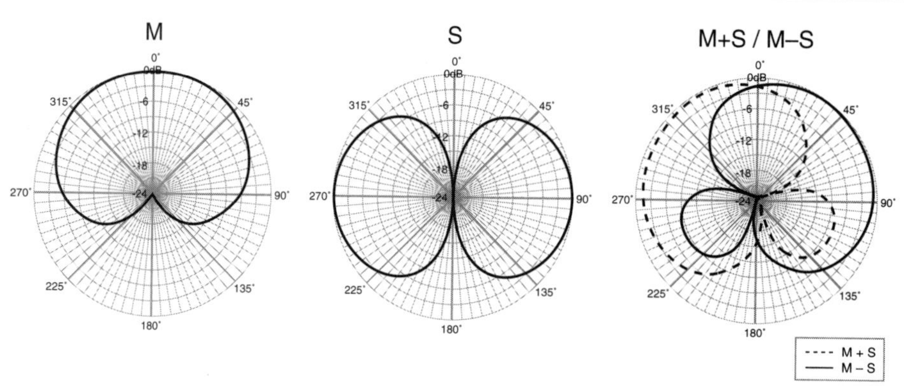

In this example, the M signal is captured using a cardioid mike (left) and the S signal is captured by a bidirectional mike (center). Adding the two signals together (M+S) creates a left channel image; subtracting one from the other (M-S) results in a right channel image (right). The polar pattern of the M+S and M-S signals may seem non-intuitive given the M and S patterns, but remember that there are phase differences in the original signals that are not shown in the polar plots.

Figure 6.2 M-S Technique

This method of processing the M and S signals to produce left and right channels is known as *matrixing*. As such, M-S is often referred to as matrixed sound.

The M-S technique allows for some flexibility not possible with other stereo recording techniques. If the M-S channels are directly stored using a two-channel recording system, the matrixing of the sound into left and right stereo channels can be done at a later time. Furthermore, the effective polar pattern of the recording can be altered by changing the relative weight of the M and S signals during matrix, as shown in Figure 6.3. Note that this altering of the pattern can occur after the original recording has been made! Of particular interest, a monophonic channel can be generated by using only the M channel.

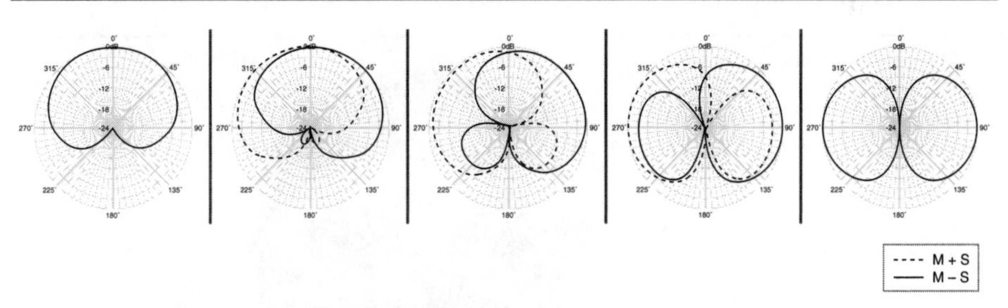

By varying the relative intensities of the M and S components, a variety of different sound response patterns can be generated. These diagrams show left to right M intensities of 0%, 25%, 50%, 75%, and 100%. S intensities are complementary: 100%, 75%, 50%, 25%, and 0%.

Figure 6.3 Variable M-S Patterns

Binaural

Binaural sound is another two-channel sound technique that stores localization cues. Stereophonic sound attempts to record and playback sound in such a way that, as it makes its way through the playback environment to the listener's ears, it has the necessary localization cues.

Binaural sound comes at the spatial reproduction problem from a different angle. As has been previously noted, sound entering the ear canal has already had a lot of additional sound cues added to it. There are amplitude differences, time delays, and phase differences. Sounds are also attenuated by frequency dependent head shadowing and have directional-dependent spectral effects added by pinnae reflections. So if you can capture the sound waves actually entering the ear canal, you should ideally have all the information you need to reproduce sounds with all the necessary localization cues.

So to record binaural sound, you simply stick microphones in people's ears. Seriously! These are obviously very small microphones. Even though different people have differently shaped ears and heads, studios have shown that we are generally able use the cues generated by someone else's head for localization.

As an alternative to using an actual person, there are commercially available head-shaped molds with self-contained microphones specifically designed for capturing binaural sound, shown in Figure 6.4. These devices include pinnae and other anatomical features so as to create reasonable approximations of sound cues generated by sound waves interacting with the human head.

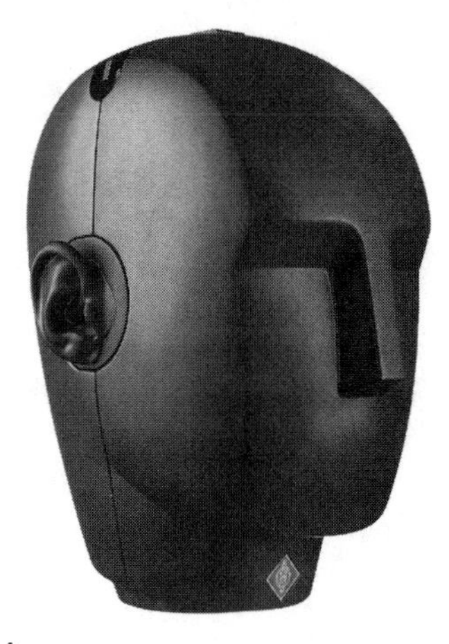

Courtesy of Neumann USA

Figure 6.4 Binaural Microphone Assembly

Binaural sound is theoretically capable of producing all the cues for localization. Whereas stereophonic recordings are typically limited to reproducing sound images to the front, binaural sound can reproduce sound from all angles. Many audiophiles insist that binaural sound is the definitive sound recording technique. Still, binaural sound recording remains rare.[2] Stereo recordings are far more dominant.

[2] For a good example, listen to Stephen King's *The Mist* Compact Disc Nightmare Edition in 3-D Sound.

Binaural sound can only be properly played back on headphones. Again, it is possible to play back a binaural recording on stereo speakers, but doing so does not reproduce the binaural image. Arguably, only earbud headphones should be used for binaural sound reproduction, because they send sound waves directly down the ear canal, right where the binaural microphones captured the sound.

Surround Sound

Stereo allows sounds to be localized along a line between the two speakers. But real-world sounds typically come from all over the place. Surround sound achieves a more immersive sound experience by placing speakers both in front and behind the listener.

Several contemporary surround systems include a separate channel dedicated to creating low-frequency sounds, such as those generated in action films by helicopters, gunfire, and explosions. This low frequency effects (LFE) channel is played by a subwoofer. Unlike the front and back speakers, the LFE does not provide any localization information; the low frequency sounds do not seem to come from a specific location.

Some surround systems also include a center channel. Designed to be placed between the front left and front right speakers, the center channel is typically used to reproduce dialogue in movie playback. The center channel helps our brains lock the character's voice to the video screen on which they appear.

Naming Conventions

There are two common naming conventions used to describe surround systems. The first nomenclature lists the number of full-range channels followed by the number of LFE channels. For instance, conventional stereo would be designated 2.0. A system with three channels in front, two in back, and one LFE is called 5.1.

An alternate naming convention is the front/back notation. The first number indicates the number of front channels. The second number indicates the number of rear channels. For instance, 2/0 refers to two front channels and zero rear channels, or stereo. This nomenclature makes no reference to LFE channels. They may or not be present. As such, both 5.0 and 5.1 sound would be noted here as 3/2. Table 6.1 lists some common shorthand definitions.

Table 6.1 Surround Nomenclature

Front/Back	Channels
1/0	Mono
2/0	Left, Right (stereo)
3/0	Left, Center, Right
2/1	Left, Right, Rear
3/1	Left, Center, Right, Rear
2/2	Left, Right, Right Left, Right Rear
3/2	Left, Center, Right, Right Left, Right Rear

Common Configurations

The first widely available consumer surround sound systems were developed in the 1970s and marketed as having quadraphonic sound. They used 2/2 sound: two front channels and two back channels. Quadraphonic sound never achieved wide success, in part because there were several different quadraphonic systems that were all incompatible with one another.

The early 1980s saw the introduction of new surround technology called Dolby† Surround. This new format offered 3/0 and 3/1 sound, as shown in Figure 6.5. Dolby Surround had the advantage of being compatible with existing stereo equipment. The surround channels were encoded inside existing stereo channels. Regular stereo equipment would not detect the encoded channels, and would just play the left and right channels. Specialized Pro Logic† decoders were able to extract the center and rear sound channels. Dolby Surround matched the surround format being used in cinemas at the time. As such, nearly all stereo VHS videotapes of feature films have Dolby Surround.

One limitation of the 3/1 format is that it uses only a single rear channel, although it may be reproduced using two speakers. As such, you can hear sounds coming from behind you. However, it is not possible to laterally localize, left to right, rearward sounds.

Probably the most popular consumer surround format in use today is the 5.1 configuration, shown in Figure 6.6. The popularity of this format is due greatly to the popularity of DVDs, and the fact that 5.1 sound is DVD's de facto surround format. Because 5.1 has two discrete rear sound channels, listeners can determine the location of sounds coming from behind them. You can hear a plane in the background fly from the left to the right. For an excellent example of 5.1 sound in action, I recommend listening to the bullet-dodging sequence in the *Matrix*. You can hear the bullets flying past you as the camera circles Neo.

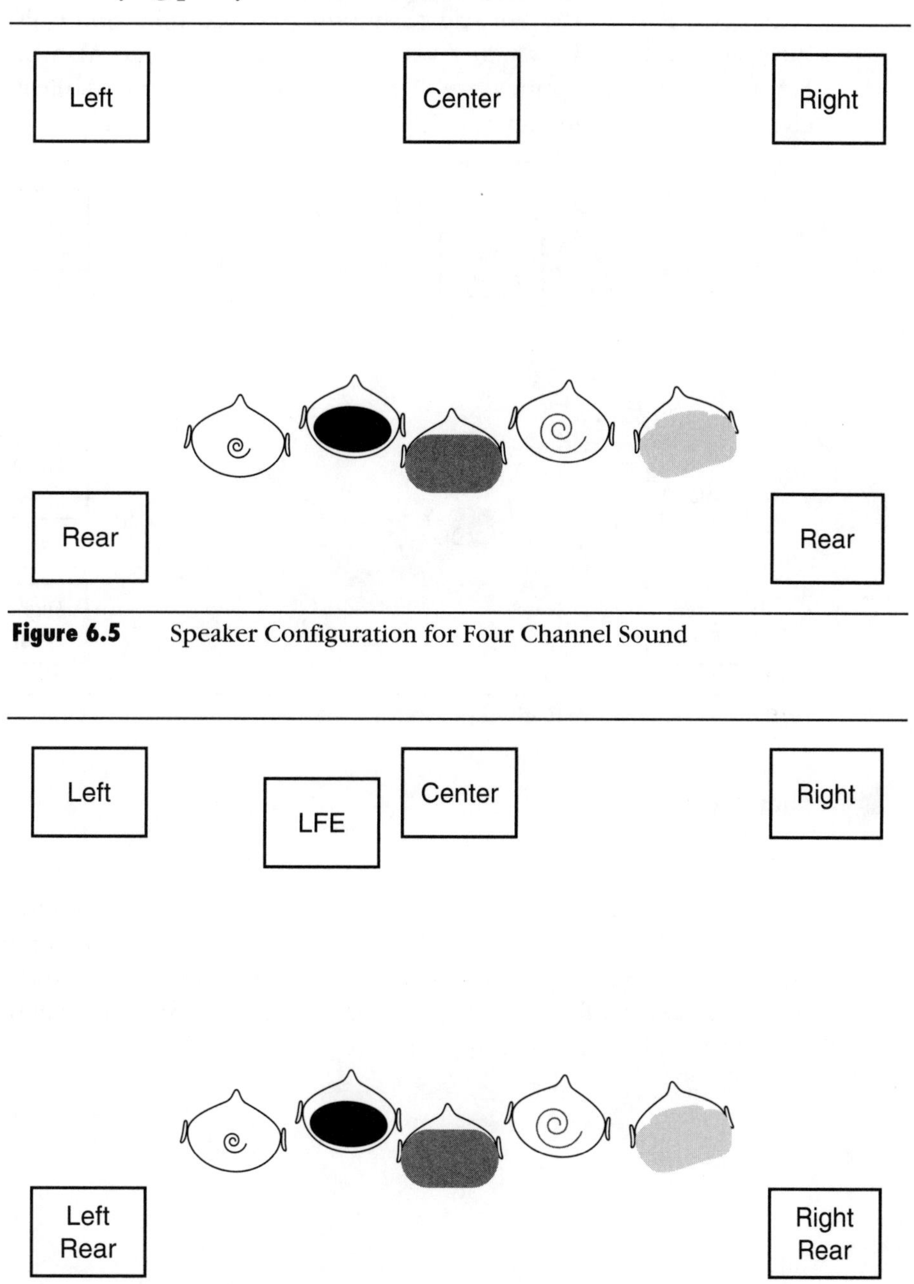

Figure 6.5 Speaker Configuration for Four Channel Sound

Figure 6.6 Speaker Configuration for 5.1 Sound

So, would you ever need more than six channels for surround sound? Well, some people feel the answer is yes, and are experimenting with 10.2 systems that add vertical positioning to the mix. Some PC sound cards now offer 6.1, which adds a rear center channel. Also becoming popular with audiophiles are 7.1 systems, which add dedicated side channels as shown in Figure 6.7.

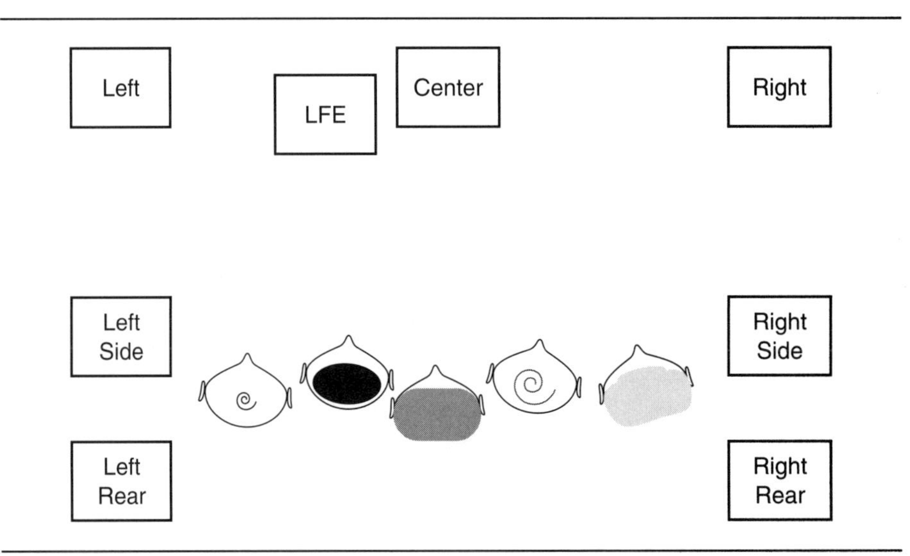

Figure 6.7 Speaker Configuration for 7.1 Sound

Summary

The first sound reproductions were monophonic, which had very limited spatialization capabilities. Stereo systems allow for lateralization: sounds can be localized along a line between the two speakers. Surround sound systems increase localization resolution by positioning speakers behind the listener as well. Many contemporary surround systems, such as 5.1, include a dedicated low frequency effects channel (LFE).

Chapter 7

Digital Audio

"Ahhh, what an awful dream! Ones and zeroes everywhere. And I thought I saw a two!"

—Bender, *Futurama*

Countless television, radio, web, and print advertisements have no doubt convinced most of the world that digital is better than analog. Tucked away in a rapidly-shrinking rainforest is a tribal hunter thinking, "Yes, my spear is good, but maybe it's time I upgrade to a digital spear." But what exactly is digital? Is it really better?

The short answer is that a digital system usually has better performance than a corresponding analog system of the same cost. In this chapter, we will explore why that is true by examining just what digital is.

Digital vs. Analog

The term analog is generally used to describe something that is a representation of something else. For instance, a graph of the ambient temperature over the course of the day is an analog of the actual temperature. In other words, the graph is analogous to the actual temperature. The first computers were analog computers, in that they used mechanical or physical systems as analogies of mathematical problems to be solved.

These first systems used continuously variable parameters. As such, the term analog (in the context of digital vs. analog) has come to refer to systems that use data consisting of continuously variable values. Clocks with hour and minute hands can be considered analog systems: the hands smoothly move from one position to another.

The term digital was originally used to refer to digits or fingers. It is likely that the habit of people counting on their fingers led to the use of the term digit being used to describe whole numbers, namely 0–9. With the development of computers that processed discrete values, 0 or 1, the term digital was further stretched to describe these computers. The term digital in the context of this book refers to systems that use data that is limited to discrete values. For example, a clock with an LED display may be considered a digital system. The minute indicator on such a display is limited to 60 discrete values, 00–59. The minutes displayed on the clock move directly from 12 to 13. There is no intermediate value.

A Metaphor

To better understand the differences between analog and digital, consider a car. This car is stopped at a red light. The light changes to green and the car accelerates to the posted speed limit. The next traffic light turns yellow as the car is approaching. The car accelerates through the intersection, trying to beat the red light, then it slows down again to its previous speed. The next light is already red, so the car slows and comes to a complete stop.

A plot of the car's velocity versus time might look like Figure 7.1.

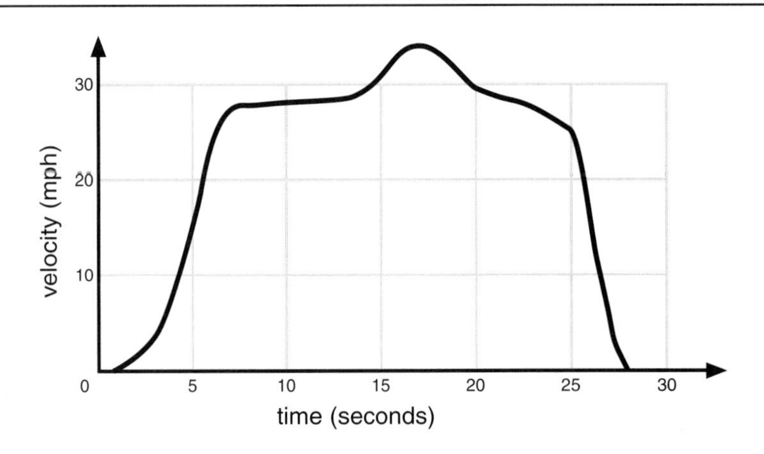

Figure 7.1 Plot of Car's Velocity vs. Time

Both axes, velocity and time, are continuous. The data plot smoothly and contiguously varies in both time and velocity. Figure 7.2 shows how examining any portion of the curve in closer detail always reveals more continuous data. The data line can never have any discontinuities. The car, for instance, never jumped from 1.0 MPH to 2.0 MPH, but rather traversed all the infinitesimal speeds in between. In essence, the graph shows an infinite number of data points. The car's velocity over time is an example of analog data.

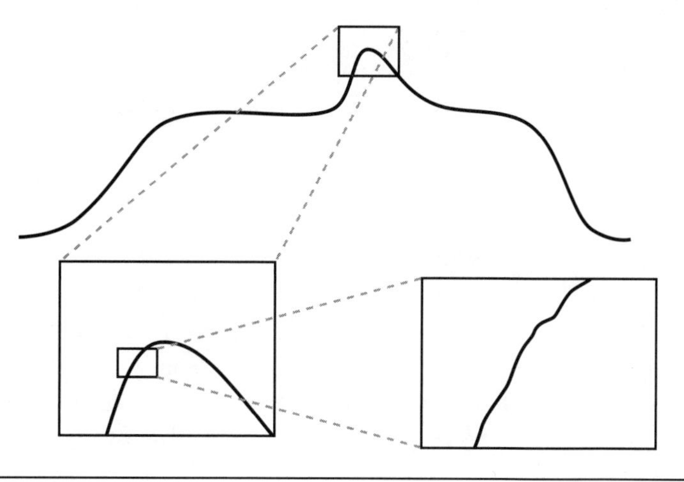

Figure 7.2 Continuous Signal

Now, although we can examine this analog data as finely as we'd like, and indeed gather an infinite amount of data points, it's simply not practical to do so. There simply isn't enough paper or time available to write down an infinite number of data points. Furthermore, there is a limit to how much data the human mind can process at one go. Providing information above and beyond that is not useful.

For example, suppose my goal is to plot the car's velocity over time and display it as I've done in Figure 7.1. My picture is going to be about five inches wide in this book. Furthermore, let us suppose that pictures can be printed by the printing press at a resolution of 300 dots per inch. So really all I need is 5 inches × 300 dpi = 1,500 samples of the analog data. Even if I gather additional data points, I won't be able to display them in my picture.

Now let's suppose I note my speed every five seconds by writing down the reading on my speedometer. The speed is still continuous, but time has now become discrete. We have sampled the original signal and now have a finite amount of data, as shown by the data points in Figure 7.3.

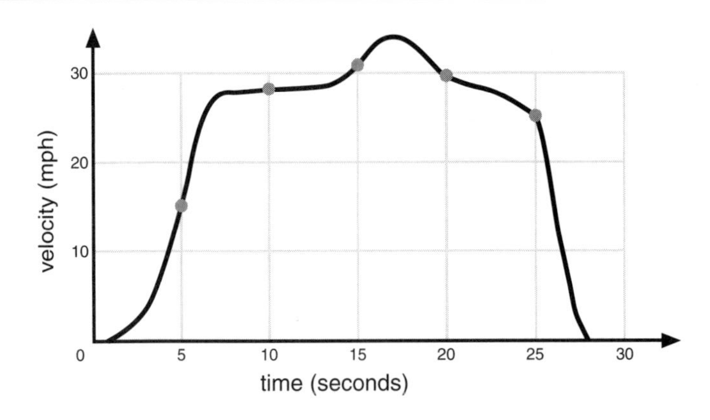

Figure 7.3 Velocity Data Points Sampled Discretely in Time and Continuously in Magnitude.

It can be difficult to read the speedometer with infinite precision, especially when I'm driving, so I'm going to round to the nearest multiple of ten as shown in Figure 7.4. Now the speed has become discretely sampled as well. The data samples show the car jumping from 0 MPH to 10 MPH. At no point in the sampled data is it moving at any speed in between. Of course the car did not really instantaneously and discontinuously change speeds; by discretely sampling the continuous curve, we have lost information. The process of discretely sampling a continuous signal is also known as *digitizing*. Discretely sampling the signal's intensity is commonly known as *quantizing*.

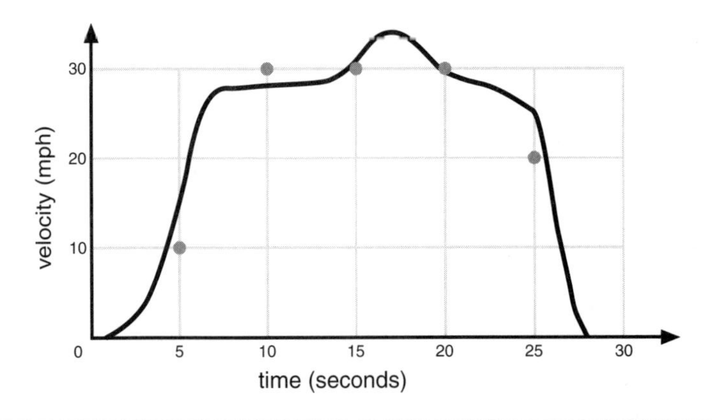

Figure 7.4 Velocity Data Points Sampled Discretely in Time and in Magnitude

We can use the digital data we gathered to recreate the original signal. There are different techniques for reproducing a signal from finite data. Counterintuitive as it may seem, given certain constraints, we can reproduce an exact copy of the original signal with only a finite number of data points. We will discuss the techniques and constraints of such a process in the upcoming section titled "Sampling." For the moment, however, let us use the very simple and crude technique of merely holding the value of the sample data, as illustrated in Figure 7.5.

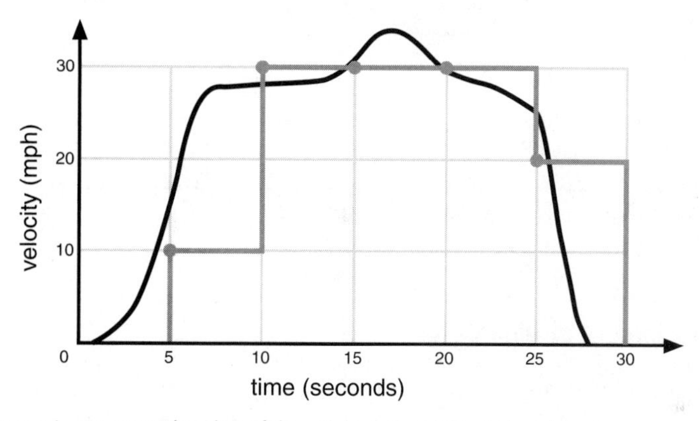

We can create an approximation of the original signal (dark line) from the discrete samples.

Figure 7.5 Signal Generation

The reconstructed signal only crudely resembles the original signal. Yet, with only seven data points, we have been able to approximate a signal containing infinite data. Being finite, it is easy to store these data, and also to move them from place to place without any degradation. These two benefits are the reason digital technology plays such an important role in today's world.

A major drawback of digital technology is that some of the original data may be lost when the original signal is digitized. In Figure 7.5 the acceleration and subsequent deceleration of the car in the 15- to 20-second time interval is not captured in this simple digital reconstruction. To increase accuracy of our reconstruction, we can increase the sampling rate. In Figure 7.6, increasing the sampling rate to once per second and the quantization resolution to every mile per hour captures the speed bump previously lost.

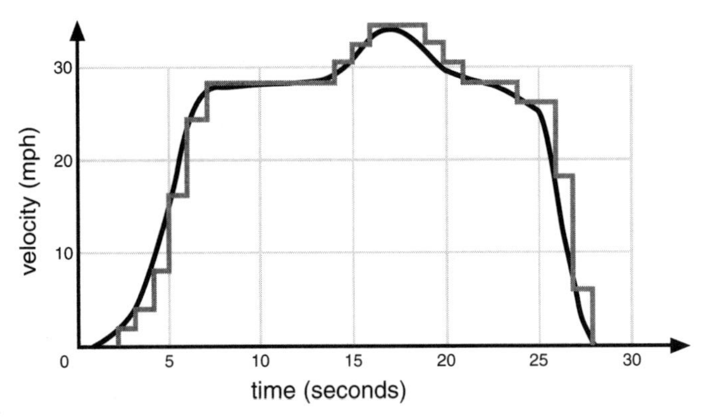

Increasing the sampling rate allows for a more accurate reproduction of the original signal.

Figure 7.6 Increased Sampling Rate

Advantages of Digital

Analog systems are inherently noisy. This noise comes from a variety of sources, such as thermal radiation from the systems' electrical components. The noise they contain is truly unpredictable and can never be completely eliminated. Moreover, each transmission of an analog signal adds further noise. If you make a copy of an analog signal such as an audio cassette tape, the copy has all the noise on the original tape plus additional noise. A copy made of that copy has still more noise and so on.

Conversely, a signal that is created in a purely digital environment can have no noise associated with it. A copy of the digital data will be exactly the same as the original data—no noise or errors are introduced. This ability to make unlimited error-free copies of copies of copies is known as *lossless multigenerational copying*. It is one of the key benefits of digital systems. Lossless multigenerational copying is also the reason why content providers such as music studios are so concerned about piracy of digital media.

So is digital always better than analog? Not necessarily. A high performance 1950 analog audio amplifier may outperform a cheap digital one from the year 2000. However, a high performance digital amplifier cannot only outperform an analog one, but can also offer capabilities impossible with its analog counterpart. As a rule of thumb, a digital system gives better performance than an analog system of the same cost.

Living in an Analog World

The majority of today's audio systems store sound digitally, as we will discuss in more detail in forthcoming chapters in this book. However, sound itself consists of continuously varying pressure waves. In a sense it is inherently analog. The microphones we have examined generate continuous signals; speakers take continuous signals as an input.[1]

In these audio systems the analog input signals must be converted to digital. This conversion is done by devices generically known as *analog to digital converters* (ADCs). The digital signals must eventually be converted back to analog output signals, a process handled by devices known as—yes—*digital to analog* converters (DACs) The analog and digital chain is shown in Figure 7.7.

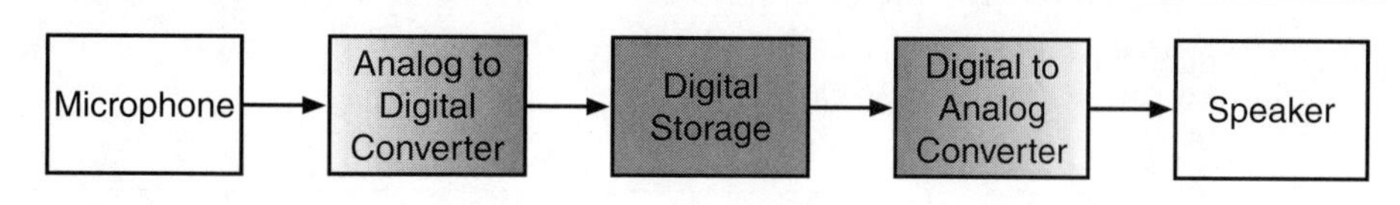

Figure 7.7 ADCs and DACs

The overall fidelity of the system depends on many factors, such as the precision used to store the digital information. However, given that such precision is typically fixed for a given standard—for instance, Compact Discs stores 32-bit digital audio samples at a rate of 44.1 kilohertz—the fidelity between two competing pieces of equipment is largely be a function of the quality of their ADCs and DACs.

We will further investigate the operation of ADCs and DACs by examining the principles between digitizing a signal along the time axis (sampling) and in the magnitude axis (quantization).

Sampling

To gain a better understanding of digital and how it applies to sound, we will first discuss ideal sampling. Following that, we will then explore some of the complications of sampling in real world situations.

[1] This is not—strictly speaking—true. Electricity comes in discrete quanta. A signal which varies from 0 to 1 volt does not do so continuously, but rather in very small but discrete steps. Furthermore, there are theories that not just energy, but space, time, and even gravity also come in discrete bits. These quanta are so small, however, that we can safely treat them as continuous phenomena for the purposes of this book.

Ideal Sampling

It would seem that if we discretely sample a continuous signal, we would not be able to perfectly reproduce the original signal from our samples. Our samples seem to be missing information: namely, the behavior of the signal between the samples. It seems that we could always approximate the original signal by interpolating the missing data, but common sense suggests that it would only be an approximation.

Contrary to intuition, the sampling theorem states that a continuous signal can be sampled without any loss of information, and that the original signal can be exactly reproduced from those samples. There are some caveats. To perfectly reproduce the signal, the sampling rate must be more than twice as high as the highest frequency contained in the signal, as explained in Equation 7.1. For example, if a signal contains frequencies up to but not including 1,000 hertz, then the signal must be sampled at a rate of at least 2,000 hertz.

Equation 7.1 Sampling Theorem

$$f_s > 2\, f_{max}$$

A signal containing a maximum frequency (f_{max}) can be completely characterized using a sample rate f_s at least twice as large.

A first pass of the sampling theorem was suggested by the prolific French mathematician—and military engineer for Napoleon—Augustin-Louis Cauchy in 1841. It was further refined by American engineer Harry Nyquist in his 1924 paper "Certain Topics in Telegraph Transmission Theory." Independently, the Russian engineer V.A. Kotelnikov published a sampling theorem proof in 1933. American mathematician Claude Shannon further codified sampling theory—and indeed founded the field of information theory—in the late 1940s.[2] It is surprising to learn that the theories governing digital signals were worked out in the first half of the 20th century, several decades before the widespread advent of digital equipment!

[2] Shannon was also an accomplished juggler and had quite the sense of humor. In an Omni magazine interview he said, "I was always interested in building things that had funny motions....especially like those dancers I used to see as a young man on the stage burlesque theatre! They had interesting motions. Cheap joke!"

Nyquist Nomenclature

Given a sampling frequency f_s, the time interval between two samples is $T_s = 1/f_s$. In acknowledgement of Nyquist's groundbreaking work, Shannon referred to this term as the Nyquist interval. Today it is much more common to refer to the sampling rate or frequency than it is to the sampling interval. As such, f_s is sometimes referred to as the Nyquist rate, Nyquist limit, or Nyquist frequency. However, all three of these terms are also used by some people to refer to the maximum frequency (f_{max}) that can be properly sampled given a sampling frequency, which can be quite confusing!

In this book, I use the term *Nyquist frequency* to refer to f_s, the minimum sampling rate required to properly sample a signal. I use the term *Nyquist limit* to refer to f_{max}.

Critical Sampling

Before we step through the details of reconstructing a signal from samples, we are first going to examine a corner case of the sampling theorem.

The case when condition $f_s = 2\ f_{max}$ is known as *critical sampling.* As we can see in Figure 7.8, it is possible to critically sample a signal and obtain enough information to fully reconstruct the original signal.

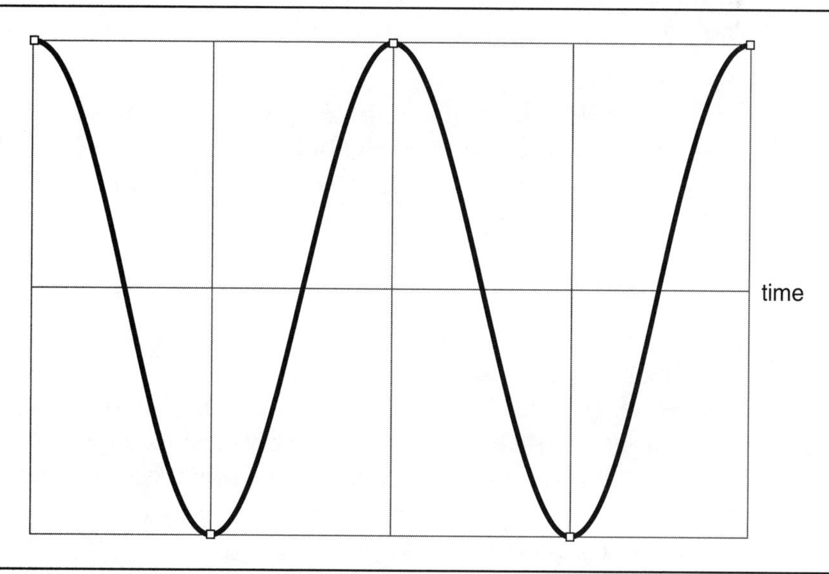

Figure 7.8 Successful Critical Sampling

However, if the original signal is shifted 90 degrees in phase, all our samples come at as zero magnitude, as shown in Figure 7.9. It is impossible for us to recreate the original signal from these zero magnitude samples. For all we know, the original signal could be f(t) = 0 or it could be a sine wave at f_{max} of magnitude *n*, where *n* could be any value.

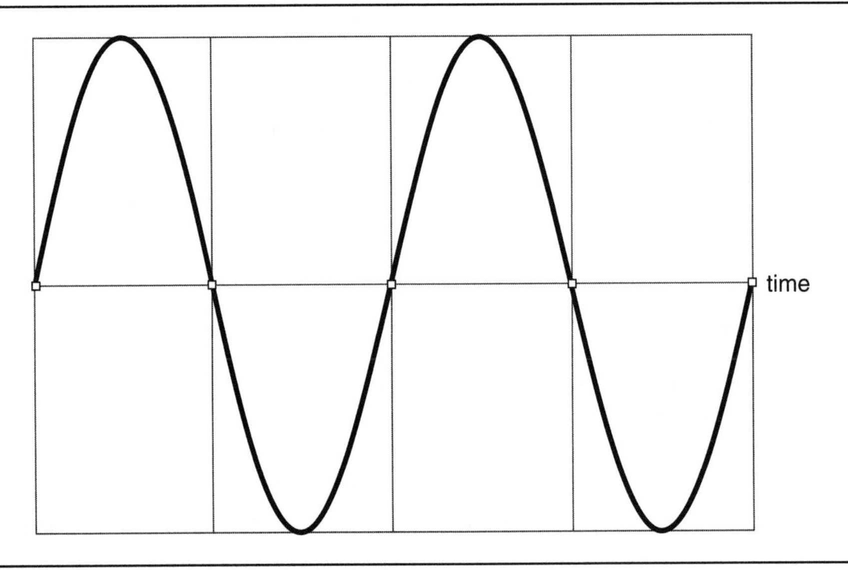

Figure 7.9 Unsuccessful Critical Sampling

In real world conditions with complex signals, this critical sampling corner case may occur very rarely, but it is still possible that it may happen. We thus need to remove the equality condition, and say that for a signal to be properly sampled $f_s > 2 \times f_{max}$.

Aperiodic Sampling

We have so far only considered the scenario of regularly spaced samples. The periodicity of the samples have allowed us to speak freely of a sampling frequency, because f = 1/T. Nonuniform also known as aperiodic, sampling is also possible. Given certain constraints, aperiodic signals can also fully characterize a signal: the original signal can be losslessly reconstructed. However, because most digital systems use uniform sampling, we will not be discussing aperiodic sampling in this text.

Reconstructing Signals

So we've said that we can reconstruct a signal, but how?

For our example, our sampling frequency is fixed at 10 hertz. Our original signal will contain 2-hertz, 4.9-hertz, and 5-hertz pure tones. This original signal and its spectrum are shown in Figure 7.10.

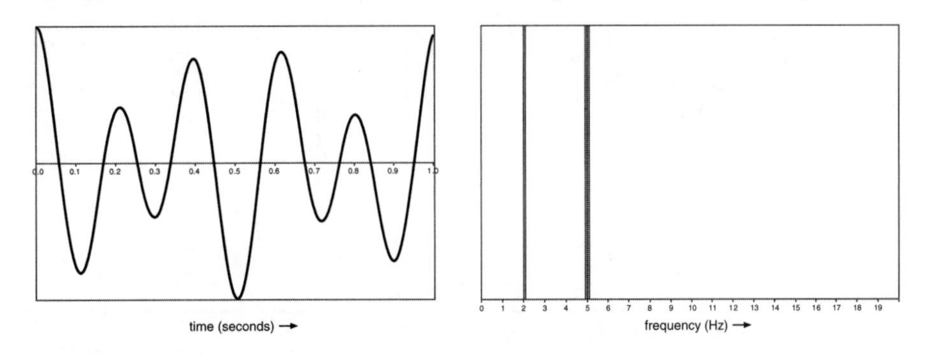

Figure 7.10 Original Signal

Our sampling rate has been set at 10 hertz. So what is the highest frequency we can safely sample? Given that $f_s > 2 \times f_{max}$ we can infer that $f_{max} < f_s / 2$. In this case, the highest frequency must be less than 5 hertz. However, our original signal contains a 5-hertz component! One option would be to increase our sampling rate. Because that is held fixed in this example, we must take the other option: remove frequencies from the original signal that we cannot properly sample.

This removal process is typically handled by running the original signal through a low-pass filter (LPF) that has a cutoff frequency at half the sampling rate. This process is also known as *band-limiting*, because the process of low-pass filtering the signal limits its bandwidth. Specifically, the bandwidth is $f_s / 2 - 0 = f_s /2$.

More precisely, the cutoff frequency needs to be less than half the sampling rate, to avoid critical sampling. However, because real-world filters are so much noisier than perfect theoretical filters, the nitpicking inequality can be safely ignored when specifying practical cutoff frequencies.

Band-limiting is a very common first step in real-world ADCs. Failing to band-limit a signal means that we would not be able to properly sample the signal due to a phenomenon known as *aliasing*. We will discuss band-limiting further in the next section.

For this example, we need to band-limit our signal to be just below 5 hertz. The resulting signal is shown in Figure 7.11. It is this band-limited signal that we can reproduce with perfect accuracy from uniform samples. Note that the 5-hertz component of the original signal has been removed.

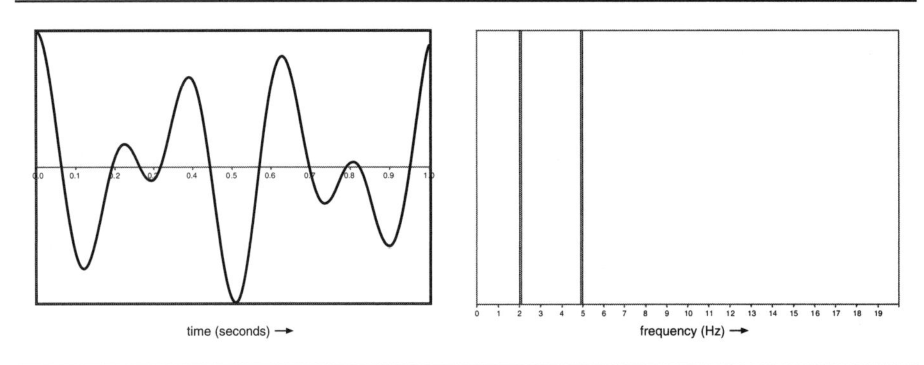

Figure 7.11 Band-limited Signal

If we go ahead and sample the band-limited signal at the indicated 10-hertz sampling rate, we get the samples shown in Figure 7.12. Imagine that we store the value of these samples on a hard drive or transmit them over the Internet. A recipient of this sample data would not have access to the original analog signal. They would need to recreate it somehow using only these samples.

As a first step to reproducing the signal, let us hold the value of the samples across the sampling interval, as shown in Figure 7.13. It is known as a zero-order hold, and is a very crude approximation of the original signal. From visual inspection, we might guess that we could get a more accurate version of the original signal by simply increasing the sampling rate. The stair steps of our zero order hold recreation would become much finer. Increasing our number of samples would certainly increase the accuracy of our held sample reproduction, but sampling theory tells us that we already have enough data to faithfully reproduce our band-limited signal. So we don't need any more samples. But how do we get rid of the blockiness of our zero-order hold recreation?

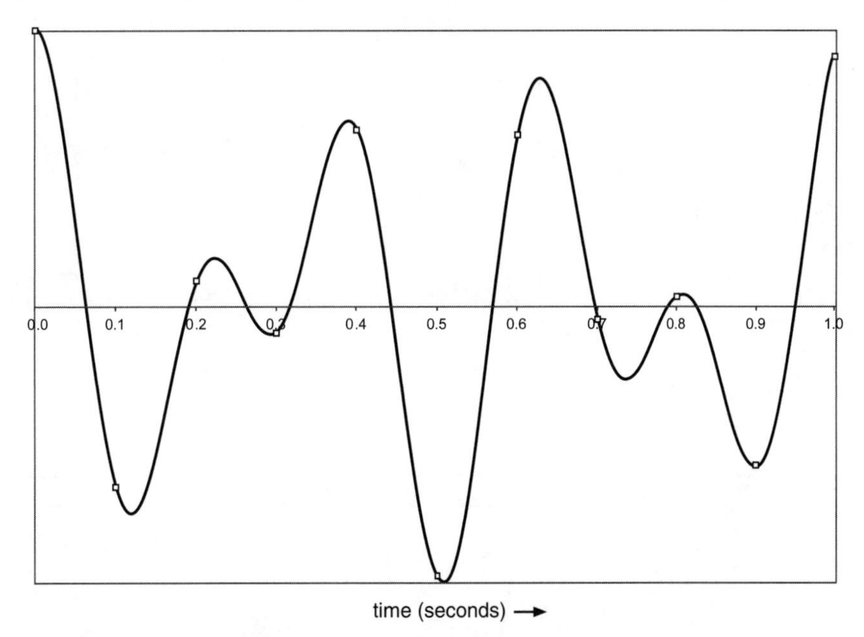

Figure 7.12 Sampled Signal

Looking at the frequency domain, we see that our zero-order hold recreation contains frequency components above $f_s/2$. Ah-ha! We know that the signal was band-limited before sampling, so we know that those frequency components were not part of the sampled signal! If we take the same low-pass filter we applied to the original signal prior to sampling it, and apply that same filter to our zero-order hold, we get the signal shown in Figure 7.14. This reproduction of the band-limited signal we originally sampled is completely accurate. Success!

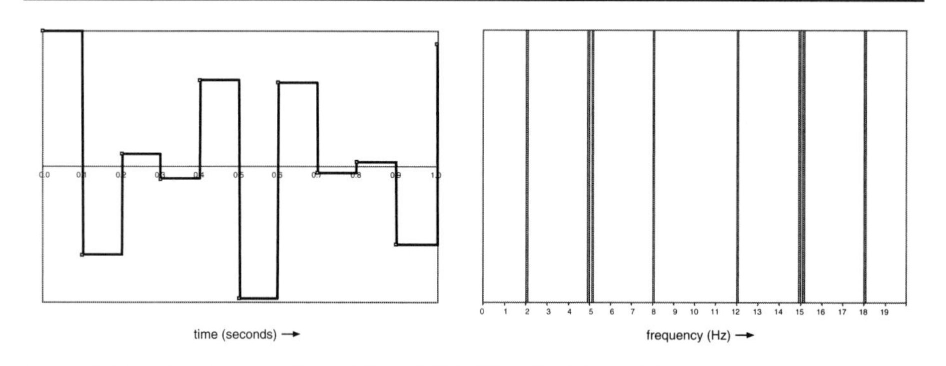

Figure 7.13 Zero-Order Hold

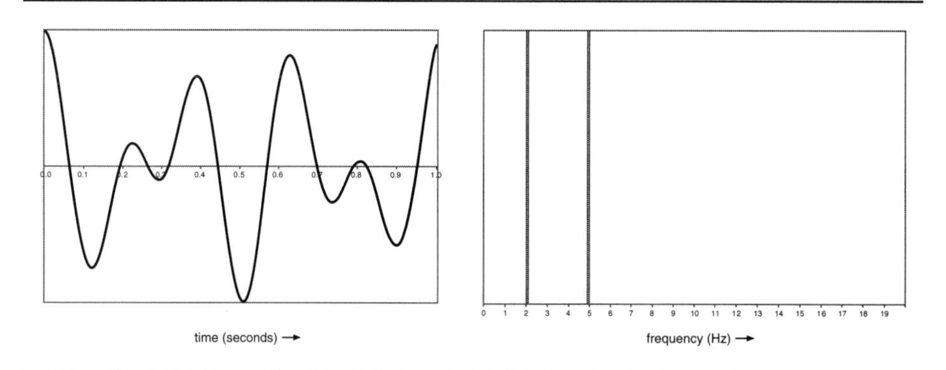

Figure 7.14 Reconstructed Signal

This LPF is known as a reconstruction filter, as it is used in the reconstruction of our analog signal from digital data.

For this initial discussion of signal reconstruction, we ignored some subtleties for the sake of conveying a high-level understanding of digital to analog conversion. We will discuss signal reconstruction in further detail in "Real World Sampling" later in this chapter.

Aliasing

So what happens if we don't band-limit the signal prior to sampling? What if we allow our signal to contain frequencies greater than half the sampling rate?

As an example, suppose we sample a 7-hertz signal at a rate of 10 hertz. The 7-hertz signal is well above the 5-hertz Nyquist limit, so we fear that something untoward is going to happen. And, indeed, when we try to reproduce the original signal using the technique described above, we create a 3-hertz signal, and not the original 7-hertz signal! This process is shown in Figure 7.15

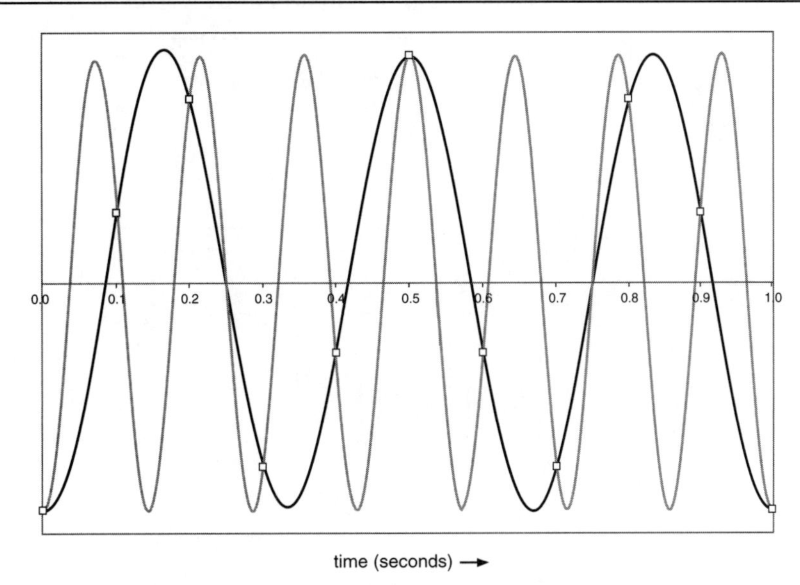

A 7-hertz signal (gray) is sampled at 10 hertz (squares). Attempting to reconstruct the signal from the samples results in a 3-hertz signal (black), not the original 7 hertz.

Figure 7.15 Aliasing

This phenomenon is known as aliasing, in reference to the way the reconstructed signals masquerade as signals that are different than the original signal. In the above example, the samples of the 7-hertz signal are indistinguishable from samples of a 3-hertz signal.

To gain a better understanding of what causes aliasing, let's review the signal reconstruction process, but this time we will pay closer attention to the frequency domain.

If we have a signal containing frequencies lower than $2f_s$, we can safely sample it at fs. The ideal sampling procedure is mathematically equivalent to multiplying the signal by a unity amplitude impulse train. A *unity amplitude impulse train* is simply a signal that has a magnitude of 1 at the times we want to take samples, and 0 at all other times. The sample times are 0, T, 2T, 3T, …, where T is the sampling interval, which is the reciprocal of the sampling frequency: $1/f_s$.

Multiplication of two functions in the time domain is equivalent to convolving their spectra. We will not go into the math of convolution at the moment, but the key takeaway in the sampling scenario is that duplicates and reflections of the original spectrum are created at multiples of f^s. This result can be seen graphically in Figure 7.16.

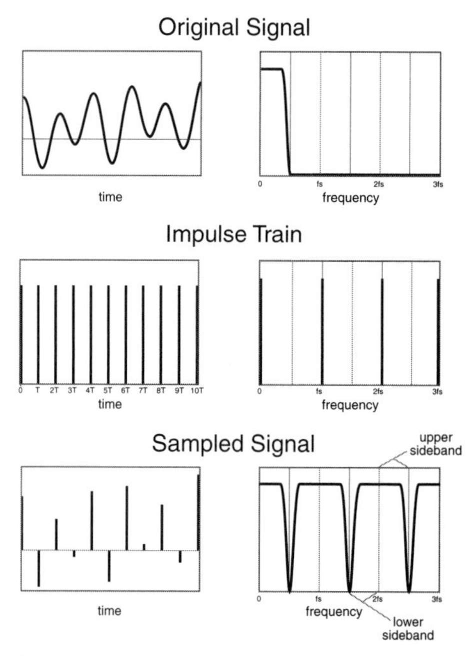

The original signal (top left) is multiplied by a unity amplitude impulse train (middle left) to produce the sampled signals (bottom left). In the frequency domain the same process is represented by taking the original spectrum (top right) convolving it with the impulse train (middle right) to produce copies of the original spectrum (lower right).

Figure 7.16 Sampling

The sampling process has created new frequencies not in the original signal! Specifically, it has created *upper sideband* frequencies, which are copies of the original spectrum shifted by $k * f_s$, where k is any integer. It has also created lower sideband frequencies, which are mirror images of the original spectrum shifted by $0.5 k * f_s$, where k is any odd integer.

This replication of the spectrum is why we needed to apply an LPF as the ultimate stage of reconstructing a sampled signal. The filter removes the copies (sidebands) and leaves us with the original spectrum (baseband) and hence the original signal.

Now let's consider the spectrum of a signal that contains frequencies that are greater than half the sampling frequency, shown in Figure 7.17.

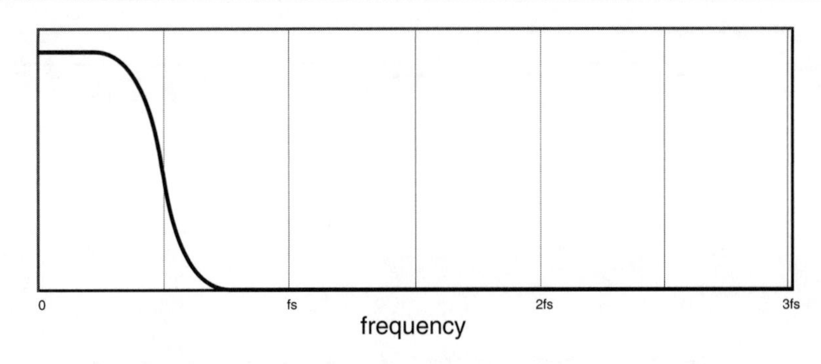

Figure 7.17 Spectrum of Undersampled Signal

When we sample the signal, we again get an infinite number of copies of the original spectrum. Previously, each sideband copy spanned a bandwidth of less than $f_s/2$. In our current example, however, the sideband signals exceed that width and actually overlap one another, as shown in Figure 7.18.

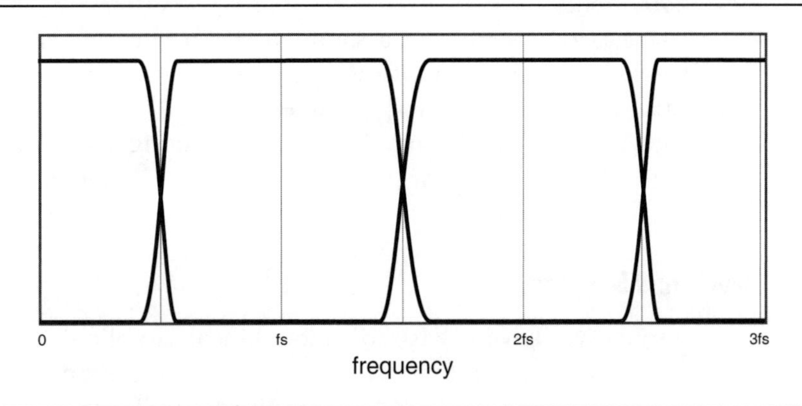

Figure 7.18 Overlapping Sidebands

When we apply our LPF, we remove all frequencies greater than $f_s/2$, but in this scenario our reconstructed signal contains elements of the first lower sideband signal, as depicted by the dotted line in Figure 7.19. This *foldback* of the sideband means that our reconstructed signal contains low frequency signals that did not exist in the original signal. They are aliases of the high frequency signals, which are reproduced as lower frequency signals during signal reconstruction.

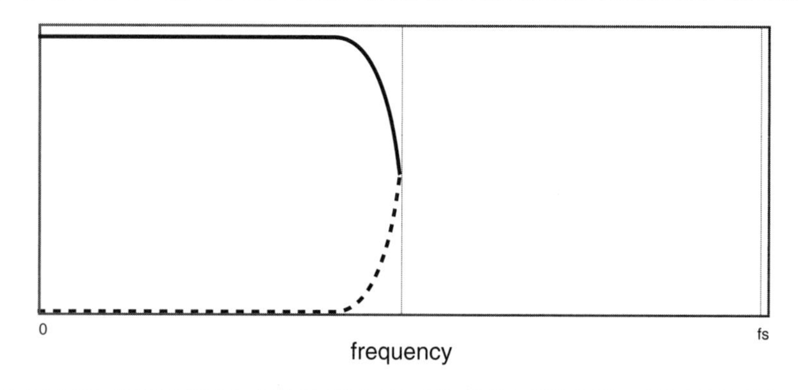

Figure 7.19 Foldback

We saw this foldback in our earlier example of sampling a 7-hertz signal at 10 hertz. When we reconstructed the signal from the samples, we created a 3-hertz signal. The higher 7-hertz frequency was aliased as a 3-hertz frequency.

Aliasing is undesirable. If a sampled signal contains aliased frequencies, it is impossible to remove them; there is no way to distinguish between aliased components and genuine signals.

Luckily, aliasing can be avoided by band-limiting a signal to $f_s/2$ before sampling it. Because this low-pass filter prevents aliasing, it is also known as an *anti-aliasing filter*.

Real World Sampling

The sampling we have discussed so far is ideal sampling; real world sampling is a bit more complex. If all you're looking for is a basic understanding of sampling, you may want to skip this section for now, going straight to quantization and coming back to this section later.

[3] Do not pass "GO." Do not collect $200.

When we discussed aliasing, we used a unity amplitude impulse train: a time-continuous signal that has a magnitude of 1 at the sample points, and 0 at all other times. This impulse train was used to generate a time-continuous signal that had the amplitude of the original signal at the sample points and 0 at all other times. It was this signal that had multiple copies and reflections of the original spectrum, which we were able to remove via an LPF.

Building a physical circuit capable of generating a true impulse train with a spike which is infinitesimally narrow is virtually impossible. Therefore we cannot use truly instantaneous sampling n the real world. Thus, most physical DACs reconstruct signals by holding the sample values to create a time-continuous staircase signal, as we did in Figure 7.13, and apply an LPF to get the final reconstructed figure.

Compared to the ideal impulse-train method, the sample-hold reconstruction's spectrum is attenuated by the magnitude of sin $(\pi f/f_s)/(\pi f/f_s)$. The function $\sin(\pi x)/(\pi x)$ is generically known as sinc(x). The magnitude of this function is shown in Figure 7.20.

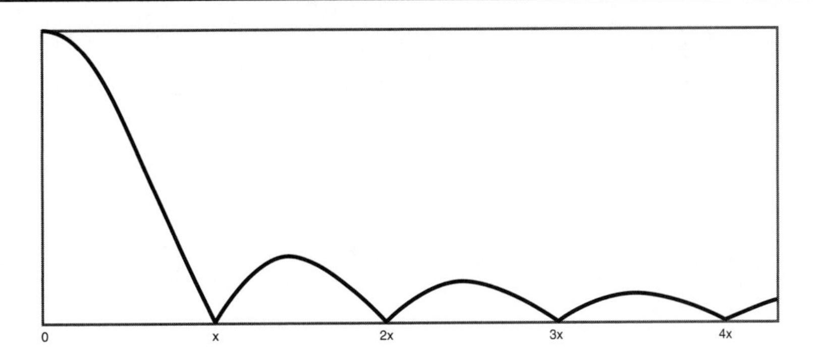

Figure 7.20 Magnitude of sinc(x)

The $\text{sinc}(f/f_s)$ attention factor of the zero-order hold has the effect of reducing the magnitude of the sidebands and the high frequencies of the baseband as well, seen in Figure 7.21. At the highest baseband frequency $(f_s / 2)$, the sinc-induced attention means the signal is roughly 4 dB down from maximum.

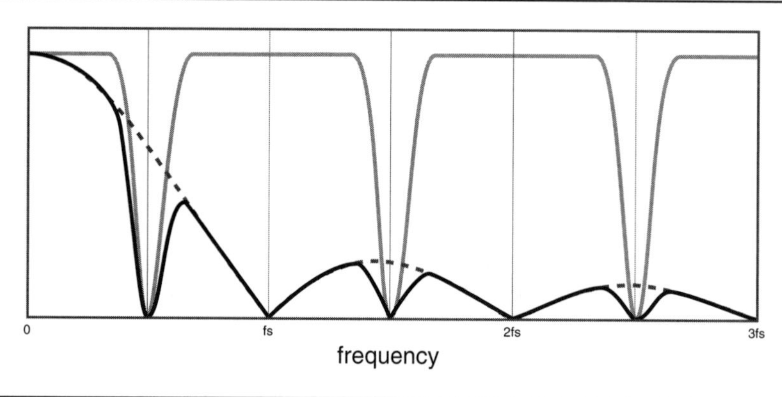

Figure 7.21 Zero-order Hold Reconstruction

Simply applying an LPF as the final step of reconstruction does not result in an accurate reproduction of the original signal. The higher frequencies are attenuated, as shown in Figure 7.22.

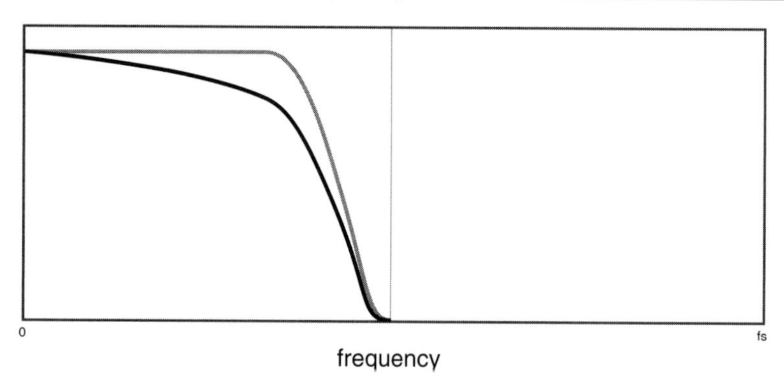

Using a simple LPF for reconstruction via zero-hold (black line) does not reproduce the original signal's spectrum (gray).

Figure 7.22 Low-Pass Filtering a Zero-order Hold

To get an accurate recreation of the original signal, we need to use a reconstruction filter that boosts the high frequencies to compensate for the sinc attenuation, such as the one in Figure 7.23.

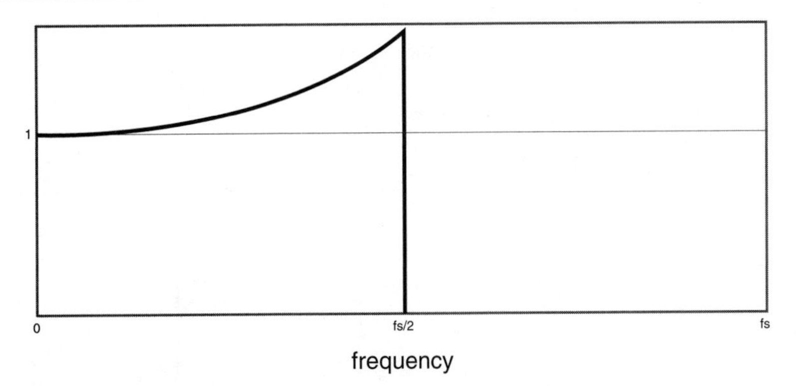

This reconstruction filter is a low-pass filter that removes sideband copies and also boosts the high frequencies to compensate for sinc attenuation brought on through zero-order hold reproduction.

Figure 7.23 Sinc-compensated Reconstruction Filter

Aperture Effect

The sinc attenuation of a zero-order hold we have just described is known as the *aperture effect.* In this context, aperture is defined as the ratio of the sample hold time (τ) over the sample interval (T_s), as shown in Figure 7.24.

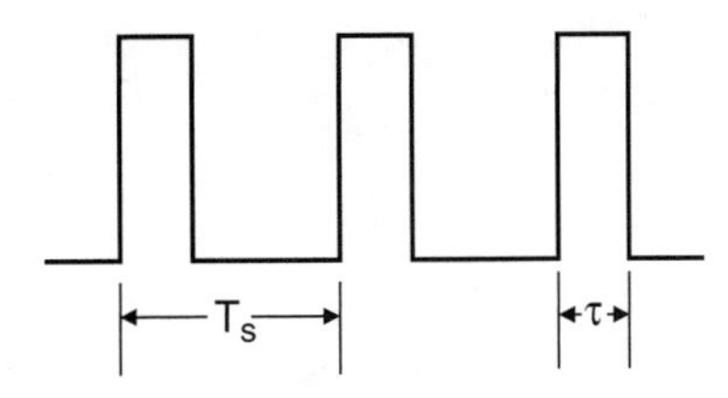

Aperture is defined as τ / T_S.

Figure 7.24 Aperture

In the zero-order hold case we have previously described, the sample values are held across the entire duration of the sampling interval. So $\tau = T_s$ and the aperture is $\tau / T_s = T_s / T_s = 100\%$.

We can reduce the aperture effect, or attenuation of the higher baseband frequencies, by decreasing the aperture. Because the sample interval is fixed, our only option is to decrease the hold time of samples. For example, by holding the sample values for only half as long as the sampling interval, we reduce the aperture to 50 percent, as shown in Figure 7.25.

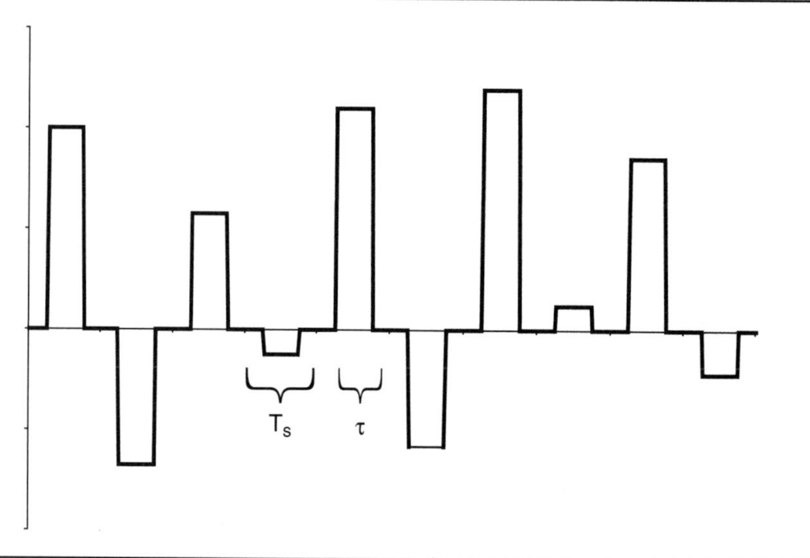

Figure 7.25 50 Percent Aperture

The effect of the aperture on the sinc attenuation of the baseband can be seen graphically in Figure 7.26. Generically, the attenuation is given by sinc((τ / T_s)*(f/f_s)). As we decrease the aperture, we get closer and closer to the mathematically ideal unity amplitude pulse gain. In practical applications, decreasing the aperture requires the use of more complex circuitry that costs more and is more sensitive to noise.

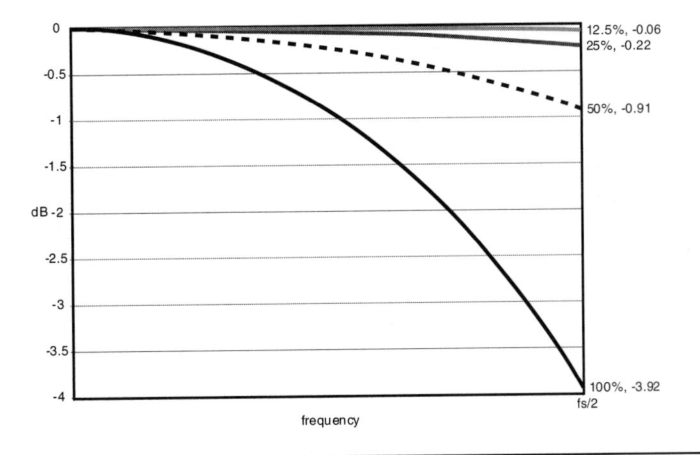

Figure 7.26 Aperture Effect

Quantization

We have just finished a discussion of sampling, which is the conversion of a time-continuous signal into a finite number of discrete data. In our sampling discussion, we placed no restrictions on the amplitude of the data samples. Because the magnitude was continuous, an infinite number of different values were possible.

Quantization is the conversion of a magnitude-continuous signal into a signal which only has values that are an integer multiple of a minimum value, known as a quantum.[4]

Quantization and sampling are separate topics, although most digital audio systems use both processes. Quantization is digitization of a signal's magnitude; sampling is digitization of a signal's time. In the following discussion of quantization, we assume the signal is time-continuous and no sampling is occurring.

A simple example of quantization is shown in Figure 7.27. A continuous signal with a signal smoothly varying in magnitude between 0.0 and 1.0 is quantized into a signal which has only eight levels, 0 through 7. Once quantized, the signal is stored and transmitted digitally. In this case, it could be stored as binary numbers in the range 000b through 111b.

---

[4] The term "quantum leap" is typically used to indicate a giant stride forward. It's interesting that a quantum is the smallest possible interval and hence a quantum leap is really the smallest possible leap you could make.

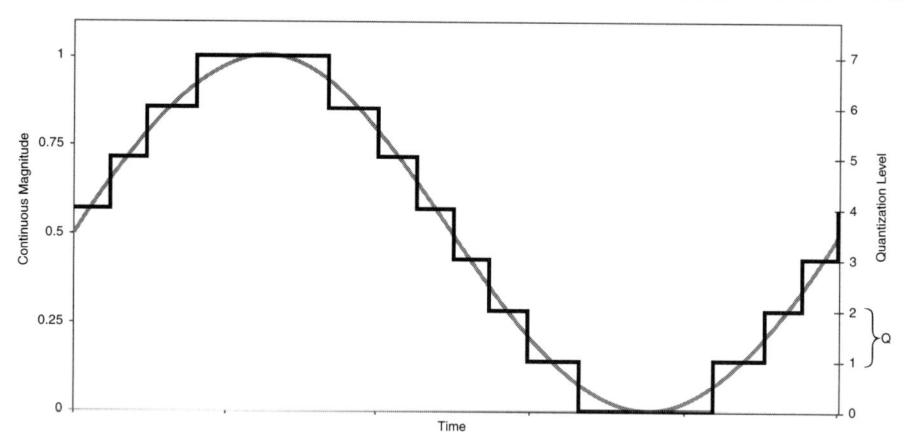

A signal that continuously varies in magnitude (gray) from 0 to 1 is quantized to eight levels (black).

Figure 7.27 Quantization

The term Q is used to describe the continuous magnitude range covered by a single quantization range. In Figure 7.27, we can determine Q by taking the range of continuous input values covered (1.0 - 0.0) and dividing that by the number of quantization levels (8) minus 1 to get $Q = 1/7 \approx 0.143$.

To reconstruct our quantized signal, we map each quantization level back to an output magnitude. In this example, the reconstructed output voltage for quantization level n would be calculated by computing $n \times Q$. For instance, quantization level 3 would map to $3 \times (1/7) \approx 0.429$. Note that our reconstructed signal looks like a staircase, as seen in Figure 7.28.

In sampling, we were able to losslessly reconstruct a signal given certain constraints. In quantization, by contrast, we are never able to completely recreate the original signal, only an approximation of it.

The accuracy of our reconstructed signal is greatly dependent upon the number of quantization levels we use. The more levels we use, the smaller our stair steps become. If we use a sufficiently large number of levels, the reconstructed signal is humanly indistinguishable from the original signal.

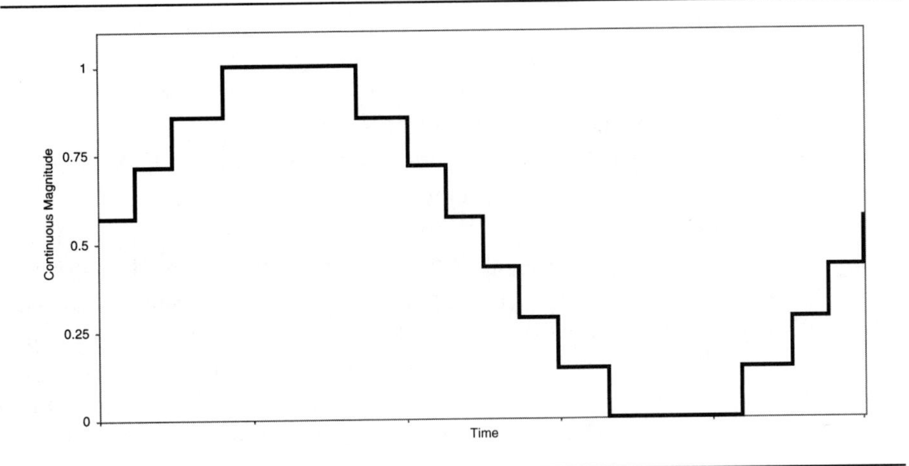

Figure 7.28 Reconstructed Signal

Quantization Errors

The difference in magnitude between our original signal and our quantized signal at any given point is known as a *quantization error.* Quantization errors are shown graphically in Figure 7.29. The quantization error is always in the range of ± Q/2. In other words, the maximum error is half the quantization interval. It makes sense: the quantized value can never get further away from the original value than half the quantization interval, because then it would get mapped to the next quantization level.

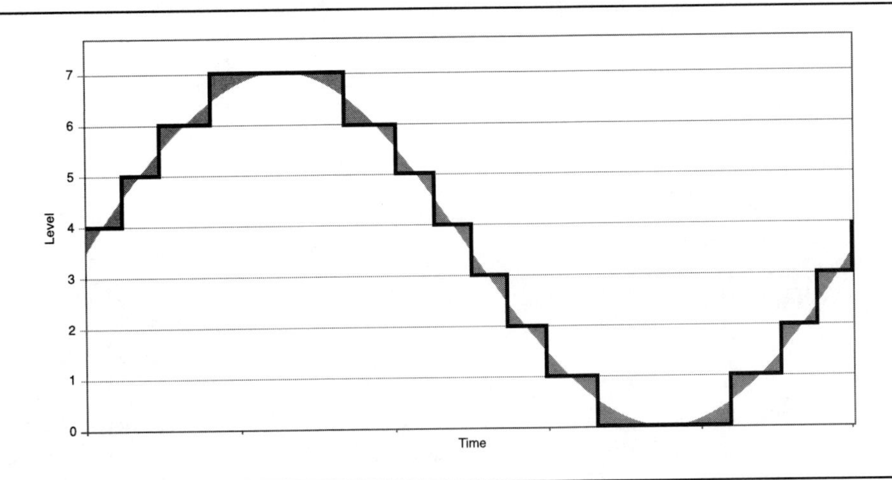

Figure 7.29 Quantization Errors

Quantization errors are not true noise—they are deterministic. If you run the same input signal through a simple quantizer, you get the exact same quantization errors each time. For a high magnitude complex signal, such as music, the quantization errors are randomly distributed in the range -Q/2 to +Q/2. The errors sound very much like low-level white noise, which is not too unpleasant to human hearing.

However, in some situations the relationship between the quantization errors and the signal is very apparent; therefore, the errors and the signal is very apparent; the errors and signal are said to be correlated. Consider, for example, a signal that varies only by a very small amount, such as that shown in Figure 7.30. Even though the signal varies in intensity, it is a small variation less than a quantization interval. All of the signal's intensities map to the same quantization level.

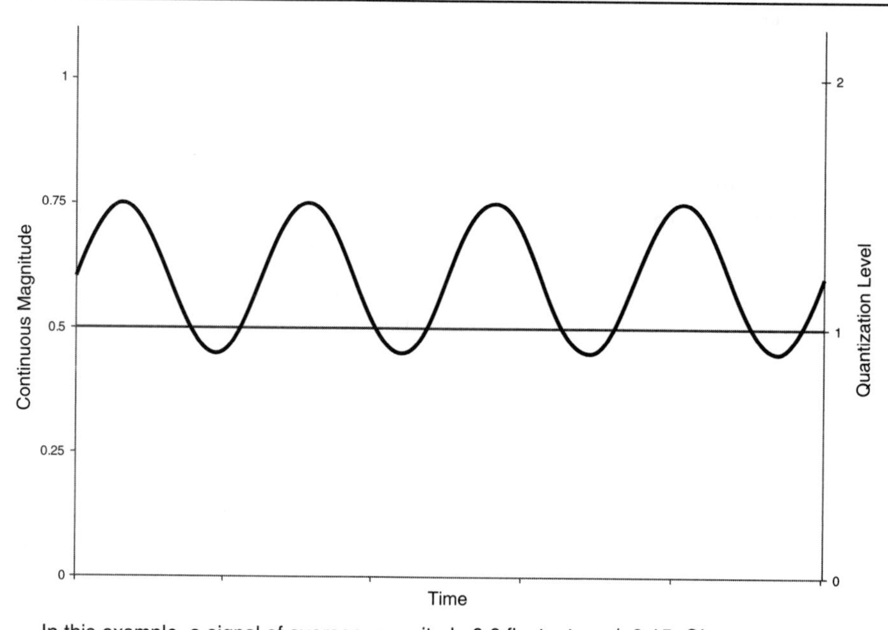

In this example, a signal of average magnitude 0.6 fluctuates +/- 0.15. Given three sample levels, the signal is always quantized to level 1.

Figure 7.30 Signal with Low-Level Variation

In this case, the quantization error is identical to the input signal! The errors and the signal are extremely correlated, causing distortion. A consequence of this distortion is the generation of harmonics of the original signal. In a practical system, which includes sampling in addition to quantization, the distortion-generated harmonics are introduced after the anti-aliasing filter has been applied, so it is very possible that aliasing will occur.

Dithering

We reduce the distortion by decorrelating, or removing the relationship, between the quantization errors and the original signal. The most common way to do this decorrelation is to add low-level noise to the quantization system.

Consider, for example, if we added noise—random values—in the range of ±Q/3 to our signal. It might look something like Figure 7.31. The noise we're adding in this context is known as *dither*. The process of adding low-level noise to a signal is known as *dithering*.

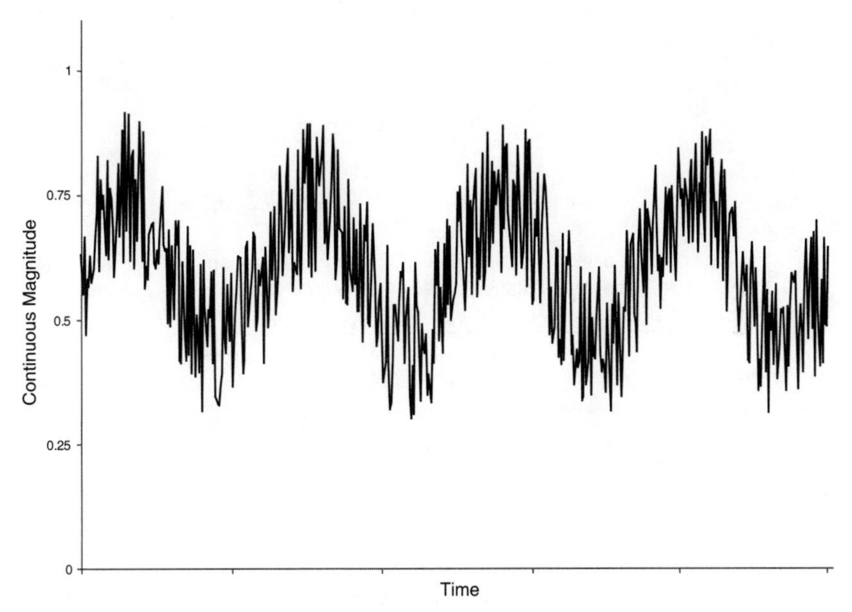

This signal is the same as Figure 7.30 with random noise of magnitude +/-Q/3 added to it.

Figure 7.31 Noise Added to Signal

If we ran this noisy signal through the quantizer, it would be randomly mapped to two different quantization levels, as shown in Figure 7.32. The quantization errors are now effectively random and decorrelated from the original signal. We have added noise to the system, but reduced distortion. The low-level noise we have added is perceptually much less objectionable than the distortion we had previously, so dithering is used almost universally in audio quantizers.

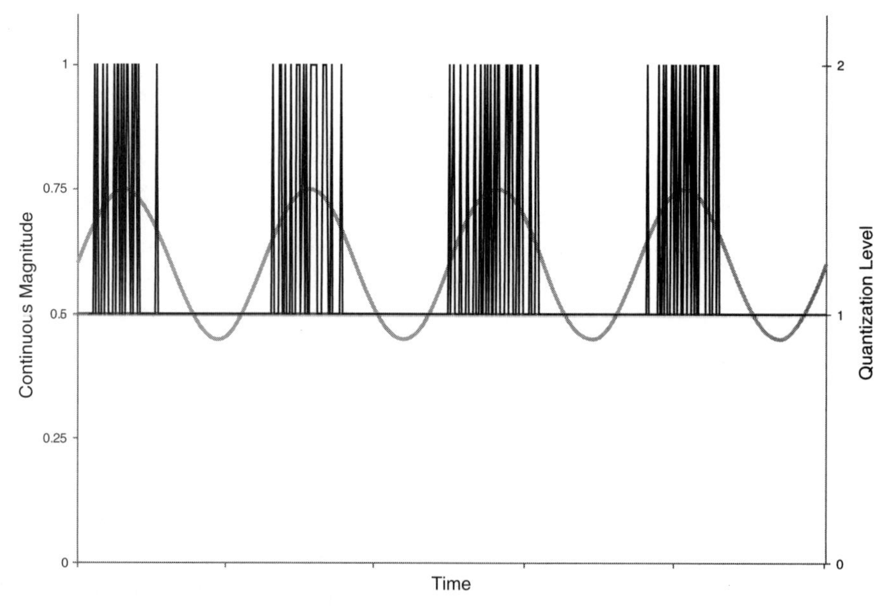

Quantization of the dithered signal in random quantization to level 1 and level 2 (black). Note the relationship between the quantization levels and the original signal (gray).

Figure 7.32 Quantized Dithered Signal

As an alternative way to look at dither, consider that our original signal had an average value of 0.6 volt. Without dither, this signal was quantized entirely to level 1 as depicted in Figure 7.30 and would subsequently be reconstructed as a 0.5-volt signal.

With dither, the signal is mapped to both level 1 and level 2. In fact, on average 20 percent of the time it is mapped to level 2 and 80 percent of the time to level 1. The reconstructed signal thus has a value of 1.0 volt 20 percent of the time and a value of 0.5 volts 80 percent of the time. The average level of the reconstructed signal is 0.6 volt—the same as our original signal. We have captured the original average magnitude of the signal with greater precision than ±Q/2, or 0.25 volt. In this sense, we have been able to increase the accuracy of our system by adding noise. We saw similar examples of how adding noise can increase signal perception in our earlier discussion of the human hearing system.

Bit Depth

Most quantization systems use a number of quantization levels that are a power of two because such numbers take full advantage of a fixed number of binary digits, or bits. With this assumption, for a given number of bits n, the corresponding number of quantization levels is given by 2^n. Three bits would give us $2^3 = 8$ levels.

It is common to refer to the depth of a quantizer in terms of the numbers of bits it uses to represent different levels. A quantizer with 256 levels would use $\log_2 256 = 8$ bits and, as such, would be said to have a depth or bit-depth of 8.

To get a feel for how much precision different quantizer depths give us, let's say we have a continuous input signal that corresponds to the height of a climber on Mt. Everest. We map the elevation range of 0 to 29,035 feet and quantize it to varying degrees of precision. If we had a 1-bit quantizer, we could specify the climber's elevation with a precision of ±14,517.5 feet. When he was below 14,517.5 feet, his elevation would map to quantization level 0. Elevations above that height would map to quantization level 1. Although it's not immediately obvious from this example, a 1-bit quantizer can actually be quite useful.

If we increase the precision of our quantizer to 8 bits, we can specify the climber's height with a precision of ±57 feet. Much better! Going to 16-bit depth, the same as used on audio Compact Discs, we can specify elevation with a precision of ±2.7 inches. That would probably be sufficient for most climbing expeditions! Going even further, we can use 24-bit depth (as supported by DVD-Audio) to get our accuracy down to ± 1/100th of an inch! With that level of precision, we could actually observe the mountain's elevation change just due to compression and rarefaction of the mountain in response to tidal forces.

Digital Clipping

Another factor that affects the accuracy of our quantization is our selection of the range of input values. Continuing our Mt. Everest example, if our climber had traveled to Death Valley—which is as much as 282 feet below sea level—his elevation would have always been mapped to quantization level 0, because it was below our specified range of 0 to 29,035 feet. Even using the 24-bit quantizer with its 0.001-inch accuracy, the climber could travel up and down the dunes in the valley, and the quantizer would continue to report his elevation as 0 feet. Similarly, if he climbed on board an airplane, as soon as his elevation exceeded 29,035 feet, the quantizer would simply map the excessive heights to the maximum quantization level.

This phenomenon, known as digital clipping, is shown in Figure 7.33.

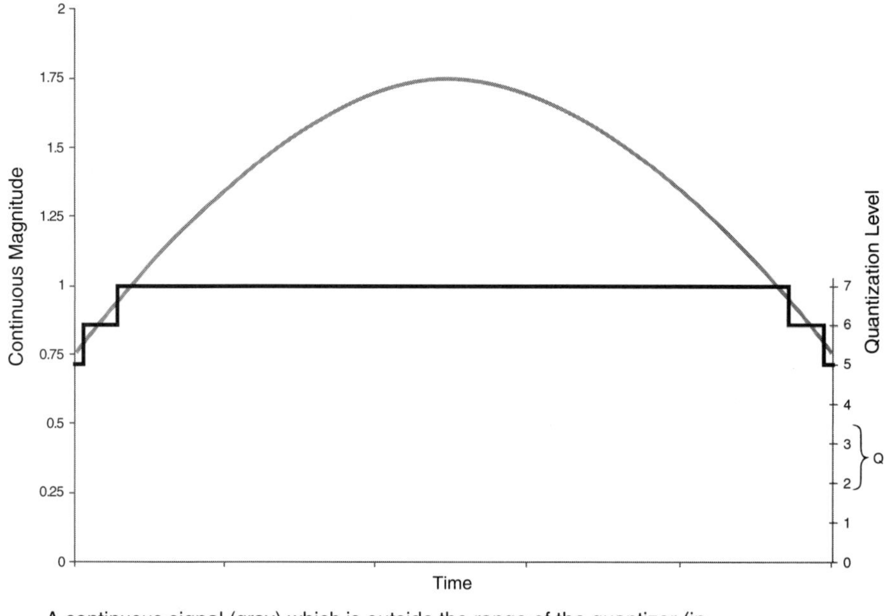

A continuous signal (gray) which is outside the range of the quantizer (in this case, 0.0-1.0) gets digitally clipped (black) to the maximum quantizer level (7).

Figure 7.33 Digital Clipping

Oversampling

For much of our discussions in this chapter, we have relied upon boxcar lowpass filters: hypothetical filters that perfectly block all frequencies above a certain point and let all the low frequencies pass through it with no alteration. Such filters make the math a lot easier, but are impossible to build in the real world. It is much cheaper and practical to build LPFs that have a slope to them.

This slope has some serious implications to our digital to analog conversion process. For instance, suppose we wanted to digitize audible sound up to a highest frequency of 20,000 hertz. Per the sampling theorem, we should then be able to sample it properly using a sample rate of 40,000 hertz. We would first need to apply an anti-alias filter. If we used a

40-dB/decade filter, and said that 40 dB down was effectively below the threshold of hearing, then we would have a problem: all the frequencies between 6,300 and 20,000 are attenuated, as shown in Figure 7.34. Such a system is not able to accurately reproduce the higher audible frequencies.

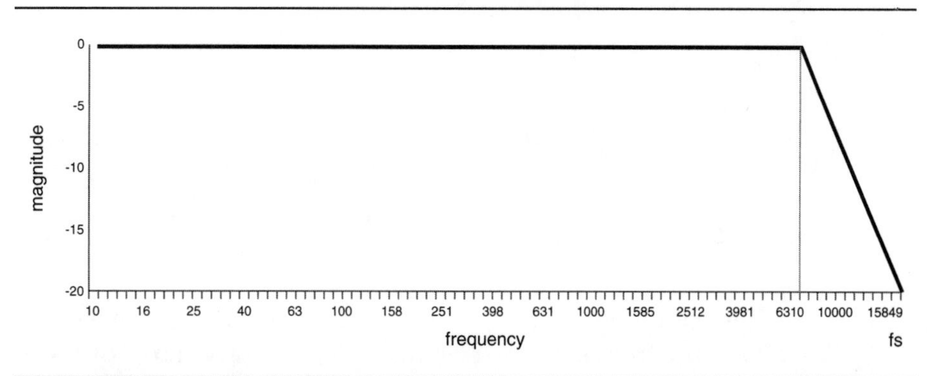

Figure 7.34 40 dB/decade Antialiasing Filter

So what can we do? We can increase the slope of our filter, using a more expensive 80-dB/decade (or steeper) anti-aliasing filter. Such an approach shrinks the range of affected frequencies, but will not completely alleviate the issue. We cannot simply shift the filter to a higher frequency, because then we get aliasing from violating the sampling theorem. What we can do is shift the filter to a higher frequency and increase the sampling rate.

If we, for instance, increase our sampling rate by a factor of 4, it means the highest frequency we can properly sample is also increased by a factor of 4 (in this case, 80,000 hertz). If we use another 40-dB/decoder antialiasing filter, we can position it so that the 40 dB down response is at 80,000 hertz to prevent aliasing. The attenuation range is now 25,300 to 80,000 hertz, as shown in Figure 7.35. Our previously indicated frequency range of interest, 0 to 20,000 hertz, is not affected at all by the antialiasing filter!

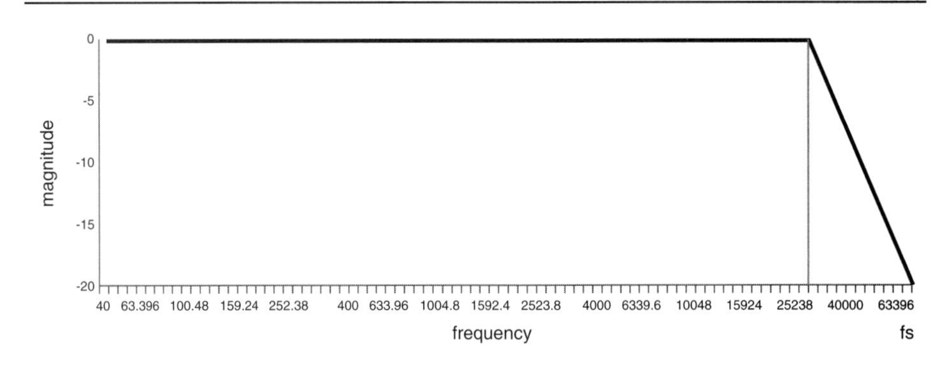

Figure 7.35 4X Oversampling

This technique of sampling in excess of the rate suggested by the sampling theorem is known as *oversampling*. The term oversampling is typically used to indicate scenarios where the sampling rate is substantially higher than the Nyquist rate. Usually, the oversampling rate is an integer multiple of the Nyquist sampling rate and is referred to by the multiple. For instance, 4X oversampling means the sampling rate used is four times higher than the Nyquist sampling rate.

Oversampling allows us to use reasonably-sloped antialiasing filters. It also reduces quantizing noise, a phenomenon we will discuss in more detail shortly. But oversampling comes with a price: we have more samples! In the 4X case, we have four times as many samples. Those samples nominally take up four times as much space to store and/or transmit. It would be nice if we could get rid of the extra samples while still keeping the aforementioned benefits of oversampling. In fact we can!

The standard analog to digital process is shown in Figure 7.36. An analog signal passes through a low-pass antialiasing filter, is sampled, and quantized, producing digital data. The digital data rate is the quantizer width times the sampling frequency. If we had a 40,000-hertz sampler and a 16-bit quantizer, the digital data rate would be 16 bits × 40,000 hertz = 640,000 bits/sec.

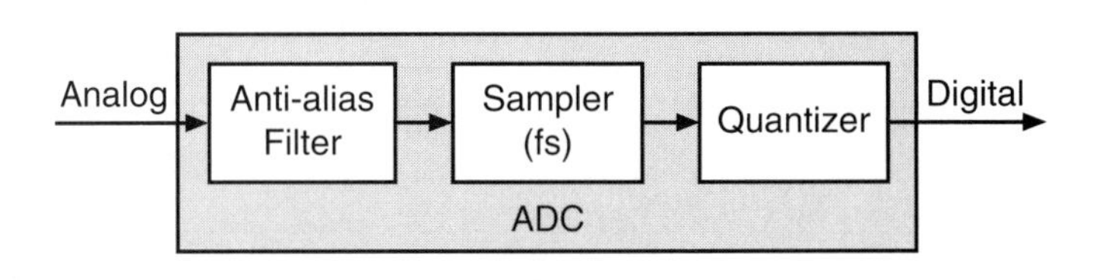

Figure 7.36 Analog to Digital Conversion (ADC)

If our ADC has a 4X oversampler, as seen in Figure 7.37, then the digital data rate coming out the quantizer is going to be four times higher (2,560,000 bits/sec).

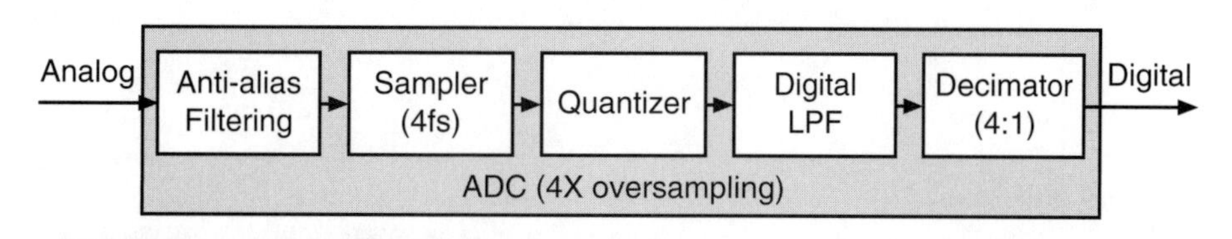

Figure 7.37 ADC with 4X Oversampling

This 4X data stream is run through a digital LPF. Digital filters behave like their analog counterparts, but operate on digital signals. The digital filter cleanly removes any frequencies below $f_s/2$. Remember that the analog antialiasing filter targeted frequencies below $4(f_s/2)$. The digital LPF removes any frequency in the range $f_s/2$ - $4(f_s/2)$. We are then able to represent the signal coming out of the digital filter using only a sample rate of f_s, in accordance with the sampling theorem.

The data rate coming out of the digital filter is still 4X, so the last step is to run it through a component known as a decimator. The decimator reduces the number of digital samples. In this example, the decimator converts every four samples into one. The final data rate coming out of the ADC is thus back down to 1X (640,000 bits/sec in this example), even though we internally oversample the signal at 4X.

The reason that oversampling is practical is that it is very expensive to build steep analog filters, but cheap to build steep digital filters. We can often realize the best combination of price and performance by using an inexpensive, low-order analog filter for anti-aliasing, oversample that signal, and then use a digital filter to bring the sampled digital data back down to the nominal sampling rate.

Noise Shaping

As has been previously noted, the quantization process introduces errors to the signal. For complex signals, these quantization errors act like true noise. This noise is spread across the entire frequency range being sampled. As a consequence, oversampling results in the noise energy being spread across a wider range, therefore lowering the quantizing noise level. In other words, in and of itself, oversampling increases the signal to noise ratio of the quantization (Figure 7.38).

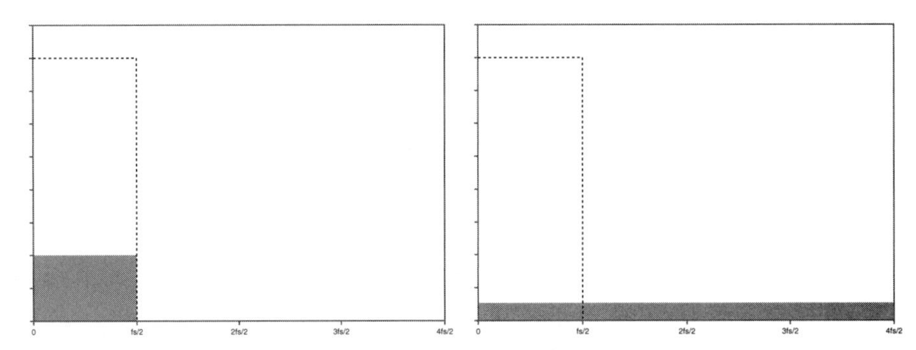

Analog to digital conversion without oversampling (left) and with oversampling (right) both introduce the same amount of noise into the system, as represented by the grey area. However, with oversampling the noise is spread over a wider area, thus reduce the noise level.

Figure 7.38 Oversampling Reduces Noise Floor

As part of the oversampling process it is possible to incorporate a feedback loop which has the effect of changing the spectrum distribution of the noise. This feedback loop decreases the intensity of the noise at lower frequencies and increases it at higher frequencies. The total amount of noise remains the same, only its distribution across frequencies is changed (Figure 7.39). Graphically, we are changing the shape of the noise, and as such this technique is known as *noise shaping*.

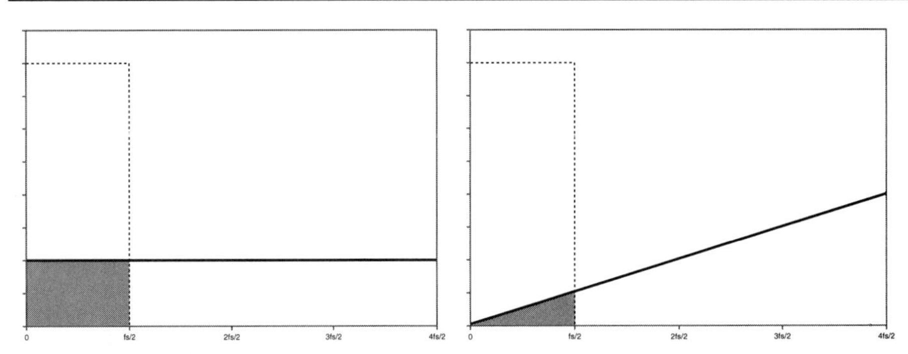

Oversampling with no-noise shaping (left) and first-order noise-shaping (right) both have the same amount of noise across the entire spectrum, as represented in each picture by the area under the black line. However, the first-order noise-shaping has significantly less noise in the frequency range of interest (0-f_s/2), as indicated by the gray areas.

Figure 7.39 Noise Shaping

Noise shaping is useful, because the digital LPF in an oversampling ADC removes all the frequencies above $f_s/2$. In other words, it removes the majority of the noise! We will not go into the details of the feedback system which affects noise shaping. However, do note that there are different orders of feedback possible. Figure 7.39 shows first-order noise-shaping. Second, third, and higher orders are also possible. The higher the order, the greater the amount of noise that is pushed to higher frequencies.

Coding Methods

We must sample and sample and quantize analog audio to store it digitally. Within these basic constraints, there are several practical ways to create and store the digital audio.

Pulse Code Modulation

Our lengthy foray into quantization and sampling in this chapter all directly apply to the concept of storing medium-sized data words at a sampling rate roughly twice of the highest audible frequencies. For example, Compact Discs store digital audio data using 16-bit audio words per channel at a rate of 44.1 kilohertz. This technique is known as *pulse code modulation* (PCM).

PCM is sometimes referred to as *linear pulse code modulation* (LPCM), because the quantization intervals are fixed. By comparison, a non-linear quantization system would have differently sized intervals for high amplitude values than for low amplitude values.

Differential Pulse Code Modulation

Differential pulse code modulation (DPCM) is—as you might guess—similar to PCM. The main difference is rather than quantizing the actual signal magnitude, DPCM quantizes the difference between the current sample and the previous sample. For instance, for the PCM sequence 0, 8, 10, 12, 11, 9, the corresponding DPCM sequence might be 0, 8, 2, 2, -1, -2.

In this sense, DPCM is a form of predictive coding; the code for the current sample is based on the previous sample. The reason DPCM is interesting is that most sounds do not have very large variations from one sample interval to another. As such, the difference in intensity between two adjacent samples can often be specified using a smaller number of bits than is used to specify the full quantization range.

The drawback to DPCM is that the rate of change is limited. For instance, suppose we had 16-bit PCM data and we wanted to store it as 8-bit DPCM. The maximum change in intensity we could store would be $2^8 = 256$ levels. If two adjacent PCM samples differed by more than that 256 levels, we would not be able to properly code the signal.

Nevertheless, a properly engineered DPCM system can be very useful and efficient.

Delta Modulation

Delta modulation (DM) is a specialized form of DPCM, the constraint being that DM uses a one-bit quantizer[5] to store the difference, or delta, between adjacent samples. The single bit is used to indicate either a fixed increase or a fixed decrease in intensity between adjacent samples, as shown in Figure 7.40. Using DM, there is no way to specify a zero-magnitude change between two adjacent samples.

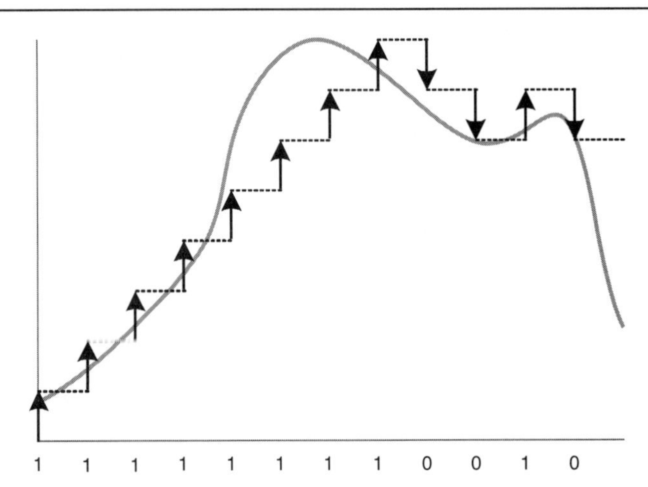

A continuous signal (gray) is coded using delta modulation (black arrows). The bottom of the diagram shows the +1 code being stored as binary 1, and a -1 code being stored as binary 0.

Figure 7.40 Delta Modulation

[5] I told you they could be useful!

Given the very limited encoding options, such as +1 or -1, it is quite possible that an input signal can vary too quickly to be accurately captured by delta modulation. This limitation can be alleviated somewhat by increasing the magnitude implied by a ±1 code, such as the height of the steps in Figure 7.40. However, such an increase causes a corresponding increase in quantization noise.

Another way to increase the accuracy of DM is to increase the coding frequency, causing a corresponding decrease in the width of the steps. To get a workable DM system, the coding frequency needs to be substantially faster than that suggested by the sampling theorem.

For instance, for a DM system to be able to fully code an n-bit PCM signal, the DM would need to be coded 2^n times faster. If we had a 16-bit PCM signal we wanted to fully realize using DM coding, our DM coding would need to be able to step across the entire quantization range from 0 to 65,535 within a single PCM sampling interval. It would, in other words, need to be able to take 65,536 steps during a single interval. A DM system hoping to fully match a 16-bit 44.1 kilohertz PCM stream would need to run at $2^{16} \times 44.1$ kilohertz = 2.89 GHz! The data rate of the DM stream would be 2.89 Gbits/s, over 4000 times higher than the corresponding PCM stream's 705 kbits/s. As such, DM is generally not a very efficient mechanism for coding high frequency audio.

Still, DM has been used as a coding scheme for transmitting voice over the telephone. DM was used in part because it is possible to reproduce discernable speech without using high frequencies.

Delta Sigma Modulation

Delta sigma modulation (DSM) was developed in 1962 as an improvement over DM. Alternately known as delta-sigma modulation, DSM uses the sum (sigma) of the current sample and the error value (delta) from the previous sample. If this sum is positive, the DSM code is +1, otherwise it is -1.

DSM is also known as *pulse density modulation* (PDM), for reasons that can be seen in Figure 7.41. When an input sinusoid is near the top or bottom of the quantization range, there are few transitions between +1 and -1. When the input signal is near the middle of the quantization range, the transitions between +1 and -1 are numerous. The density of these transitions is indicative of the nature of the original signal.

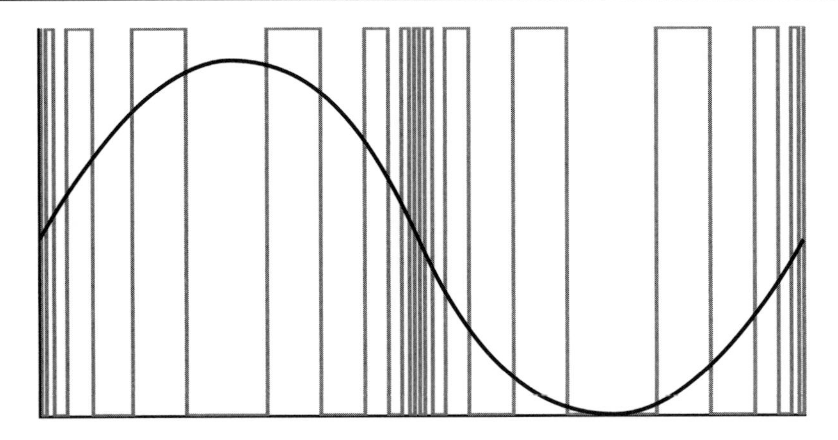

Figure 7.41 Delta Sigma Modulation

Although DSM again requires very high sampling frequencies as compared to PCM, it can use this oversampling in conjunction with high-order noise shaping to produce good performance.

Summary

Analog refers to systems that are continuously variable. Digital refers to systems that are discretely variable. Digital systems tend to be cheaper, more flexible, and better performing than similarly priced analog systems.

The process of analog-to-digital conversion is usually done by digitizing the analog data in both the time domain (sampling) and in the magnitude domain (quantizing). Sampling can be a lossless process, if the sampling frequency is twice the highest frequency being sampled. Quantization is an inherently lossy process. Real-world ADCs often achieve better performance through the use of oversampling.

Chapter 8

Connections

Habits are cobwebs at first; cables at last.

—*Chinese Proverb*

It is often desirable to move a sound signal from one piece of audio equipment to another, be it from a CD player to an amplifier, or an amplifier to speakers. Rather than permanently hard-wiring these connections together, audio components are more frequently connected using industry-standard connectors and cables. This practice of patching allows for great connectivity flexibility and the ability to buy components from different manufacturers and at different times.

Audio Signal Basics

The goal of signaling is to send data from one point to another with as little degradation as possible. Signaling is a broad field, full of devilish details. In this section, we examine a few of the topics most pertinent to audio.

Unbalanced and Balanced Signals

The simplest way to transfer a signal over wire is via two wires: one wire carries a variable voltage that matches the signal, while the other wire serves as a zero reference, or ground. Such a configuration is said to be *unbalanced*. In audio cables, the ground wire is actually a cylindrical sheath that encloses the signal wire. The ground acts as a shield, limiting the addition of external noise to the signal as it is carried along the cable.

Unbalanced cables are cheap and easy to make. A drawback to an unbalanced system is that whatever noise does get added to the signal cannot be removed. Most consumer audio connections are unbalanced.

A balanced system carries the voltage-varying signal across two lines in addition to the ground reference. One of the signal lines carries an inverted copy of the original signal. Using opposite but equal signals is generically known as differential signaling.

After the signals have traveled along the cable, both the original signal (S) and the inverted signal (-S) are likely to have picked up some external noise (N). Both lines have been exposed to the same noise (N). So the two wires are carrying (S+N) and (-S+N). Equipment receiving these balanced signals subtracts one from the other and halves the result. To wit: ((S+N)-(-S+N))/2 = S. The noise disappears!

The immunity of balanced systems to external noise is one of the reasons they are used almost exclusively for professional audio systems. They are especially important when dealing with the long cable runs associated with setting up speakers and microphones in large venues. Because balanced signals require twice as many signal lines as unbalanced systems, the cables cost more. Also, the logic required to process the signals is marginally more expensive to implement than that for an unbalanced systems. The resulting increased cost of balanced systems is why they do not appear very frequently in consumer space.

The Ground Loop

A ground loop is a condition that occurs when a nontrivial difference in potential occurs between the grounds of two connected pieces of audio equipment. This phenomenon typically occurs when a sound cable is run between two AC-powered audio devices separated by a lengthy distance. Current flows across the cable's ground wire, resulting in a low frequency hum, as described in Figure 8.1. Unbalanced systems are much more susceptible to ground loop than balanced systems.

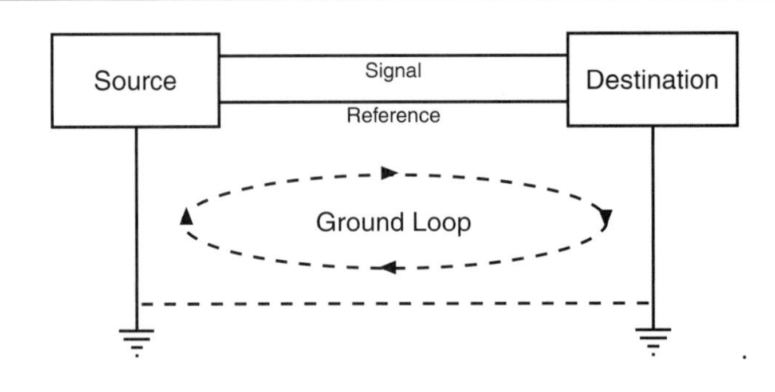

Figure 8.1 Ground Loop

Analog Levels

Audio signals run at three main voltage levels. These voltages are commonly specified in reference to 0.775 volt (1 dBu). The first two voltage levels are each known as line level. One applies to consumer equipment, the other to professional equipment. Although the same term is used to describe both levels, it is usually clear from the context or the connector which level is being discussed.

Consumer line level operates up to -10 dBu. This level is the one that is used for connecting most consumer audio equipment together, such as a CD player to an amplifier or an amplifier to speakers.

Professional line level operates up to +4 dBu. Professional amplifiers, mixing boards, and speakers are all connected using professional line levels, typically carried via XLR connectors.

Microphone level or mic level is much lower than line level: -40 dBu to -60 dBu.

SPDIF

The most common consumer digital audio interconnect is the Sony/Philips Digital Interface Format (SPDIF or S/PDIF). It is derived from the professional digital audio format commonly known as AES/EBU or AES3.

Whereas analog audio requires one channel per unbalanced line, or balanced line pair, digital formats can send multiple channels over a single line. Using only a single cable, SPDIF supports mono and stereo PCM audio with a wide variety of sampling rates up to 96 kilohertz and quantization depths up to 24 bits.

Since its introduction, SPDIF format has been extended to allow it to also carry compressed multi-channel audio in formats such as MPEG, AC3, and DTS, formats about which we will talk more in upcoming chapters. In particular, the AC3 format commonly is used to convey 5.1 sound from DVD players to home theatre amplifiers.

SPDIF includes support for the Serial Copy Management System (SCMS). SCMS is a mechanism for specifying the copy attributes of the content. A typical use of SCMS is to set a copy bit. Compliant equipment allows you to make a copy, but not a copy of a copy. You can therefore make a personal copy of prerecorded music, but are prevented from making unlicensed multigenerational copies of protected content.

The attributes are specified by a single copy bit. When the copy bit is zero on every audio frame, the content is unprotected and may be copied freely. This state is sometimes referred to as *copy always*.

When the copy bit is one on every audio frame, the content is protected and the content is coming from the original source (such as an optical disk). Content in this state can be copied once, and as such this state is sometimes known as *copy once*.

When the copy bit toggles between one and zero every five audio frames, it means that the content is protected and has already been copied. It can no longer be copied, and so this state is known as *copy never*.

Note that SCMS does not provide any cryptographic protection of the content. The copy protection status is merely carried as side-band information. A device that is not SCMS compliant can simply ignore the bits and arbitrarily copy the content.

Connecters

When connecting equipment together, the connector located on the equipment itself is known as a *jack*. The complementary connector attached to the cable is known as the *plug*. There are several jacks and plugs that are commonly used for audio.

Phone

The phone plug shown in Figure 8.2 is a very common analog connector. Its name derives from the fact that it was originally used for manually patching lines together on telephone switchboards. These original connectors were referred to as tip-ring-sleeve (TRS) connectors, in reference to the three main components of the plug. In the context of telephone patching, the tip and ring were used to carry a differential signal, and the sleeve was used for ground.

Figure 8.2 Phone Plug

The same phone connector is used today to carry unbalanced stereo signals (tip = left, ring = right, sleeve = ground). A two-conductor variation of the phone plug is also available. It is sometimes known as a *tip-sleeve* (TS) connector. It is used to carry unbalanced mono audio.

Both the mono and stereo phone plugs are available in both ¼-inch and 1/8-inch diameters. Phone plugs are mostly used in consumer applications, although the ¼-inch form factor is sometimes used for short distances in the professional space.

Phono

The phono connector shown in Figure 8.3 was originally developed to connect the tone arm of RCA phonographs to an amplifier. Known then as the phonograph plug, it has been shortened over the years to simply phono. It is also known as an RCA plug. Phono plugs carry unbalanced audio. They are widely used in the consumer space to attach audio equipment together, but almost never show up on professional equipment. Because phono plugs can only carry a single signal, they are often bundled together in pairs to carry stereo signal. One connector in the stereo pairs is colored red to indicate the right channel. The left channel is colored black or white.

Figure 8.3 Phono Plug

Phono jacks are also used to carry SPDIF signals. The same phono cables used for analog audio can be used to carry the digital SPDIF signals. The phono interconnect is often referred to as *SPDIF coaxial* when used for digital purposes.

XLR

The most popular professional audio connector is the XLR, shown in Figure 8.4. Its similar predecessor, the X connector, was developed by Canon. However, the X connector could not be secured into place—something audio professionals wanted. Canon responded with the XL connector, which added a latch (L) that would keep plugs securely attached to their sockets. As a final improvement, rubber (R) was added to the assembly, resulting in the XLR connector.

Figure 8.4 XLR Connector

The XLR connector is used to carry balanced analog audio. The three-pin version carries mono, the five-pin version carries stereo. The XLR connectors are also used to carry digital studio audio formats.

TOSLINK†

The TOSLINK† connector shown in Figure 8.5 is used to carry SPDIF. The connector's name derives from the term Toshiba Link, as the specification was defined by Toshiba. The other connectors discussed so far transmit signals over conductive wires as variations in voltage. In contrast, the TOSLINK connector is used to transmit signals as variations in brightness, as generated by a red LED. The photons are carried between connectors via a fiber optic cable.

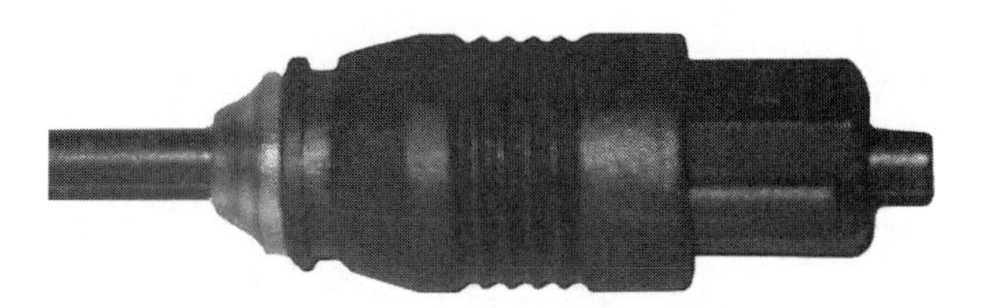

Figure 8.5 Optical Connector

Summary

Most audio systems today consist of multiple components that must be electrically attached using external cables. For instance, even very compact MP3 players require that headphones be plugged into them in order for you to hear music. There are several common connectors used to support such flexible mixing and matching of components. The signals carried across these connections are predominantly analog electrical signals, but digital electric and optical electrical signals are growing in popularity.

Chapter 9

Compact Disc

[Goodspeed's Beatles album arrives at the office]

Goodspeed:	*Oh yes! Bring it here!*
Isherwood:	*Why did you have it sent here?*
Goodspeed:	*Carla wouldn't approve. She thinks it's stupid to spend $600 on an LP.*
Isherwood:	*Carla's right. Why didn't you just spend $13 on a CD, man?*
Goodspeed:	*First of all, it's because I'm a Beatlemaniac. And second, these sound better.*

—The Rock

As the 1970s drew to a close, the dominant consumer audio formats were the cassette tape and the record.[1] Both of these formats were analog and—in a nutshell—noisy. The early 1980s saw the launch of a dramatically new audio format: the compact disc. It was the first mainstream digital audio format, and it has revolutionized the way we listen to music—and enjoy other types of content.

Overview

In the 1970s, prerecorded music was predominantly stored via two types of storage media. The first medium used variations in the physical size of materials to store information: these were records with wiggles in a

[1] At the same time, fashion trends such as bellbottoms and hiphuggers were fading away, not to be seen again until retro revivals two decades later.

groove that represented sound. The other medium used variations in magnetic field strength. The magnetic variations were stored on tape that was wound on self-contained cassettes.

In the late 70s, Sony and Philips began sharing their research on an optical storage technology. In this technology, data are stored by varying the brightness of a material. The Sony and Philips effort was focused on developing a new consumer format for prerecorded music. In June 1980, they announced the result of their efforts: the compact disc or CD.

The CD is a 12-cm (or optionally, 8-cm) disc of polycarbonate containing a stamped sheet of aluminum, shown in cross-section in Figure 9.1. The aluminum sheet contains pits, which are used to represent digital music. When illuminated by a laser, these pits cause variations in the reflected intensity of the laser. A photodetector captures these variations in brightness, which are interpreted as binary data (0s and 1s). We will discuss the details of this process in more detail later in the chapter.

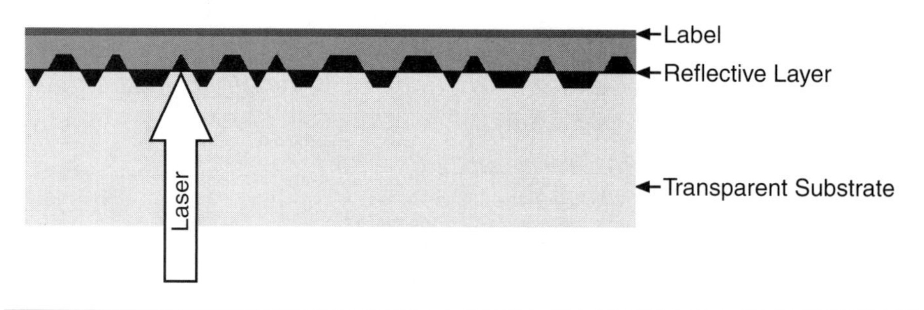

Figure 9.1 Stamped CD Cross Section

The first production CD player was the Sony CDP-101 developed by Sony, CBS/Sony, Philips, and Polygram. The CDP obviously referred to "compact disc player." The "101" was meant to be a binary interpretation of the number five, so chosen because Sony's Nobuyuki Idei felt the product to be a "medium class" device. The player launched October 1, 1982, along with the first 50 CD music albums. Of the 50 albums, Billy Joel's *52nd Street* was given the honor of being the first CD.

Although the first players sold for about $900, the compact disc format rapidly increased in popularity, with CD sales surpassing LP record sales in 1988. It remains an extremely popular format today.

Advantages

Compact discs have several advantages over the records and tapes they replaced, the most obvious being the sound quality. The high quality digital nature of CDs means that they can reproduce sounds with far greater fidelity and far less noise than either tapes or records. Also, whereas tapes and records degrade slightly with each playback, CDs can be played virtually indefinitely with no degradation of the disc or its content.

CDs also allow for very easy random accessibility. You can jump from one song to another at the push of a button. You can also have your CD player randomize the order in which the tracks are played. Record players had primitive random accessibility, in that you could pick up the tone arm and move it to a new position. Precisely moving to the start of an arbitrary song required a bit of manual dexterity, as the physical gaps between songs was fairly narrow. With tapes, random accessibility was not possible; you had to linearly rewind or fast-forward the tape to get to different points on the album.

CDs offer the longest amount of uninterrupted listening time, offering up to 74 minutes of audio on a single disc. By comparison, cassettes stored less than 60 minutes per side, and LPs typically stored less than 30 minutes per side.

One feature of CDs which has no doubt played an important role in their popularity is how well suited they are to the PC. Virtually every computer sold today includes a drive that plays back audio compact discs.

Drawbacks

The chief drawback to compact discs—at least at first—was a lack of recordability. Much like records, the CD format could only be used for playback by consumers. By comparison, recording to tape was very easy. Recordable versions of CDs are now available, but standalone audio CD recorders still remain quite expensive.

Types

There are many different types of compact discs. The specifications for them are available from Philips. These standards have different colored covers, and many of these standards are commonly referred to by the color of their covers.

Compact Disc Digital Audio (Red Book)

The Red Book defines the first CD system. The sole application of the Red Book is storing audio. This CD Digital Audio (CD-DA) standard defines an industry standard way in which high quality digital music is stored and played. Manufacturers around the world are able to produce discs and players that are fully compatible with one another. They have done so quite successfully: the CD is one of the most successful consumer electronic products ever.

In addition to being defined in the Red Book, CD-DA is also defined in IEC 60908. The specification defines both the physical nature of the discs, as well as the layout of the data on that disc. The Red Book defines a very constrained data structure that only allows for a single type of digital audio. Subsequent standards have been created which allow the compact disc format to be used for purposes other than storing audio. The Red Book is the root standard; all the other CD flavors are derived from it.

CD-ROM (Yellow Book)

The Yellow Book extends the CD format to general digital storage. This new technology is known as Compact Disc Read Only Memory (CD-ROM). The "read only" comes from the fact that CD-ROMs are produced by mass-production stamping, so the data can only be read, not written. The first CD-ROMs could store 540 Mb of data.

The first CD-ROM drives could read that data at a rate of 150 kilobits per second. Subsequent generations of drives were able to read the data at faster rates, typically reported as a multiple of the first generation data rate. For instance, a 12X driver can read CD-ROM twelve times faster than 150 kilobits per second.

Because CD-ROMs can contain arbitrary data in a wide variety of formats, they cannot be played on an audio CD player. Indeed, a CD-ROM may contain no audio data whatsoever. However, most CD-ROM drives are capable of playing CD-Audio discs.

CD-ROMs are chiefly used in association with PCs. When they were introduced, they provided a large capacity removable storage medium. The only other widely available removable storage at the time was the floppy disk—one of which could hold about 1 megabyte. A single CD-ROM could hold hundreds of times as much information as a single floppy disk. Thus, a single CD-ROM was able to eventually replace the dozens of floppy disks that were required, for example, to install an operating system.

CD-EXTRA (Blue Book)

The Blue Book defines a CD format that contains audio content that can be played on a standard audio CD player as well as additional data. For instance, Peter Gabriel's 2002 album *Up* contained PC-accessible lyrics of all the songs that you could listen to on a CD player. There were also several computer games in the 1990s that stored their soundtracks in CD-EXTRA form; the upshot of which was that you could listen to the game soundtracks away from the PC.

CD-EXTRA is also known as Enhanced Music CD and as CD Plus.

Recordable Compact Disc (Orange Book)

The Orange Book introduced recordability to CDs in 1990. Although very expensive at first, recordable CDs are very affordable nowadays, and serve as a cheap way to store lots of data.

The Orange Book includes three parts. Part I describes the now-defunct Compact Disc Magneto Optical (CD-MO) format. CD-MO used a cobalt / terbium ferrite alloy substrate that would change its optical properties under exposure to magnetic fields. As such, it was possible to store data on the disc using magnets and read back the data using a laser. Although CD-MO certainly allowed data to be written to it, it had the drawback of being susceptible to erasure by exposure to magnetic fields—a bit of an oddity for an optical format.

The CD-MO format is virtually extinct today, with the specification having been withdrawn by Philips. It has been supplanted by Parts II and III of the Orange Book.

Part II of the Orange Book defines CD Recordable (CD-R). CD-R discs can be written to once, but read a virtually unlimited number of times. This write-once, read-many capability is sometimes referred to by the acronym WORM. CD-R is also, but very rarely, referred to as CD-WO, for write once.

CD-Rs use a layer of photoreactive ink placed adjacent to a reflective aluminum layer, shown in cross-section in Figure 9.2. A relatively powerful write laser can alter the transparency of the ink. After the data has been written, a lower power read laser is either reflected through the transparent layer or absorbed by the opaque ink. This modulation in reflected intensity codes the data.

Although initially expensive, CD-Rs now cost only a few cents per disc. PC drives that record to CD-R are widely available, and are known colloquially as CD burners. CD-Rs are also very compatible, and work with most CD players and CD-ROM drivers.

Volume 1 of the CD-R specification defines discs and systems that can be written to at 1X, 2X, and 4X speeds. Volume 2 includes definitions for speeds up to 48X. A 48X CD-R burner can burn a 79-minute CD-DA disc in less than three minutes.

Figure 9.2 CD-R Cross Section

One of the obvious limitations of the CD-R format is that you can't erase them and use them over again. To address this lack of reuse, part III of the Orange Book describes CD Rewritable (CD-RW). CD-RW can be both written to and read from an arbitrary number of times.

CD-RW discs use a phase change material to encode data, shown in cross-section in Figure 9.3. This material, consisting of antimony, tellurium, indium, and silver has two stable states at room temperature: crystalline and amorphous. The crystalline state is translucent; the amorphous state is opaque. Again, a powerful write laser is used to toggle areas of the layer between the two states.

Figure 9.3 CD-RW Cross Section

CD-RWs do not reflect as much light as a stamped CD or a CD-R. As such, many older CD players developed before the CD-RW standard was defined are not able to read CD-RW discs. However, most contemporary CD players can compensate for the relative dimness of CD-RW and can play the discs without a problem.

Volume 1 of the CD-RW specification defines 1X, 2X, and 4X recording speeds. Volume 2 defines a range of recording speeds of 4X to 10X, known as high speed. These high-speed discs use a slightly different technology than Volume 1 to write discs. As such, High Speed CD-RW discs and burners are not fully compatible with Volume 1 CD-RW discs.

Volume 2 also defines Ultra Speed CD-RW discs, which have writing speeds in the range of 8X to 32X. Again, these discs are not compatible with Volume 1 CD-RW burners.

CD Interactive (Green Book)

The Green Book defines CD Interactive (CD-I). In addition to audio, it allows for the storage of video, graphics, text, and executable code. Although it allowed for the storage of audio and video in MPEG format, it is not to be confused—although it often was—with the Video CD format listed below. CD-I had a brief surge of interest in the early 1990s, but its popularity has not lasted.

Photo CD

Photo CD defines a standard data layout for storing high-resolution pictures. It was developed by Sony and Kodak. Photo CD also allows for playback of audio while viewing the pictures on the CD.

Video CD (White Book)

The White Book defines a standard layout for storing video. The Video CD (VCD) format has been quite successful in Asia, particularly China. Being based on the CD format makes VCD a cheap alternative to DVD. The quality of VCD video, MPEG-1 at a resolution of 352 x 240, is comparable to that of VHS tape. Given the large bandwidth requirements of video, a single feature length movie typically needs to be encoded on two VCDs.

Super Video CD

The Super Video CD (SVCD) format is defined in ANSI/IEC 62107. It is designed to be a replacement to VCD and offers higher resolution video as well as MPEG-2 support. Again, SVCD is based on CD, so the underlying technology is cheap. A movie typically needs to be encoded on three SVCDs.

Double Density Compact Disc (Purple Book)

The Purple Book was released in 2000. It defines Sony and Philips standard for a compact disc, which has roughly twice the capacity of a standard compact disc, while maintaining the standard CD format factor. For this reason, it is known as Double Density Compact Disc (DDCD). The Purple Book includes both recordable and rewritable versions. Although DDCD players and discs have been produced, they have not gained wide popularity, due no doubt in part to the rapid decline in price of similar DVD-based formats.

Disc Details

The Red Book includes specifications of the physical parameters of Compact Discs. These discs come in both 12-cm and 8-cm sizes, the former being far more common.

Disc Layout

CDs have a 15-mm hole in the center, as shown in Figure 9.4. CD players have a corresponding spindle upon which the CD fits. Moving outward from the center is a clamping area. The player uses this region to firmly hold the CD during playback. Next out is the lead in area, which contains the table of contents for the disc. The data area comes next. It is this region that contains the actual data corresponding to audio. It is ringed by a lead out area that indicates the end of the disc program.

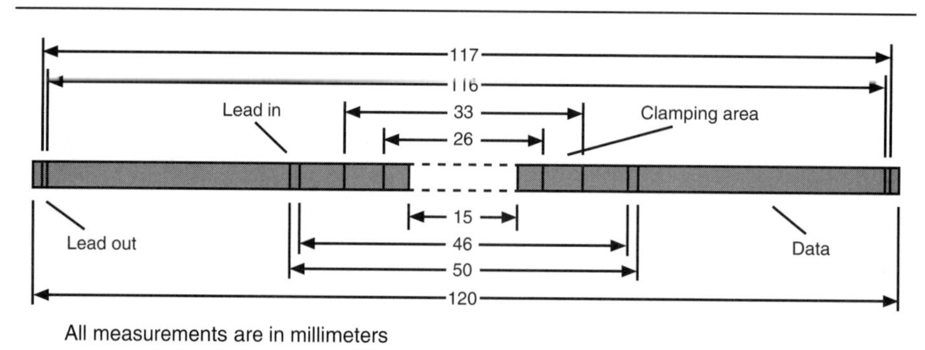

Figure 9.4 Layout of a 12-cm CD

Tracks and Pits

Data is stored on compact disc as a series of pits, shown in Figure 9.5. These pits are laid out in a single tightly packed spiral that can be three and a half miles long! The track begins at the inside of the disc and spirals outward. Even though there is but a single track, we often colloquially refer to each loop of the spiral as a separate track. For instance, we might refer to the distance between two adjacent loops of the spiral as an inter-track pitch, but keep in mind that there is really only a single spiral track.

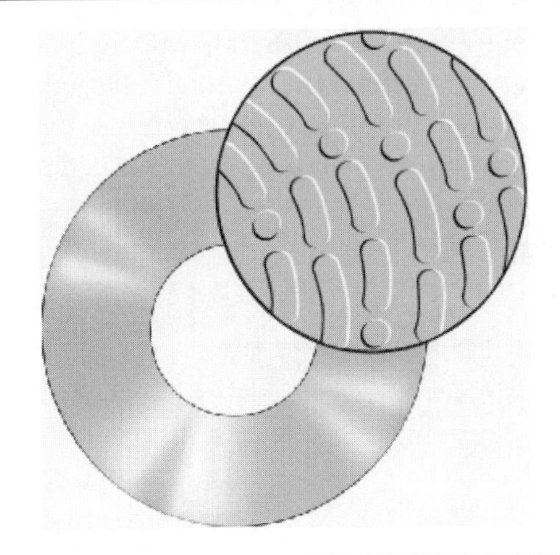

Figure 9.5 CD Spiral Track

Speaking of inter-track pitch (the distance between adjacent tracks on the CD), it happens to be 1.6 µm; see Figure 9.6. This pitch works out to be 15,875 tracks per inch! The pits themselves are about 0.6 µm wide. They are read by a laser spot which is 1.0 µm across when it reaches the pits.

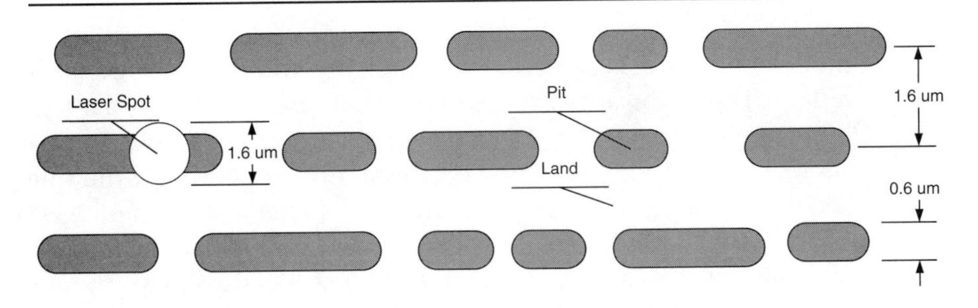

Figure 9.6 CD Track Details

The pits are stamped in a thin sheet of metal, typically aluminum. When viewed from the top of the disc, they are depressions. However, when viewed from the bottom of the disc, they are bumps. It is from the bottom of the disc that the laser reads the disc. The flat region between the bumps is known as *land*.

Pits may be one of nine different lengths, known as the "T" lengths. The nine lengths are labeled as 3T, 4T, 5T … 11T, which have nominal values ranging from 0.9 μm (3T) to 3.3 μm (11T).

CDs are read by shining a laser through a lens assembly toward the bottom of the disc. When the beam hits the reflective layer of the disc, it bounces straight back towards the emitter as shown in Figure 9.7. On its way back, it hits a beam splitter that redirects the beam toward a photodiode. This photodiode converts the intensity of the reflected beam into a voltage level from which a binary value is determined.

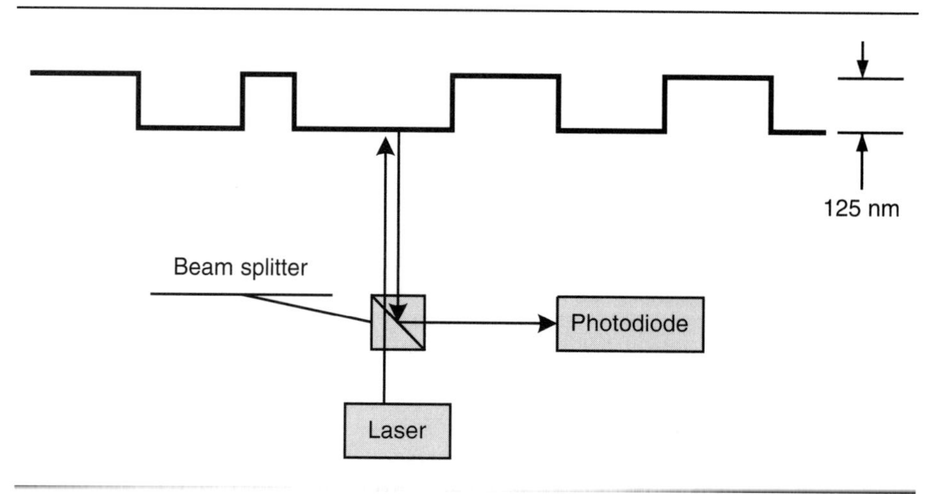

Figure 9.7 Reading Pits

At first glance, it seems like the bumps wouldn't have much effect on the reading process. Whether the laser hits the land or a bump, it is still reflected back towards the photodiode. The clever bit is that the bumps have a height that is equal to a quarter of the effective wavelength of the laser beam. As such, the laser beam energy reflecting off the bumps has half a wavelength offset in phase from the beam energy that hits the land.

Looking back at Figure 9.6 you can see that the laser spot is larger than the bump width. In fact, when the laser spot hits the bump, about half of it strikes land. So, half of the beam's energy reflects off land, and half of the energy reflects off the bump out of phase with the land reflection. The two reflection components effectively cancel each other out, resulting in a net zero intensity at the photodiode.[2]

It is a popular misconception that the pits and land each correspond to a binary value (1 and 0), but in fact, it is the *transition* from pit to land or transition from land to pit that is interpreted as a 1. The flat regions of the land and the pit itself are interpreted as 0.

Recordable and Rewritable

So, for stamped discs, the laser intensity is modulated by destructive interference of the coherent light of the laser beam. Recordable and rewritable discs, however, use a different technique. These types of CDs contain a flat reflective layer, shown in Figure 9.2 and Figure 9.3, covered by a layer with variable transparency. If this latter layer is transparent, then the laser is fully reflected into the photodiode, and it behaves just like land on a stamped disc. However, if the variable layer is made opaque, then the laser beam is absorbed and never reaches the reflective layer. The beam's energy is not reflected, and the photodiode interprets the lack of reflection just as it does a bump on a stamped disc.

Stamping Motivations

The variable opacity method used to store information on CD-Rs and CD-RWs seems a lot more intuitive than the destructive interference technique used by stamped discs. Indeed, the precision required to make stamped CDs work is quite incredible, but obviously feasible given the ubiquity of CDs in our society. So why go through all this trouble? Why bother making stamped discs at all?

The short answer is that it is very easy to mass produce stamped discs. Once a master is created, a virtually unlimited number of aluminum discs can be stamped out of it and embedded in plastic. This process can be done at a very high speed: the entire disc is pressed at once. The CD stamping process is superficially similar to how vinyl records are produced. Remember that the ability to mass produce them was one of the reasons records succeeded over wax cylinders.

By comparison, the variable opacity technique used by CD-R and CD-RW burners is much slower. The disc has to be burned sequentially, and it can take minutes to burn a single disc.

---

[2] I told you it was clever!

Rotation

During playback, the disc spins at a constant linear velocity (CLV) of 1.3 ± 0.1 meters per second. CLV means that the disc needs to rotate faster when reading tracks near the inside of the disc (500 RPM) and slower when reading tracks near the outside of the disc (200 RPM). The CLV means that a pit or land segment passes under the laser pickup at the same speed regardless of its position on the disc. The pickup is able to recognize a 3T segment without having to take into account where it is positioned on the disc.

By contrast, a record player spins at a constant angular velocity (CAV), such as 33-1/3 RPM. As such, you actually get better sound fidelity on tracks near the center of the record where the local linear velocity of the media is higher. Toward the outer edges of the record, the linear velocity is lower, and, as such, the sound quality is lower as well. The reason record players have CAV is that it was not technologically feasible or economically viable to build CLV rotation systems when the players were being developed.

CD-DA Details

Audio Compact Discs store stereo sound sampled at a rate of 44.1 kilohertz at a depth of 16 bits per channel. These parameters mean CDs have a theoretical maximum frequency response up to 22.05 kilohertz and a dynamic range of 96 dB.

A standard CD-DA can store over 74 minutes of sound, although the parameters can be fudged slightly to get up to 80 minutes of playback.

A CD can contain up to 99 audio tracks. Each audio track typically corresponds to a single song on an album, and should not be confused with the physical spiral track composed of pits.

AAD, ADD, and DDD

CD-DAs are sometimes given a three-letter descriptor that describes how the audio was handled during the production of the CD. Each letter is either D or A, corresponding to digital and analog respectively. The first letter indicates the audio form used to originally record the sound. The second letter indicates the form in which the audio was processed or edited. The third letter indicates the audio format used for mastering the CD.

Today, most CDs are DDD, indicating that they were digitally recorded, edited, and mastered. Some earlier CDs were ADD, indicating that they were recorded by an analog tape recorder, then digitally edited and mastered. Some were also AAD, indicating both the recording and editing were done on analog equipment, and only the final master was done digitally.

Because CD is a digital format, and the master is digital media, the last character is always D.

Data Format

Given the precision required to construct a CD, it is not surprising that every single CD contains errors. Invariably, some pits are improperly formed, plus scratches and smudges can mar the surface of the transparent polycarbonate. To help ensure playback without noticeable distortion, data is stored on a CD in such a fashion as to facilitate error detection and correction.

Our source data is two channels of 16-bit PCM audio at 44.1 kilohertz. These 16-bit samples go through an extensive coding process before they are actually stored to disc. The fundamental data unit used in encoding is called a frame. A frame is constructed using six samples from each channel, for a total of 12 samples. We therefore start with $12 \times 16 = 192$ bits of PCM audio data.

As a first step in the encoding process, each of the 16-bit samples is split into two 8-bit symbols, depicted in Figure 9.8.

The 24 8-bit audio data symbols are fed into a Cross-Interleave Reed-Solomon (CIRC) coder. The CIRC coder interleaves the bits from a given sample with other samples both in this frame and in several adjacent frames as well. By spreading the sample information across a wide area, chances are good that all the samples can be retrieved even if an entire frame is missing.

As part of the CIRC coding, eight 8-bit parity values are generated. It is these bits that aid in error detection and potentially error correction during playback. Four of these 8-bit parity words are inserted in the middle of the frame, four added to the back. So, we fed 24 bytes into the CIRC and got $24 + 8 = 32$ bytes out.

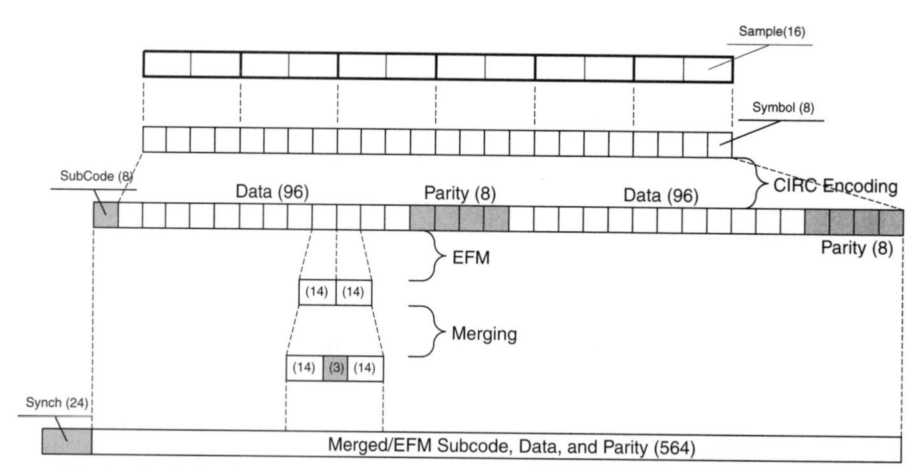

Figure 9.8 CD Data Encoding Process

At this point, eight subcode bits are concatenated to the beginning of the frame. These subcode bits are labeled P, Q, R, S, T, U, V, and W. The P and Q bits are used to store timing information about the audio disc programs, such as when each track starts and ends. The remaining bits are used to store ancillary data, such as text and graphics in the context of audio CDs.

With the addition of the subcodes, we now have 33 bytes of data in our frame. To facilitate the storage of these data into a format of pits and lands, every 8-bit data symbol is going to be translated into a 14-bit data symbol. These 14-bit data symbols are chosen such that they always have at least two zeros between ones. They also have no more than 10 zeros between ones. The number of bits between ones is known as a run length. For instance, 1001 has a run length of three.

These run length constraints [3-11] mean that our pits and land lengths can have very discrete lengths; it is easier to filter out spurious signals from dirt and scratches.

This conversion from 8-bit symbols to 14-bit symbols is known as Eight to Fourteen Modulation (EFM). Through EFM, the 33 x 8 = 264 bits in our frame so far have grown to 33 x 14 = 462 bits.

Now, we cannot simply place the 14-bit symbols adjacent to one another.[3] If one symbol ended with a 1 and the next symbol started with a 1, then our run length would be 1, which violates the [3..11] range. Therefore, merging bits are inserted between each 14-bit symbol. Although only two bits are necessary to meet our run length constraints, three bits are used for merging. The extra bit allows the low frequency characteristics of the bitstream to be controlled, as well as allowing for some flexibility in coding implementations.

Given the merging bits that need to bracket each symbol, we now have a total of 564 bits in the frame. All that remains now is to add a 24-bit synchronization word to the front of our frame. Voila! The original 192 bits of audio data have been encoded into a 588-bit frame ready to be stored on the disc.

The actual storage of the frame to the disc is done by inserting a pit-to-land or land-to-pit translation whenever a 1 appears in the bitstream, illustrated in Figure 9.9. A run-length of three is stored using a pit/land of length 3T. Run lengths of four are stored using 4T. And so on up to the maximum of 11T.

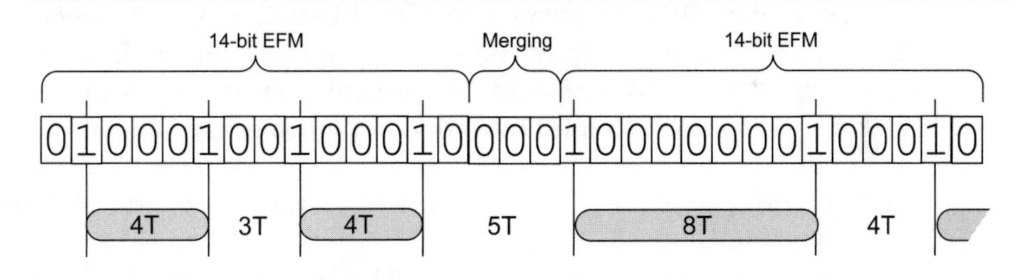

Figure 9.9 Run Length Encoding using Pits and Lands

Decoding

Retrieving PCM data from the disc follows the inverse process just described. The start of a frame is identified by the unique synch word. Every 14-bit symbol is converted back into 8-bit symbols. The merging bits can be discarded. The 8-bit symbols are fed into a CIRC decoder. At this point, the parity bits may indicate that some of the data is corrupted. Depending on the extent of the corruption, it may still be possible to recover the original signals in their entirety.

[3] No. That would be too easy.

Content Protection

The Red Book does not define any content protection mechanisms. It is very straightforward to retrieve the digital data from an audio CD—you merely stick it into your PC's CD-ROM drive. This capability allows you to use PCs to listen to CDs. Indeed, for some people, the PC is the dominant and/or only playback device they use for listening to music.

The flexibility also allows for the audio data to be ripped from the CD and stored on the PC itself, or perhaps on a different player, such as a portable MP3 player. This model allows for people to legitimately take advantage of fair use and listen to music they have purchased in a wide variety of fashions.

Alas, this same flexibility has made it very easy for people to distribute copies of the music to other people without first getting the legal right to do so from the music's copyright owner. Such infringement has led music companies to look for ways to add anti-piracy mechanisms to the existing CD-DA format.

Most of the content protection mechanisms developed so far attempt to prevent CDs from being played back at all on a PC's CD-ROM drive, or at least to introduce substantial distortion during the copy process. Hindering playback is tricky business, because, per the original specifications, all CD-DA discs should be playable on CD-ROM drives! Such content protection schemes have drawn the ire of the official CD licensing body, because they violate the specification. As such, some CDs with content protection have been produced without the official Compact Disc logo.

Licensing issues aside, there are still support issues. The same tricks that prevent the CDs from playing on a PC usually mean that the protected CDs won't play on some stand-alone CD players. For example, when BMG Entertainment released Natalie Imbruglia's *White Lilies Island* on copy-protected disc in the United Kingdom, there were so many player compatibility problems that within two weeks BMG set up a dedicated consumer hotline to handle the calls. On a positive note, BMG did replace the albums for consumers who were having playback problems.

Some of these content protection mechanisms actually cause a PC to crash when inserted into a PC! Luckily, there's often a workaround: some of the content protection schemes can be defeated by drawing on the edge of the disc with a felt-tip marker.

Recognizing that consumers want to listen to CDs on their PCs, some schemes prevent the Red Book audio tracks from being read on the PC, but make available data tracks that contain PC-friendly versions of the music. These computer music files are designed so that they can only be played on the consumer's computer, and do not play on somebody else's computer if sent to them electronically.

It remains to be seen how successfully content protection can be implemented within the existing installation base of the Red Book compliant players. Still, there is little doubt that content protection is a very real concern for the music and video industries. Later in this and subsequent chapters, we will discuss how other media formats have content protection designed into them from the beginning.

Other Audio Optical Disc Formats

Audio CDs are a revolutionary and immensely popular music format. They possess sound quality that is arguably so good that—for the average listener—the overall fidelity is limited by the environment. For instance, when listening to a CD while driving down the freeway, much of the CD's sound quality is masked by road noise. Still, there are audiophiles who insist that CDs sound too "digital." Some critics feel that CDs do not handle certain sound scenarios, such as flutes, well.

In addition, CDs are limited to stereo sound. With the advent of DVD-Video, home surround sound systems have become much more common. As such, there are platforms in place that can support the playback of music stored in surround format.

Some different optical disc formats have been developed with the intent of achieving higher sound quality and/or surround-sound support.

HCCD

High Definition Compatible Digital (HDCD) is a technology that strives to increase audio performance within the framework of standard CDs. Specifically, HDCD allows for better handling of very loud and very soft sounds, as well as high frequencies.

HDCD achieves its enhanced performance through a series of commands that are hidden in the 16-bit PCM audio data. An HDCD encoder determines when these enhancement codes need to be inserted. They insert the command one bit at a time as the least significant bit of a series of 16-bit audio samples. An HDCD decoder constantly examines the LSB of the audio data coming off the compact disc. When the decoder detects an HDCD identifier pattern and subsequent code, it performs special processing on the audio data to derive the enhanced fidelity.

The HDCD is particularly elegant in that it is very compatible with existing CD systems. A standard CD player can play an HDCD disc without a problem. It interprets any HDCD commands as pseudorandom quantization noise. An HDCD-aware player is able to play standard CDs without a problem: the LSB contains sound data, and the probability of a series of LSBs matching a valid HDCD command is very low.

The fact that HDCD-encoded discs sacrifice a bit of audio data to store commands means that such discs are marginally more noisy when played on a standard CD player, compared to a standard CD. The developers of HDCD maintain that the added noise is not detectable, due in part to the fact that not every sample needs to store HDCD commands; typically less than 5 percent of the samples are used to code HDCD via the LSB.

SACD

Super Audio CD (SACD) uses the existing CD format factor, but defines a new high-density data layer that can store up to 4.7 gigabytes of data. SACD was developed by Sony and Philips. The SACD specification is referred to colloquially as the Scarlet Book.

Whereas Red Book audio CDs store audio data as PCM, SACDs store audio in a Direct Stream Digital (DSD) format. DSD is based on 1-bit Sigma-Delta modulation, using a sampling rate of 2.8224 megahertz, which is exactly 64 times higher than 44.1 kilohertz rate used in CD-DA. SACD's DSD allows for a frequency response up to 100 kilohertz, well above the upper limits of human hearing, as well as a 120 dB dynamic range within the audible band.

A single SACD can contain separate DSD stereo and DSD six-channel surround-sound tracks. This duplicity allows for the best music mix to be played given the current playback system: stereo for two-speaker systems, six-channel for surround speaker systems. There is no need for a SACD player to down-mix a six-channel program to stereo for playback on two speaker systems.

Hybrid Discs

SACD hybrid discs store standard CD data, as well as SACD-specific data. The CD data can be played back via a standard CD player. This compatibility is accomplished by storing the SACD data using a material that is transparent to the 780-nm CD laser, as illustrated in Figure 9.10. Because it is transparent to the CD laser, the CD player is incapable of detecting the

SACD data. To the CD player, the hybrid disc looks just like a standard CD. However, an SACD player also has a 650-nm laser, to which the SACD data layer is reflective. The SACD player can thus read the SACD data.

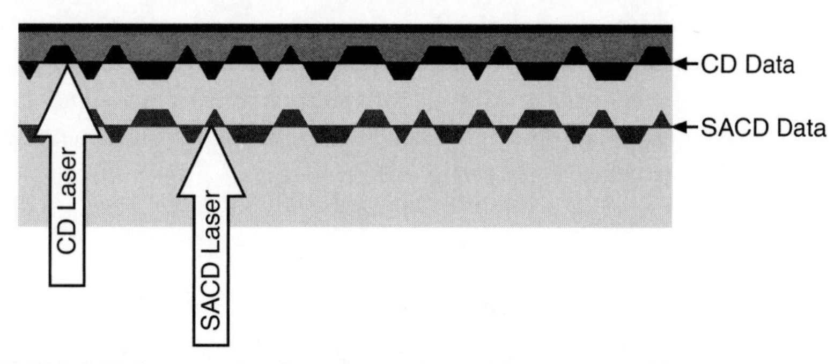

SACD hybrid discs contain a layer that can be read be a standard CD player, as well as a second layer that can only be read by an SACD player.

Figure 9.10 SACD Hybrid Disc

SACD includes several forms of content protection that make it difficult for the SACD data to be copied. For starters, there are no SACD-ROM drives for PCs, so there's no way to read the data onto a PC. Each SACD disc also includes a physical watermark known as a Pit Signal Processing Physical Disc Mark (PSP-DPM). Furthermore, the DSD data itself is scrambled.

MiniDisc

Sony announced a new music disc format in 1991 in an attempt to combine the success of their CD and Walkman[†] portable cassette player technologies. This MiniDisc (MD) format uses a small disc enclosed within a 7 cm square cartridge. Despite its smaller size, it can store up to 80 minutes of digital audio.

Whereas CDs store uncompressed audio, MiniDiscs store compressed music. The compression algorithm is known as Adaptive Transform Acoustic Coding (ATRAC[†]), a lossy technique that takes in 16-bit 44.1 kilohertz PCM—the same as CD samples—and produces a compressed data stream nearly five times smaller. MD audio is often described as near-CD quality.

In 1990, Sony expanded MD to include two new playback formats: LP2 and LP4. Based on a new (ATRAC3†) coding scheme, these formats allowed for increased playback times. LP2 provides 160 minutes on an 80-minute MD; LP4 provides 320 minutes. These long-play formats are collectively known as MDLP†.

MiniDisc includes both read-only and rewritable formats. The read-only discs are very similar in physical structure to CDs. The rewritable formats use a magneto-optical technology, similar to the withdrawn CD-MO format.

DVD

Digital audio is also available on DVD-Video and DVD-Audio optical discs. We'll discuss these formats in much greater detail in a separate chapter.

Summary

Compact Discs are a very successful consumer audio format. They store 16-bit/channel 44.1 kilohertz digital audio on optical discs. CDs are the dominant format for prerecorded music. CDs have relegated the previous audio media of LPs and cassette tapes to a minority share of the market.

CDs are available in read-only, recordable, and rewritable variations. In addition to the digital audio CD (CD-DA), generic data can be stored on CD-ROMs.

Chapter 10

MPEG

Bradley's Bromide: If computers get too powerful, we can organize them into a committee—that will do them in.

—unknown

The Moving Pictures Experts Group (MPEG) is the nickname for the International Standards Organization/International Electrotechnical Commission Joint Technical Committee 1 Sub Committee 29 Working Group 11 (ISO/IEC JTC1 SC29 WG11). The MPEG committee is comprised of technical experts from around the world who work together to create international standards for storing video and audio.

Overview

When originally formed in 1988, the MPEG committee was chartered to develop a video compression protocol. Within a year, they expanded their charter to include audio compression as well. Over the years, they have also defined additional protocols, such as ways to organize and distribute large databases of audiovisual files.

The standards that the MPEG committee has released are also named MPEG, such as MPEG-2. These standards define how to store video, audio, and ancillary data, but they do not define the actual algorithms for decoders and encoders of the formats. By avoiding implementation details, engineers are free to develop innovative and competitive mechanisms for creating and presenting MPEG compliant streams.

The term MPEG committee is used in this text to refer to the actual Moving Pictures Experts Group committee. Specific standards developed by the committee are listed as MPEG-*n*, such as MPEG-2. The term MPEG used by itself refers to the entire body of standards developed by the MPEG committee.

The MPEG standards are open in the sense that anyone can order documents describing the standards for a nominal fee. There are patents associated with several of the standards, so actually implementing and selling an MPEG device may require that the manufacturer pay royalties to a patent pool.

Royalty and licensing issues play a key role in the determination of which algorithms are selected for use in MPEG standards. Sometimes technically superior algorithms are passed over for algorithms that have worse performance but have more affordable licensing terms.

The Many Flavors of MPEG

The MPEG committee has developed several different standards, and continues to define new ones. The committee refers to each standard as a phase. The first phase was MPEG-1. The second was, naturally enough, MPEG-2. The third was, er, MPEG-4. The fourth phase is MPEG-7, and work continues on the fifth phase that is called MPEG-21.[1]

MPEG-1

MPEG-1 was approved in 1992 as a standard for storing and playing back video and audio. It had a maximum data rate of ~1.5 megabits per second and was designed to store near-VHS quality video with stereo sound onto VideoCDs. MPEG-1 also contained three layers of audio standards. MPEG-1 Audio Layer III has gained some fame under the nickname MP3.

MPEG-2

MPEG-2 built heavily on MPEG-1 and was approved in 1994. It added support for higher quality video formats (4:2:2, 4:4:4), higher resolutions, multiple audio channels, and higher data rates. MPEG-2 has since become the basis of several derived standards used in DVD, HDTV, and digital satellite broadcasts.

[1] You may wonder what the logic is in determining the number to be used for each successive phase. I came up with the following formula: $y = \frac{5}{12}x^4 - \frac{5}{2}x^3 + \frac{61}{12}x^2 - 2x + 1$

MPEG-4

The first version of MPEG-4 was approved in 1998. Several extensions to the standard have since been approved. MPEG-4 has many different uses, but is primarily targeted at multimedia and Web-based applications. For instance, MPEG-4 specifies a mechanism by which audio can be streamed across networks at various resolutions.

MPEG-7

MPEG-7 was approved in March 2001. Unlike its predecessors, it does not define a compression scheme, but rather a method for describing multimedia. MPEG-7 provides an infrastructure through which you can search and manage various forms of media. As the MPEG-7 home page cleverly puts it: "While MPEG- 1, 2, and 4 represents the content itself ('the bits'); MPEG-7 tries to represent the information about the content ('the bits about the bits')."

MPEG-21

In June 2001, work began on MPEG-21, a standard that aims to provide a framework for creating, distributing, and consuming multimedia across networks. Several parts of MPEG-21, such as the Digital Item Declaration and Digital Item Identification, have already been published, but some work items are not slated for completion until late 2004.

MPEG Audio

Because this book is about audio, we will focus on the audio compression algorithms offered by MPEG-1, MPEG-2, and MPEG-4. Although there are several different techniques encompassed within these standards, they primarily provide tools for compression audio in a lossy manner by using perceptual coding: they discard irrelevancies and redundancies in the audio signal that humans typically can't hear. The reconstructed waveform generated by the decoder does not match the original waveform, but it hopefully sounds very similar to it.

MPEG-1 Audio

One of the design goals of MPEG-1 was to store compressed movies on CDs. The 1X playback speed of the early CD drives meant that the data rate of the compressed movies had to be limited to 1.5 megabits per second. Given that uncompressed PCM audio on a standard CD takes up the full 1.5 megabits per second bandwidth of a 1X drive, the audio bit rate must be reduced to leave bandwidth for the video. In fact, the video, which is also compressed, takes up most of the 1.5 megabits per second bandwidth, so the audio bit rate must be drastically reduced.

The MPEG committee chose the approach of compressing the audio using a lossy technique. The original PCM data cannot be perfectly reconstructed from the compressed MPEG-1 audio stream. However, the MPEG-1 format is designed in such a way that ideally the human hearing system cannot hear the missing data. As such, the MPEG-1 audio format is an example of perceptual coding: a technique designed to store audio in a fashion that is perceptually lossless.

MPEG-1 supports 32-, 44.1-, and 48-kilohertz sampling rates, and allows for compressed audio bit rates of 32 to 224 kilobits per second. One study has shown that expert listeners cannot distinguish between the original audio and MPEG-1 audio compressed up to a ratio of 6:1.

Three different types of audio coding are supported under MPEG-1. They are known as Layer 1, Layer II, and Layer III. Layer I can be implemented using the simplest encoders and decoders, but it has the worst compression ratio of the three layers. Conversely, Layer III requires the most complex encoders and decoders, but offers the best compression ratio. Layer II complexity and efficiency are between those of Layers I and III.

MPEG-1 audio allows a maximum of two channels. These are typically used to carry stereo, but can also be used to store two independent mono channels. Two mono channels can be used for carrying two different languages.

MPEG-1 also supports joint stereo, a technique that uses the same waveform shape for the left and right channels for high frequencies, but scales the magnitude of the waveform differently for the two channels to create the stereo effect. Additionally, Layer III supports mid per side mode (M per s mode). As was discussed in Chapter 5, M per s stores L+R on one channel, and L-R on the other channel. These two signals can be processed to produce separate left and right channels or just as easily processed to create a monophonic signal.

Layer I

Layer I processes 384 audio samples at a time. These 384 samples are processed and split into 32 frequency *sub-bands* via a polyphase bandsplitting filter, shown graphically in Figure 10.1. These sub-bands are designed to roughly mimic the operation of the critical bands of the human hearing system. However, the sub-bands coming out of the bandsplitting filter each have the same bandwidth. By comparison, the width of critical bands varies by frequency. Higher frequencies have narrow bandwidths; lower frequencies have wider bandwidths. So while the Layer I bandsplitting filter is not the most accurate model of critical bands, it has the advantage of being very simple to implement. It should be noted that the filter bank is itself lossy: the data coming out of the bank cannot be used to exactly replicate the original signal. The loss level is, however, fairly low.

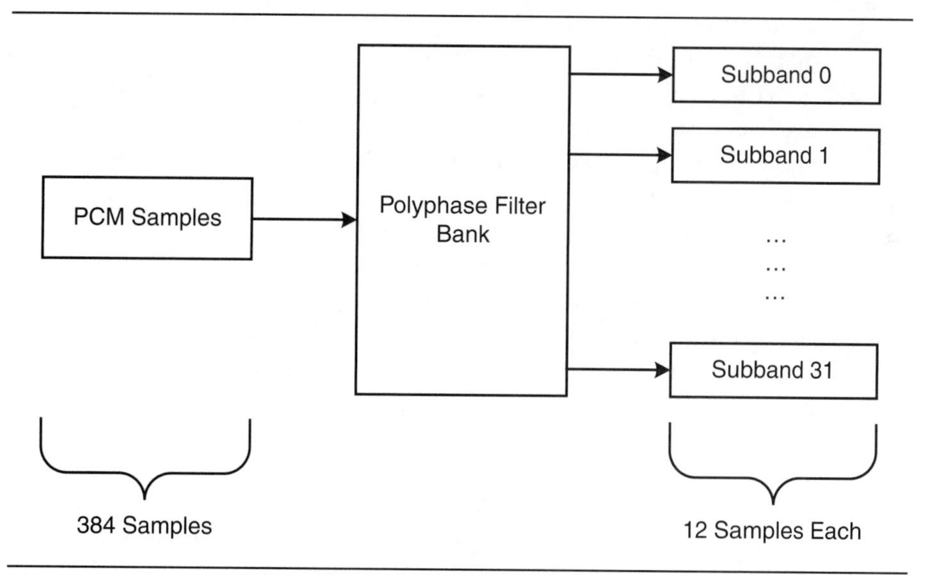

Figure 10.1 Layer I Filter Bank

Recall from Chapter 3 that the critical band model says that one sound can be masked by a simultaneous sound only if the two sounds are in the same region of the spectrum. The motivation in Layer I for splitting the original signal into sub-bands is that we can then examine each component and determine which sounds therein are heard by the average person and which ones are masked by other sounds.

After the 384 temporal samples are partitioned into 32 frequency sub-bands, each sub-band is critically decimated, or resampled at the critical frequency, resulting in 12 samples for each sub-band. These samples are shifted in frequency so that each sub-band begins at 0 hertz. This frequency-shifting technique is known as *heterodyning*.

Next, a scaling factor is chosen for each sub-band, based on the peak sample magnitude within each band. This six-bit factor is applied to all the samples in a given sub-band. Each sub-band may have a different scaling factor. This technique is known as *companding*. The signal is scaled to raise it above the noise floor. The scale factor needs to be transmitted to the decoder so that the signal can be scaled back down to its proper level for playback.

Finally, the samples in each sub-band are requantized into samples that are 0 to 15 bits long. All the samples in a given sub-band have the same length, but the requantized sample length varies from one sub-band to another. Increasing the coarseness of the quantization increases the quantization noise. The companding protects the signal to some extent, but it is important to choose the requantization level in such a way as to minimize the perceptual noise. Ideally, the encoder wants to make its choices in such a way that any quantization noise is hidden by the masking innate in human hearing. We'll discuss this concept more in the Psychoacoustical Models section later in this chapter.

Layer I streams have constant bit rate, so the compressed output of each input block must be the same size. Therefore, when the encoder is selecting quantization coarseness for the sub-bands, it needs to make its choices so that the total number of bits used to code the entire block equal a fixed number. The exact number varies based on the desired bit rate of the stream. This process of balancing the data payload across the sub-bands is known as *bit allocation*.

A compressed Layer I frame looks like Figure 10.2. It begins with a header, which contains a synchronization word, along with information about the bit stream, such as the sampling frequency and encoded bit rate. The header is optionally followed by a cyclic redundancy checksum (CRC) of the frame. Next comes bit allocation information, which indicates the bit length of the samples in each of the 32 sub-bands. Then comes scale factors for each of the 32 bands. Next are the actual requantized samples themselves. The frame may end with optional ancillary data.

Header	CRC	Bit allocation	Scale Factors	Samples	Ancillary Data
32	0 or 16	128-256	0-384		

Field sizes are in bits.

Figure 10.2 Layer I Frame

Pre-echoes

As has been previously noted, Layer I processes audio on fixed sizes frames of 384 samples. Each of these frames is a temporal window. For a 22-kilohertz sampling rate, the window is 384 / 22 kilohertz = 17.45 ms long. Because we are operating on a single window at a time, there is a risk that we may introduce coding artifacts within one window that do not appear in neighboring windows, thus causing sound discontinuity. There is also a risk that we may introduce coding artifacts that spread across a window that are not part of the original sound. An example of this later phenomenon is the pre-echo.

A pre-echo is basically quantization noise that precedes a transient sound, depicted graphically in Figure 10.3. This effect would be equivalent to hearing a faint burst of static right *before* a gunshot.[2]

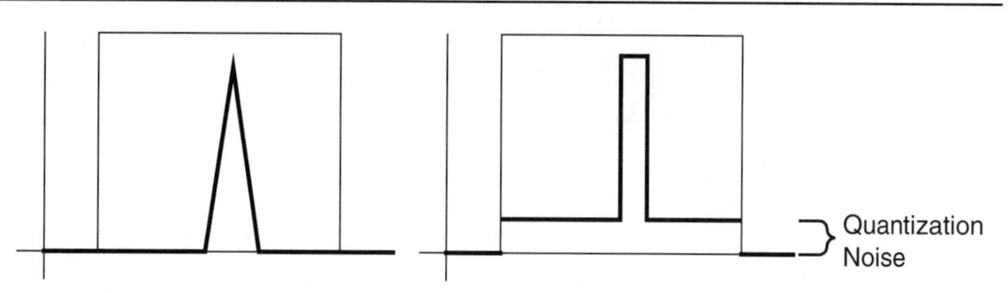

The original signal (left) consists of silence and a loud transient. When coded (right), the resulting signal includes quantization noise that precedes the transient. Neighboring windows do not include the quantization noise, making the pre-echo artifact discernable.

Figure 10.3 Pre-Echo

[2] Pre-echoes would be handy in the real world, as then you would know when to duck!

Layer II

Layer II is very similar to Layer I. However, it uses frames consisting of 1,152 samples. Each frame is broken into thirds and run through the same filter bank as Layer I. Each sub-band thus consists of three consecutive sets of 12 samples each. Layer II takes advantage of similarities among temporally adjacent sample sets to achieve increased coding efficiency.

The same companding and requantization steps from Layer I are followed for Layer II with a few differences.

For a given sub-band n, a different scale factor for each of the three temporally adjacent sample sets are used only if necessary. Often the same scale factor can be shared among two or even all three of the sets. This scale factor sharing is indicated by a field known as Scale Factor Selection Information (SCFSI). Layer II's scale factor sharing technique achieves a nominal bit rate savings of 50 percent over the scaling information bit rate of Layer I.

Layer II also takes advantage of the availability of three sets of data when storing requantized samples. Samples with certain levels of quantization do not code efficiently in a binary scheme. For instance, storing nine levels takes four bits, but only uses nine of the sixteen possible bit patterns available with four bits. Layer II addresses this inefficiency by grouping triplets of samples together into granules. These granules store more efficiently into binary space. Granules are used only when the samples have three, five, or nine levels of quantization.

As an example of granule efficiency, consider the example of five-level samples. Storing such a sample would require three bits. Independently storing three such samples would take $3 \times 3 = 9$ bits. However, if we instead considered the three samples simultaneously, we would just need to store the $5 \times 5 \times 5 = 125$ different possible combinations of levels, which we could do with only seven bits with very little waste.

In Layer I, samples in each sub-band were requantized into new samples of 0 to 15 bits. The size of each requantized sample was indicated using a four-bit bit allocation code. In Layer II, high frequency sub-bands can be requantized to 0 to 15 bits, but midrange sub-bands can only be requantized to 0 to 7 bits and low frequency sub-bands to 0 to 3 bits. As such, the bit allocation codes are respectively four, three, and two bits for high, medium and low frequency sub-bands.

The header for Layer II frames is shown in Figure 10.4. It is very similar to the Layer I header, except that it contains the additional SCFSI.

Header	CRC	Bit allocation	SCFSI	Scale Factors	Samples	Ancillary Data
32	0 or 16	26-188	0-60	0-1080		

Field sizes are in bits.

Figure 10.4 Layer II Frame

Layer III

The most complex coding scheme is Layer III. In exchange for its greater complexity, it offers the highest compression rates of the three layers. Layer III is colloquially known as MP3.

To overcome some of the deficiencies of the filter bank, Layer III coding applies a modified discrete cosine transform (MDCT) to each sub-band. The MDCT converts the samples from the time domain to the frequency domain.

Layer III defines four different window shapes that can be used to calculate the MDCT, depicted graphically in Figure 10.5. Type 0 is a wide window that covers 36 samples. It offers the highest frequency resolution: 18 discrete spectral components. Type 2 is a narrower window that covers only 12 samples. An MDCT using this window results in six spectral components. Although its spectral resolution is lower, it offers higher temporal resolution. The narrow window is typically used when there is a risk of pre-echoes.

There are two other window types. Type 1 is used to transition from a wide to a narrow window. Type 3 is used to transition from a narrow to a wide window. This transition process is shown in Figure 10.6. The fact that adjacent windows overlap by 50 percent can also be seen in this figure.

Layer III removes the ability to have individual scale factors for each sub-band. Instead, Layer III uses scale factor bands. Each scale factor band applies across multiple MDCT outputs. Each scale factor band corresponds roughly to the critical bands of human hearing.

Rather than using the linear quantization of Layers I and II, Layer III first raises the samples to the ¾th power to create a non-linear quantization. This nonlinearity helps provide signal to noise characteristics that are better aligned with human hearing.

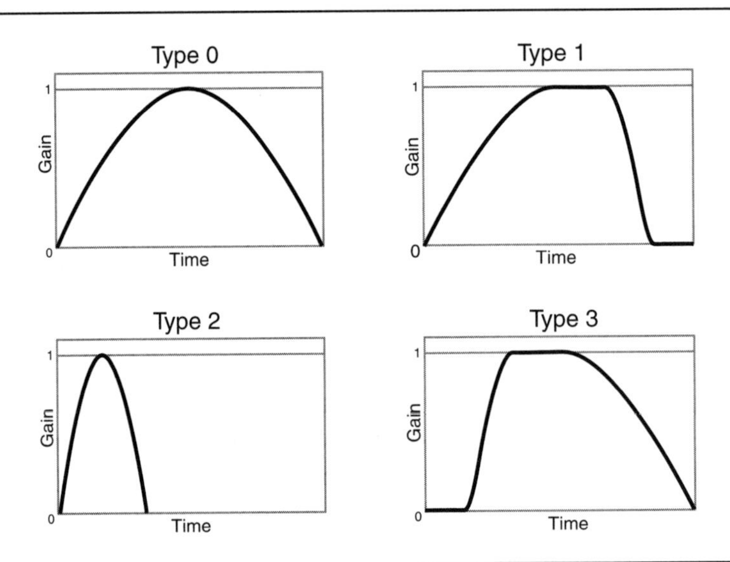

Figure 10.5 Layer III MDCT Windows

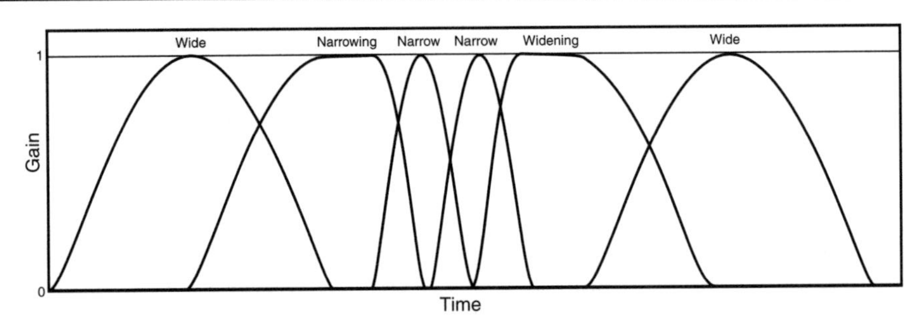

A wide type 0 window is followed by a type 1 window to create a smooth transition to type 2 windows. The transition from type 2 back to type 1 is accomplished via a type 3 window.

Figure 10.6 Window Transitions

Layer III achieves further compression by applying Huffman coding to the quantized samples. Huffman coding uses short symbols to store frequent values and longer symbols to store infrequent values. For instance, English text could be Huffman coded using the symbol 01 for the frequent letter E and 000001 for the less frequent letter Q.

To achieve a constant output bit rate while Huffman coding, Layer III uses a bit reservoir. Frames that can be coded using less than the average bit rate contribute bits to the reservoir that can be consumed by other frames that may require additional space.

ID3

Arguably, the most successful of the MPEG audio formats is Layer III in stand-alone files known as MP3 files. MP3 files became an increasingly popular way to store digital music in the late 1990s, first on PCs, and then on dedicated consumer electronic players. One of the complaints that people had with MP3 files was that there was no standard way to store information about the music content within the stream.

In 1996, Eric Kemp created a 128-byte structure for storing such information, as described in Figure 10.7. Although he created it for his own use, it quickly gained a wide following and support for it began appearing in most MP3 players. Known as an *ID3 tag*, it was appended to the end of an MP3 file. A player could go to the end of the music file and look for the TAG header in the last 128 bytes. If it was there, it could then display information about the encoded song.

ìTAGî	Title	Artist	Album	Year	Comment	Genre
3	30	30	30	4	30	1

Field sizes are in bytes.

Figure 10.7 ID3v1 Tag Structure

Notice that ID3 is not part of MPEG. In fact, it has not been sanctioned by any standards body. Independently, other people subsequently extended the original format. ID3v1.1 uses the last byte of the ID3 comment field to store the CD track number of the song and, as such, is very interoperable with ID3v1.

ID3v2 is a tagging format that is completely incompatible with ID3v1. ID3v2 is very flexible, allowing for a large number of song attributes to be stored in a tag structure that can be as large as 256 megabytes, although few real-world tags achieve this massive size. ID3v2 tags can be placed at the beginning of files, which allows for more timely retrieval of the information in streaming implementations. Most MP3 players today support ID3v2.

Psychoacoustical Models

The MPEG-1 audio standard includes two sample psychoacoustic models that an encoder may use to make intelligent bit allocation decisions. Model 1 is computationally simple, but does not provide the most accurate modeling. However, it provides sufficient performance to allow for good coding at high bit rates. Model 2 is much more complex, which means it can provide accurate coding even at low bit rates. As you might expect, model 2 is more computationally intensive than model 1.

Note that the two psychoacoustical models are not part of the normative standard, but instead are informational. Their use is entirely optional. Encoders may create their own models in an attempt to get increased fidelity.

Common Measurements

Recall that a strong signal can render a weaker signal inaudible. In other words, a masker masks a maskee. The masking is most pronounced when the masker and maskee are in the same critical band. Given a potential masker, we can describe a masking threshold. Sounds below the masking threshold are inaudible in the presence of the masker. A snippet of sound may have multiple maskers. In this case, a global masking threshold can be computed. Both types of masking thresholds vary with frequency.

The distance between the intensity of the masker and the masking threshold is known as the *signal to mask ratio (SMR)*.

For a given sub-band, the perceivable distortion is the *noise to mask ratio* (NMR). NMR can be calculated using the SMR and the signal to noise ratio, as shown in Equation 10.1.

Equation 10.1 Noise to Mask Ratio

$$NMR = SMR - SNR \quad \text{[in dB]}$$

Models 1 and 2

Superficially, the two informative models follow the same basic process. They begin by using an FFT to create a high resolution spectrum of the samples. Now, the polyphase filter already does create such a spectrum, but the FFT creates one of substantially higher resolution.

Model 1 uses a 512-sample window for Layer I and a 1,024-sample window for Layers II and III. Being powers of 2, the FFT can be efficiently implemented for the 512 and 1,024-window sizes. For Layer I, the 384 samples in a frame fit nicely within the 512-sample window. For Layers II and III, the 1,152 samples in a frame are larger than the FFT window. The samples falling outside the window are discarded in a tradeoff between coding simplicity and accuracy. Hopefully the discarded samples do not contribute significantly to the overall characteristics of the frame.

Model 2 uses a 1,024-sample window for all three layers. Again, for Layer I, the 384 samples in a frame fit within the window with no problem. For Layers II and III, a different technique is used than in model 1. The 1,024-sample FFT window is applied separately to the first 576 samples and the last 576 samples. These two sets of FFT results are considered for the psychoacoustical evaluation of the frame. All the samples are used, compared to model 1 in which some of the samples were discarded.

Next the models identify the tonal and non-tonal components of the signal. Model 1 does this classification by using heuristically-chosen maxima in each critical band. These maxima indicate a tonal component. The remainder of the signal in that band is treated as an atonal signal. From this information, a masking threshold is calculated for each sub-band along with a global masking threshold. Finally, a signal to mask ratio is computed for each sub-band. These values are passed to the bit-allocation module; it uses the information to determine which sub-bands can suffer the most quantization noise and hence be coded with the fewest number of bits.

Model 2 does not explicitly calculate the tonal and atonal components. Instead, the spectral data is split into partitions. These partitions are as wide as either one frequency line or one third of a critical band, whichever is wider at the given frequency. For each partition, the unpredictability of the spectrum is measured. A pure tone is very predictable. Noise is very unpredictable. From this unpredictability measurement, a tonality factor is derived. This tonality is used in the derivation of a masking threshold and eventually a signal to mask ratio for each of the sub-bands. Again, the SMR is fed to the encoder's bit allocation module.

MPEG-2 Audio

MPEG-2 audio has three main components: Lower Sampling Frequencies (LSF), Backwards Compatibility (BC) and Advanced Audio Coding (AAC). MPEG-2 LSF and MPEG-2 BC are defined in ISO/IEC 13818-3, which was finalized in November 1994. MPEG-2 AAC was finalized in April 1997 as ISO/IEC 13818-7.

MPEG-2 LSF

Recall that MPEG-1 only supports sampling frequencies of 32, 44.1, and 48 kilohertz. MPEG-2 LSF uses the same format MPEG-1, but also adds support for the lower sampling rates of 16, 22.05, and 24 kilohertz. All three layers are supported.

An MPEG-2 LSF decoder can thus play existing MPEG-1 audio files. However, an MPEG-1 decoder is not necessarily able to play an audio file encoded by an MPEG-2 LSF encoder; the sampling rate may not be supported.

Note also that there are also coders and streams which use sampling frequencies of 8, 11.025, and 12 kilohertz. Such frequency support may be colloquially referred to as MPEG-2.5, but there is no such MPEG phase; these very low frequencies are not part of any MPEG ISO/IEC standard.

MPEG-2 BC

Recall that MPEG-1 audio supports a maximum of two channels. MPEG-2 BC was designed to add support for additional channels, and to do so in such a way as to maintain compatibility with MPEG-1. This compatibility is achieved by taking advantage of the fact that MPEG-1 frames may contain ancillary data. The format and function of such data is unspecified, so an MPEG-1 compliant decoder ignores them.

An MPEG-2 BC encoder stores the L and R channels in the two channels supported by MPEG-1. The encoder stores additional channels in the portion of the MPEG-1 frame reserved for ancillary data.

If a multichannel MPEG-2 BC stream is sent to an MPEG-1 decoder, the decoder properly recovers a useful stereo signal. It is for this reason that MPEG-2 BC is considered backwards compatible with MPEG-1. If the same stream is sent to an MPEG-2 BC decoder, the decoder is able to recover the additional channels.

Notice that an MPEG-2 BC decoder can also play any stream generated by an MPEG-1 encoder. For this reason, MPEG-2 BC may also be considered forward compatible with MPEG-1.

MPEG-2 BC elegantly adds multichannel support while maintaining very good cross compatibility with MPEG-1. It achieves this compatibility at a price: it cannot make use of some of the coding efficiencies that would be possible under a scheme that natively comprehended multichannel sound.

Also, even though MPEG-1 allows for arbitrary ancillary data lengths, the overall stream has a maximum bit rate to which it must adhere. Coding the surround channels may very well come at the expense of the main channels. Care must taken when coding the surround channels so that when combined with the main channels the final stream does not exceed the maximum permitted bit rate.

MPEG-2 AAC

To address some of the limitations of MPEG-2 BC, a new scheme was devised for compressing multichannel audio streams without the constraint of being backwards compatible to MPEG-1. Known originally by the somewhat unwieldy moniker of MPEG-2 Non-Backward Compatible, it has since been renamed MPEG-2 Advanced Audio Coding (AAC).

AAC allows up to 48 main channels, 16 LFE channels, 16 alternate language channels, and 16 ancillary data streams. An AAC stream may contain up to 16 different programs, each of which is a unique combination of the aforementioned elements. The use of multiple programs allows a movie's score and sound effects to be stored on one set of channels and dialog in a variety of languages to be stored on different sets of channels. The playback language can be easily switched during playback, and efficiency is realized by not repeatedly encoding the score and effects channels for every language.

MPEG-2 AAC supports sampling frequencies from 8,000 to 96,000 hertz. It supports bit rates as low as 8 and as high as 576 kilobits per second per channel.

Tools

AAC encoding is accomplished via a set of tools or modules. They include:

- Gain control
- Filter bank
- Prediction
- Quantization and coding
- Bit-stream multiplexing
- Temporal noise shaping (TNS)
- Mid per side (M per s) stereo coding and intensity stereo coding.

These tools are used by an encoder to compress an audio stream (and the tools' inverses are used to decode that stream). A sample MPEG-2 AAC encoder is shown in Figure 10.8.

Profiles

The actual selection of tools used varies depending on the profile used. A profile defines a set of constraints that are a subset of the MPEG-2 AAC specification. By setting pre-defined profiles, less expensive encoders and decoders can be built that meet a certain application space. Without the profiles, every decoder would need to be capable of processing the full gamut of MPEG-2 AAC compliant streams—a feat which would add often unnecessary complexity and cost to the decoder.

AAC includes three profiles: main, low complexity, and scalable sampling rate.

The main profile provides the best audio quality. As a rule of thumb, a main profile MPEG-2 AAC stream can provide the same audio fidelity as an MPEG-2 BC stream with twice the bit rate. For the main profile, all tools except the gain control tool may be used. Main profile decoders are also capable of playing low complexity profile streams.

The low complexity (LC) profile requires less processing power and a smaller memory footprint to decode than the main profile does. The gain control and prediction controls may not be used in this profile, and restrictions are placed on the use of TNS.

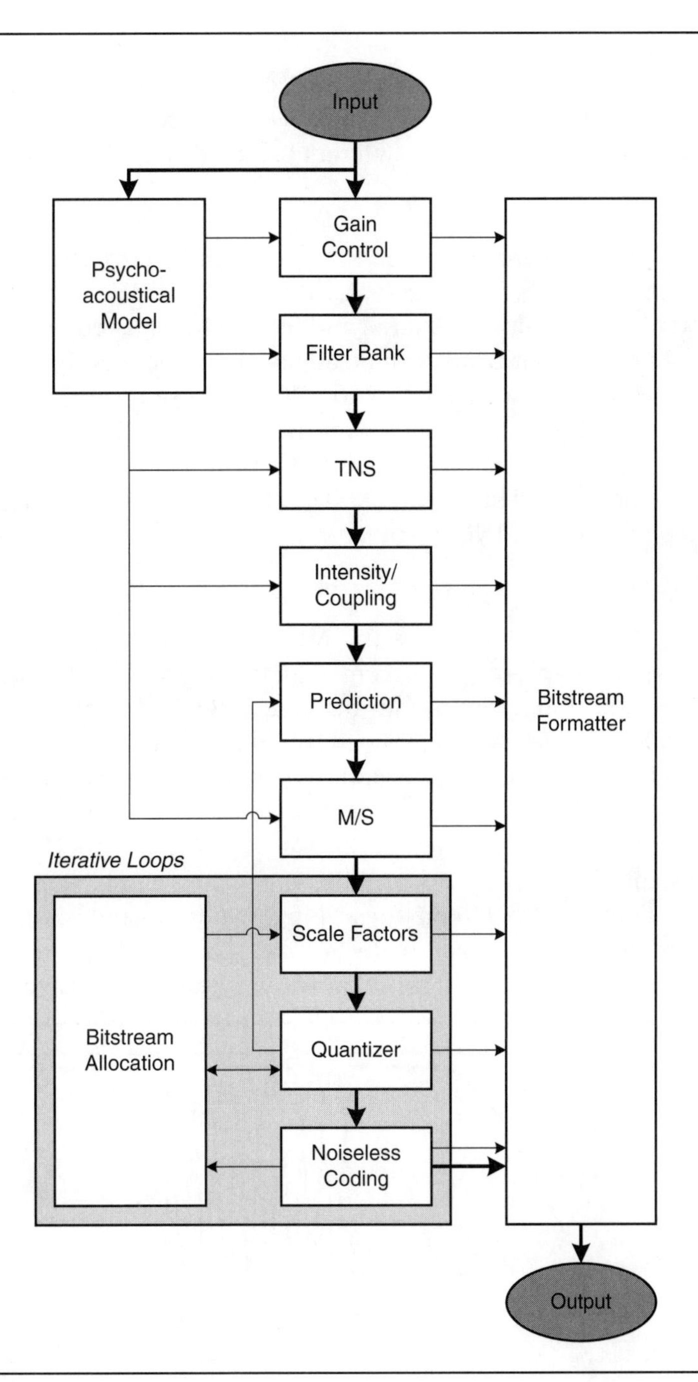

Figure 10.8 MPEG-2 AAC Encoder

The scalable sampling rate (SSR) profile is the least complex of the profiles. It requires the use of the gain control tool, but forbids use of the prediction tool. Again, the TNS usage is restricted. The scalability of SSR refers to the fact that streams of different bandwidth can be easily generated.

Gain Control

The gain control tool splits each channel into four equally sized frequency bands using a Polyphase Quadrature Filter (PQF). The PQF outputs are critically decimated and their gain adjusted. Note that the gain of each of the four bands can be adjusted independently.

When all four bands of the PQF are used, the gain tool has a bandwidth of 24 kilohertz. However, by discarding the output of one or more of the multiple bands, the output bandwidth can be changed to 18, 12, or 6 kilohertz. This ease of scalability means that decoders can be simplified for low bandwidth streams.

Filter Bank

The AAC filter bank uses the MDCT. As with Layer III, the MDCT windows overlap by 50 percent and there are two fundamental window sizes. The long window in this case is 2,048 samples, whereas the short window is 256 samples. Again, the short window is best suited for transients, while the longer window is better for steadier signals. The short windows must be used in sets of eight so as to stay in phase with the long windows that may be in use by other channels for the same time instant.

Transition between these long windows and short windows is accomplished via transitional start and stop windows, as shown in Figure 10.9. Again, this handling of transitions is similar to Layer III.

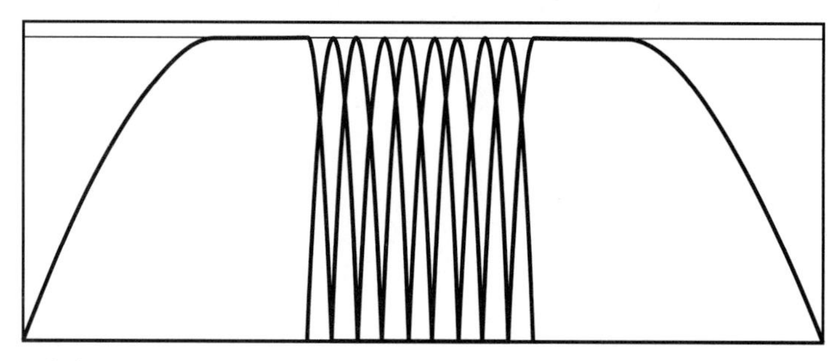

A start window, eight short windows, and a stop window.

Figure 10.9 AAC Window Transitions

In addition to window sizes, AAC supports two different window shapes. The Kaiser-Bessel derived (KBD) window rolls off very steeply and is good at separating signals that are more than 220 hertz apart. The sine window rolls off less steeply, but produces good separation of densely packed spectral components (< 70 hertz apart). AAC allows the encoder to switch seamlessly between the two window shapes, so that the most efficient shape for the given signal can be chosen on a frame-by-frame basis.

TNS

Temporal Noise Shaping is a technique designed to reduce pre-echo effects. TNS allows for fine grain control over the spectral components within a single block coming out of the filter bank. The use of TNS is optional and may be toggled on or off on a block by block basis.

TNS works by applying predictive coding in the frequency domain. Predictive coding is the technique of coding the differences between adjacent samples, rather than explicitly coding the explicit values of the samples. Given the duality of time and frequency, predictive coding in the context of TNS means that quantization noise is shaped like the input signal. As a result, TNS makes it much more feasible to mask quantization noise below transient signal levels across an entire block.

Prediction

In addition to explicitly coding the intensity of spectral components of a signal, AAC allows for the difference between the current and previous frames' intensities to be coded. This technique is known as *prediction*, because the current values are derived from previous values. Prediction allows for increases in coding efficiency in slow-changing signals where the difference from one frame to another of each spectral component is very small, and hence the difference can be coded with fewer bits than explicitly coding the actual levels for each frame.

Prediction is not effective for rapidly-varying signals, and for this reason may not be used for short windows (which are assumed to only be used for rapidly-varying signals). Prediction is optional and may be selected on a frame by frame basis.

Quantization

AAC uses non-uniform quantization where the input values are raised to the 0.75 power.

Noiseless Coding

Noiseless coding is a lossless compression technique. It does not use perceptual techniques, but achieves compression by using entropy coding (specifically, Huffman coding). It is similar to the coding scheme used in Layer III, but provides a larger number of codebooks as well as increased flexibility in the application of those books.

MPEG-4 Audio

MPEG-1 and MPEG-2 define mechanisms for coding arbitrary audio waveforms. MPEG-4 also includes mechanisms for coding such general audio as well. Additionally, MPEG-4 has techniques designed explicitly for coding speech. MPEG-4 also has tools wherein structured data is used to convey audio information, rather than waveform-derived data.

The main intent of MPEG-4 is to store audio at low bit rates. These bit rates have a nominal range from 2 to 64 kilobits per second, although excursions from this range are possible in certain configurations. Even though the bit rates are lower than MPEG-1 and MPEG-2, it is still possible to achieve CD quality sound using MPEG-4 coding.

The first version of MPEG-4 was finalized in October 1998. Additional tools were added to MPEG-4 with version 2, which was finalized in December 1999. Additional tools have since further augmented the specifications.

General Audio Coding

MPEG-4 has three main schemes for coding general audio: AAC, Transform-Domain Weighted Interleave Vector Quantization (TwinVQ), and Harmonic and Individual Lines plus Noise (HILN). Although there are no hard and fast rules, AAC is best suited for higher bit rates, TwinVQ for midrange bit rates, and HILN for the lowest bit rates.

AAC

The MPEG-4 AAC toolset includes all of the MPEG-2 AAC tools. As such, an appropriate MPEG-4 decoder can play MPEG-2 AAC streams. Some of the MPEG-2 AAC tools have been given a few new capabilities in the context of MPEG-4, allowing for greater flexibility and performance. An MPEG-4 stream generated using these new capabilities would mean that such an MPEG-2 AAC decoder would not be able to play the stream.

In addition to the MPEG-2 AAC tools, MPEG-4 also adds new tools: Perceptual Noise Substitution and Long Term Prediction.

Perceptual Noise Substitution (PNS) is a tool that allows noise-like elements in the input audio to be stored as parametric data, rather than explicitly coding the random waveform. When using PNS, the noise-like elements of the stream are identified and removed from the stream prior to subsequent coding and quantization. The noise is coded independently by setting a noise substitution flag and storing a power level for the removed noise. The decoder generates random noise of the indicated intensity and injects it back into the reconstructed audio waveform.

So why are we inserting noise back into the system? It may not actually be true noise; it is a noise-like component that existed in the original signal. For instance, rainfall or sizzling bacon sounds like noise, yet could be the sound we're trying to record. Because one of our coding goals is to maintain the perceptual characteristics of that original signal, we cannot discard the noise-like signal.

Long Term Prediction (LTP) achieves signal compression by removing redundancy in unchanging sounds such as pure tones. Whereas the normal Prediction tool works within a single frame, LTP is applied across multiple frames.

TwinVQ

Transform-Domain Weighted Interleave Vector Quantization is a tool designed to replace the AAC's scale and quantization tools. TwinVQ is well suited to low bit rates of 6 to 40 kilobits per second and nominally gives better performance than AAC for bit rates below 16 kilobits per second.

TwinVQ works by taking spectral coefficients, such as the input signal vector in Figure 10.10, and interleaving them into subvectors. These subvectors are weighted using values from the perceptual model being used. The resulting values are run through a weighted vector quantization (VQ) process to produce indices that are coded into the stream.

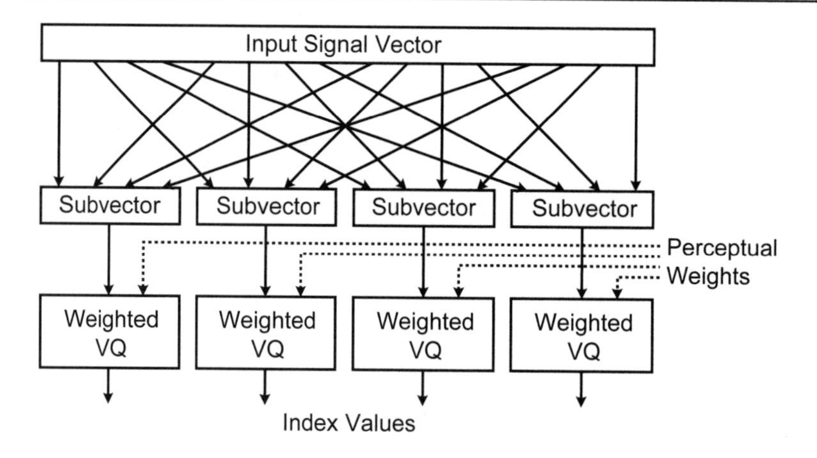

Figure 10.10 TwinVQ

HILN

Harmonic and Individual Line plus Noise (HILN) is a parametric coding technique. It works by breaking down the input signal into basic audio objects and then coding the parameters of these objects into the stream. As an analogy, consider the idea of parametrically coding a real-world environment using basic objects of blocks and cylinders. An office building might be parametrically coded as a block 100 feet by 150 feet by 200 feet. A tire on a car in the parking lot out front could be coded as a cylinder 6 inches wide and 18 inches in diameter. Of course, the shape of complex objects such as a car would be very hard to code using only a cylinder and a block as primitives.

HILN uses three audio primitives: harmonic lines, individual lines, and noise. It is from these primitives that HILN derives its name.

The harmonic lines refer to a harmonic tone. Such objects have parameters of a fundamental frequency as well as the amplitudes of the harmonic components. Individual lines refer to sinusoid or pure tones. The parameters used to represent these objects are the frequency and amplitude of the tone. Noise is represented by parameters that define its spectral shape.

HILN encoding works by first identifying and coding the harmonic lines. The harmonic components are removed from the sound being coded, and the result is parsed for individual lines. These lines are coded and similarly removed from the sound. The remaining sound element has had all harmonic and sinusoidal elements removed. It is considered to be noise-like and is coded as such.

The parameters of the objects are compressed into the stream using prediction, quantization, and entropy coding.

One interesting aspect of parametric coding is that the speed and pitch of the audio waveform can be easily altered during playback.

Speech Coding

In addition to the general audio coding tools described above, MPEG-4 also defines tools that are explicitly targeted for coding human speech.[3] The two toolsets are Harmonic Vector Excitation Coder (HVXC) and Code Excitation Linear Prediction (CELP). HVXC supports constant bit rates of 2 and 4 kilobits per second and variable bit rates from 1.2 to 1.7 kilobits per second. CELP supports bit rates from 4 to 24 kilobits per second.

Humans speak by pushing air out from their lungs, through the glottis, or vocal chords, and into the vocal tract, which consists of the upper esophagus and oral cavity. Air is often directed into the nasal cavity as well. Speech is a complex modulation of air flow controlled by distortion of the glottis, vocal tract, and nasal tract.

The vocal tract is shaped roughly like a tube and as such has resonant frequencies. These frequencies are known as *formant frequencies* or simply as *formants*. Because the vocal tract's shape changes over time, so too do the formants.

The primitive sounds of human speech are placed into three categories: *voiced*, *unvoiced*, and *plosive*. Voiced sounds are quasic-period air pulses generated by a vibrating glottis. The "oo" sound in "moo" is an example of a voiced sound. Unvoiced sounds are generated by creating a constriction on the vocal tract coupled with sufficient air velocity so as to produce turbulent flow. Unvoiced sounds have broad, noisy spectra. They are also known as fricative sounds. The "sh" sound in "fish" is an example of an unvoiced sound. Plosive sounds are those formed by completely closing the tract, building up pressure, and then explosively releasing that pressure. The "p" sounds in "pop" are examples of plosive sounds.

---

[3] You might think that the term "human speech" is redundant, but I've got a feeling those dolphins are talking about something. Maybe, "So long, and thanks for all the fish?"

CELP Coding

CELP is an extension of a speed coding technique known as Linear Predictive Coding (LPC). In a nutshell, LPC works by predicting the current speech sample by doing a linear combination of several previous samples. LPC uses a model that assumes that speech consists of voiced and unvoiced sounds.

LPC speech is synthesized by sending signals into a time-varying digital filter designed to mimic characteristics of the vocal tract, as represented in Figure 10.11. This filter is known as an LPC filter. Voiced sounds are generated by sending impulses to the filter; unvoiced sounds are generated by sending noise into the filter. Only one type of excitation, impulse train or noise, can be fed into the LPC filter at a time. Both types of excitations are modulated by a gain (G), which is an analog of air flow within the vocal tract.

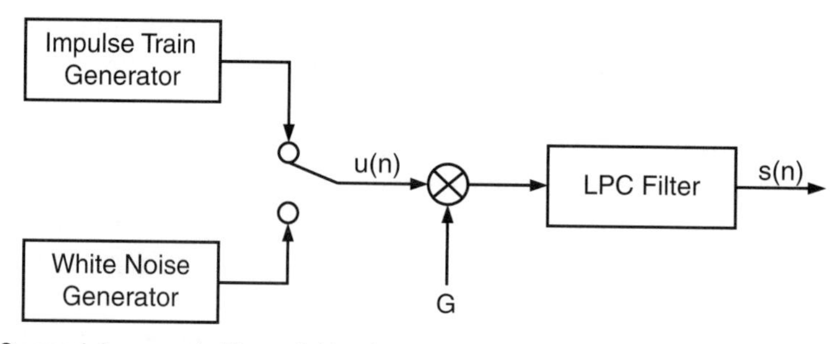

LPC speech is generated by switching between impulse trains and noise. These excitations u(n) are modified by a gain parameter G and fed to the time-varying LPC filter to generate the speech signal s(n).

Figure 10.11 LPC Speech Synthesizer

The process of determining the LPC filter coefficients, gain, voiced, and unvoiced components for every frame is known as LPC analysis. It is these parameters that are the output of LPC analysis which are coded into a stream. To reproduce speech, these parameters are recovered from the stream and used to configure the LPC synthesizer diagrammed above in Figure 10.11.

One of the drawbacks of LPC is that its analysis procedure requires each speech segment to be categorized as either voiced or unvoiced, when in fact a speech segment may include both voiced and unvoiced components. CELP overcomes this limitation.

CELP continues to use linear prediction to provide a rough estimation of the current speech sample based on previous samples. However, this estimation is almost always slightly different than the original speech sample. The difference between the two is known as the *error* or the *residual*. In CELP, this residual signal is stored as a vector quantized random sequence of pulses. These random pulses are used to excite the LPC filter.

MPEG-4 CELP supports two bandwidths: narrowband (8 kilohertz) and wideband (16 kilohertz). Narrowband is most applicable for a single person speaking. Wideband is better suited for coding multiple speakers.[4]

HVXC

HVXC is also based on LPC. Unlike CELP, it does make a distinction between voiced and unvoiced speech segments. For voiced portions, the residuals are coded using vector quantization, similar to CELP. For the unvoiced portions, the residual is coded using Vector Excitation Coding (VXC).

The HVXC parametric coding scheme is similar to the HILN structure. In fact, HVXC and HILN can be supported in a single parametric decoder, shown graphically in Figure 10.12 that supports switching between HVXC and HILN on a frame-by-frame basis. The optimal algorithm can be selected depending on whether the content is pure speech or more general audio.

Synthetic Sound

MPEG-4 also defines mechanisms for coding synthetic sounds. The intent of these schemes is not to store existing waveforms but instead to code general information that can be reconstructed or rendered in a variety of ways.

So rather than coding the recorded waveform of an orchestra playing a symphony, you would instead just code the sheet music for the symphony. Rather than coding the recorded waveform of a person speaking, you would instead code the text of their speech.

By their very nature, synthetic sound schemes are not useful for reproducing a specific person's voice or a specific musician's performance. The synthetic schemes are useful in that they can convey generic speech and musical information using very low bit rates. The decoder also has great flexibility in rendering synthetic sound. Different instruments and voice types can be easily substituted for the originals.

---

[4] For instance, if you had James Earl Jones talking to Tweety Bird, you would almost certainly want to use wideband.

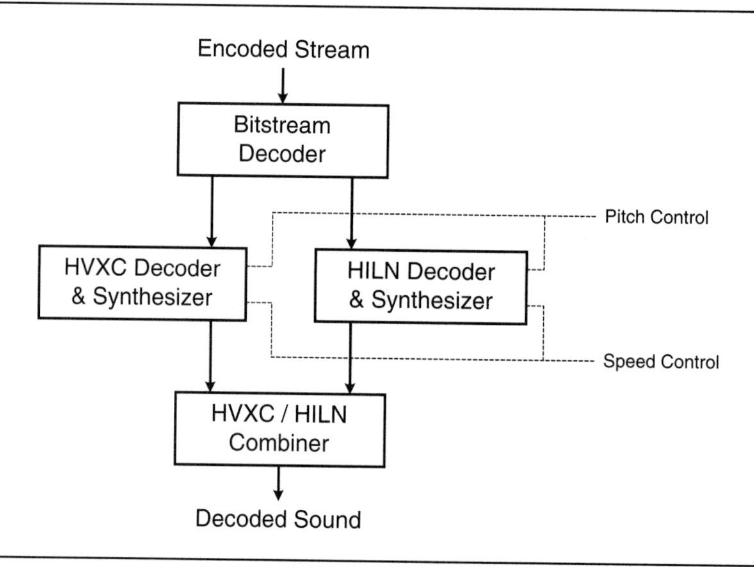

Figure 10.12 Parametric Decoder

The two synthetic speech categories supported by MPEG-4 are Text to Speech (TTS) and Structured Audio.

Text to Speech

The MPEG-4 Text to Speech (TTS) is used to transmit speech data. TTS supports bit rates from 0.2 to 1.2 kilobits per second.

In its simplest form, TTS simply codes the text of the speech. However, the data can be greatly augmented to include information such as the speaker's gender, age, and rate of speech. The TTS stream may also include detailed information about the intensity and duration of the fundamental speech components known as *phonemes*.

MPEG-4 TTS also includes support for Facial Animation Parameters (FAP), which allow the synthetic speech to be reconstructed in concert with a computer-generated synthetic face. The FAPs are again generic, so the lip shapes, eye blinks, and so forth that they describe can be applied to an arbitrary face.

TTS allows for novel usage models, such as virtual newscasters. The news story can be delivered at a very low bit rate and a synthetic human face created to actually deliver the story. The newscaster can—at the click of a button—be changed by the viewer. The avatar's voice and face changes, but the TTS bit stream remains unaltered.

Structured Audio

Structured Audio, also known as Score Driven Synthesis, allows for the transmission of music and sound effects. Structured Audio basically works by defining a set of instruments and then sending notes or control information to those instruments.

Each instrument is a signal-processing unit. An instrument may take in data and controls and output a waveform, analogous to a traditional instrument, or it may be an intermediary which sends out processed data and controls to other instruments. An MPEG-4 instrument can actually represent several real-world instruments, such as an orchestra's entire wind section. Alternatively, multiple MPEG-4 instruments may be used to represent a single real-world instrument, especially if the real-world instrument has wide-ranging characteristics. For instance, a real-world piano sounds different if the sostenuto pedal is depressed.

The Structured Audio Orchestra Language (SAOL) is used to define a set of instruments required to render the stream. The set of instruments is known as an *orchestra*. Note that the instrument definitions are part of the stream itself.

Now that we have defined the instruments, we need to tell them what to play. This feat is accomplished via the Structured Audio Score Language (SASL). The scores that are coded via SASL are also known as scripts.

SA also includes the Structured Audio Sample Bank Format (SASBF), which allows audio samples to be used as the basis of custom instruments. SASBF includes support for signal processing of the samples. For instance, you could record a sample of a helicopter hovering and define a Doppler control. You could then use SASBF to synthesize an entire fleet of helicopters flying to and fro.

Musical Instrument Digital Interface (MIDI) support is included as part of MPEG-4 Structured Audio. MIDI is a very popular format for transmitting musical information between computers and electronic musical instruments.

Scalability

One of the main features of MPEG-4 is scalability. In this context, scalability refers to the ability of the decoder to select a subset of the bit stream and still recover a useful signal from it. Such simplified decoders are typically cheaper to build. Alternatively, scalability also refers to the ability of the stream transmitter to easily send down streams of different bit rates.

For instance, a web site might offer several instantiations of a sound coded at different bit rates, so that you could pick the one that was most compatible with your Internet connection speed.

MPEG-4 version 1 offered coarse scalability. As an example, a scalable stream might include one 24-kilobits per second base layer and two 16-kilobits per second enhancement layers. The base layer might just carry a mono version of the sound. Adding the first enhancement layer to the base stream might allow for stereo, while adding the third layer on top of that might allow high quality stereo.

A drawback to this form of scalability is its coarseness. In the example above, a person with a 24-kilobits per second connection can only receive mono. If the connection speed is increased up to 39 kilobits per second, they can still receive only mono. It is not until they can sustain a connection speed of 40-kilobits per second that they are able to receive the 24-kilobits per second base layer and 16-kilobits per second enhancement layer, and thus suddenly receive stereo.

MPEG-4 version 2 introduced support for Fine Grain Scalability (FGS) via the Bit-Sliced Arithmetic Coding (BSAC) tool for general audio. BSAC offers support for scalability steps of 1 kilobit per second per audio channel. This fine grain allows for run-time adjustment of the bit rate. If your 40-kilobits per second connection degrades to 39-kilobits per second, the BSAC allows for the bit stream to be throttled back to that level, providing you with a graceful degradation in service, rather than suddenly switching from stereo to mono.

BSAC basically works by storing the most significant bits of the quantized spectral values into the base stream. The less significant bits are arranged into selectable enhancement layers. The full stream includes all the bits. With the removal of each enhancement layer, the remaining least significant bit is removed. 16-bit values, for instance, would degrade to 15-bit values. As such, it is possible to still convey the general characteristics of the sound even as the overall quality of the sound is reduced.

Profiles and Levels

MPEG-4 defines a large number of profiles, several of which are shown in Table 10.1. These profiles are for audio objects. Recall that a single MPEG-4 stream may contain multiple objects.

Table 10.1 MPEG-4 Audio Object Profiles

Profile	Hierarchy	Supported Tools
AAC Main	contains AAC LC	13818-7 main profile PNS
AAC LC		13818-7 LC profile PNS
AAC SSR		13818-7 SSR profile PNS
T/F		13818-7 LC profile PNS LTP
T/F Main scalable	contains T/F LC scalable	13818-7 main profile PNS LTP BSAC tools for large step scalability (TLSS) core codecs: CELP, TwinVQ, HILN
T/F LC scalable		13818-7 LC PNS LTP BSAC TLSS
TwinVQ core		TwinVQ
CELP		CELP
HVXC		HVXC
HILN		HILN
TTSI		TTSI
Main Synthetic	contains Wavetable Synthesis	all structured audio tools
Wavetable Synthesis		SASBF MIDI

MPEG-4 also defines combination profiles. The combination profiles define a set of supported audio object profiles. They are shown in Table 10.2.

Table 10.2 MPEG-4 Audio Combination Profiles

Combination Profile	Hierarchy	Supported Audio Object Profiles
Main	Contains Scalable, Speech and Low Rate Synthetic	AAC Main, LC, SSR T/F, T/F Main Scalable, T/F LC Scalable TwinVQ core CELP HVXC HILN Main Synthetic TTSI
Scalable	Contains Speech	T/F LC Scalable AAC-LC or/and T/F CELP HVXC TwinVQ core HILN Wavetable Synthesis TTSI
Speech		CELP HVXC TTSI
Low Rate Synthesis		Wavetable Synthesis TTSI

Summary

The MPEG committee has designed and released several different open standards that provide many different ways for storing compressed audio. Most of the MPEG audio schemes use lossy perceptual coders: they achieve compression—in part—by discarding irrelevant and redundant information from the original sound that humans cannot hear.

MPEG-1 and MPEG-2 have three different coding schemes known as Layer I, II, and III. The higher numbered layers indicate increased encoder and decoder complexity in exchange for better fidelity. MPEG-1 supports a maximum of two channels, but MPEG-2 supports surround sound. Layer III is colloquially known as MP3, a very popular format for digital music.

In addition to supporting and extending the three layers of MPEG-1, MPEG-2 also supports Advanced Audio Coding. MPEG-2 AAC supports a wide range of bit rates, channels, and sampling frequencies. Because it is not constrained to be MPEG-1 backward compatible, it is able to achieve better compression ratios than Layers I-III.

MPEG-4 introduces several new audio-coding tools to the mix. It supports and extends the MPEG-2 AAC tools, and includes new tools such as Long Term Prediction and Transform-Domain Weighted Interleave Vector Quantization.

In addition to providing these tools for coding general audio, MPEG-4 also offers tools designed explicitly to efficiently code speech and synthetic sounds. Because these tools are targeted at a subset of general audio, they are able to achieve very low bit rates.

MPEG-4 has a recurring theme of scalability. Various tools within MPEG-4 offer a coarse level of scalability, such as the ability to pick quartiles of the TwinVQ output, as well as Fine Grain Scalability that allows a stream to be scaled in increments as small as 1 kilobit per second.

All in all, the MPEG audio methods appear in numerous applications such as DVD and digital television.

Chapter 11

DVD

"What is a DVD player? Is it for pornography?"

—*Everybody Loves Raymond*

The DVD family is a very popular optical-disc format that has revolutionized how we watch movies, as well as providing affordable ways to make high quality home movies, to store massive amounts of data for the PC, and to listen to high resolution surround sound.

Overview

The development of DVD technology began many years ago and continues to this day.

History of DVD

In the early 1990s, several efforts were made to store video on CD. In 1993, several different incompatible concepts were demonstrated. In an effort to prevent another VHS vs. Beta debacle, several key players in the motion picture industry set forth a set of requirements for a videodisc system. Some of these requirements were:

- Store 135 minutes on a single side
- Better video resolution than Laserdisc
- CD-quality surround sound
- Three to five audio tracks per disc

- Four to six subtitles per disc
- Copy protection

One of the proposed video on CD formats was Video CD. VCD stores quarter-resolution MPEG-1 video on standard CDs. VCDs require special decoders or can be played back on computers with appropriate software. A single VCD can hold 74 minutes of video at a resolution roughly equivalent to VHS tape. Although VCD became quite popular in Asia, it did not meet the Hollywood committee's requirements. So the race was on to develop a higher density disc able to fulfill Hollywood's desires.

In 1995, Philips and Sony demonstrated their Multimedia CD (MMCD) technology while Toshiba and Time Warner demonstrated their Super Disc (SD). Of course, the two systems were incompatible with one another. Isn't it interesting how history repeats itself? Luckily, before the year was out, everyone was able to reach a compromise. They formed a group known as the DVD Consortium. Under its auspices, they released a unified videodisc standard called, yes, DVD.

Originally, DVD stood for Digital Video Disc. Then it stood for Digital Versatile Disc. Nowadays, it apparently stands for nothing. No longer an acronym, it is just three letters.

The first DVD players launched in late 1996. DVD has not yet replaced VHS as the de facto video standard, but it's certainly on track to do so. In 2001, there were over 15,000 different DVD titles available. By mid 2003, there were over 30,000 titles available!

DVD Specifications

In 1997, the DVD Consortium morphed into the DVD Forum. The DVD Forum continues to revise and expand upon the original DVD specification.

The DVD Format/Logo Licensing Corporation (DVD FLLC) licenses use of the DVD formats and DVD logos. They also define conformance tests that products must pass before they can use the DVD logo.

The DVD Forum has defined several sets of DVD specifications for each of the following formats:

- Read-Only Disc
- Recordable Disc
- Rewritable Disc
- Re-recordable Disc

At first glance, rewritable and re-recordable seem to mean the same thing. However, the terms have slightly different connotations within the DVD paradigm, as we will discuss below.

Format Overview

Multiple formats are defined under these specifications. Grouped by category, the formats approved by the DVD Forum are as follows:

- Read-Only Discs:
  - DVD-Read Only Memory (ROM)
  - DVD-Video
  - DVD-Audio
- Recordable:
  - DVD-Recordable (R) 1.0
  - DVD-R 2.x for General
  - DVD-R 2.x for Authoring
- Rewritable:
  - DVD-Random Access Memory (RAM) 1.x
  - DVD-RAM 2.x
- Re-recordable:
  - DVD-Readable/Writeable (RW)

The capacity and physical structure of the discs varies across the formats. Also, each format has a different purpose. Two other DVD formats are: DVD+R and DVD+RW. These two formats are being promoted by the DVD+RW Alliance, but have not been approved by the DVD Forum. The DVD+RW Alliance believes its formats have merit, and indeed DVD+RW media and drives are readily available today.

DVD-ROM

DVD-ROM is the root format in DVD. You can think of it as a high-density CD-ROM. On DVD-ROM, the files can be laid out in virtually any hierarchy, as long as they conform to the UDF-Bridge file system. Any type of file can be stored on DVD-ROMs, not just video. Typically DVD-ROM is used to store a large set of files that would take several CD-ROM discs to store. For instance, Douglas Adams' game *Starship Titanic* was released on DVD-ROM because it took up 1.7 gigabytes of space.

The equipment necessary to make DVD-ROMs is very expensive. The DVD-ROM mastering process involves creating molds and physically stamping depressions onto discs. As such, it is likely to always remain cost-prohibitive for consumer use.

DVD-Video

DVD-Video is the format designed to satisfy the requirements of the Hollywood committee. DVD-Video is used for storing and viewing movies and other video content. A single disc can store as much as 17 gigabytes of data corresponding to over two hours of high quality video. DVD-Video is a read-only format. DVD-Video discs can be watched on a set-top DVD player or a properly equipped computer.

DVD-Audio

DVD-Audio is a high-fidelity audio format, with sound quality better than audio CDs. DVD-Audio also allows for surround sound, a feature not supported on standard CDs.

DVD-R

DVD-R is a write once, read many (WORM) format. Data can be written to it once. Once written, the data can only be read. It is similar to CD-R, but a DVD-R disc stores up to 4.7 billion bytes of data. It is useful for archiving large amounts of data or storing home videos.

There are three flavors of DVD-R. The first iteration of DVD-R was version 1.0, and it had a maximum capacity of 3.9 billion bytes. The DVD-R format then forked into two versions of the 2.0 standard, each capable of storing 4.7 GB. The two formats are DVD-R for General and DVD R for Authoring, often referred to as DVD-R(G) and DVD-R(A).

DVD-R(A) adds a few features above and beyond DVD-R(G) that are useful when the disc is to be used as a master for creating mass quantities of DVD-ROMs.

DVD-RW

DVD-RW discs can be written to repeatedly. They are designed primarily for sequential access, and as such are very useful for DVD development houses. DVD images destined to become mass-produced DVD-Video or DVD-ROM titles can first be burned to DVD-RW for testing. Any mistakes can be easily overwritten.

DVD-RAM

DVD-RAM is another writeable format. Whereas DVD-RW is targeted at sequential operations, DVD-RAM is specifically designed for fast random access of the disc. DVD-RAMs can thus be used much like a hard disc.

Format Compatibility

By design, there is a lot of similarity among the DVD formats. However, the formats are not all compatible with one another.

A DVD-ROM, for instance, may not contain MPEG streams, or may contain MPEG streams that do not meet DVD-Video constraints. A DVD Video player is not able to play such a DVD-ROM because there is no content that it understands. However, if DVD-Video compliant MPEG streams are placed onto a DVD-ROM in addition to other files, a DVD-Video player ignores the extraneous files and plays the DVD just like a standard DVD-Video. Indeed, many DVD-Videos are also DVD-ROMs and contain software that allows you to watch the DVD on computers.

Similarly, if videos are stored on any of the writable DVD formats compliant with the DVD-Video specification, a set-top DVD-player may be able to play back the video. The different rewritable formats use different technologies to store the data, so although it may be in the proper data format, the DVD-Video player may not be able to physically read the data from the disc. Many DVD-Video players can play back content burned onto a DVD-R; however, most cannot play back content stored on a DVD-RAM.

This situation of inconsistent compatibilities among players and disc formats is similar to the incompatibilities between early CD drives and writable CD formats. The audio CD players were not required to read files from CD-R or CD-RW discs. However, as consumers began burning audio CDs on CD-R, public demand for audio players capable of reading CD-R grew. Manufacturers responded to the demand. I have an antique CD player that cannot play back my CD-R discs, but the CD-player in my car can. However, my car's CD player can't play CD-RW discs, but those new models down at the electronics store can!

The DVD industry is following a similar trend so that hopefully in a few years all DVD drives will be able to read all the different DVD formats. Along these lines, DVD FLLC has announced the DVD Multi logo. For a DVD player sport a DVD Multi logo, it must be able to read DVD-ROM, DVD-R(G), DVD-RAM, and DVD-RW discs. A DVD Multi recorder must be able to read all these formats, as well as be able to write to

DVD-R(G), DVD-RAM, and DVD-RW discs. If successful, the DVD Multi program will make great strides in alleviating consumers of format compatibility headaches.

Note, however, that DVD Multi does not comprehend the two formats advocated by the DVD+RW Alliance, as they have not been approved by the DVD Forum. Still, DVD+RW drives and media are readily available and have the backing of some major manufacturers.

Physical Structure

The form factor of DVDs is—intentionally—very similar to CDs, as can be seen in Figure 11.1. The similar shape allows for DVD drives to be capable of physically accepting CDs. Most DVD players sold today can play audio compact discs.

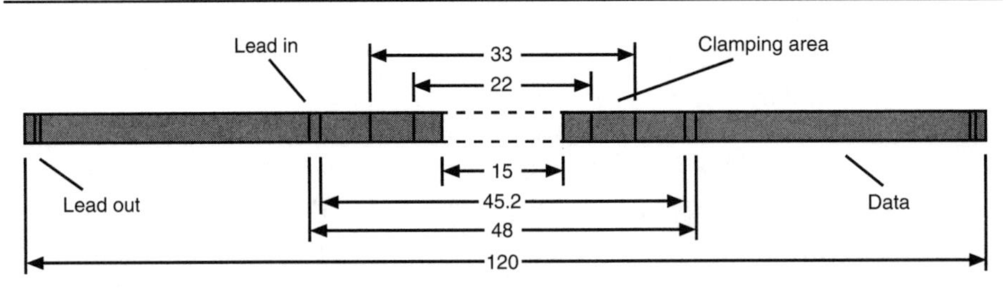

Figure 11.1 Layout of a 12-cm DVD

Again, similar to CDs, information is stored on DVDs as a series of pits laid out in a spiral track. The pits are shorter, ranging from 0.400 μm to 2.054 μm. The tracks are narrower than CDs, having a pitch of 0.74 μm. 1X DVDs spin faster than 1X CDs, at a rate of 3.49 ± 0.03 meters per second for single layer discs and 3.84 ± 0.03 meters per second for dual layer discs. We haven't yet discussed the difference between single layer and dual layer discs, but fear not: we tackle it in the next section!

Sides, Layers and Capacities

DVDs consist of two substrates glued together. A substrate is just a disc of plastic that may contain one or two reflective layers that store data. Each substrate is 0.6 mm thick, making the combined substrates 1.2 mm thick, the same thickness as a CD. There are four permitted ways to use the two substrates:

- Single Sided/Single Layer (SS/SL)
- Single Sided/Dual Layer (SS/DL)
- Dual Sided/Single Layer (DS/SL)
- Dual Sided/Dual Layer (DS/DL)

Single Sided/Single Layer discs contain a single reflective layer that stores data as shown in Figure 11.2. Because SS/SL discs can only be read on one side, a label can be printed on the other side. SS/SL is also known as DVD-5.

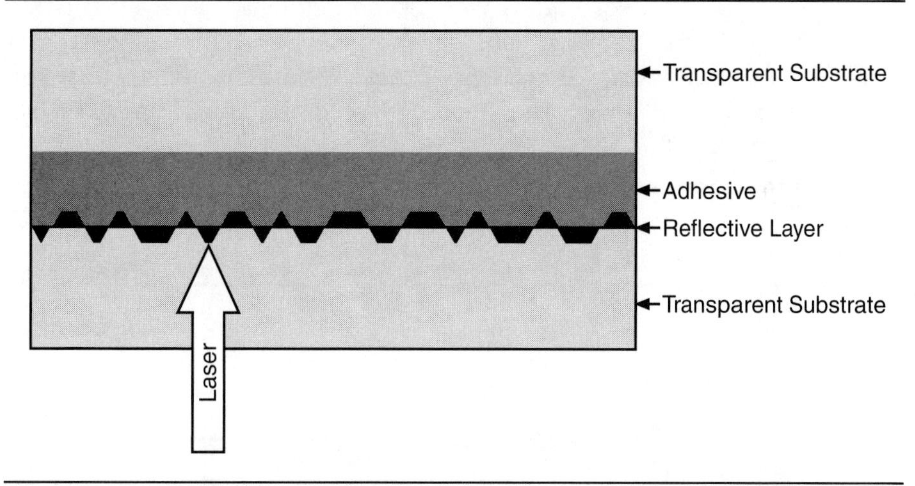

Figure 11.2 Single Sided/Single Layer Disc

Single Sided/Dual Layer discs contain the same reflective layer present in SS/SL discs, but add a semi-reflective layer, shown in Figure 11.3, as well. The laser can read from either of these surfaces. SS/DL is also known as DVD-9.

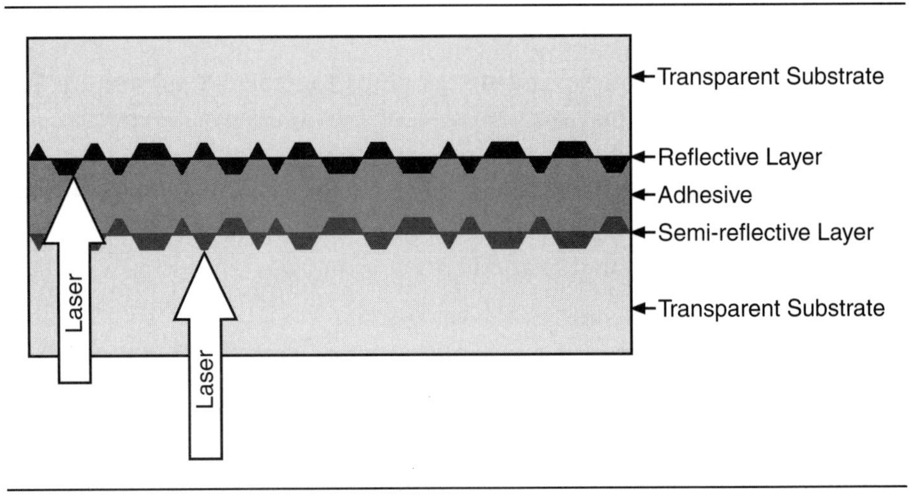

Figure 11.3 Single Sided/Double Layer Disc

A Dual Sided/Single Layer disc, shown in Figure 11.4, is effectively just two data-carrying substrates from a SS/SL disc glued together. Because each layer is completely reflective, the disc needs to be physically flipped over before the laser can read the other layer. DS/SL is also known as DVD-10.

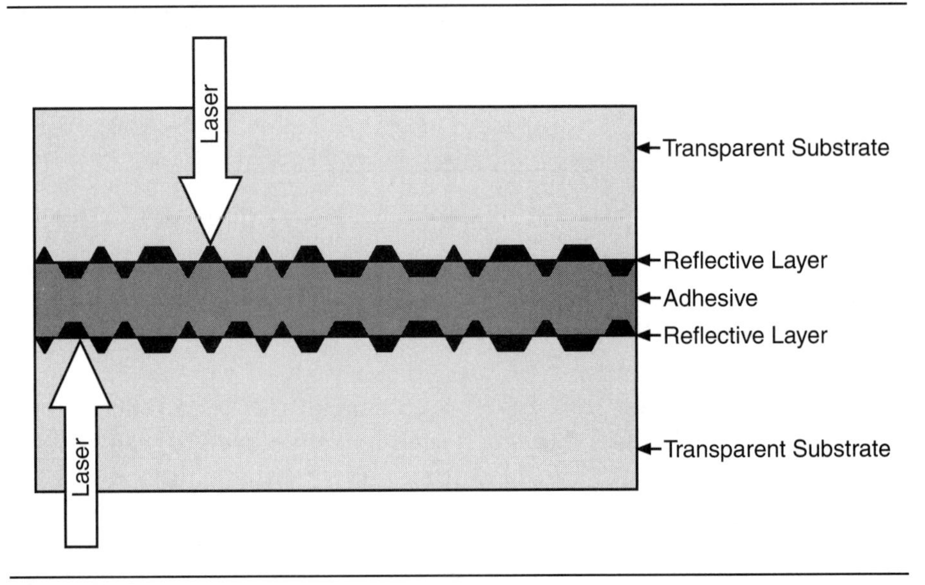

Figure 11.4 Dual Sided/Single Layer Disc

The Dual Sided/Dual Layer disc shown in Figure 11.5 contains four layers, and is akin to two SS/DL discs glued together. On each side, the laser can read from both the reflective and the semi-reflective data layers. The two layers on the opposite side of the disc can only be accessed by physically flipping the disc over. DS/DL discs are extremely difficult to manufacture. For example, the first copies of the *Terminator 2: Judgment Day: The Ultimate Edition* DVD were released on DS/DL discs. Manufacturing problems led to later copies being distributed as two SS/DL discs. DS/DL is also known as DVD-18.

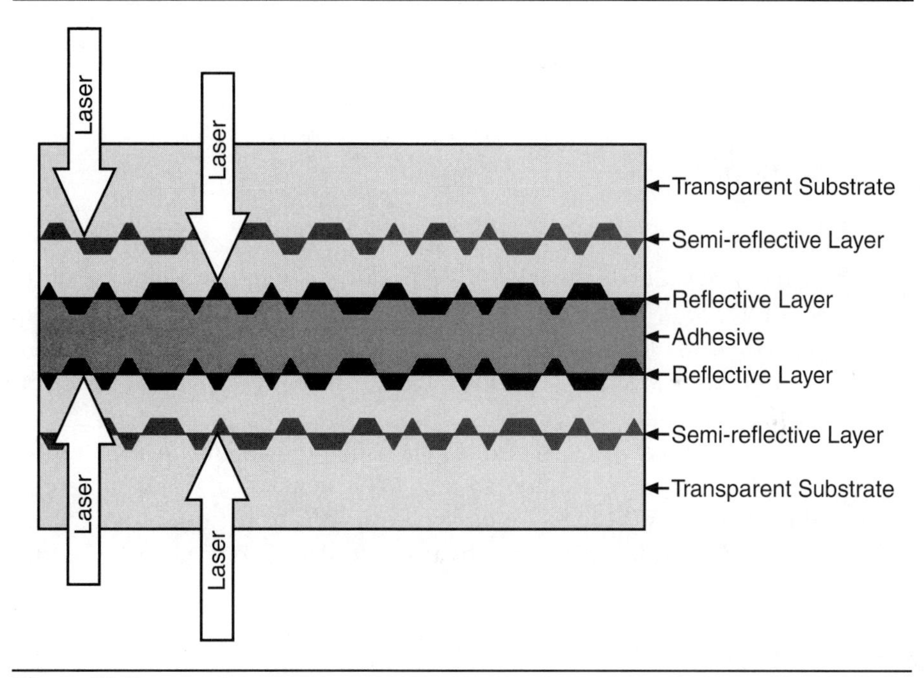

Figure 11.5 Double Sided/Double Layer Disc

The storage capacity of a DVD disc is dependent on its format, diameter, and number of layers and sides. A summary of capacities is shown in Table 11.1.

Table 11.1 Capacities of Different DVD Formats

Format	Diameter	SS/SL	SS/DL	DS/SL	DS/DL
Read-only	12 cm	4.7	8.5	9.4	17.0
	8 cm	1.5	2.7	2.9	5.3
DVD-R (1.0)	12 cm	3.9	N/A	N/A	N/A
DVD-R(G/A)	12 cm	4.7	N/A	9.4	N/A
DVD-RW	12 cm	4.7	N/A	9.4	N/A
DVD-RAM	12 cm	4.7	N/A	9.4	N/A
	8 cm	1.5	N/A	2.9	N/A

All values are in billions of bytes.

DVD-Video

Because this book focuses on audio, I will not delve too deeply into the many video details of DVD-Video,[1] but we will examine the different audio formats it supports. Bear in mind that DVD-Video discs are designed for video playback, and all of the audio used in DVD-Video is associated with a video stream. DVD-Video is not intended to be an audio-only playback system like CD-Audio is.

DVD-Video discs may be built using any of the forms described previously (SS/SL, SS/DL, and so on). What makes the DVD discs eligible for the official DVD-Video is the structure of the data contained on the disc itself. DVD-Video files are always stored in the VIDEO_TS folder in the disc's root directory.

Features

DVD-Video has several features that distinguish it from its predecessor formats. In this section, we will briefly discuss some of the non-audio components of DVD-Video.

High-quality Video

DVD-Video supports resolutions up to 720 × 480 pixels for NTSC and 720 × 576 pixels for PAL in 4:2:0 color. The video is digital 4:2:0 color. The picture quality is substantially better than VHS, which stores video as

---

[1] To learn more about the video aspects of DVD, I highly recommend reading *Video in the 21st Century.*

analog composite signals. The picture quality is also better than that of laser discs, which store video as digital composite signals.

Menus

DVD menus are mechanisms that allow you to interact with the video in a way not previously possible. Menus define hotspots on a still image or motion video. When a viewer selects the hotspot using a remote control, various actions can occur. Menus can be created that allow you to jump to a specific chapter in a movie, watch behind the scenes footage, select their desired subtitle language, select their desired audio track, take a quiz, or play a simple game.

Sub-pictures

Sub-pictures are used for subtitles and karaoke. Up to 32 different tracks of sub-pictures can be stored on a DVD. Sub-pictures are graphics that are overlaid on top of the video. Sub-pictures can be changed with every frame, so they can be used to create animations such as a ball bouncing across the top of song lyrics.

Regional Coding

DVD-Video titles may contain regional coding. The region code indicates in which regions of the world that particular title may be played. A DVD coded for the United States may not be played by a compliant DVD player in the United Kingdom. The different regions are shown in Table 11.2. DVDs coded as Region 0 are playable in all regions.

Table 11.2 DVD Regions

Region	Geographic Areas
0	All
1	United States, Canada
2	Europe, Japan, South Africa, Middle East
3	Southeast Asia
4	Mexico, Central America, South America, Australia
5	Russian Federation, remainder of Africa, India, Pakistan, North Korea
6	China

The region coding was added to the DVD-Video specification to allow DVD publishers the ability to release DVDs at different times in different parts of the world, much in the same way that international films are released across the world. For example, some DVDs of popular films are released in the United States before the film has actually arrived in theatres in other countries. If people in these countries were able to just get the DVD, they might simply rent the DVD rather than going to the theatre. Such a practice would result in decreased studio revenue, so the film industry was quite keen on regional coding.

The bulk of DVD-Videos released today are coded for Region 1. DVD-Videos of the same Hollywood film for other regions are released later in time and tend to have far fewer features than their Region 1 counterparts. As such, there has been great demand in these regions for DVD-Video players that do not check the region coding. Such players are in violation of the spec and cannot bear the DVD-Video logo. There are several players that by default properly support regional coding, but you can disable the regional coding by entering a specific sequence of keys on the remote control. The DVD FLLC has been cracking down on these players.

Content Protection

One of Hollywood's biggest concerns with video discs is piracy. Each time you make a copy of a VHS tape, the image degrades. Because DVDs store data digitally, you could make unlimited copies with no loss in picture quality.

DVD offers three features designed to protect content: copyright management information, Macrovision, and Content Scrambling System (CSS). DVD players must properly support all three of these features. A DVD disc may have any combination of the three features; it may also have none of these features.

Copyright management information indicates whether or not the material on a disc is copyrighted. It also indicates how many copies may be made of the material, with the valid options being zero, one, or infinity. Different sectors of the disc may contain different copyright information.

Macrovision is a system used to protect the decoded picture information sent over an analog display interface, such as the RCA video jack in the back of most DVD players. The video signal is modified in such a way that it can be displayed on a television, but cannot be recorded to video tape. Macrovision has long been used on pre-recorded videotapes to thwart unauthorized duplication. This mechanism prevents someone from renting DVDs or videotapes and making VHS bootleg copies of them.

The final and most infamous of the content protection schemes supported by DVD is CSS. CSS is a mechanism for protecting the compressed video and audio data stored on a DVD. The data is scrambled prior to being stored on DVD. Before the data can be decoded, it must first be descrambled. Descrambling is done by the decoder and requires retrieving keys from the DVD drive and the DVD-Video disc.

If you copy the contents of a scrambled DVD to your hard drive, you cannot watch them with a PC DVD player, because some of the necessary security information is uncopyable from the DVD. Similarly, burning a copy of a scrambled DVD onto a DVD-R won't work as that same security information is still uncopyable.

To get the necessary keys and algorithms to scramble and descramble DVDs, you need to sign the CSS license offered by the DVD Copy Control Association (DVD CCA), a fairly nontrivial and expensive endeavor. CSS allows only authorized DVD players to decode scrambled content when stored on the original DVD discs.

At least, that used to be the case. Seems some teenage hackers got together and cracked CSS, posting a utility called DeCSS to the Internet in late October 1999. DeCSS makes a descrambled copy of a scrambled DVD. It goes without saying that DeCSS is not licensed by DVD CCA.

Proponents of DeCSS argue that it is not a piracy tool, but rather a way for them to watch DVDs on Linux-based computers. Alas, this argument does not address why the widely popular version of DeCSS runs on Windows instead of Linux. The argument also disregards the fact that DVD players supporting scrambled content are available for Linux.

Even though methods to defeat CSS are available, manufacturers of DVD players and discs must still adhere to the CSS license.

File Layout and Logical Structures

A DVD-Video consists of many nested logical structures. Figure 11.6 shows that at the root level, a DVD-Video begins with a Video Manager (VMG) structure followed by multiple Video Title Set (VTS) structures. There must be at least one VTS and no more than 99 of them.

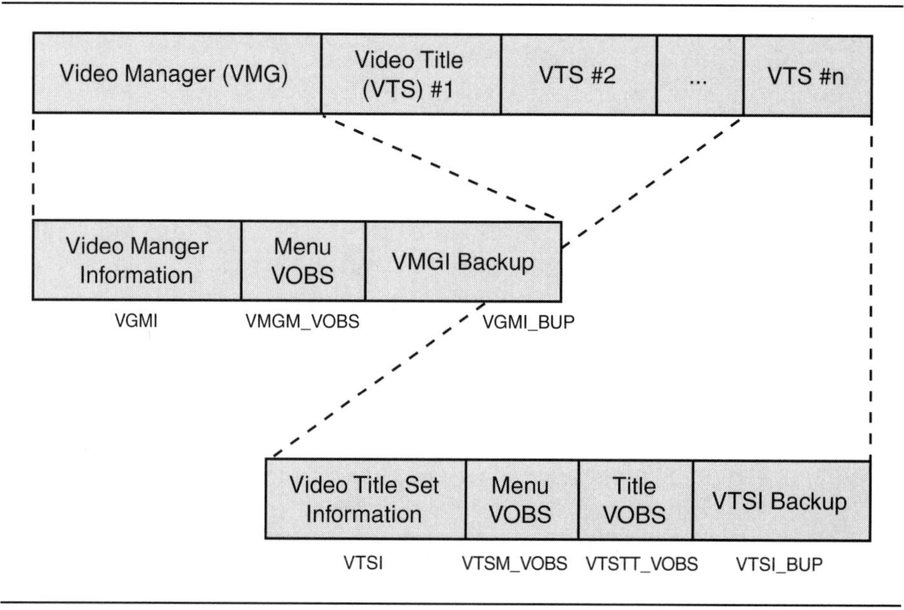

Figure 11.6 Logical Structure of DVD-Video

The Video Manager is basically a table of contents of all the Video Title Sets on the disc. The Video Manager Information (VMGI) stores information about the contents of the disc and where they are physically located. The backup of the VMGI is an exact copy of the original control data. The Video Manager may optionally contain a Menu Video Object Set (VOBS). A VOBS contains the actual video, audio, and sub-picture data, as shown in Figure 11.7. The Menu VOBS is optional. If included, it is the main menu that appears when the DVD is first inserted into a player.

A DVD may contain 1 to 99 VTSs. Many DVDs only contain one. Some DVDs use one VTS for a widescreen version of the movie and another VTS for the cropped version. A collection of TV episodes might store each episode as a different title. Or it could store all the episodes on a single title.

Each VTS begins with Video Title Set Information (VTSI). The VTSI stores information about the VTS, including the number of audio and sub-picture streams it contains. An exact duplicate of the VTSI is also stored on the disk as the VTSI Backup (VTSI_BUP).

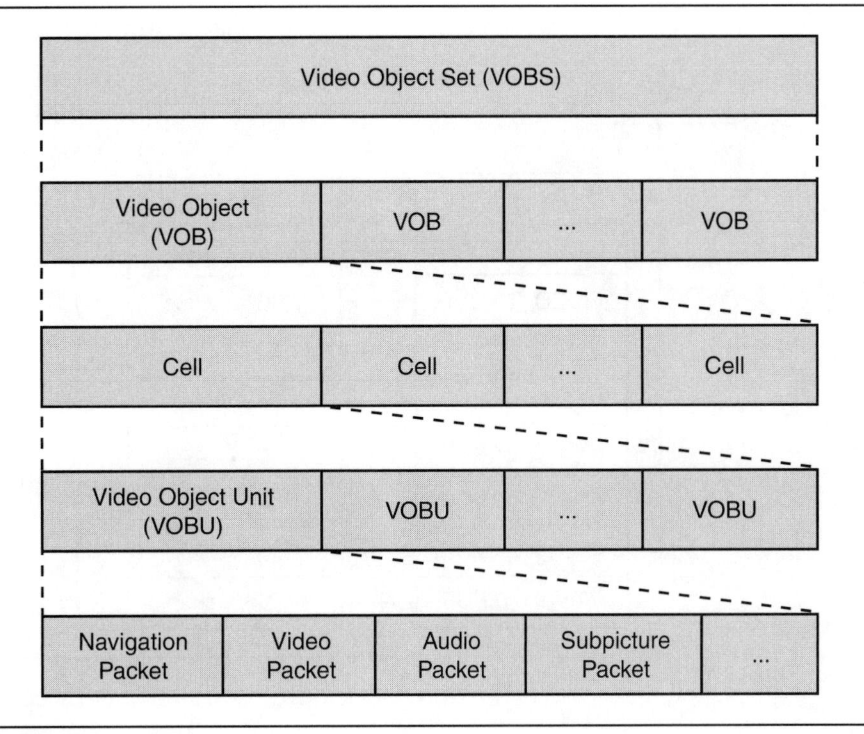

Figure 11.7 VOBS

The VTS can contain a Menu VOBS. It serves as the Title Menu, a menu specific to that title.

The Video Title Set Title Video Object Set (VTSTT_VOBS) is the entity containing the video, audio, and subtitles that comprise the feature presentation of the disc.

The logical structures described so far all correspond to a single file on a DVD-Video disc, with the exception of the Title VOBS. The Title VOBS may be spread across as many as nine files. Figure 11.8 shows a sample layout of files on a DVD and how these files correspond to the logical structures.

Notice that for a DVD-Video, these files must reside in the VIDEO_TS directory. DVD-Video players may safely ignore files outside this directory, with the exception of files in the JACKET_P directory, an optional directory used to store pictures of the DVD jacket. The jacket pictures are designed for systems that store multiple DVDs, so you can graphically browse the titles.

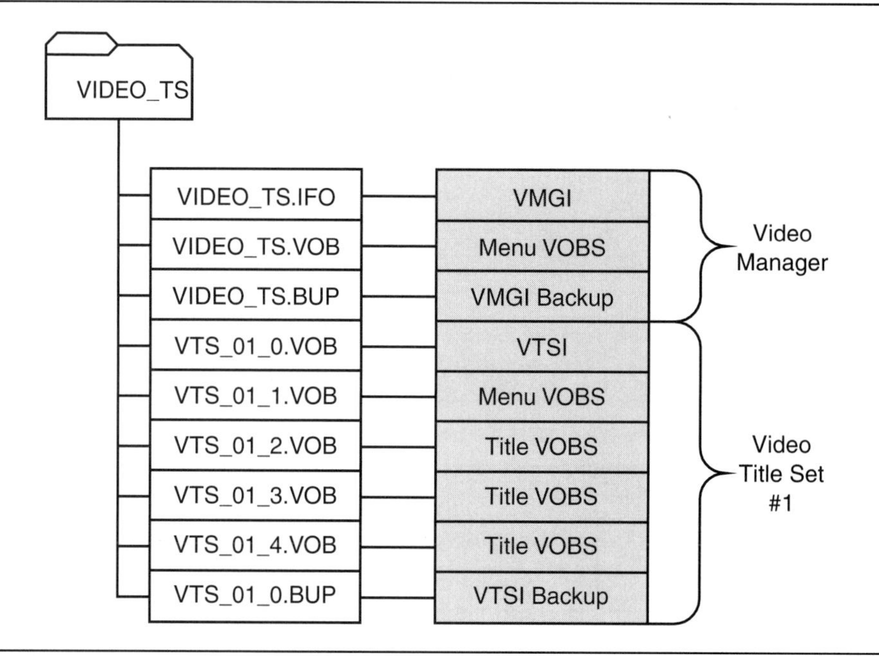

Figure 11.8 Sample DVD file structure.

Many DVDs produced today contain files outside VIDEO_TS and JACKET_P. These DVD-ROM files are designed for PC-based DVD players, and indeed these files may even *be* a PC DVD player.

Audio Formats

DVD-Video supports up to eight independent streams of audio. Each stream can have a maximum bit rate of 6.144 megabits per second, although the total of all the tracks on a single disc may not exceed 9.80 megabits per second. The multiple tracks allow for a single DVD to contain the dialogue for a movie in several different languages. This feature is also commonly used to provide a director's running commentary of the film. Each of the streams may contain up to eight sound channels, which allows for 7.1 surround sound. Each stream may be in one of five different audio formats.

The five audio formats supported by DVD-Video are:

- Linear PCM
- AC-3
- MPEG
- DTS
- SDDS

PCM and AC-3 are mandatory formats: all DVD-Video players must be able to play both PCM and AC-3 audio streams. DVD Video discs must contain at least one audio stream in either PCM or AC-3.

The MPEG, DTS, and SDDS formats are optional. A DVD-Video player does not have to support them, nor does a DVD-Video disc have to include them. MPEG audio was originally a required format in certain geographies, but was later made optional.

PCM

DVD uses PCM, which we have already discussed in the chapters on digital audio and compact discs. In DVD-Video, PCM may be sampled at either 48 or 96 kilohertz with 16, 20, or 24 bits per sample. As the number of channels increase, restrictions are placed on the sample frequency and sample size so that the audio channel does not exceed the maximum bit rate allotted to audio streams. The permitted combinations of channels, sampling frequency, and sample size are shown in Table 11.3. In practice, PCM is generally only used for encoding stereo sound on DVDs. Encoding the six channels for 5.1 surround sound would take at least 4.6 megabits per second and not leave very much bandwidth for the video and sub-picture streams.

MPEG

DVD-Video supports Layer II MPEG. DVD-Video constrains the bit rate of MPEG-1 mono streams to the range 64 to 192 kilobits per second. MPEG-1 stereo streams are constrained to the range 64 to 384 kilobits per second. MPEG-2 surround streams may range from 64 to 912 kilobits per second for DVD-video; all the MPEG audio streams have a sampling frequency of 48 kilohertz.

Table 11.3 Supported PCM Formats for DVD-Video

Number of Channels	Sampling Frequency (kHz)	Bits per Sample
1	48 or 96	16
	48 or 96	20
	48 or 96	24
2	48 or 96	16
	48 or 96	20
	48 or 96	24
3	48 or 96	16
	48 or 96	20
	48	24
4	48 or 96	16
	48	20
	48	24
5	48	16
	48	20
	48	24
6	48	16

MPEG audio was originally a mandatory format for 525/60 DVD players. Due to low adoption rates, however, the format was made optional.

AC-3

AC-3 is a lossy compression algorithm developed by Dolby Laboratories (AC-3 is marketed by Dolby as Dolby Digital). The AC-3 algorithm was developed for use with DTV. AC-3 uses knowledge of the way the human ear perceives sound waves to discard information from the original signal that humans can't hear. Much like the human eye perceives both a full-spectrum light and a red-green-blue light to be white, so too does the human ear perceive certain sounds as being the same, even when one of the sounds is a subset of the other.

AC-3 on DVD-Video supports 1/0, 2/0, 3/0, 2/1, 2/2, and 3/2 channel configurations, with an LFE channel available for each configuration. The compressed bit rate ranges from 64 to 448 kilobits per second. In general, an AC-3 5.1 stream uses less than 10 percent of the bandwidth of PCM 5.1 stream. Even though the AC-3 compression system is lossy, the Dolby Laboratories Web site offers the opinion that "...the 448 kilobits per second rate used on DVDs (the maximum allowable) provides sound quality that critical listening tests have consistently confirmed as on a par with original master tapes." By taking up less room on the disc, AC-3 allows for higher quality video to be stored on the same disc, or alternatively multiple surround-sound streams.

We will examine AC-3 in more detail in the forthcoming chapter on digital television.

DTS

In 1993, you may have gone to see *Jurassic Park*. Before the movie, a giant compact disc flew onto the screen and exploded, bursting your eardrums. This sound was Digital Theater Systems (DTS). Traditionally, audio tracks for films were stored as analog signals in a magnetic strip adjacent to the film cells, but DTS soundtracks were stored digitally on specialized CDs synchronized to the film projector. A derivative of DTS is supported on DVD-Video as an optional format.

DTS on DVD-Video is a lossy compression algorithm with a sampling frequency of 48 kilohertz. Like Dolby Digital, it supports 1/0, 2/0, 3/0, 2/1, 2/2 and 3/2 channel configurations, with an LFE channel available in each of the modes. The bit rate allowed for DTS audio streams on DVD-Video ranges from 64 to 1,536 kilobits per second.

Unlike PCM, MPEG, and AC-3, DTS is a proprietary format. The details of its implementation are not available.

DTS versus Dolby Digital

DTS does not compress audio as much as Dolby's AC-3 algorithm. As such, a 5.1 DTS audio stream takes up significantly more space than a 5.1 Dolby Digital audio stream. There is an ongoing debate between audiophiles as to which of the two formats is superior. Dolby and DTS each seem to feel that their format is the best.

The fact that DTS takes up more space on the DVD has meant that some studios have removed bonus material from the DTS 5.1 release of some of their longer films compared to the Dolby Digital 5.1 release. For instance, the version of *Saving Private Ryan* (161 minutes) with Dolby Digital 5.1 sound includes behind-the-scenes footage not available on the DTS version. On the other hand, *102 Dalmatians* (100 minutes) has both a 5.1 Dolby Digital and 5.1 DTS version of the soundtrack on the same DVD, as well as a director's commentary in stereo and behind-the scenes footage.

SDDS

Sony Dynamic Digital Sound (SDDS) is an eight-channel surround system available only in theatres. It places five channels in the front and two in the rear, with the eighth channel used for low frequency effects.

SDDS for DVD-Video is a lossy compression algorithm with a sample frequency of 48 kilohertz. Surround sound up to 7.1 is supported with bit rates up to 1,280 kilobits per second. Although the DVD-Video specification calls out SDDS as an optional audio format, the official SDDS home page says, “Sony has no current plans to develop a consumer version of SDDS”. Indeed, no DVD discs are available with SDDS, nor are SDDS-capable DVD players.

DVD-Audio

DVD-Audio is an audio format designed to exceed the capabilities of CD-Audio, while taking advantage of the existing infrastructure of DVD, which has been created due to the popularity of the DVD-Video format. DVD-Audio includes support for sampling rates and bit depths well beyond those supported by CD-Audio. It also includes support for surround sound and offers copy protection. The first DVD-Audio album was Gordon Goodwin's *Big Phat Band*, released in October 2000.

DVD-Audio was developed by Working Group 4 (WG4) of the DVD Forum. Some of the goals WG4 targeted were based on requirements set by the International Steering Committee (ISC). The ISC consisted of the International Federation of the Phonographic Industry (IFPI), the Recording Industry Association of America (RIAA), and the Recording Industry Association of Japan (RIAJ). Some of the ISC’s recommended features for the new format were:

- Six audio channels of the highest possible sound quality
- Minimum playing time of 74 minutes at maximum quality
- Slide show during audio playback
- Content protection
- Support audio, video, and data
- Compatible with CD format

Features

DVD-Audio is distinct from DVD-Video, but uses the same DVD disc technology. DVD-Audio discs can be created using any of the disc layouts, such as SS/SL.

Video

Although DVD-Audio is primarily an audio format, it does include limited support for video as well. A pure DVD-Audio disc can include still images that may be displayed on an attached monitor in a slide show fashion. The transition between images may be a simple cut, a dissolve, or a wipe.

Full motion video is also supported. Specifically, a portion of a DVD-Audio disc may contain a *video zone* that contains DVD-Video compliant streams.

Content Protection

DVD-Audio was originally slated to offer CSS II encryption, but the very public cracking of the original CSS led WG4 to select a different technique. They chose the Content Protection for Pre-recorded Media (CPPM) scheme developed by 4C (IBM, Intel, MEI, and Toshiba). Compared to CSS's 40-bit keys, CPPM uses 56-bit keys. As a rule of thumb, the longer the key length, the harder it is to crack a cryptographic method. CPPM uses the Cryptomeria[2] Cipher (C2) to actually encrypt the disc content.

In addition to encryption, CPPM also includes a revocation mechanism. Each disc contains a large number of keys stored in a Media Key Block (MKB). Each DVD-Audio title has a unique MKB; new MKBs are required to be used every three months. Every licensed DVD-Audio decoder has its own set of keys, known as *device keys*. A decoder uses its device key in conjunction with the disc's MKB to recover the actual key needed to successfully decrypt the disc.

If a particular decoder model becomes compromised, the MKB of future discs can be altered in such a way that the compromised device keys cannot recover the decryption key. In short, the decoder's ability to play back discs is revoked. It is still able to play older discs that were released prior to revocation, but it is not able to play any discs released after the revocation.

---

[2] Cryptomeria, by the way, is a Japanese cedar. And the first entry after "cryptography" in many encyclopedias. Coincidence?

By comparison, DVD-Video has no concept of revocation. A tool such as DeCSS can decrypt all DVD-Videos, even those released long after DeCSS was created.

Watermarking

Originally, a watermark was a pattern made in a piece of paper indicating the manufacturer. The watermark is not visible during normal usage. However, when you hold it up to the light, it appears because it is thinner and therefore more translucent than the surrounding paper.

DVD-Audio includes support for a form of watermarking. This unique type of watermark is designed to be transparent in that you cannot hear it during playback, but it can still be detected by audio equipment. The watermark includes copy control information that allows a recording device to determine whether or not it is licensed to make a copy of it.

The watermark is part of the actual audio signal; even if the signal is transmitted via analog means, the watermark is still detectable.

File Layout and Logical Structures

Mandatory DVD-Audio files are stored in the AUDIO_TS folder in the root directory. A DVD-Audio disc may also contain audio streams that are DVD-Video compliant. Such files are stored in the VIDEO_TS folder, where they can be recognized and played by a DVD-Video player. The data in AUDIO_TS is known as the *audio zone*, while the VIDEO_TS folder is known as the *video zone*. Extra files such as PC applications can be stored in other, arbitrarily named folders on the disc.

The AUDIO_TS folder contains four types of files:

- Simple Audio Manager (SAMG)
- Audio Manager (AMG)
- Audio Objects (AOBs)
- Audio Still Video Set (ASVS)

The SAMG is similar to the table of contents of an audio CD; it allows the disc to be played by an audio-only DVD-Audio player with no external display attached. The Audio Manager is a more detailed table of contents; it contains information about the content in both the audio and video zones, as well as menu information. The AOBs contain the audio data itself. The ASVS files contain optional still pictures, such as album cover art.

Each DVD-Audio disc is considered to be a logical entity known as an *album* as illustrated in Figure 11.9. Each album can be subdivided into up to nine groups. A group consists of a section of audio content that should be played back sequentially.

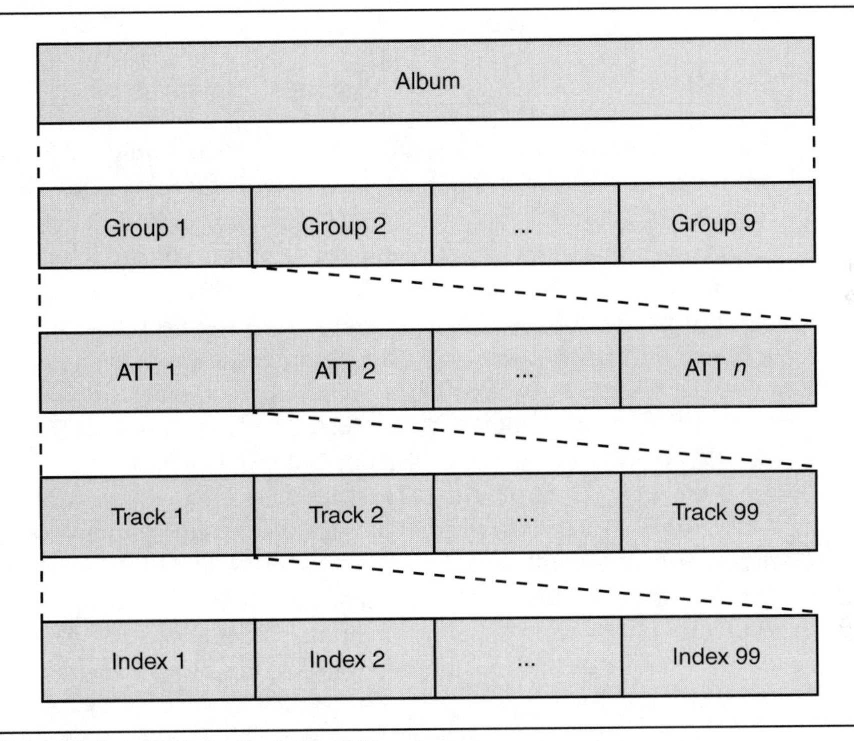

Figure 11.9 DVD-Audio Logical Structure

A group can contain up to 99 different Audio Titles (ATTs), with a concurrent limitation that each album contain no more than 99 ATTs. An ATT is equivalent to a DVD-Video Video Title Set. An ATT contains audio and navigation data that defines the program that can be listened to with a single operation, such as pushing the play button. One ATT may include the 5.1 version of the content, while another ATT could indicate the stereo mix of that same content. Note that audio-only players disregard the ATTs and use only the SAMG for determining the playback sequence.

Each ATT may contain up to 99 tracks. A track is an audio sub-unit to which a listener can quickly navigate. For instance, each song on a music album is typically stored as a separate track. Each track may contain up to 99 indices that allow still finer access granularity.

Audio Formats

DVD-Audio allows for audio streams up to 9.6 megabits per second, compared to DVD-Video's maximum of 6.144 megabits per second. Although DVD-Video supports several different audio formats, the audio zone on DVD-Audio only supports one: PCM.

PCM

DVD-Audio supports up to six channels of PCM sound. The quantization depth can be 16, 20, or 24, meaning the dynamic range can be as large as 144 dB. The sampling rate can be 44.1, 48, 88.2, or 96 kilohertz. For stereo streams, sampling rates of 176.4 and 192 kilohertz are also supported.

These bit depths and sampling rates far exceed those offered by CD audio or even DVD-Video. These higher depths and rates mean more data needs to be stored to disc. Storing such a large amount of uncompressed audio data is not possible on DVD-Video, because the video data takes up most of the space on the disc. However, with DVD-Audio, the majority of the DVD disc can be used for storing audio data.

Even with the large capacity offered by DVD discs, we can still run out of room. For instance, a DVD only has enough room to store 65 minutes worth of six full-range channels of 24-bit PCM at 96 kilohertz. Sixty-five minutes is certainly long enough to store most music albums, but not all of them. CDs store at least 74 minutes of audio, so DVD-Audio would ideally need to be able to achieve this playing time. Indeed, it can, as we will soon see.

In addition to requiring a large amount of space, six channels of 96/24 sound also requires a high data rate of 13.8 megabits per second. Unfortunately, this data rate exceeds the 9.8 megabits per second limit of DVD.

DVD-Video overcame both disc space and bit stream bandwidth concerns by using lossy audio compression (MPEG, AC-3, and DTS). By definition, each of these compression formats does not exactly reproduce the original PCM audio. They are designed so the reproduced signal is ideally perceptually indistinguishable from the original, but everyone's hearing capabilities and tastes are different. Many audiophiles consider any form of lossy compression unacceptable.[3] So DVD-Audio solved the space and bandwidth problems differently by using a lossless compression technique.

---

[3] So I'm a bit confused why they continue to spend—to this day—hundreds of dollars on super premium record players.

Meridian Lossless Packing

DVD-Audio supports the compression of PCM data using a technique known as Meridian Lossless Packing (MLP). MLP is a lossless coding technique, as you might guess from its name. It takes advantage of the similarities between channels and similarities between temporally adjacent samples, as well as applying entropy coding to store the PCM in a compressed manner. Unpacking the MLP data results in an exact reproduction of the original PCM bits. An overview of the MLP encoder is shown in Figure 11.10

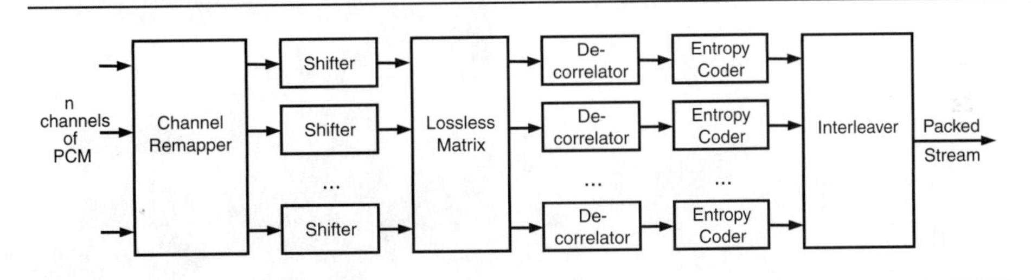

Figure 11.10 MLP Encoder

The efficiency of MLP varies based on the content being packed, but compression ratios of 2:1 are typical. Therefore, with MPL, you can fit at least 74 minutes of 96/24 sound onto a single disc and also meet the stream bandwidth restrictions.

Channel Groups

DVD-Audio allows for different channels to have different bit rates and sampling frequencies. This feature is useful, because the audio associated with surround and LFE channels typically requires a narrower bandwidth than the front stereo channels. Grouping channels into different sampling rates and bit depths allows for optimal usage of the finite DVD-Audio bit rate.

Not every permutation of sampling rates and bit depths are supported across all the channels. Instead, there are 21 defined channel groupings, listed in Table 11.4. The audio channels are distributed across one or two groups. All channels within the same group must have the same sampling rate and bit depth.

Table 11.4 Channel Group Allocations

	Ch1	Ch2	Ch3	Ch4	Ch5	Ch6
1	C					
2	L	R				
3	L	R	S			
4	L	R	LS	RS		
5	L	R	LFE			
6	L	R	LFE	S		
7	L	R	LFE	LS	RS	
8	L	R	C			
9	L	R	C	S		
10	L	R	C	LS	RS	
11	L	R	C	LFE		
12	L	R	C	LFE	S	
13	L	R	C	LFE	LS	RS
14	L	R	C	S		
15	L	R	C	LS	RS	
16	L	R	C	LFE		
17	L	R	C	LFE	S	
18	L	R	C	LFE	LS	RS
19	L	R	LS	RS	LFE	
20	L	R	LS	RS	C	
21	L	R	LS	RS	C	LFE

Channel Group 1 Channel Group 2 L: Left, R: Right, C: Center, LFE: Low Frequency Effects, S: Surround, LS: Left Surround, RS: Right Surround

The sampling frequency and bit depth of channel group 1 must be greater than or equal to the sampling frequency and bit depth of group 2. Also, the sampling frequency of group 1 must be an integer multiple of group 2. For instance, if group 1 had a sampling rate of 96 kilohertz, group 2 could be at 96 kilohertz or 48 kilohertz, but not 44.1 kilohertz.

Audio streams with 176.4 or 192 kilohertz sample rates can only have a single channel group. Remember that a maximum of two channels is supported for those sampling rates, so the single channel group is not a severe limitation.

SMART Content

A recurring issue with surround sound is how to listen to it on non-surround systems. For instance, you may have a great set of surround speakers at home, but suppose you want to listen to your DVD-Audio disc on your car's stereo speakers or on headphones? You cannot simply discard the surround channels, as they may contain essential sound elements. DVD-Video discs typically address the topic by explicitly coding two different audio streams: one in stereo and one in surround. The stereo track is down-mixed from the surround in the production studio. You'll recognize some obvious deficiencies here. Because the stereo track is wholly derived from the surround track, the stereo stream is, in a sense, redundant information that is taking up valuable disc space.

Although DVD-Audio also supports multiple audio tracks, it provides another mechanism for down-mixing: System Managed Audio Resource Technique (SMART). Such SMART content consists of a surround sound track and a set of coefficients that a DVD-Audio player can use to do the down-mixing itself. The down-mix formula is shown in Equation 11.1.

Equation 11.1 Surround to Stereo Down-mix

$$L_{mix} = {}_0L + {}_1R + {}_2C + {}_3LS + {}_4RS + {}_5LFE$$
$$R_{mix} = {}_0L + {}_1R + {}_2C + {}_3LS + {}_4RS + {}_5LFE$$

Compatibility

By the time the first DVD-Audio players hit the streets, DVD-Video had become one of the fastest ramping consumer electronics technologies. DVD-Video players were becoming increasingly affordable, there were a large number of DVD-Video discs available which you could rent at the local video store, and DVD-Video playback on the PC was transitioning from a cool new feature to an expected feature.

Given such an environment, it was desirable that the DVD-Audio discs work at least in some fashion with DVD-Video players. To meet this backward compatibility requirement, many DVD-Audio discs contain a video zone that contains a DVD-Video compatible version of the audio content. The video zone content can be in any of the audio formats supported by DVD-Video; it can be in surround sound or simply in stereo. DVD-Audio discs containing a video zone sport the DVD-Video logo in addition to the DVD-Audio logo.

Nearly all the DVD-Audio players available today are capable of playing the audio portion of DVD-Video discs.

DVD-Audio vs. SACD

Currently, an audiophile format war is being waged between DVD-Audio and SACD. Both offer high-resolution surround audio. DVD-Audio is based on PCM coding, while SACD uses DSD coding. SACD discs cannot be played on the PC, but DVD-Audio discs can. Although most players support either one format or the other, there are a limited number of players available that support both DVD-Audio and SACD.

Each technology has its proponents, and it remains to be seen which format will emerge as the dominant format in the years to come.

Summary

DVD-Video introduced consumers to a whole new way of watching movies. Its video quality, small form factor, flexibility, and random access were unprecedented. DVD-Video brought with it high quality surround sound. The popularity of DVD-Video also ushered in an increase in the availability of surround sound systems targeted at consumers who would never think to describe themselves as audiophiles.

DVD-Audio is targeted to exceed the audio quality offered by DVD-Video and become the dominant audio CD replacement technology. It has the capability of drafting off the success of DVD-Video while still being a format that is viable in an audio-only playback setting, such as part of a car's sound system.

Chapter 12

Digital TV and Radio

"Who the hell wants to hear actors talk?"

—Harry M. Warner, Warner Brothers Studios, 1927

Commercial analog radio and television services are relics of the early 20th century. These technologies have served us well for several decades, but they are outdated. DVDs have better quality and features than a standard definition television broadcast. CDs have better quality than radio broadcasts. As the 21st century begins, digital broadcasts of both television and radio programs are slowly but steadily beginning to replace their analog counterparts.

Digital broadcasts offer higher quality pictures and sound, as well as being able to provide a wealth of ancillary data in the broadcast stream.

Digital Television

Digital television (DTV) refers to the broadcast of video and sound. Ancillary data may be included in the broadcast. The ancillary data may contain episode guides, detailed biographies of the actors, or even executable software that can be run on a computer. To minimize the spectrum needed, the audiovisual data is typically broadcast in a compressed format that must be decompressed before it can be seen and heard.

DTV comes in many different flavors. Some versions have a video resolution comparable with that of analog TV. Such resolutions are known *as standard definition* (SD). Other DTV formats offer increased resolution and are known as *high definition* (HD) TV.

Television broadcasts may be sent from earth-based transmitters to TV sets located within a range of a few dozen miles. This technique is known as *terrestrial broadcasting*.

Alternatively, the broadcasts may be sent by copper or optical cables several miles in length that directly connect from a local transmitter to household receivers. This technique is known as *cable broadcasting* or *cablecasting*.

Finally, the broadcasts may be sent from satellites orbiting the Earth to household antennas. Such satellite broadcasts travel thousands of miles and typically can serve a large geographical region.

Satellites in low orbits move through the sky from the vantage point of a person on the ground. The satellites spend about half their time below the horizon, so multiple satellites are necessary to provide a signal 24 hours a day. Satellites may be placed in a geosynchronous orbit, in which case they orbit the Earth once every 24 hours and hence appear fixed in the sky. Noted science fiction author Sir Arthur C. Clarke devised the concept of geosynchronous satellites in a 1945 letter to *Wireless World* magazine.

There are two dominant sets of digital television standards in the world. One is known as ATSC, as it was developed by the Advanced Television Steering Committee. The other set is known as Digital Video Broadcasting (DVB). The term digital video broadcasting is also used generically. As such, the ATSC format is an example of digital video broadcasting, although it is a different format than Digital Video Broadcasting.

ATSC

In 1995, the FCC adopted the DTV system proposed by the ATSC for use in the United States. The format uses MPEG-2 transport streams to transmit high definition video (up to 1920 x 1080 pixels), audio, and optional ancillary data. The video is compressed using MPEG-2 video compression. The audio format is AC-3. ATSC allows for the simultaneous broadcast of multiple audio and video programs on the same channel.

Broadcasting

An ATSC broadcast requires the video, audio, and any data streams to be time-interleaved into a MPEG-2 transport stream, shown graphically in Figure 12.1. This process is known as *multiplexing* or *muxing*. The transport stream is converted to an appropriate radio frequency and then transmitted via a large antenna out over the broadcast area.

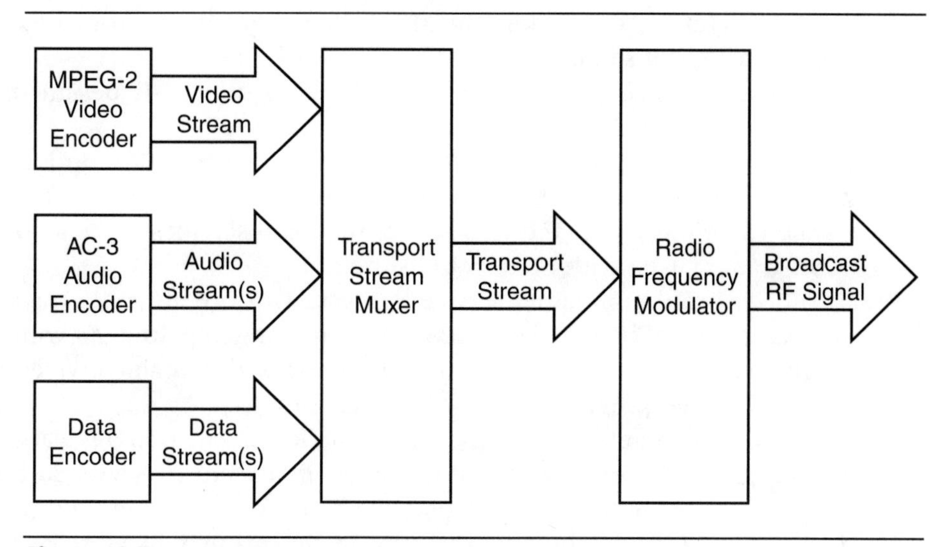

Figure 12.1 ATSC Broadcasting

An ATSC receiver must follow the inverse process. The received RF signal is demodulated to recover the transport stream. The transport stream is then demultiplexed to recover the video, audio, and data streams. These streams are then sent to the appropriate type of decoder.

Audio Services

DTV defines two types of main audio service and six associated services. The two main services are complete main (CM) and music and effects (ME). The six associated services are dialogue (D), visually impaired (VI), hearing impaired (HI), commentary (C), emergency message (E), and voice-over (VO).

The complete main service contains all the elements of a complete audio program. This is the default service and contains dialogue, music, and effects. CM may contain from 1 to 5.1 audio channels of sound.

The music and effects service contains the entire audio program with the exception of dialogue. The ME service can be mixed with one of the associated services to form a complete audio program. For instance, an associated dialogue service can be mixed with the ME service to form the complete program. The advantage of separating the services in this manner is that multiple dialogue services can be part of a single DTV program, each in a different language. It is thus simple to change languages while watching a program. The ME service may contain from 1 to 5.1 audio channels of sound.

The dialogue service contains only dialogue and is designed to be mixed into an ME service, as noted above.

The visually impaired service is meant to carry a description of the video content for use by people who are visually impaired. The VI service can either be mixed into one of the main services or be a complete program in itself with up to 5.1 channels.

The hearing impaired service is meant to store an audio track of increased intelligibility for people who are hearing impaired. As with the VI service, the HI service can either be mixed with a main service or be a self-contained program with up to 5.1 channels.

The commentary service contains audio information ancillary to the main program. For example, it may contain a scene-by-scene description of the movie by the editor. Alternatively, it could contain jokes made at the expense of the original dialogue in the manner of *Mystery Science Theatre 3000*. The C service may be either mixed with a main service or be a self-contained program with up to 5.1 channels.

The emergency message service is a single channel that takes priority over all the other audio services. If a decoder receives a DTV program with an E service, it must mute the main service and play back the E service instead. Note that the E service may be used for purposes other than announcing emergencies.

The voice-over service is a single channel that is mixed into the center channel of a main service. It is second in priority only to the E service. The VO service may be mixed into a main service at volumes controlled by the broadcaster. A local station might use the VO service to add an announcement during the end credits of a movie stating that viewers should stay tuned for the upcoming nightly news. By taking advantage of the VO service, they would not have to re-encode the main service with their advertisement inserted into the mix.

AC-3

The AC-3 format was developed by Dolby explicitly for DTV and is specified in the ATSC's document A/52. The actual audio format sanctioned for DTV is a subset of the AC-3 format documented in A/52. For instance, AC-3 supports bit rates up to 640 kilobits per second for a single audio stream, but the permitted bit rates for DTV are lower to keep decoder cost reasonable.

A main audio service or auxiliary service containing a complete program is limited to 384 kilobits per second. Mono associated services designed to be mixed with a main service are limited to 128 kilobits per second. Stereo associated services designed to be mixed with a main service are limited to 192 kilobits per second. Furthermore, the combined data rate of a main service and associated service designed to be mixed together may not exceed 512 kilobits per second.

In all cases, DTV audio has a sampling frequency of 48 kilohertz.

An overview of the AC-3 encoding process is shown in Figure 12.2. The encoder first transforms input samples into the frequency domain via a filter bank. These frequency domain components are represented as binary exponents and mantissas. The exponents are used to generate a rough representation of the original signal, which is called the spectral envelope. The envelope is used to determine how many bits to use in the quantization of the mantissas.

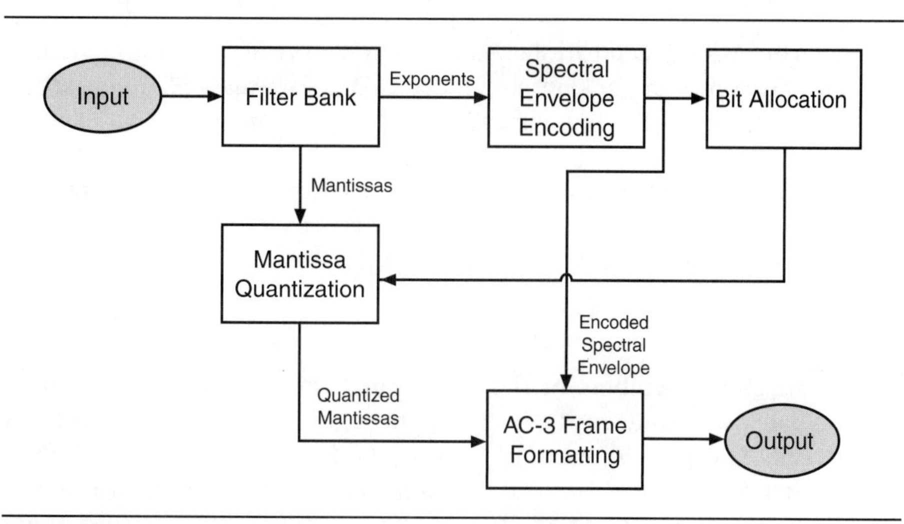

Figure 12.2 AC-3 Encoding

The AC-3 filter bank uses 50 percent overlapping blocks of 512 samples. Thus, each block contains 256 new samples as well as 256 samples from the previous blocks. To help reduce pre-echoes, each block may optionally be split into two 256 sub-blocks to create a narrower transform window.

Sets of six audio blocks are organized into synchronization frames, shown in Figure 12.3. The sync frame begins with a synchronization information (SI) header, which contains a synchronization pattern indicating the start of the frame. The SI also includes the length of the frame. Following the SI header is the bit stream information (BSI) header. The BSI contains information about the stream format, such as the number of channels, time codes, and other information. The BSI is followed by the six audio blocks, which may be followed by auxiliary data. The frame ends with a checksum.

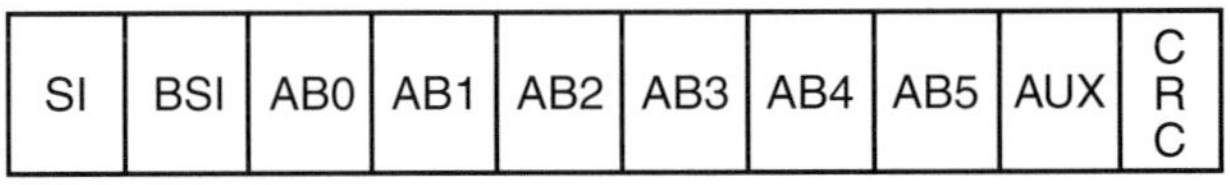

SI	BSI	AB0	AB1	AB2	AB3	AB4	AB5	AUX	CRC

Figure 12.3 AC-3 Synchronization Frame

Karaoke

The AC-3 specification includes details on how to implement karaoke.[1] When running in karaoke mode, an AC-3 stream's channels are no longer L, R, C, LS, RS, but instead L, R, M (guide melody), V1, and V2 (vocal tracks).

A karaoke-aware AC-3 decoder plays the channels of a karaoke stream at the relative levels specified by the stream. A karaoke-capable decoder allows you to independently adjust the channel levels during playback.

DVB

In 1991, members of the European television broadcasting industry began discussing ways to implement digital television. In September 1993, this European Launching Group (ELG) drafted a Memorandum of Understanding (MoU) that laid down ground rules for the various—and often competing—television stakeholders to work together in defining digital

[1] To quote Zapp Brannigan: "There's only one surefire way back into a woman's heart and parts beyond. I speak, of course, of karaoke."

television. Coincident with the MoU, the ELG renamed itself the Digital Video Broadcasting (DVB) Project. The DVB continues promoting MPEG-2 based digital television standards today.

DVB has defined three main sets of standards; one for satellite, one for cable, and one for terrestrial broadcasts. The standard families are known respectively as DVB-S, DVB-C, and DVB-T.

Like ATSC, DVB uses MPEG-2 transport streams as the fundamental broadcast format.

The mandatory DVB audio formats are MPEG-1 and MPEG-2 Layer I and II. Optionally, MPEG-2 Layer II Backwards Compatible multichannel audio and AC-3 formats are supported. Layer I streams may have bit rates from 32 to 448 kilobits per second; Layer II streams may have bit rates from 32 to 384 kilobits per second. For MPEG-2 BC streams, an extension bit stream can be used to surpass the 384 kilobits per second limitation.

Primary audio programs have a sampling rate of 32, 44.1, and 48 kilohertz. Secondary programs can have sampling rates from 16 to 48 kilohertz.

Digital Terrestrial Radio

Today there are two main digital radio formats being used for terrestrial broadcasts. One is known as Digital Audio Broadcasting (DAB), the other as In Band On Channel (IBOC). IBOC is being used in the United States. DAB is being used everywhere else in the world.

DAB

In 1987, the EUREKA-147 Consortium was founded to define a digital radio system that was capable of terrestrial and satellite broadcasting and of being received by stationary and mobile receivers. The EUREKA-147 system became known as Digital Audio Broadcasting (DAB). Eleven years later in 1998 the first DAB receivers became available. Soon after, the EUREKA-147 Consortium evolved into the World DAB Forum, a non-governmental body designed to promote the digital radio format around the world.

DAB offers CD-like audio quality and less interference than traditional AM/FM radio broadcasts. In addition to digital audio, DAB also supports limited text and graphics that can augment the audio stream. Regular and pilot DAB broadcasts are available today in many European countries and Australia.

Broadcast

DAB programs consist of MPEG Layer II audio and ancillary data. In preparation for broadcast, audio and data packets are processed by a channel coder that adds error protection and time interleaved; the process flow is shown in Figure 12.4. The output of the channel coders are mixed together in the Main Service Channel (MSC) multiplexer.

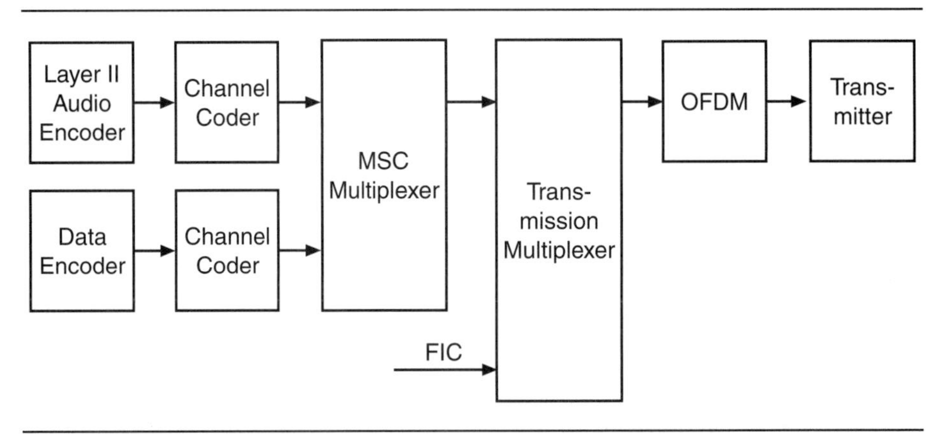

Figure 12.4 DAB Broadcast Flow

The MSC is then mixed with the Fast Information Channel (FIC). The FIC is fast because data can be extracted from it by a receiver without having to demultiplex the MSC stream. Whereas the MSC contains audio and in-program data, the FIC contains Service Information and Multiplex Configuration Information (MCI). The Service Information includes data such as the radio station name and current song title, as well as links to related DAB audio programs and legacy analog simulcast frequencies. The MIC contains information on how the fundamental audio and data streams have been multiplexed into the MSC. The FIC may also contain a Traffic Message Channel (TMC) and an Emergency Warning System (EWS).

The FIC and MSC are combined and then processed using Orthogonal Frequency Division Multiplexing (OFDM) as a final step prior to broadcast. OFDM divides channel data into a large number (192, 384, 768 or 1,536) of independent low bit rate streams, each of which is sent over an independent carrier signal. The collection of carriers is known as an *ensemble*. Even if a few of the carrier signals are blocked, the majority of the ensemble is likely to arrive at the receiver and a useful version of the audio reconstructed. By comparison, if an analog radio station's signal is blocked, then no audio can be heard.

Redundancy and temporal and frequency interleaving among the OFDM carriers help protect DAB broadcasts from multi-path interference as well as temporary signal fades associated with a mobile receiver.

For analog radio broadcasts, each station is allocated a small portion of the radio frequency (RF) spectrum. The stations use this entire allotment to send a single audio program. In contrast, a DAB ensemble may contain multiple audio programs.

Audio Format

DAB uses MPEG Layer II for audio coding. The nominal sampling rate is 48 kilohertz, but 24-kilohertz sampling is also available for situations requiring reduced bandwidth. The 24-kilohertz mode is sometimes referred to as half sampling. Sampling at 48 kilohertz uses MPEG-1 Layer II; sampling at 24 kilohertz uses MPEG-2 Layer II.

Mono, stereo, and joint stereo modes are supported. There have been proposals to add multichannel support, but they have yet to be formally adopted. Individual audio channels may use bit rates from 8 to 192 kilobits per second.

Each audio frame ends with two bytes that contain Program Associated Data (PAD). The PAD begins with a two-byte structure known as the Fixed Program Associated Data (F-PAD). The F-PAD contains information that is relevant to the adjacent audio samples, such as whether the content is music or speech, and dynamic range control data. Although the F-PAD structure is a mandatory part of the DAB audio frame, the use of the F-PAD fields themselves is optional.

The F-PAD also contains flags indicating whether or not Extended Program Associated Data (X-PAD) is contained in the frame. X-PAD may be stored in fixed-size short packets four bytes long or may be variably sized. X-PAD may consist of information such as dynamic textual labels or application-specific data.

Conditional Access

DAB also includes provisions for conditional access (CA). *Conditional access* means that the broadcast content is scrambled, thereby preventing unauthorized people from listening to it. Authorized listeners, typically consumers who pay a provider for premium content, have the necessary information to descramble and listen to CA radio.

IBOC

In 1990 in the United States, the FCC began investigating digital radio. In the mid 1990s, as part of this activity, the National Radio System Committee (NRSC) and the Consumer Electronics Manufacturing Association (CEMA) tested several different experimental digital radio systems. One category of systems they tested was In Band On-Channel (IBOC). The IBOC name refers to the fact that the digital radio broadcasts occur within the existing analog radio spectrum, and further that the digital broadcast from a particular radio station is in the same spectrum allocation as its existing analog channel.

In 1997, the digital audio radio subcommittee's final report indicated that IBOC was not yet ready for commercialization. Both CEMA and National Public Radio (NPR) urged the FCC to consider non-IBOC systems, such as EUREKA 147's DAB.

In 1999, the FCC began revaluating DAB solutions. They eventually decided that out-of-band solutions such as DAB that required new airwave spectrum to be allocated were not feasible. In the interim, IBOC technology had become much more mature. The only IBOC developer at this point was iBiquity Digital Corporation. The FCC ran a series of IBOC tests using MPEG-2 AAC coding. Satisfied with the results, they re-ran a series of tests using iBiquity's proprietary Perceptual Audio Coder (PAC) format. Again, the results were satisfactory.

In October 2002, the FCC formally adopted IBOC as the digital radio format to replace existing analog FM and daytime AM broadcasts. Sanctioning of IBOC for nighttime AM broadcasting was withheld until further testing could be completed, because nighttime radio wave propagation is substantially different than the daytime equivalent.

IBOC offers the usual advantages of digital systems over legacy analog: increased signal quality and ancillary data services. For instance, many of today's IBOC broadcasts contain ID3 tag information that describes the song being played. IBOC-aware receivers can display this information to the listener.

Hybrid Mode

FM and AM radio stations have a narrow frequency band in which they are licensed to transmit. FM stations lie in the band from 88 to 108 megahertz. Adjacent FM stations are separated in the spectrum by at least 200 kilohertz. Each station may broadcast signals ±75 kilohertz from their center frequency, leaving a 25-kilohertz guard band to help minimize interference between adjacent stations. AM stations are in the band between 535 to 1,700 kilohertz. AM stations may be separated by only 10 kilohertz.

The existing IBOC broadcasts are a hybrid. They contain analog FM and AM broadcasts at a somewhat narrower than normal bandwidth and bracket these analog signals with digital signals.

For FM hybrid broadcasts, the analog signal is flanked by a lower and upper digital sideband, as shown in Figure 12.5. The digital signal is capable of producing CD-like sound.

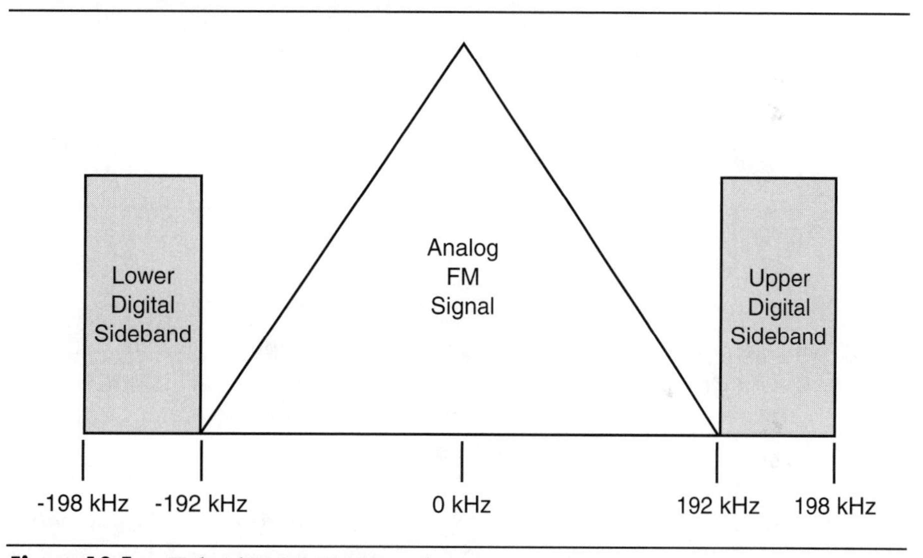

Figure 12.5 Hybrid IBOC FM Waveform

For AM hybrid broadcasts, the analog signal is flanked by primary and secondary digital sidebands, as shown in Figure 12.6. Furthermore, a pair of tertiary sidebands overlaps the bandwidth of the analog signal. It is possible to distinguish the analog and tertiary digital signals because the two signal sets are 90 degrees out of phase with one another. The hybrid waveform constraints mean that only monophonic AM broadcasts can be supported by the analog signal. The digital signal offers FM-quality sound.

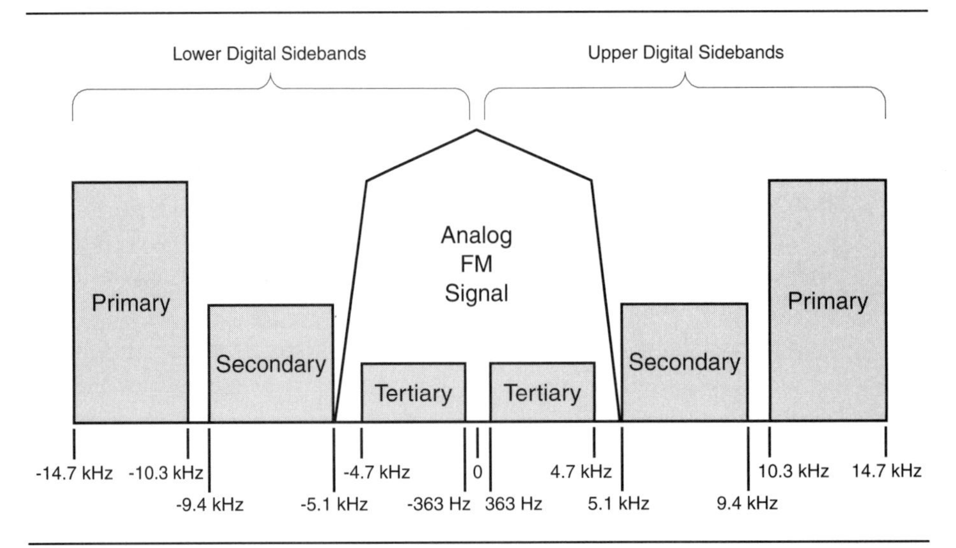

Figure 12.6 Hybrid IBOC AM Waveform

The hybrid formats offer an easy transition path between existing analog and future digital systems. Legacy radio receivers can decode the analog portion of the hybrid broadcast. New digital receivers are able to achieve increased performance by recovering the digital signal.

In the case that the digital signal is unrecoverable, as might be the case at the edge of the broadcast area, a digital radio can fall back to the analog signal. This use of the analog signal allows for a graceful degradation of the radio program, rather than the sudden cliff-edge effect that happens when a digital program can no longer be received.

The hybrid formats can cause some interference with existing broadcasts. However, the interference is primarily outside the protected service contour of existing stations. The FCC deemed the slight increase in analog interference to be a reasonable tradeoff for the overall increased quality and features offered by the digital service.

In the future, the analog broadcasts may be discontinued, in which case the entire spectrum allocation of a radio station could be used for transmitting the digital signal. The audio quality of such all-digital IBOC broadcasts would be better than that of hybrid broadcasts.

Digital Satellite Radio

Digital satellite radio broadcasts offer the same features as digital terrestrial radio broadcasts; namely, excellent audio quality, conditional access, and data services. The three digital satellite radio service providers today are Worldspace, XM, and Sirius.

All the satellite radio services require listeners to purchase proprietary receivers that work only with that particular service. Listeners have to pay a monthly fee for listening to the service. Additional premium channels are typically available for an extra fee. Because satellite radio typically covers continent-sized geographical areas, they do not provide local channels. Therefore, many satellite radio receivers also include legacy FM/AM receivers.

Worldspace

On October 21, 1999, Worldspace began broadcasting over 25 channels of digital audio to the African continent via its geosynchronous AfriStar satellite. It subsequently launched another geosynchronous satellite called AsiaStar which provides service to—yes, you guessed it—Asia. Each satellite broadcasts three slightly overlapping beams. Each beam provides a unique program selection, but listeners can only select from the channels offered by a single beam. Worldspace also has plans to launch AmeriStar, a satellite that will provide coverage to South America.

Worldspace uses MPEG-2 Layer III audio compression at bit rates from 16 to 128 kilobits per second. In addition to audio programs, a datacasting service is available. It is being used for distance learning and distributing stock and weather information.

XM

XM Satellite Radio began offering service September 25, 2001. The service uses two geosynchronous satellites called Rock and Roll to provide coverage of the continental United States. XM Satellite Radio currently offers over 120 digital channels.

XM encodes its audio streams in compliance with the MPEG-4 High Efficiency AAC profile. The profile uses MPEG-4 AAC and Spectral Band Replication (SBR). SBR works by reconstructing high frequency information from analysis of the low frequency components of the signal in conjunction with a low data rate side channel. Prior to standardization, the combination of AAC and SBR was known as aacPlus.

Sirius

Sirius Satellite Radio began offering service February 14, 2002. Sirius uses a constellation of three satellites in highly inclined elliptical orbits. Sirius offers 100 channels of audio and has also demonstrated experimental video broadcasting.

Sirius uses iBiquity's proprietary PAC technology for audio compression. Sirius also uses statistical multiplexing for dynamically allocating the satellite broadcast bandwidth to the channels that need it most. Sirius refers to this technique as S>PLEX.

Summary

Digital broadcast services are available today that have either replaced or are in the process of replacing legacy analog broadcasts. These broadcasts include both television and radio delivered by satellite, cable, and terrestrial means.

Digital broadcasts typically offer greater sound quality than their analog predecessors. These new broadcasts also offer new capabilities, such as offering multiple concurrent audio programs on a single channel and providing ancillary data that supplements the audio stream. Digital broadcasting also allows easy support for conditional access programs; content is scrambled prior to broadcast and only authorized people are able to descramble and listen to the program.

Chapter 13

Audio on the PC

"A lot of features of the Apple II went in because I had designed Breakout *for Atari. ... I got this ball bouncing around, and I said, 'Well it needs sound,' and I had to add a speaker to the Apple II. It wasn't planned, it was just accidental..."*

—Steve Wozniak

One of the first widely successful personal computers (PC) was the Apple II. Introduced in 1977, it was powered by a 1 megahertz processor. A mere 25 years later, the processor frequencies in PCs were literally 2,000 times faster! If the automobile industry had been able to follow the same rate of performance growth, cars would travel at speeds exceeding that of the fastest jet fighter.[1] The increase in computer processing power has brought with it a similarly dramatic growth in sound capabilities.

Evolution of PC Sound

The first personal computers had very limited sound capabilities—if they had any at all. The aforementioned Apple II came standard with a simple speaker that could be toggled between two positions via software. To produce any sort of tone, a subroutine had to be written that would

[1] But, as the joke goes, the car would explode at least once a day for no apparent reason.

toggle the speaker at the desired frequency. The resulting motion generated monophonic square wave sound.

In 1981, the Commodore VIC-20 computer was introduced. The VIC-20 was the first PC model of which over a million units were shipped. It offered three square wave generators that could be run simultaneously. Each generator spanned three octaves and was limited to producing 128 different tones. The VIC-20 also included a white noise generator that could be combined with the square wave generators.

1981 also saw the launch of the IBM PC (Model 5150), the first in a long family of computers based on Intel® processors that continues to this day. The IBM PC sported a single channel square wave generator. The resulting sound has come to be known as *PC Speaker*.

Sound Cards

By 1987, IBM had introduced multiple successors to the original IBM PC. Furthermore, compatible IBM clones were being sold by an increasing number of companies around the world. All these computers continued to use monophonic PC Speaker sound. Competing computer systems offered superior sound capabilities. For instance, the Apple Macintosh II supported four channels of 8-bit 44.1 kilohertz digital stereo sound.

However, 1987 was a milestone in IBM PC sound, as it saw the introduction of a new sound card from AdLib. The AdLib card used a technique known as frequency modulation (FM) to reproduce the sound of musical instruments far more accurately than was possible with a single square wave. The AdLib card was capable of simultaneously playing nine sound channels or six sound channels and five hit instruments, such as drums and cymbals. While the AdLib card dramatically improved the musical soundtracks of games, the remaining sound effects, such as a spaceship firing its weapons, still had to be rendered via the monophonic PC Speaker.

In 1989, Creative Labs introduced a new sound card, called the Sound Blaster, which contained the same FM synthesis chip used by AdLib and also included the ability to play 8-bit 22 kilohertz digital samples. While still a far cry from the built-in capabilities of the Apple computers, the $300 Sound Blaster marked the start of a whole new era of sound on PCs. The Sound Blaster quickly became the best-selling computer peripheral. A 1991 version of Sound Blaster added stereo sound support. A 1992 version supported stereo and 16-bit digital sound.

Hardware Abstraction Layer

By 1995, a wide variety of sound cards were available from numerous manufacturers. Cards were available that supported 44.1 kilohertz 16-bit stereo sound, CD-Audio playback, and S/PDIF connectors. Not all of these cards were compatible with one another. Typically, for a piece of software to support a particular sound card family, support for the card would need to be explicitly coded. When buying a game, consumers had to make sure they had a compatible sound card. The effort required to support a large number of sound cards was nontrivial, so it was difficult for every piece of software to support every sound card. Because there were a large number of sound card clones, applications would often support only basic features that were common to most cards.

Compatibility was such a problem that avid gamers would often have an assortment of floppy boot disks, each of which contained different hardware and operating system configuration information. For instance, if you wanted to play *Doom* you would boot your computer with one disk, but then you'd have to reboot with a different disk if you wanted to start playing *Sam and Max Hit the Road*, and reboot with still a different disk if you then wanted to play *Ultima VII*.

One way to solve the combinatorial complexity of large numbers of software applications and hardware devices is to define a hardware abstraction layer (HAL), as shown in Figure 13.1. The HAL defines a standardized set of high-level commands. These commands are available to applications via a software library module. Each sound card manufacturer provides a specialized piece of software known as a *driver*. The driver takes each high-level command and does all the custom configuration and programming of the sound card required to implement the feature.

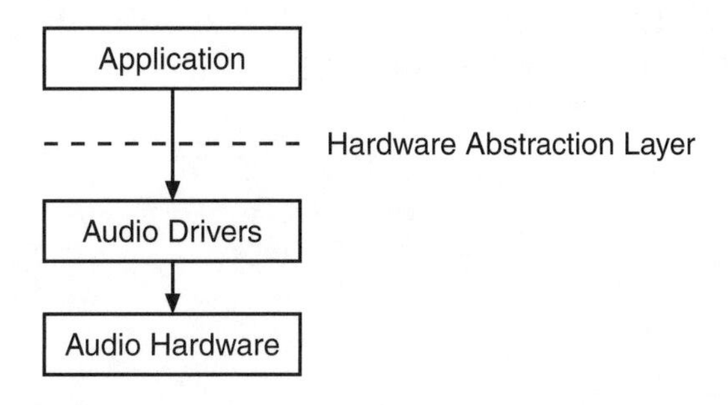

Figure 13.1 Hardware Abstraction Layer

The practical upshot of having a HAL is that a software application no longer needs to know all the details of how the audio hardware is implemented. Developers need merely to code their software using standardized commands such as SetVolume(), and they can rely on the appropriate audio drivers to make that command work on the associated sound card. With a HAL, the software application works on all sound devices, as long as there are drivers for the device.

In 1995, Microsoft launched a HAL to be used with their Windows 95 operating system. Known as DirectX 1.0, it included a component called DirectSound that specified a HAL for audio devices. DirectX completely changed the sound ecosystem under Windows. Users no longer needed to manually configure their sound cards to work with different games. As DirectX evolved and became adopted throughout the industry, users were able to buy virtually any piece of software and be confident that it would almost certainly work with their sound card.

Soft Sound

The collection of hardware responsible for receiving raw sound data from the PC's operating system and converting it to signals that drive a speaker is known as an *audio controller*. An audio controller may also take in external audio signals and make them available for use on the PC. These external signals may come from a microphone or consumer electronics (CE) device such as a CD player.

The first audio controllers were often mounted on add-in cards that were compatible with an industry standard peripheral interface such as the Industry Standard Architecture (ISA) bus or Peripheral Component Interface (PCI). Interfaces such as PCI are generic and can be used to support a large number of peripheral types; they are not specific to audio. The PCI interface on most PCs is supported by a chip known as the Input/Output Controller Hub (ICH), as shown in Figure 13.2.

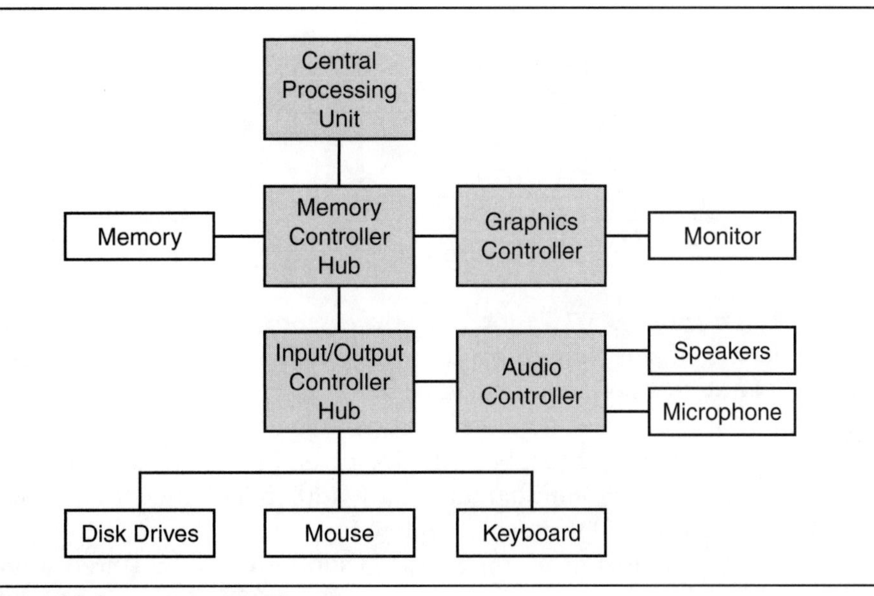

Figure 13.2 Schematic of a PC

Add-in sound cards from the mid-1990's era had dedicated hardware to perform all the necessary processing of the sound, such as mixing multiple voices together into a single sound channel and doing digital-to-analog conversion. One reason such dedicated hardware was required was because there was not sufficient processing power elsewhere in the PC capable of handling the sound processing.

However, the computational power of PCs has continued to double every one to two years. So it came to pass that CPUs became sufficiently powerful to take on some of the sound processing tasks. To this end, Intel introduced the Audio Codec 1997 (AC97) protocol in 1997. AC97 allows sound processing tasks such as sample rate conversion and mixing to be handled by the CPU.

AC97 is implemented by adding logic known as the *AC97 digital controller* to the ICH, shown in Figure 13.3. The digital controller logic sends and receives processed digital audio to an external piece of silicon known as an *AC97 analog codec*. The purpose of the codec is to convert the digital audio data into analog signals that were used to drive speakers. The codec also converts external analog sources into digital data that is fed back to the main memory space via the AC97 link.

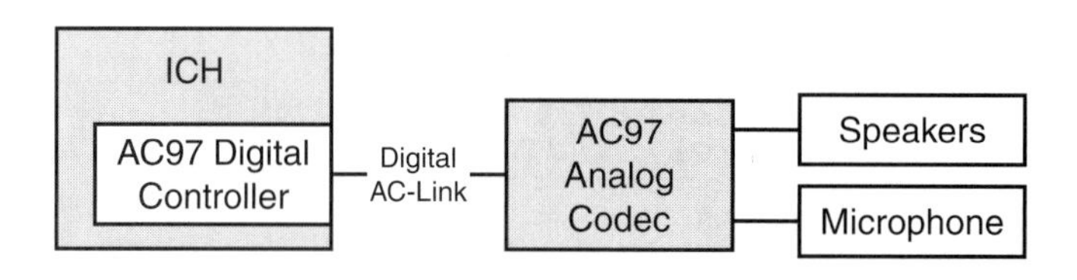

Figure 13.3 AC97

Because AC97 offloads many of the sound processing tasks from dedicated hardware to software that runs on the general purpose CPU, it is known as *software sound* or *soft sound*. An AC97 analog codec is significantly cheaper than a full-blown sound chip, so it is an inexpensive way to add sound to a PC. The decreased price comes at the cost of some of the CPU's computational bandwidth being used to process sound. Typically, the CPU usage is negligible.

The original AC97 specification supported 16-bit stereo sound output at 48 kilohertz. The specification was expanded in subsequent years to include support for 20-bit 96-kilohertz stereo sound output, four-channel and six-channel sound configurations, and S/PDIF.

In 2003, Intel announced Intel® High Definition Audio (Intel® HD Audio), an AC97 replacement codec. The new codec, formerly code-named Azalia, is thematically similar to AC97 but supports many new features. For instance, Intel HD Audio can support 32-bit 192-kilohertz surround sound out.

An Intel HD Audio controller can simultaneously handle four input and four output streams, enabling many usage models not possible under AC97. One such model is microphone arrays, where the inputs from multiple mikes are used to reduce environmental noise and echoes, thus allowing for cleaner voice signals. Microphone arrays are of particular interest to voice recognition systems, which require a very clean voice signal.

Usage Models

Today's PCs are capable of recording and playing back sounds with extremely high quality. In addition to these basic capabilities, the power and flexibility of computers has enabled usage models for listening to, creating, and distributing sounds that were not previously possible.

Editing

Audio editing was originally accomplished by physically cutting and splicing magnetic tapes together. Consumers eventually were able to duplicate this simple type of editing by using a separate tape player hooked up to a tape recorder. Such a system could be used to create mix tapes or do simple editing of audio tracks, but anything more sophisticated required expensive professional equipment.

As PCs became more powerful, it became possible to do a wide variety of sound editing techniques. By 1990, an off-the-shelf PC coupled with shareware software could perform cross-fades between multiple CD-quality digital audio tracks. Furthermore, the PC could easily do more complex effects that were previously only possible with extremely expensive equipment, such as adding arbitrary reverb and echoes, pitch bending, and adjusting the tempo.

Ripping

The addition of CD-ROM drives to PCs meant that you could listen to audio CDs on their PCs. It also allowed the possibility of copying the audio from the CD to the PC's hard disk, a process that has come to be known as *ripping*. After the CD has been ripped to disk, you can listen to the music even without the CD in the CD-ROM drive.

Initially, ripping was not used very widely. Because the audio files were uncompressed, they took up large amounts of space. In the first years of CD-ROM drives, the average hard drive capacity was on the same order of magnitude as the CDs themselves.

Ripping became more interesting in the late 1990s. Hard drive capacities were continually increasing, even as their prices continued to decrease. Additionally, CPUs became sufficiently powerful to do real time MPEG Layer III encoding and decoding of music files. It became feasible to rip several CDs worth of songs onto your computer's hard drive as MP3s. You could then listen to songs all day long without ever having to swap CDs. You could create custom play lists that would play just the songs on the albums that you liked. In effect, it allowed people to create their own personalized radio station.

Burning

Having MP3 collections on the PC gives us great flexibility in how we listen to music. However, this flexibility was initially only available while people stayed in front of the PC. It was not until 1999 that audio CE devices such as CD and DVD players began supporting MP3 files. Nowadays you can listen to MP3s on a wide variety of playback systems.

As compact disc burners became available for the PC, and the price of blank media dropped below $1, it became feasible to convert MP3 files into audio CD format and record them onto CD-R discs. This technique is known as *burning*. Burning CDs allows you to create custom collections of their favorite tracks from their pre-recorded CD collection, much as people previously created mix tapes using dual-deck tape recorders.

These burned discs can then be listened to on older CD equipment, such as stand-alone players in the living room and car stereos. Burned CDs do not necessarily have to come from existing CDs. Burning also allows you to listen to music originating in the MP3 format on traditional equipment that does not natively support MP3.

Downloading

The popularity of MP3s and other proprietary compressed music formats brought with it new audio distribution models. One such model is the ability to download songs on demand. An audio download could be an MP3 file created by an amateur musician and posted on their website for free download. Or it could be the work of a popular artist recorded in a proprietary format with a digital rights management (DRM) system that restricts how it can be played. Some studios release tracks from upcoming albums for free download that expire when the album itself is released.

The download of the music itself may be slower than real time. In other words, a three-minute song may take more than three minutes to download, depending on the connection speed between the user and the file server. Once downloaded, the file resides on the user's local hard drive. In general, a downloaded file can be listened to repeatedly, although DRM-protected content may have playback limitations. The downloaded file can also be burned to CD or copied to a stand-alone MP3 player; although, again, DRM may limit the permitted operations.

The ability for virtually anyone to post content for download means that aspiring artists can distribute their work far more widely than was ever previously possible. Now, in the early years of the 21st century, numerous commercial music download services are available. Boasting the same albums available for sale in brick and mortar stores, these music sites allow you to download music regardless of where you are or what time it is. Several sites allow listeners to download individual tracks from an album, so they only have to pay for the songs they like.

As a point of fact, this possibility is a topic of concern for some record labels, who presumably make more money selling a Baha Boys album for $15 than they do selling the single track "Who Let the Dogs Out?" for $1. For instance, on Apple's iTunes† music store, you can buy individual tracks of Dirty Vegas' self-titled album, but you cannot buy as a single track their extremely popular song "Days Go By." The only way to get that song is to pay for the entire album.

Streaming

Another distribution model made possible by the Internet is streaming audio. As is the case with downloading, sound data are sent from a file server to a client PC. The difference is that streaming sound files are temporary—they exist on the local hard drive just long enough to be played back. Soon after they have been played, the sound data are overwritten by newer sound data.

Streaming is also different from downloading in that streaming files must be sent no slower than real time. A three-minute song must be transmitted in no more than three minutes. Otherwise the audio playback pauses or skips while the player waits for the next chunk of data.

Streaming files are available in both open-source formats, such as MP3, and proprietary formats, such as those offered by Apple, RealNetworks, and Microsoft. Because connection speeds to the Internet vary widely—from 56 kilobits per second modems to 44 megabits per second T3 lines—sites usually provide streams at multiple bit rates.

Streaming audio can be on demand. For instance, many on-line stores that sell audio CDs offer 30-second audio stream previews of tracks on the CDs. Streaming audio can also be in the form of a broadcast. When you tune into a particular broadcast stream, you cannot begin at the beginning, but instead you hear the stream at the point it happens to be, much like a traditional radio broadcast. In fact, this technique is often known as Internet radio.

A specialized type of streaming is Internet Protocol (IP) telephony, which is the technique of making phone calls to and/or from a PC. The technique is also known as Voice Over Internet Protocol (VoIP). VoIP requires two streams: one for talking and one for listening. The streams move in opposite directions. When calling from one PC to another, the audio data remains entirely on the Internet. However, when one of the endpoints is regular telephone, specialized equipment converts between the IP streams and the Public Switched Telephone Network (PSTN) that handles traditional phone calls. The VoIP system also handles the routing of the audio streams to and from the desired telephone number.

File Sharing

The fact that millions of computers are connected together via the Internet makes possible a technique known as *peer-to-peer file sharing*. You can make files on your computer accessible to another person—any other person—also connected to the Internet.

There are different variations of file sharing implementations. A centralized system uses one or more servers to keep track of which files are available on which PCs. When you begin using such a file-sharing service, a list of your shared files is sent to the server. When you search for a particular file, the query is handled by one of the centralized servers. The centralized server returns a list of all the PCs that are currently sharing the file. You can select from which PC you want to download the file and begin doing just that.

A centralized sharing network requires that one or more people run servers that are dedicated to maintaining the ever-changing inventory of user's PCs. The servers do not store any of the content themselves; the content remains on the client PCs.

A distributed file sharing system does not use a centralized server. Users simply run client software. The task of inventorying and distributing the list of who has what is distributed across the clients.

Both centralized and distributed file-sharing systems can support parallel file transfers—the simultaneous transfer of different pieces of the same file from different locations. Parallel systems offer the potential of higher speed transfers. For instance, if there are 10 copies of a particular file located on machines connected to the network via 300 kilobits per second modems, you could receive a tenth of each file simultaneously, therefore receiving the file at 3,000 kilobits per second. To achieve the higher throughput, you would need to have a sufficiently speedy network connection. If in the previous example you were also connected to the network at 300 kilobits per second, you would not be able to realize any file transfer speedup.

Another advantage of parallel transfers is that if one segment is lost—as might happen if one of the hosting PCs disconnects from the Internet—only that particular segment needs to be recovered. The remaining segments are still valid. If a file transfer is interrupted, some file-sharing systems allow the transfer to resume from the point of interruption, even if the download resumes using a different PC as the source.

File-sharing networks are used by some companies on their corporate intranets to distribute large files throughout their global offices. If an employee in Taipei needs a particular file, the catalog server ideally identifies and uses a local copy in the same office as a source. Only if none are available locally does it begin the slower transfer of the file from the home office in San Francisco.

Napster

In 1999, a student named Shawn Fanning was frustrated that he could not find a lot of music available on line for download. To solve this problem, he created a file-sharing program known as Napster. Launched in May, the program became very popular. Soon, tens of millions of people began sharing music files. As more and more copies of a particular song because available on the network, it was easier and faster to download a copy. As more and more people began using Napster, each added their own collection of audio files to the collection.

In its heyday, an incredible amount of audio content was available on Napster. You could find almost any piece of music ever produced in the history of recorded sound: 1940s radio programs, TV themes from the 1970s, Presidential speeches, historical newscasts, the latest Britney Spears song, and even the "U Stink But I ♥ U" song by Billy and the Boingers, from the floppy record included in the Bloom County comic strip collection of the same name.

People were less interested in hearing a recording of a local artist's garage band then they were in hearing the latest hits from popular recording stars. Napster users would often rip their prerecorded audio CDs to their hard drive and then share them, allowing an unlimited number of other Napster users to make copies of it. The problem was that very few—if any—of the Napster users first got permission from the copyright owners to distribute their content in such a fashion.

Now, most interpretation of copyright law permits content owners to make a reasonable number of backup copies of artistic content they buy, but it is a bit of a stretch to suggest that the backup concept extends to providing an untold number of strangers from around the world with a high-quality copy.

Napster was so popular and contained so many copyrighted works that it became easy to download an entire album. You could burn it to a CD and have a free copy of a popular album. In fact, it was sometimes possible to download an album via Napster before it was even commercially released.

In December—just seven months after the Napster began—the Recording Industry Association of America (RIAA) sued Napster for copyright infringement on behalf of the artists it represented. Thus began a lengthy series of court battles. As the months progressed, Napster made a series of concessions. Given a list of copyrighted songs by the RIAA, Napster modified their servers to block the transfer of audio files with those names. Napster users responded to this tactic by devising protocols for scrambling the file names in a deterministic manner. Because the scrambled file names did not match the RIAA list, the Napster servers allowed them to be swapped.

The RIAA complained that Napster was still permitting copyright infringement. Napster continued updating its servers in an effort to block such content, including using audio fingerprint algorithms to identify songs based on their audio content rather than file name. But, in July 2001, Napster was ordered by U.S. District Judge Marilyn Hall Patel to take their servers offline.[2]

Challenges Continue

This end to the original instantiation of Napster was not the end of audio file sharing. Even as Napster's legal battles continued, several new file-sharing systems were created. Rather than the centralized system used by Napster, many of these new systems used a distributed approach. Because there are no centralized servers or company responsible for the maintenance of these file-sharing systems, there is no immediately obvious litigation target in the case of copyright infringement. And, indeed, much of the content on these new file-sharing systems was indeed copyrighted material.

---

[2] This seems like a good time to mention a *Futurama* episode that aired just before the court decision. The episode was about a company called Nappster.com wherein one of the characters said, "You can't shut us down! The Internet is about the free exchange and sale of other people's ideas. We've done nothing wrong!"

Several of these peer-to-peer systems remain in use today, and the recording industry continues its efforts to prevent unlicensed distribution of its songs. In the summer of 2003, the RIAA began subpoenaing ISPs for lists of individual users with the stated intent of suing those sharing copyrighted material.

Although it remains to be seen how the litigable aspects of file sharing will conclude, artists and studios are engaged in other activities to thwart sharing of their content. For instance, in the spring of 2003 copies of Madonna's new single began appearing on file-sharing networks. Users who downloaded the song were surprised to hear not the song, but instead a loop of Madonna scolding them for trying to do so.

File sharing is not in and of itself illegal. File-sharing networks can be quite legitimately used to share and distribute music that might otherwise not get a wide distribution.

Digital Home

The popularity of the DVD-Video format and its support for surround sound encouraged many manufacturers to produce low-cost surround sound speaker and amplifier systems. Several such systems were intended for use with PCs. Prior to the introduction of DVD-Video, consumer surround sound systems were quite expensive and enjoyed by a limited number of audiophiles. The increasing availability of low-cost systems means that many PC users have a better sound system attached to their computer than they do elsewhere in the house. The PC, for many, has become the primary mechanism for enjoying immersive sound, be it from DVD-Video or audio-only formats such as DVD-Audio.

The advent of surround sound systems for the PC in turn had led computer game manufacturers to add surround support. Now players can hear bullets whizzing past them in a truly immersive fashion.

The cost of building both wired and wireless networks has continued to decrease, leading many people to build home networks. One thing that most people want to be able to do with their home networks is share content across their PCs. Perhaps a home server stores a person's entire music collection, ripped from CDs and downloaded from on-line music providers. People want to be able to listen to that music not just while sitting in front of that computer, but while using other computers in the house or using the living room sound system.

Small devices called Digital Media Adapters (DMA) that bridge the gap between PCs and CE equipment are beginning to appear. They can receive local streams from a home server and convert them into a standard analog audio signal that can drive a standard CE audio input.

Several different ad-hoc systems are available today for implementing such a digital home, but it still requires that the user have a fair amount of technical expertise to cobble together a working system. Industry groups such as the Digital Home Working Group (DHWG) are forming with the intent of standardizing protocols for delivering media throughout the home. Hopefully it will soon be a simple matter for the average consumer to just plug in components and have everything work.

Summary

Sound on the PC began as monophonic square waves. Within 25 years, it evolved to the point of being on par with most stand-alone consumer audio equipment. Today's PCs can play 24-bit 192-kilohertz digital sound and support 6.1 surround sound. The ever-increasing processing power of the PC continues to bring with it new audio capabilities. Computer games once went 'beep beep,' but now they surround the gamer in immersive sound effects while simultaneously serenading them with movie-quality soundtracks.

The connection of all these powerful PCs together via the Internet has created new usage models that are unparalleled in history. People can listen to a huge library of music on demand at any time from all across the planet. Artists can likewise offer their creations to the world at large without having to worry about the costs associated with physical distribution. Music aficionados can create their own radio stations and broadcast the songs they like out to the world without having to build a massive radio antenna that would only reach a few hundred square miles anyway. Home networks promise to let us listen to our personal music collection throughout the house, whether we are in front of a computer or not.

Chapter 14

That Which is Yet to Come

"Where a calculator on the ENIAC is equipped with 18,000 vacuum tubes and weighs 30 tons, computers of the future may have only 1,000 vacuum tubes and perhaps weigh 1-½ tons."

—*Popular Mechanics*, March 1949

It is generally accepted by physicists that time travel into the future is indeed possible. Moving at relativistic velocities—those close to the speed of light—will cause time to pass more slowly for the traveler than it will for stationary observers. So if you get into a space ship and go on a very high-speed journey, centuries may pass on Earth even though you only age a few months.

Now, moving backward through time is a bit more problematic. There are some very good proposals for how to go about doing just that, but they all involve squeezing through a wormhole that is smaller than an atom, shaping a cosmic string that is tens of thousands of light years across, or spinning a cylinder which has a mass greater than that of our entire solar system. In short, nothing that is immediately practical given our species' current state of technological development.[1]

Given this current state of affairs, predicting the future remains an uncertain business. Although we can send someone to the future to see what is coming, there is no way today for that person to transmit that information back to us. And even if they could, some theories hold that

[1] Heck, I'm still trying to make it through the day without my computer crashing!

the returning time traveler would return to a new instantiation of the Universe, one which is identical throughout its history to the original, right up to the point of the traveler's return, whereupon it begins to diverge. In other words, what the future the traveler has seen will not necessarily come to pass.

Ruminations

So, allow me to speculate on the continued evolution and revolution of audio technologies. Just understand that due to budgetary constraints and further limitations imposed by the framework of physical laws of the Universe in which we live, these are merely informed guesses and not guaranteed previews.

The Persistence of Speakers and Microphones

Despite incredible changes in how audio is stored, the mechanisms for getting sound in and out of the system—namely, speakers and microphones—have remained fundamentally unchanged for decades. Although the performance of speakers and microphones will no doubt continue to asymptotically improve with the advance of new materials, the basic structure of the equipment is likely to remain unchanged.

The Death of Analog

It's a pretty safe bet that audio will be increasingly stored in a digital format and that analog storage and transmission formats will become obsolete. In general, digital systems offer increased flexibility, higher performance, and lower cost than their analog analogs. Already, it is increasingly difficult to buy analog audiotapes and records in the United States. Almost all prerecorded music is sold on compact disc.[2]

Although audio can be stored and transmitted digitally, the full audio chain will never be a strictly digital technology, because sound pressure waves are continuous phenomena. Microphones will always be needed to convert the analog waves into discrete digital signals, and speakers will always need to convert digital signals back into analog waves. To that point, the overall quality of audio systems will depend greatly on the performance of the analog-to-digital and digital-to-analog converters used.

---

[2] Still, there will always be those audiophiles who spend massive sums of money for records and high performance players.

CD sound is 16-bit 44.1-kilohertz digital audio. It is the benchmark against which most new sound formats are compared, as in "MP3 encoded at 160 kilobits per second offers CD-quality sound." There are multiple competing high definition audio formats entering the market today. Will they raise the bar for mainstream sound quality? Perhaps. The high definition formats, offering sound up to 24-bit 192 kilohertz certainly offer higher fidelity than a CD, but will the average person be able to hear that increased quality in a typical setting?

When my mom saw a movie on DVD-Video, she immediately noticed how much better the video quality was compared to VHS tape. That obvious increase in quality was sufficient motivation for her to switch from tape to disc. Unless consumers have the same experience when comparing CDs and high definition sound, I suspect they will not readily adopt HD audio.

What may spur the transfer to new audio formats is not the increased fidelity, but instead a new feature: surround sound. CD is just stereo, but the new disc formats offer surround sound. Since surround systems are becoming increasingly affordable for both home theatre and PC settings, audio-only multi-channel formats may become popular.

Smaller, Faster, Cheaper

In 1965, Gordon Moore wrote a paper titled "Cramming more Components onto Integrated Circuits," in which he noted that the number of transistors per integrated circuit was doubling every year. He further predicted that this trend would continue for several years. Although this original prediction was slightly optimistic, the doubling of transistor density every one to two years has continued for 30 years. There has been a corresponding exponential increase in performance and decrease in cost. This doubling trend cannot continue indefinitely, but it looks to continue for several more years. As Moore himself put it in 2003: "No exponential is forever... but we can delay 'forever'."

In short, electronic devices will continue to shrink in size even as their price and performance continue to increase. This trend will make possible new audio devices. For instance, one new type of audio player is the MP3 USB key, a finger-sized device that can play several hours worth of music. The three main components of these devices are a flash memory chip, a processing chip that decodes MP3 and controls the USB interface, and the USB connector itself. Today, the two chips are on par in size with the actual connector. As the chips shrink, the limiting feature in size reduction will be the external connector, rather than the silicon chips.

Coin-sized audio players are in the works, starting with ones the size of a US dollar. These will no doubt shrink in size toward dimes, but this shrinking will not continue indefinitely: at some point the devices become so small that human fingers can no longer push the play button. But the fact that these devices will be so small, light, and cheap means that it will become easy to carry around the music you like. Imagine key fobs that are music players. They can contain slots for tiny earbud headphones with retractable cords. Music personalized to your preference becomes ubiquitous.

Take the concept a step further. Remove the external physical connector and replace it with a tiny wireless transceiver. To fill the player with music, just put it near enough to your computer to be within its wireless range. Keep shrinking the chips, and put them actually inside the earbuds.

New Distribution Models

Historically, each audio format has been engineered to meet or exceed the listener's expectations of the previous format. We still speak of music CDs today as albums, a reference to the fact that the first records were so short that it required multiple records to record a single symphony. These record sets were bound together into storage sleeves called an album. The LP that replaced the first generation of records was designed so you could play an entire album of the older records without having to flip the disc over. In particular, a single record side was targeted to store a single classical symphony. The first cassette tapes—30 minutes on a side—mimicked record capabilities. CDs are long enough to play both sides of a record or tape without having to flip anything over. The fact that today's music artists release albums that are nominally 60 minutes long are due in part to the evolution of audio formats and the fact that symphonies composed in the 18th century were typically under 30 minutes long.

However, I see no reason for this trend to continue in the future. The fact that music can be distributed digitally over the network means that an album can be arbitrarily sized. Numerous independent artists release albums that only contain two or three songs monthly via the Internet. Since there is no physical media to be distributed, it is cost effective to release songs in such a manner. It remains to be seen whether or not mainstream recording artists and the studios that represent them will embrace these more flexible models. It is clear from the popularity of peer-to-peer file-sharing systems and commercial download-on-demand sites that consumers desire the ability to buy only the songs they want instead of having to buy an entire disc.

One challenge that will have to be addressed with the new models is the matter of permanence. When you buy a CD today, you can rip copies of the music to your PC and portable MP3 player. If your hard drive crashes or you accidentally delete the file, you still have the original CD from which you can make more copies. If you buy a song via an Internet download and the file gets deleted, that song is gone forever and you will need to repurchase it. The onus can certainly be placed on consumers. Backing up your hard drive regularly can protect your music, but it can be a difficult task keeping track of which files are where as you transfer them out to smaller capacity portable players or upgrade to a new computer.

The Digital Home

One of the recurring themes in future audio is ubiquity: being able to access music at any time from any location. In recent years, audio on the PC has become quite mature. On your computer, you can listen to CDs, play games that immerse you in surround sound effects, or listen to Internet radio stations. But for most people, the PC has been relegated to the den or home office. It remains a discrete system from the TV and stereo system in the living room. Shuttling content between the two arenas typically involves carrying a CD back and forth or running really long audio cables between the two rooms. With them wired, you'd still need to run back and forth between rooms to hit the play button and adjust the volume

To an engineer, that just screams, "I am an inelegant, stop-gap solution!" Luckily, new types of devices are beginning to emerge. There are stand-alone CD players that include an internal hard drive. Listeners can rip songs from their CDs and create an extensive audio library on the hard drive. These devices also include network connections so they can wirelessly stream music to receivers in other rooms. Some of these devices are sophisticated enough to stream a different audio program to every receiver station: each person can sit in a different bedroom and listen to any song from the family library, regardless of what other family members are listening to.

This wireless hard drive-based player system offers a great deal of flexibility in playback. The chief drawback of this system is its expensive price, although that will certainly decline in time. Such a device is a CE product that has PC-like capabilities. But it still can't get content off my PC, or let me listen to the music stored on my PC.

Coming at the problem from the other angle are Digital Media Adapters (DMA), which can wirelessly receive audio data streams from a PC and convert them to standard analog audio electrical signals. While DMAs can access the media library stored on a PC, they are currently limited in their playback bandwidth. They cannot, for instance, receive high definition uncompressed DVD.

Also, both types of media player devices described above currently use proprietary technologies. Although several of them may store audio as MP3s, they all have their own way of organizing and transmitting files. One type of system cannot interoperate with another. Bodies such as the Digital Home Working Group (DHWG) are endeavoring to define industry-standard protocols for exchanging audio/video data throughout the home. These first sets of standards are targeting stereo CD sound quality, but future versions will no doubt incorporate high definition surround sound as well.

These are interesting times. The long-talked about convergence between PCs and CE devices is gradually coming to pass. With the creation of new types of devices that lie between the bounds of traditional PCs and CE devices, there is concern by CE manufacturers that they will lose market segment share to PC manufacturers, and vice versa. It seems likely that the line between PC and CE will continue to blur, and we will see more companies sell products across the full spectrum.

The Universal Network

The digital home concept is cool. I can listen to any piece of music that I own anywhere in my house. Ubiquitous sound. But a limitation of the digital home is that it stops when I walk out the front door. While in my digital home, I can burn songs to a CD to listen to in my car, or download them onto my MP3 player to listen to while I go rollerblading. But once I go out, I'm limited to whatever I happened to download. And having to transport physical media just so I can listen to it, that's just so 20th century.

Another limitation of the digital home manifests itself when you stay inside, but try to listen to music from outside via the Internet. You can download music files today, but there's no guarantee you can do it in real time. If it takes an hour to download a 3-minute song, it might be just as fast to run out to the store and buy the whole album. It's affordable to set up a wired home network that moves data around at 100 megabits per second. But the speed at which you can connect to the Internet is limited by your modem speed. A DSL or cable modem has a bandwidth on the order of 1 megabit per second. A plain old telephone service modem has substantially less bandwidth.

Latency is another problem with getting data from the Internet. Even if the host and client have a high-speed T3 connection to the Internet, there's no guarantee that a particular packet of data will make it from one point to the other in a specified period of time. Even when listening to a 128-kilobits per second Internet radio station via T3, you can still get dropouts. The Internet offers incredible connectivity and robustness. Even if a large number of network nodes are damaged, it is still possible for the remaining computers to communicate with one another. A trade-off of this design is that there can be no guaranteed maximum latency.

To expand the digital home to the digital world and offer everybody truly ubiquitous sound, we are going to need high bandwidth network connections, or fat pipes, into every home. This universal network would need to overcome latency limitations and offer high-speed wireless connectivity for mobile users. Wherever you go in the house, in the car, at a friend's house, on a plane, or at the beach, you can get into the network.[3]

Ignoring for a moment the technical complexities involved in building the universal network, consider what such a network would offer. You could store all your music files on your PC and be able to listen to them wherever in the world you went. You could buy music on demand and listen to it in real-time as you downloaded it. Since this network would be universal, it could be used as the transport mechanism for several legacy communication systems. All telephone traffic could be routed via this network, as well as digital television and radio.

It may sound a bit far-fetched to imagine putting all our eggs in one basket and relying on a single mechanism for all our data transmission. But consider that that is precisely what we do today with utility services. The water we use at home for drinking, showering, and irrigation all comes in through a single pipe. All the electricity we use at home for running TVs, vacuum cleaners, and computers comes in through a single wire pair. The universal network is just another utility: a data service. And, yes, you'll have to pay for it each month.

If this universal network becomes a reality and achieves the same reliability as our current utilities, then you no longer need to store music files on your PC or on CDs. All the music is stored on industrial-grade server farms scattered throughout the world. Tucked away in a database is a list of all the songs that you are licensed to listen to. Whenever you want to listen to a song, you just select it from your list, hit play, and it'll

---

[3] Tricky. I can't even get cell phone reception at work unless I stand on the building's exposed girders.

be streamed to you in real time. There's no need to burn the files to disc, or download them to a portable player: the universal network is available 24 × 7. Local storage becomes obsolete. A playback device can simply be a headphone with an embedded antenna and decoder chip.

Want to add more songs to your list? No problem. Just have your credit card ready. Of course, some content will always be available for free, such as radio netcasts. Their revenue stream will come from advertisers. And since it's all digital, there is potential for new flexibility. Imagine radio commercials that are targeted very specifically at you or your location. "Hope you're enjoying your drive up Interstate 5. Why not take Exit 142 in half a mile and visit the local Starbucks?"

Unfortunately, increases in personalization invariably bring with them a decrease in privacy. This tension is one of many that will need to be balanced on the universal network. Other concerns include defending premium content from piracy, securing the network itself from worm and virus attacks, and limiting new forms of spam. Imagine every speaker in your house suddenly playing an unsolicited audio message offering free inkjet cartridges, or low mortgage rates, or a new wonder drug that "adds inches" during Thanksgiving dinner.

All these issues aside, the fundamental matter of designing and building such a universal network is a fiendishly complex problem. Guaranteeing that billions of people can simultaneously pull down huge amounts of data around the world is no mean feat, perhaps on par with spinning a cylinder a billion miles long.

Glossary

5.1 A surround sound format with five full range channels (front left, front center, front right, rear right, rear left) and one low frequency effects channel.

AC-3 A multi-channel audio compression algorithm used in DTV and DVD.

AC97 A soft sound infrastructure developed by Intel.

acoustic energy The amount of energy an object uses to make sounds.

ADC An acronym for an analog-to-digital converter. A device that converts an analog signal into a digital signal.

aliasing The introduction of spectral components into a reconstructed signal that did not exist in the original signal. Aliasing is caused by sampling a signal with spectral components above the Nyquist limit.

anechoic chamber A specially-designed room with acoustically absorbent walls used for sound measurements. In such a room there are no reflections, and hence no diffuse sounds.

angle of acceptance The angle within which the microphone will pick up sounds within a specified sensitivity.

anti-aliasing filter A low-pass filter designed to band-limit a signal prior to sampling. A properly designed anti-aliasing filter will prevent aliasing during sampling.

audio controller PC hardware responsible for transporting sound signals from within the computer out to speakers and for bringing external sound signals into the computer.

audio zone The portion of a DVD that contains DVD-Audio information. Audio zone files are stored in the AUDIO_TS folder.

backward masking A type of masking that occurs when the signal precedes the masker in time.

balanced Refers to a transferring a signal using three wires. One wire carries a variable voltage that corresponds to the signal itself, a second wire carries negative equivalent to the first wire. The third wire serves as a zero reference, or ground.

band-limiting Running a signal through a low-pass filter so that it contains no frequencies above Nyquist limit. Failure to band-limit a signal will result in aliasing of the signal when it is sampled.

beaming The phenomenon of sound becoming increasingly directional as the frequency of the sound increases when using a single driver.

bi-directional A microphone pickup pattern that is most sensitive to sounds directly in front and directly behind.

binaural Two-channel sound that creates spatial cues by directly feeding pressure waves into the audio canals.

bit allocation The process of balancing a data payload across sub-bands, particularly in the context of MPEG audio.

burning Writing files to an optical disc. Often used to refer to placing audio files onto a CD-R in such a way that they can be played by a standard CD-Audio player.

capsule The actual transducer element in a microphone.

cardioid A microphone pickup pattern that is most sensitive to sounds directly in front. The cardioid family includes the pure cardioid, the super-cardioid, and the hyper-cardioid.

companding Independently scaling each sub-band in order to achieve optimal signal-to-noise ratios during compression.

copy always A protection state indicating the associated content can be freely copied an unlimited number of times.

copy never A protection state indicating the associated content can never be copied.

copy once A protection state indicating the associated content can be copied only once. Copies of the copy are not permitted.

critical band A range of frequencies that stimulate the same portion of the basilar membrane.

critical bandwidth The width of the auditory filter associated with a single critical band.

critical sampling Sampling a signal at exactly twice the frequency of the highest frequency in the signal.

crossover A circuit that splits an incoming audio signal into two or more bands. For instance, a two-way crossover splits a signal into low frequency and high frequency components. The low frequency output is sent to a woofer, the high frequency output to a tweeter.

DAC An acronym for a digital-to-analog converter. A device that converts a digital signal into an analog signal.

diaphragm A large thin surface designed to interact with the air. In a speaker, the diaphragm is the component that actually creates sound pressure waves. In a microphone, the diaphragm is the component that actually receives sound pressure waves.

diffraction The tendency of waves to bend around obstructions in their path.

digital clipping The mapping of an input signal to the highest or lowest quantization level when the signal is outside the quantization range.

digitizing The process of discretely sampling a continuous signal.

dither Low-level noise that is added to a signal to reduce certain quantization artifacts.

DM An acronym for delta modulation. A specialized form of DPCM that uses a one-bit quantizer to store the difference between adjacent samples. The single bit is used to indicate either a fixed increase or a fixed decrease in intensity between adjacent samples.

DPCM An acronym for differential pulse code modulation. A form of PCM where, rather than quantizing the actual signal magnitude, the difference between the current sample and the previous sample is quantized.

DRF An acronym for directivity factor. The ratio of a microphone's response to a diffuse sound field versus an on-axis sound.

driver A piece of software that converts high-level commands from an operating system or application into instructions that are specific to the hardware associated with the driver.

driver The actual transducer element in a speaker.

DSF See Q.

DSM An acronym for delta signal modulation. A digital coding technique that uses the sum of the current sample and the error value from the previous sample. DSM stores single-bit values at a very high frequency.

DTS Acronym for Digital Theatre Sound. A proprietary multi-channel sound scheme used in DVDs and digital radio.

DTV An acronym for digital television. Refers to the broadcast of video and sound in a digital format. Ancillary data may be included in the broadcast. The ancillary data may contain episode guides, detailed biographies of the actors, or even executable software that can be run on a computer.

DVD A high quality audio and video optical disc format. Also used as a generic high-capacity storage medium.

DVD+R A write-once, read-many DVD format defined by the DVD+RW Alliance.

DVD+RW A rewritable DVD format defined by the DVD+RW Alliance.

DVD-Audio A DVD designed primarily to store high quality audio.

DVD-R A write-once, read-many DVD format.

DVD-RAM A rewritable DVD format designed for random access.

DVD-RW A rewritable DVD format designed for sequential access.

DVD-Video A DVD designed primarily to store high quality video and associated audio.

electret A substance that has a permanent electrical charge. It is the electrical equivalent of a permanent magnet.

equivalent noise level The intensity an external sound source would need to have in order to generate a voltage level in the mike equal to the voltage the mike generates as self-noise. Also known as **equivalent noise rating**.

excursion The maximum range of diaphragm movement in a driver.

foldback The reflection of upper sideband signals above the Nyquist limit into the lower sideband.

formants Resonant frequencies in the vocal tract that form a pivotal role in forming vowel sounds.

forward masking A type of masking that occurs when the masker precedes the signal in time.

frequency response The measurement of a frequency-varying parameter across the spectrum. Commonly used to measure the sensitivity of a microphone or the intensity a speaker can create.

frequency selectivity The ability to differentiate two pure tones. Also known as **frequency resolution**.

frequency The rate at which a wave repeats. The inverse of period.

front wave The sound wave created by the front of a speaker diaphragm.

full range Refers to equipment that can handle sounds across the entire spectrum of human hearing.

fundamental The lowest or base frequency in a set of harmonics.

fusion The phenomenon of two sounds with similar frequencies being perceived as a signal sound.

hard room A specially-designed room with acoustically reflective walls used for sound measurements. Regardless of where a sound is generated in the room, its intensity will generally be the same throughout the room due to all the reflections.

harmonic A frequency that is an integer multiple of a fundamental. The second harmonic has twice the frequency of the fundamental. The third harmonic has three times the frequency of the fundamental. And so on. Sometimes the fundamental is referred to as the first harmonic.

HD An acronym for high definition. Used to describe video or audio signals that have superior quality to standard definition signals.

HDTV An acronym for High Definition Television.

heterodyning Shifting the frequency of a signal. For instance, a sub-band with the range 1,000 to 2,000 Hz and a sub-band with the range 3,000 to 4,000 Hz can both be heterodyned to the range 0 to 1,000 Hz so that they can both be processed by a single device that only operates on frequencies in the range 0 to 1,000 Hz.

Hz An abbreviation of hertz. Denotes units of "per second," typically used when measuring frequency.

ID3 tag A

IEC International Electrotechnical Commission. A global organization that prepares and promotes electrical and electronic standards.

impedance The opposition to the flow of alternating current.

in room Conducting measurements of the audio equipment in a chamber with walls that produce echoes. The intent is to reproduce the acoustic behavior of a typical real world setting.

ISO International Organization for Standardization. A network of national standards committees. You might think the proper acronym would be "IOS." Or perhaps the organization's name in another language forms "ISO." In fact, "ISO" is apparently not an acronym at all, but rather a reference to the root "iso-" which means "equal."

ITU-R International Telecommunications Union, Radio Sector. Coordinates efforts within different countries in the field of radio communications.

jack A connector attached to a piece of equipment. See **plug**.

JND An acronym for just noticeable difference. Refers to the smallest consistently perceivable change for a given stimulus.

land The flat region between bumps on an optical disc such as a compact disc or DVD.

LFE An acronym for Low Frequency Effects. Refers to a sound channel that is designed to carry only low frequencies. LFE channels are typically played using a subwoofer.

lossless A system in which information is not lost. Typically used to describe compression algorithms in which the original signal can be exactly reconstructed from the compressed version.

lossy A system in which information is lost. Typically used to describe compression algorithms in which the original signal cannot be exactly reconstructed from the compressed version.

loudness adaptation The psychoacoustical phenomenon of sounds of constant intensity decreasing in loudness over time.

loudness The subjective equivalent of intensity.

LPCM An acronym for linear pulse code modulation. A form of PCM that uses a linear quantizer. In other words, the levels between adjacent quantization levels remain constant across the entire signal range.

maskee The sound that is hidden by a masker.

masker The sound that is responsible for rendering a signal undetectable.

masking The phenomenon of a sound being rendered undetectable due to the presence of another sound.

matrixing The process of encoding multiple audio channels into sound channels. For instance, surround channel information can be matrixed into two channels that also carry front stereo information.

mel A unit of pitch. One thousand mels are defined to equal the pitch of a 1,000-Hz pure tone. A 2,000-mel tone is one that sounds to a listener twice as high as a 1,000-hertz tone. A 500-mel tone is one that sounds twice as low as a 1,000-mel tone.

microphone A collection of one or more capsules encased within an enclosure. A microphone converts sound pressure waves into electrical signals. Also known as a mike or mic.

mid-range A driver optimized to create medium frequency sounds.

monophonic Single-channel sound. Also known as mono.

MP3 An acronym for MPEG Layer III audio. A popular music compression format.

MPEG Moving Pictures Experts Group. An ISO/IEC subcommittee that develops international standards for storing, transmitting, and organizing digital audio and video.

MPEG-1 A video and audio compression standard. It supports a maximum bit rate of 1.5 megabits per second.

MPEG-2 An extension of MPEG-1 that adds support for higher quality audio and video. The base format of DVD-Video.

MPEG-4 A versatile format that allows for multiple concurrent audio and video channels.

MPEG-7 An infrastructure for searching and managing multimedia. Unlike its predecessors, it is not an audio/video compression format.

multigenerational copying Making a copy of a copy.

multiplexing Chronologically interleaving packets of data together. For instance, MPEG-2 streams consist of discrete audio and video packets that contain information that are intended to be played back at the same time. For transmission or storage purposes, the packets are multiplexed: placed one after another in a single stream. Also known as **muxing**.

NMR An acronym for noise-to-mask ratio. A measurement of the perceivable distortion of a compressed signal.

noise shaping Using a feedback loop and oversampling to change the spectrum of noise. Specifically, noise energy is redistributed so that most of it exists at higher frequencies, and as such, is easily removed by a low-pass filter.

nonlinear PCM A form of PCM wherein the quantization levels are unevenly spaced.

Nyquist frequency The minimum sampling rate required to properly sample a signal. If the highest frequency in the signal is f_{max}, then the Nyquist frequency is $2f_{max}$.

Nyquist limit. Given a fixed sampling rate, the highest frequency that a signal may contain and still be properly sampled. If the sampling rate is f_s, then the Nyquist limit is $f_s/2$.

off-axis Any and all directions that are not directly in front of a microphone or speaker.

off-axis colorization The tendency of microphones to have an increasingly distorted frequency response as sounds originate further away from on-axis.

ohm The unit of resistance and impedance.

omnidirectional A microphone pickup pattern that is equally sensitive to sounds in all directions.

on-axis The direction directly in front of a microphone or speaker.

oversampling Sampling a signal at a much higher rate than Nyquist frequency.

PC Speaker The single-channel square wave sound generator that originated on the IBM PC.

PCM An acronym for pulse code modulation. A digital coding scheme wherein samples are stored as multi-bit data words at the sampling rate.

PDM an acronym for pulse density modulation. A synonym for DSM.

Peer-to-peer file sharing A scheme for directly sending and receiving files among networked PCs.

perfect pitch The ability to identify the pitch of a tone without a reference tone.

period The time required for a wave to complete a cycle. The inverse of frequency.

phantom power A technique for supplying power to microphones that need it over the very same lines used to transmit the sound signals. Phantom power is designed in such a way that it does not interfere with microphones that do not require power.

phase opposition When two waves are 180 degrees out of phase.

phase quadrature When two waves are ±90 degrees out of phase.

phoneme A distinctive sound that is a fundamental unit of speech.

pickup pattern A polar graph that indicates the sensitivity of a microphone to sounds originating from different directions.

piezoelectric A material that physically changes shape when electricity is applied. Changing the shape of the material causes it to generate electricity.

pitch The subjective equivalent of frequency.

plug A connector attached to a cable. See **jack**.

polar patterns See **pickup patterns**.

precedence effect The psychoacoustical phenomenon wherein two similar sounds arrive within milliseconds of each other at each ear and are fused together into a single perceived sound. The fused sound is localized in the direction of the sound the reaches the ears first. This effect is also known the **Haas effect**, and the **law of the first wave front**.

prediction A compression technique where the current value is determined from previous values.

proximity effect The phenomenon of certain microphones becoming increasingly sensitive to low frequencies as the sound source nears the diaphragm.

Q or **distance factor**. A measurement of a microphone's reach.

quantization error The difference in magnitude between the original signal and the quantized version of the signal.

quantizing The process of discretely sampling a signal's intensity.

reach The point at which a microphone is equally sensitive to direct sounds and ambient sounds.

rear wave The sound wave created by the rear of a speaker diaphragm.

REE An acronym for random energy efficiency. The measurement of a microphone's ability to pick up sounds from the front direction while rejecting ambient noises.

residual A term used in compression to denote the difference between a predicted value and the actual value. Also known as an error.

resistance The opposition to the flow of direct current.

ripping Copying media files from an optical disc to a PC's hard drive. Often used to describe copying audio files from an audio CD to a PC. Also used to describe copying video and audio from a DVD to a PC.

SCMS An acronym for Serial Copy Management System. A copy protection system wherein compliant equipment prevents unlicensed multigenerational copies from being made.

SD An acronym for standard definition. May be used to describe either video or audio signals.

self-noise The amount of sound a microphone generates when it is placed in an absolutely quiet environment. Self-noise originates from phenomenon such as thermal noise in electrical components.

SMR An acronym for signal-to-mask ratio. Refers to the distance between the intensity of the masker and the masking threshold.

soft sound A scheme for handling audio on the PC where much of the processing of the sound is handled by the CPU, rather than specialized audio hardware. Also known as **software sound**.

sonogram A plot of how a sound's spectrum changes over time.

SPDIF An acronym for the Sony/Philips Digital Interface Format. The most popular consumer digital audio interconnect. It carries a wide variety of formats including compressed multi channel audio across a single cable.

speaker A collection of one or more drivers and potentially a crossover encased within an enclosure. Speakers convert electrical signals into sound pressure waves.

spectrum A plot of a sound's intensity at different frequencies.

spider The flexible structure in a driver that attaches the voice coil to the frame. The spider keeps the voice coil centered within the permanent magnet.

sub-band A subset of the audible audio spectrum. Used in compression schemes such as MPEG audio. Allows different portion of the spectrum to be concurrently compressed with different quality.

subwoofer A drive optimized to create very low frequency sounds.

suspension The flexible component of a driver that attaches the diaphragm to the frame.

threshold of feeling The highest intensity a sound can have before it causes sensations of prickling and pain. Nominally on the order of 120 to 130 dB-SPL. Also known as the **threshold of pain**.

threshold of hearing The lowest intensity a sound can have and still be audible. Nominally 0 dB-SPL, although the exact level will vary from person to person.

timbre The psychoacoustical assessment that allows us to differentiate between two sounds that have the same pitch and loudness.

tip-ring-sleeve A three-conductor phone plug typically used to carry unbalanced stereo audio.

tip-sleeve A two-conductor phone plug typically used to carry unbalanced mono audio.

transducer A device that converts energy from one medium to another. For instance, speakers convert energy from electricity to air.

tweeter A driver optimized to create high frequency sounds.

unbalanced Refers to a transferring a signal using two wires. One wire carries a variable voltage that corresponds to the signal itself, while the other wire serves as a zero reference, or ground.

video zone The portion of a DVD that contains DVD-Video information. The video zone typically includes both video and audio information. Video zone files are stored in the VIDEO_TS folder.

voice coil The electromagnet in a driver that is used to modulate the diaphragm.

waveform A plot of a sound's intensity over time.

woofer A driver optimized to create low frequency sounds.

Selected Bibliography

Advanced Television Systems Committee. 1995. *A/52 Digital Audio Compression Standard (AC-3).*

Advanced Television Systems Committee. 2001. *A/53B Digital Television Standard.*

Audio Engineering Society. 1998. *AES Standard for Professional Audio Equipment — Application of Connectors, Part 1, XLR-type Polarity and Gender.*

Ballou, Glen, ed. 1987. *Handbook for Sound Engineers: The New Audio Cyclopedia.* Indianapolis, IN: Howard W. Sams & Co.

Bartlett, Bruce. 1987. *Introduction to Professional Recording Techniques.* Indianapolis, IN: Howard W. Sams & Company.

Baudino, Joseph E. and John M. Kittross. 1977. "Broadcasting's Oldest Stations: An Examination of Four Claimants." *Journal of Broadcasting.* Winter:61-82.

Borwick, John, ed. 1987. *Sound Recording Practice*, 3rd ed. Association of Professional Recording Studios. New York, NY: Oxford University Press.

Bosi, M., K. Brandenburg, S. Quackenbush, L. Fielder, K. Akagiri, H. Fuchs, M. Dietz, J. Herre, G. Davidson, and Y. Oikawa. 1996. "ISO/IEC MPEG-2 Advanced Audio Coding." AES 101st Convention. Los Angeles, California USA.

Buddine, Laura and Elizabeth Young. 1987. *The Brady Guide to CD-ROM*. New York, NY: Prentice Hall Press.

Camras, Marvin. 1988. *Magnetic Recording Handbook*. New York, NY: Van Nostrand Reinhold Company.

Casson, Henry N. 1911. *The History of the Telephone*. Chicago, IL: A.C. McClurge & Co.

Coe, Lewis. 1996. *Wireless Radio: A Brief History*. Jefferson, NC: McFarland & Company.

Colloms, Martin. 1997. *High Performance Loudspeakers*, 5th ed. New York, NY: Wiley & Sons.

Dolby Laboratories. 2001. *The Selection of Audio Coding Technologies for Digital Delivery Systems*.

Eargle, John. 1976. *Sound Recording*. New York, NY: Van Nostrand Reinhold Co.

European Broadcasting Union. 2000. ETSI TR 101 496-1 v1.1.1 *Digital Audio Broadcasting; Guidelines and Rules for Implementation and Operation, Part 1: System Outline*.

—. 2000. ETSI TR 101 496-2 v1.1.2 *Digital Audio Broadcasting; Guidelines and Rules for Implementation and Operation, Part 2: System Features*.

—. 2000. ETSI TR 101 496-3 v1.1.1 *Digital Audio Broadcasting; Guidelines and Rules for Implementation and Operation, Part 3: Broadcast Network*.

—. 2000. ETSI TR 101 154 v1.4.1 *Digital Video Broadcasting, Implementation Guidelines for the use of MPEG-2 Systems, Video and Audio in Satellite, Cable and Terrestrial Broadcasting Applications*.

Farley, Tom. 2001. *Telephone History Series*. TelecomWriting.com.

Federal Communications Commission. 2002. *Digital Audio Broadcasting Systems and their Impact on the Terrestrial Radio Broadcast Service, First Report and Order*. October 10.

Fletcher, Harvey and W.A. Munson. 1933. "Loudness, Its Definition, Measurement, and Calculation." *Journal of the Acoustical Society of America*. 5:82-108.

Furui, Sadaoki. 2001. *Digital Speech Processing, Synthesis, and Recognition*, 2nd edition. New York, NY: Marcel Dekker.

Gelatt, Roland. 1966. *The Fabulous Phonograph, From Edison to Stereo*. New York, NY: Appleton-Century.

Gelfand, Stanley A. 1998. *Hearing, An Introduction to Psychological and Physiological Acoustics*, 3rd edition. New York, NY: Marcel Dekker.

Gerzon, M.A., P.G. Craven, J.R. Stuart, M.J. Law, and R.J. Wilson, 1999. "The MLP Lossless Compression System." AES 17th International Conference on High Quality Audio Coding. Florence, Italy.

Grill, Bernhard. 1999. "MPEG-4 Scalable Audio Coding." AES 106th Convention. Munich, Germany.

Gould, Stephen J. 1993. "An Earful of Jaw," *Eight Little Piggies: Reflections in Natural History*. New York, NY: W.M. Norton & Company.

Hawkins, J.E. and S.S. Stevens. 1950. "The Masking of Pure Tones and Speech by White Noise." *Journal of the Acoustical Society of America*. 22:6–13.

Herre, Jürgen. 1999. "MPEG-4 General Audio Coding." AES 106th Convention. Munich, Germany.

—. 1999. "TNS, Quantization, and Coding Methods." AES 17th International Conference on High-Quality Audio Coding. Florence, Italy.

Huber, David M. and Robert E. Runstein. 1989. *Modern Recording Techniques*, 3rd ed. Indianapolis, IN: Howard W. Sams & Company.

Huopaniemi, Jyri. 1999. "AudioBIFS: Audio Composition in MPEG-4 version 1." AES 106th Convention. Munich, Germany.

Institution of Electrical Engineers. 1995. *International Conference on 100 Years of Radio* (London, England).

Intel Corporation. 2002. *Audio Codec '97*, revision 2.3.

International Electrotechnical Commission. 1987. *IEC 268-12: Sound System Equipment Part 12: Application of Connectors for Broadcast and Similar Use*.

ISO/IEC 11172-3:1993 Information technology—Coding of moving pictures and associated audio for digital storage media at up to about 1.5 Mbit/s -Part 3: Audio, (MPEG-1 Audio)

ISO/IEC 13818-3:1993 Information technology—Generic coding of moving pictures and associated audio information — Part 3: Audio (MPEG-2 BC Audio)

ISO/IEC 13818-7:1997 Information technology—Generic coding of moving pictures and associated audio information—Part 7: Advanced Audio Coding (AAC) (MPEG2-AAC)

ISO/IEC 14496-3:1998 Information technology—Coding of audio-visual objects—Part 3: Audio (MPEG-4 Audio)

Janus, Scott. 2002. *Video in the 21st Century*. Hillsboro, OR: Intel Press.

Jarrar, Abdul and Ernesto Martinez. 2003. "Designing in Azalia for High Performance Audio." Intel Developer's Forum. San Jose, United States.

Jesteadt, Walt, Sid P. Bacon, and James R. Lehman. 1982. "Forward Masking as a Function of Frequency, Masker Level, and Signal Delay." *Journal of the Acoustical Society of America* 71. 4 (April):950-962.

Johnson, Keith O. and Michael W. Pflaumer. 1996. "Compatible Resolution Enhancement in Digital Audio Systems." AES 101st Convention. Los Angeles, United States.

Jorgensen, Finn. 1996. *The Complete Handbook of Magnetic Recording*. New York, NY: TAB Books.

Lide, David R., ed. 2003. *CRC Handbook of Chemistry and Physics*, 84th ed. Cleveland, OH: CRC Press.

Lyons, Richard G. 1997. *Understanding Digital Signal Processing*. Reading, MA: Addison-Wesley Publishing.

Manley, Geoffrey A. 1986. "The Evolution of the Mechanisms of Frequency Selectivity in Vertebrates." *Auditory Frequency Selectivity*. Edited by Brian C. J. Moore and Roy D. Patterson. Plenum Press.

Marco, Guy, ed. 1993. *Encyclopedia of Recorded Sound in the United States*. New York, NY: Garland Publishing.

McNicol, Donald. 1917. "The Early Days of Radio in America." *The Electrical Experimenter*. (April):893-911.

Moore, Brian C.J., ed. 1995. *Hearing, Handbook of Perception and Cognition*, 2nd edition. San Diego, CA: Academic Press.

Moore, Brian C. J. and Brian R. Glasberg. 1981. "Auditory Filter Shapes Derived In Simultaneous and Forward Masking" *Journal of the Acoustical Society of America* 70. 4 (October):1003-1014.

—. 1983. "Suggested Formulae for Calculating Auditory-filter Bandwidths and Excitation Patterns." *Journal of the Acoustical Society of America*. 74. 3 (September):750-753.

Nahin, Paul J. 1996. *The Science of Radio*. Woodbury, NY: American Institute of Physics.

Noll, Peter. 1997. "MPEG Digital Audio Coding." IEEE Signal Processing Magazine. (September):59-81.

Nyquist, H. 1924. "Certain Factors Affecting Telegraph Speed." *Transactions of the American Institute of Electrical Engineers*. XLIII (February):412-422.

Oliver, B.M., J.R. Pierce, and C.E. Shannon. 1948. "The Philosophy of PCM." *Proceedings Institute of Radio Engineers*. 36:1324-1331.

Pan, Davis. 1995. "A Tutorial on MPEG/Audio Compression." IEEE Multimedia 2. 7:60-74.

Park, Sangil. 1990. "Motorola Digital Signal Processors: Principles of Sigma-Delta Modulation for Analog-to-Digital Converters." Motorola.

Patterson, Roy D. and Brian C.J. Moore. 1986. "Auditory Filters and Excitation Patterns as Representations of Frequency Resolution" *Frequency Selectivity in Hearing*. Edited by B.C.J. Moore. Academic Press Limited.

Patterson, Roy D. 1974. "Auditory Filter Shape." *Journal of the Acoustical Society of America* 55. 4 (April):802-809.

—. 1976. "Auditory Filter shapes Derived with Noise Stimuli." *Journal of the Acoustical Society of America* 59. 3 (March):640-654.

Philips, 2002. "High Speed CD-RW." Document 21/01/02-3122 783 0121 2.

—. 2002. "SACD Content Protection."

—. 2002. "SACD Format."

—. 2002. "SACD General Overview."

—. 2002. "SACD Hybrid."

—. 2003. "Product Catalogue." Document 17/02/03-3122 783 0027 2.

Pohlmann, Ken C. 2000. *Principles of Digital Audio*, 4th edition. New York, NY: McGraw-Hill Professional.

Quackenbush, Schuyler. 1999. "MPEG-4 Speech Coding." AES 106th Convention. Munich, Germany.

Rabiner, L. R. and R.W. Schafer. 1978. *Digital Processing of Speech Signals*. Englewood Cliffs, NJ: Prentice-Hall.

Rhodes, Frederick Leland. 1929. *Beginnings of Telephony*. New York, NY: Harper & Brothers.

Royal Scottish Museum. 1977. *Phonographs and Gramophones*. Edinburgh, Scottland.

Rumsey, Francis and Tim McCormick. 1992. *Sound and Recording: an Introduction*. Boston, MA: Focal Press.

Scheirer, Eric D. 1999. "MPEG-4 Structured Audio." AES 106th Convention. Munich, Germany.

Schicke, Charles A. 1974. *Revolution in Sound*. Boston, MA: Little, Brown & Co.

Schubert, Paul. 1928. *The Electric Word*. New York, NY: MacMillan Company.

Shannon, Claude E. and Warren Weaver. 1949. *The Mathematical Theory of Communication*. Urbana, IL: The University of Illinois Press.

Sharpless, Graham. 2003. "New Formats for Music: DVD & SACD." Disctronics.

Shlien, Seymour. 1994. "Guide to MPEG-1 Audio Standard." IEEE Transactions on Broadcasting 40. 4 (December):206-218.

Sloane, N.J.A. and Aaron D Wyner, ed. 1993. *Claude Elwood Shannon, Collected Papers*. New York, NY: IEEE Press.

Smith, Steven W. 1999. *The Scientist and Engineer's Guide to Digital Signal Processing*, 2nd edition. San Diego, CA: California Technical Publishing.

Sony. 1991. "Sony Unveils Mini Disc System for Portable Audio Market." Press Release, May 16.

—. 2003. "A Great Invention 100 Years On." www.sony.net.

Stevens, S.S., J. Volkmann, and E.B. Newman. 1937. "A Scale for the Measurement of the Psychological Magnitude of Pitch." *Journal of the Acoustical Society of America* 8. 3:185–190.

Strang, Gilbert. 2000. "Signal Processing for Everyone." *Computational Mathematics Driven by Industrial Problems*. Edited by V. Capasso, H. Engl, and J. Periaux. Springer.

Strum, Robert D., and Donald E. Kirk (contributor). 1988. *First Principles of Discrete Systems and Digital Signal Processing*. Reading, MA: Addison-Wesley Publishing Company.

Tipler, Frank. 1974. "Rotating Cylinders and the Possibility of Global Causality Violation." *Physical Review*. D 9.

Toshiba Corporation. *DVD Specifications for Read-Only Disc, Part 1: Physical Specifications*.

—. *DVD Specifications for Read-Only Disc, Part 2: File System Specifications*.

—. *DVD Specifications for Read-Only Disc, Part 3: Video Specifications*.

—. *DVD Specifications for Read-Only Disc, Part 4: Audio Specifications*.

Watkinson, John. 2001. *The MPEG Handbook*. Woburn, MA: Focal Press.

Wagner, Ronald. 1987. *Electrostatic Loudspeaker Design and Construction*. Blue Ridge Summit, PA: Tab Books.

Worm, John M. 1989. *Sound Recording Handbook*. Indianapolis, IN: Howard W. Sams & Company.

Zuckerman, Art. 1978. *Stereo High-Fidelity Speaker Systems*. Indianapolis, IN: Howard W. Sams & Company.

Zwicker, E. H. and H. Fastl. 1990. *Psychoacoustics: Facts and Models*. New York, NY: Springer-Verlag.

Index

D

J

K

L

M

Q

R

S

T

X

Y

Z

“As the pace of technology introduction increases it’s difficult to keep up. Intel Press has established an impressive portfolio. The breadth of topics is a reflection of both Intel’s diversity as well as our commitment to serve a broad technical community.

I hope you will take advantage of these products to further your technical education.”

Patrick Gelsinger
Senior Vice President and Chief Technology Officer
Intel Corporation

Turn the page to learn about titles from Intel Press for system developers

ESSENTIAL BOOKS FOR SYSTEM DEVELOPERS

A comprehensive reference for the digital video engineer

Video in the 21st Century

By Scott Janus
ISBN 0-9712887-5-5

Filled with useful video information, this book benefits hardware and software designers who create digital multimedia products.

In the past few years, video technology has made huge advancements. Since the DVD format was launched, it has gained wide consumer acceptance. HDTV has gone from specification to reality, with broadcasts now occurring daily throughout the U.S. *Video in the 21st Century* explores the key technologies that have made all of this possible.

Starting with basic video concepts, this book provides an easy-to-read tutorial for novices, and serves as a useful reference for experienced engineers.

An easy-to-read tutorial for novices and a useful reference for experienced engineers

Peer-to-Peer Computing

Technologies for Sharing and Collaborating on the Net
By David Barkai
ISBN 0-9702846-7-5

Written for application developers, IT professionals, and end users, this book reveals what the P2P buzz is all about. To show how P2P computing is a viable set of technologies and a computing model for business and the enterprise, the author describes pioneering innovations and early successes as the foundation on which self-managed online communities of consumers might be built.

See how P2P enhances and complements network computing

Please go to this Web site

www.intel.com/intelpress/bookbundles.htm

for complete information about
our popular book bundles.
Each bundle is designed to
ensure that you read important
complementary topics together,
while enjoying a total purchase
price that is far less than the
combined prices of the
individual books.

About Intel Press

Intel Press is the authoritative source of timely, highly relevant, and innovative books to help software and hardware developers speed up their development process. We collaborate only with leading industry experts to deliver reliable, first-to-market information about the latest technologies, processes, and strategies.

Our products are planned with the help of many people in the developer community and we encourage you to consider becoming a customer advisor. If you would like to help us and gain additional advance insight to the latest technologies, we encourage you to consider the Intel Press Customer Advisor Program. You can **register** here:

www.intel.com/intelpress/register.htm

For information about bulk orders or corporate sales, please send email to **bulkbooksales@intel.com**.

Other Developer Resources from Intel

At these Web sites you can also find valuable technical information and resources for developers:

developer.intel.com	general information for developers
www.intel.com/IDS	content, tools, training, and the Early Access Program for software developers
www.intel.com/software/products	programming tools to help you develop high-performance applications
shale.intel.com/softwarecollege	the Intel Software College provides training tools and technologies from the people who know processors
www.intel.com/idf	world-wide technical conference, the Intel Developer Forum